IN TIME OF WAR

CHICAGO STUDIES IN AMERICAN POLITICS

*A series edited by Benjamin I. Page, Susan Herbst,
Lawrence R. Jacobs, and James Druckman*

ALSO IN THE SERIES:

*Us Against Them: Ethnocentric Foundations
of American Opinion*
by Donald R. Kinder and Cindy D. Kam

*The Partisan Sort: How Liberals
Became Democrats and Conservatives
Became Republicans*
by Matthew Levendusky

*Democracy at Risk: How Terrorist Threats
Affect the Public*
by Jennifer L. Merolla and
Elizabeth J. Zechmeister

*Agendas and Instability in American Politics,
Second Edition*
by Frank R. Baumgartner and Bryan D. Jones

The Private Abuse of the Public Interest
by Lawrence D. Brown and Lawrence R. Jacobs

*The Party Decides: Presidential Nominations
Before and After Reform*
by Marty Cohen, David Karol, Hans Noel,
and John Zaller

*Same Sex, Different Politics: Success
and Failure in the Struggles over Gay Rights*
by Gary Mucciaroni

IN TIME OF WAR

Understanding American Public Opinion
from World War II to Iraq

ADAM J. BERINSKY

The University of Chicago Press CHICAGO & LONDON

ADAM J. BERINSKY is associate professor
of political science at Massachusetts Institute
of Technology.

The University of Chicago Press, Chicago 60637
The University of Chicago Press, Ltd., London
© 2009 by The University of Chicago
All rights reserved. Published 2009
Printed in the United States of America

18 17 16 15 14 13 12 11 10 09   1 2 3 4 5

ISBN-13: 978-0-226-04358-6 (cloth)
ISBN-13: 978-0-226-04359-3 (paper)
ISBN-10: 0-226-04358-4 (cloth)
ISBN-10: 0-226-04359-2 (paper)

Library of Congress
Cataloging-in-Publication Data

Berinsky, Adam J., 1970–
In time of war : understanding American
public opinion from World War II to Iraq /
Adam J. Berinsky.
p. cm. — (Chicago studies in American
politics)
Includes bibliographical references and index.
ISBN-13: 978-0-226-04358-6 (cloth: alk. paper)
ISBN-13: 978-0-226-04359-3 (pbk.: alk. paper)
ISBN-10: 0-226-04358-4 (cloth: alk. paper)
ISBN-10: 0-226-04359-2 (pbk.: alk. paper)
1. War and society—United States. 2. World
War, 1939–1945—United States—Public
opinion. 3. Korean War, 1950–1953—United
States—Public opinion. 4. Vietnam War,
1961–1975—United States—Public opinion.
5. Iraq War, 2003—Public opinion. I. Title.
II. Series: Chicago studies in American politics.
HM554.B475 2009
303.6′60973—dc22

2008053228

⊗ The paper used in this publication
meets the minimum requirements of the
American National Standard for Information
Sciences—Permanence of Paper for Printed
Library Materials, ANSI Z39.48-1992.

To Deirdre, Benjamin, and Lila

CONTENTS

List of Figures / ix

List of Tables / xii

Acknowledgments / xv

1 Introduction: America at War / 1

PART I. HISTORICAL PERSPECTIVE

2 Public Opinion and War: A Historical Perspective / 13

3 The Myths and Meaning of Public Opinion and World War II / 33

PART II. THE STRUCTURE OF SUPPORT FOR WAR

4 The Calculation of Costs: An Innocent Public / 61

5 Partisan Structure of War Support: Events, Elites, and the Public / 85

6 Ethnic Groups: Attachments, Enmities, and Support for War / 127

PART III. PUBLIC OPINION AND WAR: BACK TO THE WATER'S EDGE

7 Civil Liberties and War / 155

8 Elections during Wartime / 178

9 Conclusions / 207

APPENDIX A: Description of Data and Weighting / 222

APPENDIX B: Iraq War Casualty Survey Analysis / 229

APPENDIX C: *Congressional Record* Content Analysis / 234

APPENDIX D: Statistical Significance of Ethnic Variables / 246

APPENDIX E: Relationship between Support for War and Support for Restricting Civil Liberties / 251

APPENDIX F: NES Analysis of Retrospective War Support / 256

Notes / 265

References / 309

Index / 327

FIGURES

2.1. Trends in support for the Korean War / 16

2.2. Trends in support for the Vietnam War / 21

2.3. Trends in support for the Gulf War / 23

2.4A. Trends in support for the Afghanistan War, 2001–2 / 28

2.4B. Trends in support for the Afghanistan War, 2006–7 / 28

2.5. Trends in support for the Iraq War / 32

3.1. Trends in opposition to making peace with Germans / 48

3.2. Trends in support for helping England and defeating Germany over staying out of the war / 49

3.3. Trends in support for using U.S. convoy ships to carry war materials to Britain / 51

3.4. Gender gap in support for helping England over staying out of the war / 54

3.5. Gender gap in opposition to peace with the German army / 54

3.6. Gender gap on support for taking an internationalist position after the war / 56

5.1. Parties and war rhetoric in Congress, 1938–45 / 89

5.2A. Evidence of polarization pattern, Gallup, November 1939: Approve of changes to neutrality law / 93

5.2B. Evidence of polarization pattern, OPOR, January 1941: More important to help England than stay out of war / 93

5.2C. Evidence of polarization pattern, Gallup, June 1941: Let Germany keep land in exchange for peace / 94

5.2D. Evidence of polarization pattern, Gallup, June 1941: Use U.S. navy to convoy ships to England? / 94

5.2E. Evidence of polarization pattern, Gallup, August 1941: Use U.S. Navy to convoy ships to England? / 95

5.3A. Evidence of mainstream pattern, OPOR, June 1942: Take active part in world affairs after the war / 96

5.3B. Evidence of mainstream pattern, OPOR, June 1942: Do not make peace with Hitler / 96

5.3C. Evidence of mainstream pattern, Roper, March 1943: United States should take active role in international organization after war / 97

5.3D. Evidence of mainstream pattern, Gallup, August 1943: Oppose peace with Germany even if Hitler overthrown / 97

5.3E. Evidence of mainstream pattern, OPOR, January 1944: Oppose peace with Germany even if Hitler overthrown / 98

5.4. Distinctiveness of domestic policy, February 1944 / 98

5.5A. Evidence of mainstream pattern, Gallup, October 1940: Help England if British lose war without aid? / 101

5.5B. Evidence of mainstream pattern, Gallup, October 1940: Send airplanes to England? / 101

5.6. Partisan trends in support for Iraq War, 2003–8 / 102

5.7A. Patterns of polarization in Iraq War attitudes, August 2004: Current war in Iraq has been worth fighting / 104

5.7B. Patterns of polarization in Iraq War attitudes, August 2004: United States made the right decision in using military force against Iraq / 104

5.8. Partisan trends in estimates of Iraq War success, 2003–7 / 106

5.9. Patterns of polarization in estimates of Iraq War success, August 2004 / 106

5.10A. Patterns of polarization in estimates of how well the Iraq War is going, January 2004 / 107

5.10B. Patterns of polarization in estimates of how well the Iraq War is going, July 2005 / 107

5.10C. Patterns of polarization in estimates of how well the Iraq War is going, January 2006 / 108

5.10D. Patterns of polarization in estimates of how well the Iraq War is going, August 2006 / 108

5.11A. Opinions on attitudes toward war, 2004 NES, Iraq / 110

5.11B. Opinions on attitudes toward War, 2004 NES, Afghanistan / 110

5.12A. Vietnam analysis: Opposition to de-escalation, 1964 / 113

5.12B. Vietnam analysis: Opposition to de-escalation, 1966 / 113

5.12C. Vietnam analysis: Opposition to de-escalation, 1968 / 114

5.12D. Vietnam analysis: Opposition to de-escalation, 1970 / 114

5.13A. Vietnam analysis: United States did not make a mistake, 1964 / 116

5.13B. Vietnam analysis: United States did not make a mistake, 1966 / 116

5.13C. Vietnam analysis: United States did not make a mistake, 1968 / 117

5.13D. Vietnam analysis: United States did not make a mistake, 1970 / 117

5.13E. Vietnam analysis: United States did not make a mistake, 1972 / 118

5.14. Partisan trends in support for the Vietnam War, Gallup Poll / 119

6.1. Should the United States trust Russia after the war? / 141

6.2. Should the United States trust England after the war? / 141

6.3. England is fighting only to preserve democracy / 142

6.4. Oppose peace with the German army / 143

6.5. Make peace treaty more severe than last war? / 144

7.1. Support for civil liberties, 1996–2006 / 165

7.2. Partisan gap in support for civil liberties, 1996–2006 / 167

7.3. Partisan polarization in support for civil liberties, January 2006 / 167

7.4. Relationship between support for retaliation for 9/11 and support for restricting civil liberties, September 2001 / 169

7.5. Relationship between support for the Iraq War and negative civil liberties judgments, 2001–6 / 169

7.6. Support for Vietnam War and civil liberties judgments / 172

7.7. Support for civil liberties, 1938–45 / 174

7.8. Support for World War II and negative civil liberties judgments / 176

7.9. Support for World War II and allowing free speech for radicals / 176

8.1. Estimated net contribution of retrospective evaluations of war on presidential voting / 183

8.2. Johnson's, Nixon's, and Humphrey's placement on the Vietnam future action scale / 185

8.3. Weighted change in real disposable income as a predictor of the incumbent's vote share of a two-party vote / 187

8.4. Trends in fear of terrorism, 2001–7 / 194

8.5. Bush's feeling thermometer ratings, 2000–2004 / 195

8.6. Bush's leadership ratings, 2000–2004 / 196

8.7. Relationship between Bush's leadership and Bush's feeling thermometer, 2000–2004 / 196

8.8. British political preferences, BIPO polls 1943–45 / 203

9.1. Polarization between parties in the House of Representatives, 1877–2005 / 221

TABLES

3.1. The Gender Gap on Questions of Intervention, August 1939 / 53

4.1. Effect of Partisanship and Information on Predicted Probability of Estimating Correct Casualty Level / 78

4.2. Experimental Effect of Casualty Information on Support for the Iraq War / 81

4.3. Experimental Effect of War Information on Support for the Iraq War, Autumn 2005 / 84

5.1. Korea Experiment, 2006 / 121

6.1. Racial Variables and Support for Sanctions against South Africa, 1986 / 134

6.2. The Power of Ethnic Attachments, before the United States' Entry into World War II / 137

6.3. Distribution of Ethnic-Group Attachments and Enmities, August 1939 / 145

6.4. Group Attachments and Enmities and Support for Isolationist Positions, August 1939 / 149

8.1. Estimated Effect of Opposition to War on the Vote for the Incumbent Candidate / 181

8.2. War Scenarios and percent Vote for FDR in the 1940 Election / 198

8.3. War Scenarios and percent Vote for FDR in the 1944 Election / 199

8.4. Estimate of Effect of War on the Vote for FDR in the 1944 Election / 201

8.5. War Scenarios and the Strength of FDR Support, October 1944 / 201

8.6. Class Cleavages on Churchill Approval and Conservative Party Support / 204

B.1. Multinomial Logit Analysis of Determinants of Estimates of War Deaths / 233

B.2. Probit Analysis of the War Effects of Casualty Estimates on Support for the Iraq War / 233

C.1. Support for the Neutrality Act, November 1939 / 240

C.2. Support for U.S. Navy convoys, July–August 1941 / 241

C.3. Statistical Test of Differences: Support for the Neutrality Act, November 1939 / 242

C.4. Statistical Test of Differences: Support for U.S. Navy convoys, July–August 1941 / 243

C.5. Probit Results of the Iraq War Casualty Survey / 244

D.1. The Power of Ethnic Attachments, before the United States' Entry into World War II / 247

D.2. The Power of Ethnic Attachments, before the United States' Entry into World War II / 248

D.3. The Power of Ethnic Attachments, after the United States' Entry into World War II / 249

D.4. Bivariate probit selection model analysis of sanctions against South Africa / 250

E.1. Partisan Polarization on Civil Liberties Restrictions, 2006 / 252

E.2. Support for War and Support for Civil Liberties, 2002 / 253

E.3. Effect of Support for the Vietnam War on Civil Liberties Judgments / 254

E.4. Effect of Support for World War II on Negative Civil Liberties Judgments, November 1940 / 255

F.1. 1952 NES Election Analysis of the Retrospective War-Support Measure / 257

F.2. 1952 NES Election Analysis of the Prospective War-Support Measure / 258

F.3. 1968 NES Election Analysis of the Retrospective War-Support Measure / 259

F.4. 1968 NES Election Analysis of the Prospective War-Support Measure / 260

F.5. 1968 NES Election Analysis of the Hawk–Dove War-Support Measure / 261

F.6. 1972 NES Election Analysis of the Retrospective War-Support Measure / 262

F.7. 1972 NES Election Analysis of the Hawk–Dove War-Support Measure / 263

F.8. 2004 NES Election Analysis of the Retrospective War-Support Measure / 264

ACKNOWLEDGMENTS

I like reading acknowledgments. They give us a sense of the intellectual history of a project and shed some light on the twists and turns taken by the researcher as he or she brought the book to completion. Because you are reading this section, you must like acknowledgments too, so please indulge me—this represents the culmination of a long journey.

This book is the product of nearly six years of work conducted at four different institutions, but its roots run deep into my intellectual past. In fact, I can think of three distinct events that shaped the project.

The first occurred in the fall of 1990, when, as a junior at Wesleyan University, I took a class on public opinion and foreign policy with Richard Boyd. Although I read many of the works that ended up in this book's reference list, what I remember most was a question on the final exam, which asked us, in December 1990, to predict the dynamics of opinion change in the face of what would surely be mounting casualties once a ground war began in Iraq. Needless to say, my analysis was far off the mark, but I was hooked on political science.

The next summer I worked as a research assistant for Richard on a study reexamining the role of foreign policy in the 1948 election. Richard taught me some basic statistics and off we went. Or, should I say, off he went, with me along for the ride. For the life of me, when looking at the output from the mainframe computer, I could never keep straight which number I wanted to be big (right, the coefficient) and which number I wanted to be small (ah, yes, the p-value). Still, I stuck with it, and in the spring of 1992, Richard paid my way to the Midwest Political Science

Association conference so we could present our research, and introduced me to the professional side of political science.

At the same time, I was writing a senior thesis on the relationship between television and terrorism in the modern era with Martha Crenshaw. This thesis solidified my interest in work at the intersection of U.S. politics and international relations. So when—at the urging of Martha and Richard—I went off to graduate school at the University of Michigan in 1994, I assumed I would continue along this path.

I soon received some sage advice that reshaped my career plans. This second event occurred in the office of John Kingdon sometime early in the fall of 1994. Kingdon asked me what I wanted to study, and I told him my plan to examine the relationship among the media, the public, and government officials in the realm of foreign policy. To this he replied (as best I can remember), "Oh no, you don't want to do that. You seem like a smart guy. Let me tell you what's going to happen. You'll write a good dissertation and all the Americanists will say, 'he's great, you should hire him as an IR guy.' And all the IR people will say 'he's terrific, you should hire him as an Americanist.' Then you'll never get a job. Here's my advice. You should put that on hold, do something else, and then when you get a job, come back to that idea."

I followed Kingdon's advice to a T. I wrote my dissertation (and first book, *Silent Voices*) on the subject of nonresponse in opinion surveys and got a job at Princeton—as an Americanist. Still, foreign policy lurked in the background of my work. The final chapter of *Silent Voices* was a study of public opinion during the Vietnam War. Subconsciously, at least, I was returning to my roots.

In the year after the completion of *Silent Voices*, a circuitous path led me back to foreign policy. In pursuit of my "second project," I began a study of political cognition growing out of some work that Don Kinder and I had done while I was a graduate student at Michigan. I sent a grant proposal off to the National Science Foundation (NSF), and that fall it came back with a resounding thud. Although the initial project about Kosovo seemed interesting, my proposed extensions of the project were, with the benefit of hindsight, admittedly banal. Three reviewers wrote, essentially, "Berinsky is a smart guy who should be doing something else." With this high inter-coder reliability, I was convinced. But the question remained; what should that "something else" be?

In the fall of 2002, I was back at Michigan as a National Elections Study fellow and had some time to explore other projects. Combing though the Roper Data Center archives one night, I happened on a trove of old data from the 1930s and 1940s. A search though JSTOR revealed that in fact these data were largely untouched since the 1950s. With war in the air—in the wake of 9/11 and the road to Iraq clear—it seemed that a study of public opinion about World War II could be timely. And with the data in hand, I thought it seemed a straightforward task.

For a variety of reasons, this was not to be, and as a result, the project took much longer than I expected. The problems began with the data. The old surveys had largely not been touched for over fifty years and showed their age. I learned just what "dirty" data were. In some data sets, I found a stray q where a number should be. In other data sets, there were random—and unexplained—symbols where I expected numbers. In addition, it was not clear how best to analyze this old data. Surveys conducted in the 1930s and 1940s were collected using a form of sampling that had long been discredited—namely, quota-controlled sample surveys. A search for the appropriate methods of analysis came up empty. Almost no one, it seemed, had thought about these data since the controversy that emerged after the 1948 presidential election. Thus, I spent another year trying to figure out how best to process the rich trove of old opinion data.

In the meantime, world events changed the substantive focus of the manuscript as well. Originally this book was intended to be about public opinion during World War II. As years went on, however, I found it hard to ignore the concurrent war in Iraq. I therefore expanded the focus to draw lessons from across history. I am not a historian, however: I hope this book does not do violence to the historical record.

And so here I am at the end. With so long a path through so many institutions, I have many people to thank. This project has been very data intensive, so I owe a great deal to a veritable army of research assistants. I am grateful to Gabe Lenz, Erik Lin-Greenberg, Matthew Gusella, Laura Kelly, John Lovett, Colin Moore, Lara Rogers, Alice Savage, Jonathan West, and Adam Ziegfeld for first-rate help. Nicole Fox and Tiffany Washburn each served a year as the project research assistant for the data reclamation project and slogged though a lot of the unpleasant but necessary work that made this book possible. They are both in graduate school now, so I can only hope that someday they can find research assistants as excellent as they. Above all, I thank Ellie Powell and Ian Yohai. They helped design and implement the weighting programs used to bring the data from the 1930s and 1940s back to life. They also heeded my calls for research assistance at all hours of the day and night and always performed superbly.

For valuable discussions regarding this project, I thank Steve Ansolabehere, Larry Bartels, Matt Baum, Jake Bowers, John Brehm, Paul Brewer, Andrea Campbell, Michael Cobb, Kathy Cramer-Walsh, Sarah Croco, Jamie Druckman, Zachary Elkins, Taylor Fravel, Andrew Gelman, Kim Gross, Ben Hansen, Steve Heeringa, Susan Herbst, Marc Hetherington, Sunshine Hillygus, Vince Hutchings, Larry Jacobs, Don Kinder, Doug Kriner, Yanna Krupnikov, Shana Kushner Gadarian, Jonathan Ladd, Chappell Lawson, Gabe Lenz, Jim Lepkowski, Deirdre Logan, Tali Mendelberg, Marty Gilens, Ben Page, Marcus Prior, Kris Ramsey, Ken Scheve, John Sides, David Singer, Sarah Sled, Jim Snyder, Marco Steenbergen, Lily Tsai, Nick Valentino, and seminar participants at Binghamton University, Columbia University, Dartmouth College, Emory University, Harvard University, MIT, the Northeast Political Psychology Meeting, the University of Chicago, the University of Michigan, the University of Minnesota, and Yale University (and almost certainly other deserving people whom I have forgotten). Larry Bartels generously hosted a one-day conference on this book in October 2007 at Princeton. The feedback I received there demonstrated that the book was not as close to being done as I had thought, but this final product is much stronger for the experience. I owe special thanks to Eric Schickler, who was a coconspirator in the data reclamation project that made this book possible and served as a sounding board for almost all the ideas in the book over the last five years.

Given the massive data management tasks needed to produce this book, this project was extraordinarily expensive, and I have a long list of benefactors to thank. Financial support was provided by the National Science Foundation (SES-0550431), Princeton University, MIT, the University of Michigan, and the Center for International Studies at MIT. I also thank the Time-Sharing Experiments for the Social Sciences project for collecting the 2004 Iraq data and the 2006 Korea data, as well as the Public Opinion Research Training Lab at MIT for collecting the 2005 Iraq data.

Last, and certainly not least, this book is dedicated to the Blogan clan. Over the six years I worked on this book, we grew from a newly married couple to a family of four. Ben's and Lila's arrivals almost certainly delayed the completion of this book, but they have made life all the more fun in the process.

CHAPTER ONE

INTRODUCTION: AMERICA AT WAR

In early 2006, with the initial successes in Iraq a distant memory, public opinion seemed to have turned against the war. Republicans continued to support President Bush's foreign policies, but the nation as a whole did not. Although support for the war had remained fairly stable since the beginning of 2004 (Jacobson 2008), not since March 2004 had a majority of Americans agreed that the United States "did the right thing in taking military action against Iraq."[1] Bush's public reaction to this grim news was to belittle the polls. At an appearance at Freedom House in March 2006, he exclaimed, "You don't need a president chasing polls and focus groups in order to make tough decisions. You need presidents who make decisions based on sound principles."[2]

Bush's public face, however, hid a more complicated political reality. From the beginning of the war, the Bush administration planned and executed military strategy with the public firmly in mind. There is, in fact, clear evidence that the administration was paying close attention to the polls. On November 30, 2005, Bush outlined his future strategy for Iraq in a speech at the U.S. Naval Academy. As the *New York Times* subsequently reported, Bush heavily emphasized the concept of "victory," using the word fifteen times in his speech, posting "Plan for Victory" signs on the podium, and titling an accompanying National Security Council report "National Strategy for Victory in Iraq." The origins of this "victory" theme can be found in the public opinion research of National Security Council (NSC) advisor Peter Feaver, a political scientist at Duke University who has argued that support for war depends on citizens' beliefs about the correctness of war and its likelihood of success.[3] Bush's strategy was therefore not only a response to opinion polls; it was an attempt to influence those polls by emphasizing the prospect of eventual success in Iraq.

Bush's attention to public opinion polls in the realm of foreign policy puts him in good company among modern presidents. Lyndon Johnson tracked public opinion on Vietnam beginning in 1965, employing specialists to analyze both media and private opinion surveys and to draw conclusions about the direction of the public mood. The scope of this data collection and analysis effort was immense; under Johnson, according to Jacobs and Shapiro, the White House became "a veritable warehouse of opinion surveys" (1999, 595). The introduction of opinion polls into the war-making decision process in fact dates back to the 1930s. As long as there have been surveys, polls have played a central role in the formation of policy concerning matters of war and peace. Franklin D. Roosevelt's interest in public opinion is well known. Throughout his presidency, Roosevelt carefully cultivated various "channels to the public mind" (Steele 1974). Many of these techniques were methods well tested by politicians.[4] But unlike his predecessors, Roosevelt had considerable access to scientific opinion surveys. The early years of FDR's presidency, after all, coincided with the rise of opinion polling in America. Given that the public's voice has long held great consequence for politicians, how are we to understand the meaning of that voice and its place in the political process?

In this book, I argue that the lessons learned from studies of public opinion on domestic issues ought to inform our knowledge of public opinion in the foreign realm. Much of our understanding of opinion during wartime has proceeded from the notion that times of war are unique moments in political history. I argue that such thinking is incorrect. Instead, public opinion about war is shaped by the same attitudes and orientations that shape domestic politics. Public opinion during times of war is properly viewed as a continuation of the same processes that shape public opinion during times of peace.

PUBLIC OPINION AND WAR

Considering the importance of the relationship between public opinion and foreign policy, it is not surprising that the study of war and public opinion is a flourishing industry within political science. Some scholars of international relations have studied "audience costs"—the public's potential to punish politicians who do not follow through on military threats—by exploring the way these costs enable leaders to signal their resolve in international crises (Fearon 1994; Baum 2004; Schultz 1998). Others have investigated the way in which an organized political opposition affects the process of crisis bargaining (Schultz 1998). In addition, a large literature has grown up around "the democratic peace"—the question of whether democratic governments are less prone to international conflict than states with other forms of government (Doyle 1983, 1986; Gowa 1999; Huth and Allee 2003; Maoz 1998; Morrow 2002; Russett 1993; Small and Singer 1982). These scholars often look to the mass public as the primary cause of military action or inaction. As Reiter and Stam (2002) argue, democracies cannot wage war without at least the tacit consent of their citizens. According to these scholars, it is the fear of an unreceptive public that often keeps the dogs of war at bay in democracies.

Public opinion scholars have taken up this theme and closely examined the nature of the public's preferences in times of crisis, conducting systematic studies of individual conflicts and series of wars in an attempt to determine what it is that leads citizens to rally to war or to reject an internationalist position.[5] The result of this vast literature, however, is an inconclusive set of findings. Early authors such as Almond (1960) and Lippmann (1922) argued that Americans' preferences in foreign policy were largely incoherent—nothing more than shifting and changing "moods." More recently, authors such as Feaver and Gelpi (2004), Gelpi, Feaver, and Reifler (2005–6), and Larson (1996) have taken the opposite view, arguing that opinions about foreign policy adjust directly to dynamic world events in sensible ways. Furthermore, with rare exceptions (Aldrich, Sullivan, and Borgida 1989; Baum and Groeling 2004), the study of foreign policy attitudes has mostly been divorced from the study of domestic politics. In fact, a largely separate literature has developed on public opinion concerning foreign policy (see Holsti 2004 for a comprehensive review). As a result, the study of public opinion and war lacks a coherent center.

An additional problem with the existing work on public opinion and foreign policy is that scholars have mainly focused on developments in the cold war and post–cold war periods in isolation, one war at a time. What we know about mass reaction to war, we have learned from failed international interventions—such as those in Korea and Vietnam—and relatively short-term military excursions—such the 1991 Gulf War, Kosovo, and Afghanistan. In the process, studies of public opinion during wartime have seemingly forgotten the rise of the polling industry in the 1930s and 1940s and have almost completely ignored World War II—a war that was in many ways a unique event in American history. World War II was the only war in the last two centuries in which Americans were directly attacked by another nation before becoming engaged in active combat. Furthermore, unlike recent wars, World War II was waged with and against some of the same European nations that had provided generations of immigrants to America.

Seminal studies of public opinion and war have largely set aside such concerns. Mueller's (1973) pathbreaking book, *War, Presidents, and Public Opinion*, for instance, devotes only three pages to World War II. More recently, Holsti's (2004) comprehensive treatment, *Public Opinion and American Foreign Policy,* devotes less than ten pages to the Second World War. Thus, paradoxically, the systematic study of the relationship between government and the public during wartime, at least the work conducted by political scientists in the last forty years, has overlooked the largest and most important international conflict in U.S. history—one with potentially important lessons for the study of public opinion and war more generally. In fact, as I discuss in greater detail in the chapters that follow, to the extent that scholars have drawn lessons from the Second World War, these lessons have been based on a faulty understanding of the public's reaction to that war, in part because the surveys from the 1930s and 1940s have been neglected.

This book is an attempt to fill this gap in our knowledge. In the pages that follow, I consider the United States' experience during six wars: World War II, the Korean War, the Vietnam War, the Gulf War, the Afghanistan War, and the Iraq War. In advancing a general theory of public opinion and war, I therefore address a number of conflicts in American history but maintain a particular focus on World War II. Thus, this book brings our understanding of the dynamics of a conflict that was in many ways a unique effort into the general study of public opinion and war, thereby enriching both our knowledge of that war and our general understanding of how public opinion is forged in times of crisis. I make use of a rich trove of opinion data that were collected from 1935 to 1945, but—for reasons I make clear—have remained largely untouched for almost sixty years. I also draw on polls from familiar contemporary cases. The conflicts I consider range from relatively minor military interventions—such as the 1999 Kosovo conflict—to large-scale wars spanning many years—such as World War II and Vietnam. Although these wars differ in many respects, I find common patterns in the organization of public opinion during wartime that can change our understanding of public opinion in both the foreign and domestic arenas.

In this book I argue that public opinion during times of crisis—and during war in particular—is shaped by many of the same affections and enmities found on the domestic stage. Although these individual attachments may not fully account for changes in collective opinion, looking at wartime opinion through the lens of domestic politics yields some striking insights. Thus, to properly understand international relations and domestic politics, we need to unify the two areas of study.

The public may be directly influenced by some dramatic events, such as Pearl Harbor and 9/11, but—as in the domestic arena—public opinion is primarily structured by the ebb and flow of partisan and group-based political conflict.[6] These factors shape support for policies of war just as they shape policies of peace. Moreover, we can better understand critical public choices during times of international conflict—notably, support for civil liberties and the election of political leaders—by looking to the same factors that shape opinion on the domestic stage. In these realms, the feelings of threat and fear generated by international conflict influence opinions and choices in the same ways that they influence public decisions surrounding domestic policies. In short, the study of domestic politics and international affairs—at least in the realm of public opinion—can and should proceed from a common foundation. Considering public opinion and foreign policy in isolation from the rest of the field of public opinion is not only unnecessary; it is a misguided enterprise. My book therefore builds on the work of other scholars—such as Hurwitz and Peffley (1987) and Zaller (1992)—who have applied the lessons gleaned through years of research on domestic public opinion to understand public opinion about matters lying beyond the water's edge. By revisiting faulty lessons from World War II and drawing on seemingly disparate survey evidence from more than sixty years of American involvement in international affairs, I draw broader conclusions about the roots of public attitudes toward foreign policy. In doing so, I provide a coherent understanding of public opinion during times of crisis that brings together several divergent lines of research in the fields of international relations and American politics.

My findings also have important implications for the study of domestic politics. Just as our study of domestic opinion can inform our study of public opinion and foreign policy, the study of public opinion and war can shed new light on the nature of public opinion more generally. In domestic politics, the positions of prominent political elites have—with rare exception—changed only gradually if at all. The two parties have long taken firm positions on many political controversies. Whereas the intensity and salience of these positions may wax and wane over electoral cycles, the relative locations of the two parties are relatively stable. It is difficult in these circumstances to disentangle the relative importance of mass preferences and elite positions. In the realm of war, however, elite positions are sometimes more malleable, especially given the wide latitude politicians often have in the foreign realm. In the last decade alone, both Democratic and Republican presidents have rallied the nation to military action at different times using very similar justifications. Moreover, once foreign commitments have been launched, it is difficult for leaders to extract the country from involvement abroad. Vietnam, for instance, may have been Johnson's folly, but after 1968 it became "Nixon's war." Given the sometimes abrupt changes in elite positioning and rhetoric on critical foreign policy issues by particular party leaders, the study of public opinion and war can illuminate the dynamics of public opinion more generally in a way that the study of domestic politics cannot easily do. Times of war may be distinctive in several respects, but they can inform our general understanding of the formation and expression of public opinion in important ways.

OVERVIEW

In part 1 of this book, I set the stage for the analysis that follows by providing a historical overview of the different military interventions and conflicts. In chapter 2, I discuss the Korean War, the Vietnam War, the Gulf War, the war in Afghanistan, and the Iraq War. In chapter 3, I take up World War II. In both chapters, I make the case that we can learn much by comparing and contrasting the trends and relationships in the patterns of public opinion across the different wars. I pay special attention here to the Second World War, a conflict that looms large in American history, but also one that has mostly been passed over by scholars of public opinion. Generations of researchers have ignored the vast stores of information concerning the public's preferences during this crucial moment in American political life, in large part because these data are difficult to work with and were collected using procedures that—from a modern perspective— seem arcane. I use methods that account for the shortcomings of these early survey efforts, however, and dispel several myths that have arisen concerning the nature of public support for World War II; in doing so, I bring the Second World War into the systematic study of public opinion and war.

The two parts of the book that follow take up topics central to the formation and expression of public opinion during times of war. I first examine the roots of public support for war in chapters 4–6. This section makes a simple point: domestic politics has a great impact on how people think about war. There is a growing consensus among political scientists, and even some policymakers, that citizens on the whole hold views of foreign policy generally, and war specifically, that move in response to changes in salient world events that reflect on American interests (Holsti 1992, 2004; Jentleson 1992; Nincic 1988, 1992; Page and Shapiro 1992; Feaver and Gelpi 2004; Gelpi, Feaver, and Reifler 2005–6). For instance, a prominent line of argument in this vein is what Burk (1999) calls the "casualties hypothesis," the view that the American people will shy away from international involvement in the face of war deaths (Mueller 1973). Although recognizing the important contributions of these authors, I question the assumption of scholars in this tradition. In chapter 4, I review the literature on the influence of events on public opinion concerning war. Existing accounts of the roots of public support for military action fail to specify the mechanism by which members of the public process information concerning the events of war. Although events may ultimately help shape public opinion, the mechanism by which these events exert influence on opinion is complex. Foreign policy events seldom directly affect opinion in and of themselves. Facts are often ambiguous and little known by citizens. Instead, factors that shape opinions on other policies—attachments and enmities forged on the domestic political scene—also shape public opinion on war.

I begin to explore these factors in chapter 5. Using data from a variety of conflicts that seem to differ in their particulars—Vietnam, the war in Iraq, and World War II—I find a common structure to opinion: above all else, patterns of conflict among partisan political actors shape mass opinion on war. Here, the revised picture of public opinion during World War II is especially significant. Even in a war in which—according to conventional wisdom—the public rallied as one in direct response to the notorious attack at Pearl Harbor, the residue of partisan political conflict emerges as a powerful influence on public opinion. Opinions on foreign and domestic policies, it seems, are formed using similar processes. In this framework we can see how the tides of war may matter for public opinion. There is little reason to suspect that the public can independently evaluate the political implications of ambiguous wartime events. However, political elites with a stake in the outcome of policy decisions have the power to shape the meaning of those events for the public. Objective events are evaluated by elites through the lens of their own beliefs, values, and ideologies. These politicians then communicate their evaluations to ordinary citizens. Thus, patterns of consensus and dissensus on the interpretation of wartime events by politicians—who have partisan and career aspirations—shape public opinion.

In chapter 6, I turn to another factor that influences opinion, namely, feelings about particular groups in society. Beliefs about the groups to which individuals feel attachment or enmity may be forged in the domestic arena, but these beliefs also structure individuals' attitudes in the foreign policy realm. To provide evidence for this contention, I draw primarily on data from World War II—a time when internal ethnic divisions were a highly visible part of the social sphere. Large segments of the American population were able to trace their ancestry to the very countries the United States fought with and against. Before the United States entered the war, those citizens with ties to Allied countries were more likely to support intervention, whereas those from Axis countries advocated isolationist policies. The entry of the United States into war diminished differences between citizens whose parents were born in Allied countries and those whose parents were born in the United States, but the differences in support for war between these groups and citizens with lineal connections to Axis countries persisted. Thus, in some circumstances, even large-scale unifying events cannot erase long-standing ethnic differences. I also demonstrate that one's feelings toward other groups can shape public opinion. Affection or hostility toward Germans, Italians, and Jewish citizens—opinions that had most likely been formed independent of foreign events—had a significant impact on individuals' opinions about involvement in the war. Negative feelings toward groups from Axis countries and positive feelings toward individuals with lineal connections to Allied countries were correlated with more interventionist attitudes. Negative feelings toward Jews, on the other hand, were correlated with anti-interventionist sentiment.

In the third part of the book, I move beyond explaining attitudes toward war and investigate how normal democratic processes are shaped by the public's experiences during wartime. Chapter 7 explores how political judgments critical for the foundation of democracy are generated in times of war. Specifically, I investigate civil liberties judgments during World War II, Vietnam, and the period following the terrorist attacks of September 11, 2001. Consistent with the themes of this book, I find that the basic structure of civil liberties judgments remains the same in times of war and peace. Although the particular conditions of war may change the manner in which members of the public judge the desirability of restrictions on civil liberties, those factors that scholars have used to gauge support for civil liberties—most notably perceptions of threat—shape civil liberties opinions in times of war as well. The specific nature of threats may differ in times of war and times of peace, but in both cases it is the presence of a perceived threat that diminishes support for civil liberties. In general, attacks on America—or the onset of war—increase citizens' willingness to limit civil liberties, at least for a time. However, as threats recede, citizens begin to resist encroachments on their basic values. Thus, although the particular circumstances of war may be unique, they influence civil liberties judgments through mechanisms that are familiar from studies of domestic politics.

In chapter 8, I examine the role of war in shaping presidential elections. I begin by examining the effect of judgments about particular wars on the vote. A number of scholars have argued that opinion concerning the Iraq War crucially shaped the outcome of the 2004 election. I make the case that this conclusion is erroneous. Given the partisan nature of support for war discussed in chapter 5, I argue that it is impossible to uncover the effects of war on the vote by examining a single election in isolation. During war, people judge the correctness of military actions through the lens of their partisan predispositions, not vice versa. Any analysis that treats such attitudes as causally prior to vote choice is therefore inherently erroneous. I instead take a longer view of electoral history, considering every presidential election from 1952 to 2004. I find that war can affect electoral outcomes in two ways, both of which are crucially rooted in the normal political process. First, war—like the economy—can serve as a performance issue for leaders. Just as leaders may be punished for poor economic performance, they might also be hurt by bad news coming from abroad. Second, I find that the emotions of fear and threat that are brought about by war—not war itself—can change the dynamics of elections. Specifically, foreign crises can cause citizens to place a high value on leadership, thereby advantaging the party in power. Both Franklin D. Roosevelt and George W. Bush, it seems, benefited from the conditions of crisis that began under their respective watches.

PART I   Historical Perspective

PUBLIC OPINION AND WAR:
A HISTORICAL PERSPECTIVE

The era of public opinion polling began in the 1930s and has spanned wars great and small. Because the particulars of some of these conflicts might not be familiar to readers, in this chapter I take up the period from 1950 to the present. I briefly describe the conflicts discussed in this book to lay the groundwork for the analysis to follow. These treatments are not intended as a comprehensive overview of the different wars the United States has fought since the beginning of the cold war; I leave that task to other authors. For instance, Mueller has written excellent accounts of the Korean and Vietnam wars (1973) and the Gulf War (1994). Furthermore, I set aside some important interventions in U.S. history, such as the 1992–93 military involvement in Somalia. Here I merely provide an overview of major wartime events and a picture of the broad outlines of public support for those wars I take up in this book.[1]

There is, however, one conflict into which I do dive into the details. In a departure from much work on public opinion and war conducted since the 1950s, in this book I pay special attention to public opinion during World War II. Considering World War II alongside other conflicts in U.S. history is, however, a somewhat controversial undertaking. As some scholars have argued, the exceptional nature of the threat posed by that war and the unprecedented military effort that followed may make comparisons with other wars difficult. Thus, in the next chapter I investigate the World War II era with an eye toward exposing certain myths that have developed about the "exceptional nature" of public opinion concerning war during the 1930s and 1940s. In debunking these myths, I set straight the empirical record on one of the most important conflicts in American history, but also lay the foundation for the broader points I make in the chapters that follow. As I demonstrate in the rest of this book, by expanding our historical reach to include the most important war of the twentieth century, it is possible to draw broad conclusions about the roots of public attitudes toward foreign policy more generally.

KOREA

The Korean War was the first direct military action of the cold war.[2] Its roots, however, lie in the final days of the Second World War. After the Allies' defeat of Germany and with the end of the war in the Pacific in sight, the future of those territories occupied by Japan, such as Korea, was in question. The United States and Russia decided on a policy of joint administration. The initial decision to divide Korea was made at the Potsdam Conference in the summer of 1945, followed a few weeks later by an agreement between the United States and the Soviet Union that placed the dividing line along the 38th parallel. Soviet forces would invade, occupy, and receive Japanese prisoners of war north of this point, while the United States handled the south. At the Moscow Conference of Foreign Ministers in December 1945, it was decided that Korea would regain independence after four years of international control. However, the creation of competing governments in the north and south—which were handpicked by the Soviet Union and the United States, respectively—made such a long-term arrangement unlikely.

In 1948, South Korea took its first steps toward independence by holding elections. The winner was Syngman Rhee, an anti-Communist, American-educated candidate. Meanwhile, the Soviet Union established a Communist government in the north headed by General Secretary Kim Il-Sung. With each government claiming the right to rule the entire peninsula after the period of occupation had ended, tensions began to rise in 1949, building toward a civil war. Supplied with arms from the Soviet Union, the North began military attacks across the border, while the South was given only limited support by the United States.

By 1950, tensions had escalated considerably, coming to a head that summer. In the predawn hours of June 25, 135,000 North Korean troops launched a surprise attack across the 38th parallel.[3] Within days, South Korean forces found themselves outnumbered and in full retreat. North Korean forces occupied the South Korean capital of Seoul just three days after the initial attack.

Faced with the prospect of a united communist Korea, the United States led a call for international intervention at the United Nations. Taking advantage of the absence of the Soviet Union from the Security Council, the United States pushed through the adoption of Security Council Resolution 82, which cleared the way for direct American involvement in the conflict.[4] The resolution called for an end to all hostilities and a withdrawal of North Korean troops across the 38th parallel, the formation of a UN Commission in Korea to monitor the situation, and a prohibition on UN member states from providing assistance to North Korean authorities.

At first, the U.S. involvement did little to change the tide of the war. The first UN forces to see combat, which included a sizable U.S. presence, were defeated with heavy losses, and the North Korean army continued its advance. By August, the South Korean forces and the U.S. Army had been pushed back to a small area in the southeast corner of the Korean peninsula. A bold move by General MacArthur, the UN commander in chief, soon turned the tide, however. MacArthur planned an amphibious landing at Inchon, well behind the North Korean front lines, near the 38th parallel. On September 15, the landing was made, and U.S. forces were met with only light resistance. Seoul was recaptured, and the North Koreans, cut off, quickly retreated northward.

Although public opinion data from this time are spotty, the surveys that exist suggest that the American public was initially supportive of the military effort. Early polling was conducted by Gallup—which asked whether "the United States made a mistake in going into the war in Korea, or not"—and by the National Opinion Research Center (NORC)—which asked, "Do you think the United States was right or wrong in sending American troops to stop the Communist invasion of South Korea?" (beginning in mid-1952, NORC also asked, "As things stand now, do you feel that the war in Korea has been (was) worth fighting, or not?"). Figure 2.1 presents the percentage of Americans who supported the war from 1950 to 1953. The remaining respondents opposed the war or said they did not have an opinion. As the figure demonstrates, although public support was higher when the anti-Communist version of the question employed by NORC was asked, both forms of the question elicited strong support for the U.S. effort through the summer and early fall of 1950 (see Mueller 1973 for a comprehensive discussion of this question-wording effect).

With the public firmly behind the effort, victory seemed close at hand. On October 7, 1950, American troops crossed the 38th parallel and

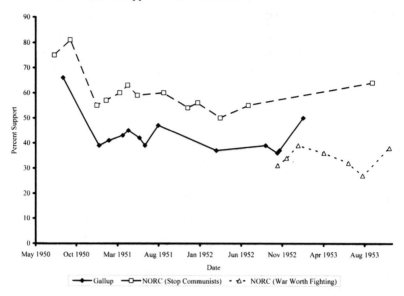

FIGURE 2.1. Trends in support for the Korean War.

continued their advance northward. MacArthur's aggressive move, however, soon triggered a counterresponse from China. Mao Zedong decided in October to mobilize the Chinese army to reinforce North Korean forces, sending 270,000 Chinese troops into the conflict. In early November, the Chinese army began to engage U.S. forces. The entrance of the Chinese turned the tide of battle, and by the new year, United Nations troops had pulled back and lost control of Seoul.

The entrance of Chinese forces also corresponded with a large dip in public support for the war (see fig. 2.1). The percentage of respondents who supported the war dropped over twenty points from September to December, coinciding with the events of October and November. Given the gap in the temporal coverage of the survey data, we cannot know precisely when the tide turned against U.S. involvement, but it is clear that late 1950 represented a defining moment in the Korean conflict.

In the spring of 1951, the UN forces rebounded, advancing north once again to the 38th parallel. Their advance was again stopped, however, and both sides stalled at the dividing line for the remaining two years of the conflict. Opinion poll data suggest that the public's reaction to the war ossified as well. After the initial drop following the entry of the Chinese forces, public support for the American effort remained stable, even rebounding somewhat through early 1951. As Mueller aptly notes,

> It was the entry of China into the war that apparently altered . . . the basic support for war. More striking than the drop in support caused by the Chinese entry is the near-absence of further decline for the remaining 2½ years of the war. From early 1951 until the end of the war in the summer of 1953, basic support for the war [remained constant]—this despite the continually mounting casualties and despite a number of important events: the recall of General MacArthur; the beginning, breaking off, and then intermittent restarting of peace talks; the launching of offensives and counteroffensives. (1973, 51)

In chapter 4, I return to the question of the power of particular wartime events, but Mueller's observation is telling. Figure 2.1 demonstrates that opinion was remarkably stable from the end of 1950 onward. In fact, through 1951 at least, there was not a serious base of opposition to the war. The picture painted in figure 2.1 overstates the steady level of dissatisfaction with the war because, following convention, it treats "don't know" responses as a substantive answer, on par with opposing the war. From April 1951 through the end of the year, in fact, with the exception of a single poll, fewer respondents said the United States made a mistake than said the war was the right thing to do (with the rest abstaining).[5] Even in that one poll—a Gallup poll taken in late June 1951—the opponents of the war barely outnumbered the supporters of the war, by a margin of 43 percent to 39 percent. Come 1952, the opponents of the war began to outnumber its supporters, but on no survey did a majority express opposition to the war. Moreover, a majority of the public always expressed support for war in response to the "stop the Communist invasion" version of the question.

The long stalemate that began in the middle of 1951 facilitated the beginning of truce talks, which continued through the following year. As would be the case in Vietnam sixteen years later, the control of the presidency shifted hands during the war. However, in the 1950s, unlike the Vietnam era, the new Republican leadership sought a quick end to the conflict. In November 1952, the president-elect Dwight Eisenhower began negotiations with both Korean governments. After several months of bargaining, in July 1953, an armistice was reached. Both sides withdrew from their front lines, and a UN commission was set up to enforce the armistice. The status quo produced by that war persists more than fifty years later.

VIETNAM

Like the origins of the Korean War, those of the Vietnam War can be found in the early years of the cold war.[6] The conflict in Vietnam began shortly after World War II as a colonial war between France and revolutionary forces in Vietnam. In the summer of 1954, the French government ended its century of rule over Vietnam by agreeing to the Geneva Peace Accords, which partitioned Vietnam at the 17th parallel.[7] This arrangement was supposed to be temporary, but, under President Eisenhower, the United States sought the creation of a counterrevolutionary government south of the dividing line—the Republic of Vietnam (or South Vietnam). This government proved unstable and—in the late 1950s and early 1960s—a revolutionary movement known as the National Liberation Front emerged to fight the South Vietnamese government, with at least the tacit support of the Democratic Republic of Vietnam (or North Vietnam). In response, President Kennedy increased U.S. military involvement in Vietnam, through arms and advisors. This buildup continued under President Johnson.

Direct U.S. involvement in the conflict began in 1964. In response to what the Johnson administration claimed were attacks on U.S. naval destroyers by North Vietnam in August of that year, Congress passed the Gulf of Tonkin Resolution. This bill was supported unanimously in the House and met with only two dissenting votes in the Senate. The resolution gave the president broad war powers to pursue the conflict in Vietnam, and in March 1965, the first American combat troops were sent to Vietnam to prevent the weak South Vietnamese government from collapsing. The United States was now fully committed to supporting that government. More importantly, given the strong support for the Gulf of Tonkin Resolution, the U.S. government was fully united behind an interventionist strategy. Conversations concerning the Vietnam War within the government consisted largely of a steady and mostly unchallenged stream of rhetoric reminiscent of Lyndon Johnson's contention that the issue of Vietnam "is the future of southeast Asia as a whole. A threat to any nation in that region is a threat to all, and a threat to us. . . . This is not just a jungle war, but a struggle for freedom on every front of human activity."[8]

Through the mid-1960s, the United States became increasingly embroiled in the conflict. The commitment of U.S. troops surged from an average of 23,000 in 1964, to almost 500,000 by 1967 (Mueller 1973, 28). At the same time, the strong pro-intervention message continued among both government officials and the news media. Zaller's (1992) content analysis of news magazine coverage of the Vietnam War finds that the prowar message was much stronger than the antiwar message in the period from 1964 to 1968, reaching its greatest disparity in 1966.

With hearings held by Senator William Fulbright in 1966, opposition to the war began to emerge within the U.S. government. In 1967, there were some attempts in Congress to cut off funding for the war. The defeat of these bills by large margins, however, indicated continuing strong support for the war within the government (Zaller 1992). In the next year, though, the balance of support began to shift. In 1968 on Tet, the Vietnamese New Year, North Vietnam launched coordinated attacks on several southern cities. Meant to break American will, the attacks had mixed results; Communist forces suffered large casualties in the South, but indiscriminate violence against non-Communists in the North created local ill will. Still, the Tet offensive was widely viewed as a setback for U.S. forces, and politicians within the Democratic Party opposed to the war began to gain prominence. In the face of antiwar candidate Eugene McCarthy's surprising showing in the New Hampshire primary in March 1968, Johnson announced that he would not seek reelection.

In the years after 1968, the anti-intervention message signaled by Fulbright's actions and McCarthy's candidacy gathered steam. At the turn of the decade, the proportion of pro- and anti-intervention messages in the media, although not quite balanced, contained strong messages to appeal to both those groups predisposed to support the war and those predisposed to oppose the U.S. effort (see Zaller 1992).

This shift in the balance of elite rhetoric on war had important implications for the nature of public support for that conflict. As I have demonstrated elsewhere (Berinsky 2004), the opening of the lines of elite communication facilitated the expression of latent antiwar sentiment among the public. The political mechanisms of the late 1960s also had important partisan implications, however. As the balance of pro- and antiwar messages shifted, the fault line of support for war at the elite level did not initially track party lines. Vietnam is unusual among the wars of the last sixty-five years in that, during Johnson's time as president, polarization occurred *within* the Democratic Party, not across the parties. After all, the first real hints of opposition within Congress came through hearings conducted by Fulbright, a Democrat, in 1966. This debate grew and spilled into the 1968 campaign, splintering the Democratic Party into rival factions in the primaries and beyond. At the same time, rhetoric from the

Republican side did not change appreciably—a trend that continued into the Nixon administration.

Nixon's election in 1968 signaled the beginning of a strategy of Vietnamization, which involved turning over much of the fighting responsibility to the South Vietnamese government while removing U.S. troops and continuing air strikes on North Vietnam. In June 1969, Nixon announced that he would bring 25,000 troops home by August of that year. Further withdrawals were announced in September and November. The direct U.S. presence on the ground was clearly on the decline. In other ways, however, the pace of the United States' involvement in Southeast Asia increased, with the invasions of Cambodia and Laos in 1970. Thus, although Nixon followed through on his campaign promise to end the war in Vietnam, the period of continued U.S. involvement made Vietnam "Nixon's war." The net result of these actions was to shift the dispute over the correctness of the action in Vietnam from one within the Democratic Party to one between the two major parties.

The Vietnamization strategy also signaled the dawn of a period of military stalemate. For the next three years, the North and the South made little progress toward peace. At the end of 1972, U.S. secretary of state Henry Kissinger and North Vietnamese representatives Xuan Thuy and Le Duc Tho produced a draft peace agreement, but that agreement was quickly rejected by the warring parties. The conflict intensified in the following month, culminating in a series of large-scale bombings of North Vietnam's largest cities. In January 1973, the sides returned to the bargaining table and came to a final agreement. On January 23, the final draft was initialed, officially ending hostilities between the United States and North Vietnam.

Trends in support for the Vietnam War are presented in figure 2.2. In some ways, the pattern of support is reminiscent of that shown by the Korean War data presented in figure 2.1. There are, however, important differences in the path of public opinion as well. Rather than the quick drop in support found at the beginning of the Korean War, support for Vietnam seems to have followed a path of slow and steady decline, punctuated by several turning points in 1968, 1969, and 1970. Moreover, unlike its response to Korea, the public did not react to the change in presidential administrations in 1968 with an increase in support for the war. The postelection increase in support for Vietnam was on the order of a couple of percentage points—a far cry from the ten-point increase following the election of Eisenhower in 1952. In fact, the decline in support for the war continued from 1969 onward. As I discuss further in chapter 5, this pat-

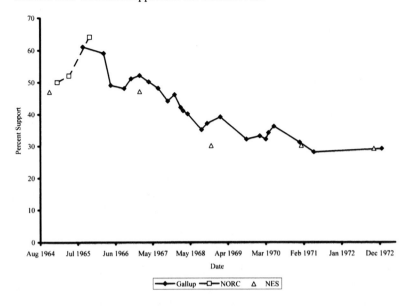

FIGURE 2.2. Trends in support for the Vietnam War.

tern of decay can be explained by a shift in the impact of partisanship on Nixon's ascension to the presidency. For now, however, what is important is that the paths of public support for the two wars in Southeast Asia converged and diverged in important ways.

GULF WAR

Although the United States generally shied away from large-scale military commitments in the wake of the Vietnam War, America was involved in a number of military interventions from the mid-1970s through the 1980s, including missions in Lebanon, Grenada, and Panama. These actions, however, paled in comparison to the depth of U.S. involvement in the Persian Gulf in the early 1990s.

The Persian Gulf region was, for many years, of central strategic importance to the United States. Throughout the 1980s, the United States contributed military and economic aid to Iraq in an attempt to balance Iran's influence and to promote stability in the Gulf. By 1990, however, tensions had developed between the United States and its erstwhile ally over a number of issues, including reported human rights abuses, Iraq's continued military buildup, and relations with Israel.

In the summer of 1990 these tensions came to a boil. Iraq began to make a series of aggressive demands on Kuwait, its neighbor to the south.

At the end of July, after negotiations between the two countries had stalled, Iraqi soldiers were sent to the border of Iraq and Kuwait. When Kuwait refused to submit to Iraq's demands, Iraqi leader Saddam Hussein ordered an invasion. Troops crossed the border on August 2, 1990. Within a week, Iraq annexed the whole of Kuwait, declaring parts of it to be extensions of the province of Basra and the rest to be the nineteenth province of Iraq.

The international community quickly condemned Hussein's action. The UN Security Council passed Resolution 660, which demanded the withdrawal of Iraqi troops, and Resolution 661, which placed economic sanctions on Iraq. On August 7, the United States became directly involved in the crisis. George H. W. Bush commenced Operation Desert Shield, ordering the immediate deployment of U.S. troops to Saudi Arabia to defend that country from possible attack. By the end of August, over 60,000 U.S. troops were in Saudi Arabia to place pressure on Hussein.

In this initial phase of the Gulf crisis, bipartisan support for Bush's policies ran high. As Zaller (1994) notes, there was no open opposition to the deployment of U.S. forces to the Gulf, and—more importantly—most leaders in the Democratic-controlled Congress backed Bush's actions. By and large, the public followed suit. Mueller (1994) provides an excellent review of public opinion concerning conflict. To condense his presentation, in figure 2.3 I provide four time series measuring support for military action. As the figure shows, through the early fall of 1990, even with the dissipation of the initial rally, a large majority of the public approved of the decision to send U.S. troops to the Gulf. Although Republican identifiers were more supportive than Democrats of military action (Jacobson 2008; Zaller 1994), a substantial majority of the public supported the hard line taken by Bush.

All the while, the international community sought to ratchet up the pressure on Iraq. In October and November, the UN Security Council passed a further series of resolutions, most notably Resolution 678, which set a deadline of January 15, 1991, for Iraqi withdrawal. For the first time since the Korean War, the UN authorized the use of force against a nation-state.

Domestically, talk also moved from sanctions to the use of force. Two days after the 1990 midterm congressional elections, Bush announced that he would send several hundred thousand additional troops to Saudi Arabia. This move began to stir Democratic resistance and sparked debate over the need for immediate military action. Prominent congressional Democrats began to speak against the Bush administration's chosen course of action. Senator Sam Nunn of Georgia, chairman of the Armed Services

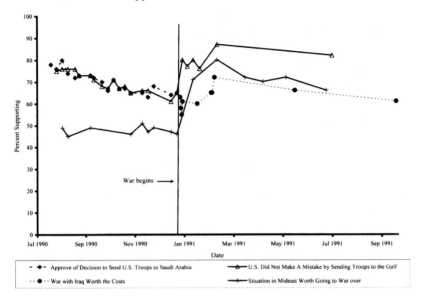

FIGURE 2.3. Trends in support for the Gulf War.

Committee, for instance, championed a policy of continued sanctions. Administration officials responded to this resistance by accusing Democrats in the House and Senate of providing "comfort" to Saddam Hussein.[9] Meanwhile talks between Iraq and the United States made little progress. The United States maintained that only a full, unconditional surrender and withdrawal of Iraqi troops would provide an acceptable resolution to the crisis. Iraq, on the other hand, insisted that it would not withdraw its troops unless Israeli troops withdrew from Palestinian territory and Syrian troops withdrew from Lebanon. A series of proposed talks in December did not come to fruition, and the crisis in the Gulf continued to escalate.

During this time, although support for strong U.S. action remained fairly high, the public preferred sanctions over war. In mid-November, 70 percent of the public thought that Bush should "wait to see if economic and diplomatic sanctions are effective" rather than "quickly begin military action."[10] As figure 2.3 shows, throughout November and December 1990, only once did a majority of the public think that the current situation in the Mideast was worth going to war over. A December Gallup poll also found that a majority of Americans wanted to wait to see if sanctions would be effective rather than commence military action on January 15.[11]

It quickly became apparent, however, that Iraq and the United States were on a clear path to war. On January 9, President Bush urged Congress to adopt a resolution authorizing the use of "all necessary means" against Iraq if it did not pull out before the deadline.[12] Debate on the Senate resolution, proposed by John Warner (R-VA) and thirty-four cosponsors, began January 11. Senator Nunn, along with George Mitchell (D-ME), introduced a counterproposal, which would continue sanctions. The House considered both a bill authorizing force—introduced by Rob Michel (R-IL) alongside thirty-one cosponsors—and another in favor of continuing sanctions, proposed by Reps. Lee Hamilton (D-IN) and Richard Gephardt (D-MS).[13]

The partisan wrangling over the wisdom of force, which had bubbled up in December, led, predictably, to a series of highly partisan votes over the proposals. The Authorization for Use of Military Force against Iraq Resolution of 1991 passed both houses of Congress on January 12, by a vote of 52–47 in the Senate and 250–183 in the House. These majorities obscured large party differences in levels of support. Nearly all the Republican legislators—42 of 44 senators and 164 of 167 congressmen—supported the action. Over two-thirds of Democrats in both chambers opposed the resolution, however; 45 of 55 senators and 179 of 265 congressmen voted against it. The bipartisan consensus of the fall clearly gave way to a splintered political coalition on the eve of the war.

Although Democratic identifiers among the public did not split as starkly as did members of Congress in early January, large gaps emerged between the two parties on the wisdom of war. Among Democrats, 57 percent thought that the United States had "done enough to seek a diplomatic solution to the Persian Gulf situation," compared with 80 percent of Republicans.[14] Similarly, 46 percent of Democrats thought that sanctions should be given more time, compared with only 24 percent of Republicans.[15]

Regardless of Democratic misgivings, with congressional authorization in place and the UN deadline of January 15 clear, war soon came. Operation Desert Storm was launched on January 17, 1991, with a series of initial air strikes. Iraqi radar sites near the Saudi Arabian border were destroyed first, followed by attacks on targets in Baghdad, government headquarters, Iraqi television stations, air force fields, presidential palaces, and command and communication facilities. This air campaign continued for over one month. During this time, the U.S. military and its allies prepared for further action. About 600,000 troops from thirty-four countries had by that time joined the U.S.-led coalition, and ground forces entered the conflict by February 24. Iraqi forces began a retreat on February 26, setting fire to the Kuwaiti oil fields as they went. Coalition forces continued to pursue retreating units over the border and back into Iraq.

The end of active hostilities was declared on February 27, one hundred hours after the ground campaign started. The cost in terms of lives was relatively modest, contrary to even the most optimistic forecasts. U.S. combat casualties totaled 148, including 35 deaths by friendly fire, whereas injuries totaled 776 coalition troops, including 467 Americans. [16] As figure 2.3 shows, the quick end to the fighting did not increase support for the war. Given the size of the initial rally in mid-January, however, such opinion dynamics are not surprising. Unlike the Vietnam and Korean wars, the Gulf War was almost as popular at its end as it was at its beginning.

9/11, AFGHANISTAN, AND IRAQ

During the 1990s, the United States was involved in a number of other military interventions throughout the world, including actions in Somalia during the early 1990s and in the former Yugoslavia during the mid- to late 1990s. A large body of work exists that considers the public's reactions to these interventions.[17] In this book, I set aside a consideration of such conflicts not because they are unimportant but because I do not address them in the analysis in the chapters that follow. I therefore pick up my narrative after the turn of the century with the two major incidents that occurred in the wake of the terrorist attacks on September 11, 2001—the Afghan and Iraq wars.

9/11 and Afghanistan

Afghanistan has long been a troubled country, but these troubles continued with a power struggle that emerged after the withdrawal of Soviet forces in February 1989. The Soviet Union continued to back the incumbent government, led by the People's Democratic Party of Afghanistan, against a diverse group of guerrillas known as the mujahideen. With the collapse of the Soviet Union in 1991, this aid dried up, and soon thereafter, in early 1992, the government collapsed. After taking power, the mujahideen experienced political splits, and the country entered a period of renewed civil war. In late 1994, a faction of religious scholars and former mujahideen, known as the Taliban, emerged in the south of the country. By 1996, this group took control of the capital, establishing a government based on strict religious principles. By 1998, the Taliban secured control of almost 90 percent of the country. The opposition to the Taliban—the remnants of the coalition government that had ruled between 1992 and 1996—organized with other opposition groups as the Northern Alliance and continued to fight a losing battle against the regime.

Around this time, Osama bin Laden, who, with his group al Qaeda, had been based in Sudan since 1991, returned to Afghanistan, where they had first formed in the 1980s. Although the Taliban regime did not formally sanction the actions of al Qaeda, the Taliban provided sanctuary for bin Laden and his followers. This implicit policy of protection led to considerable friction with the United States. In 1998, in response to attacks on U.S. embassies in Kenya and Tanzania, the United States launched a targeted bombing campaign against terrorist training camps established by al Qaeda. Aside from this incident, however, al Qaeda proceeded unimpeded.

On September 11, 2001, two planes struck the World Trade Center towers in New York, and another crashed into the Pentagon in Washington, D.C., killing nearly three thousand people and beginning a new phase in U.S. foreign policy. Within hours of the attack, the trail of evidence led to al Qaeda. On September 14, Congress passed the Authorization for Use of Military Force against Terrorists Act by an overwhelming majority, with only one dissenting vote in the House. The act authorized the president to "use all necessary and appropriate force against those nations, organizations, or persons he determines planned, authorized, committed, or aided the terrorist attacks that occurred on September 11, 2001, or harbored such organizations or persons, in order to prevent any future acts of international terrorism against the United States by such nations, organizations or persons." Following the Taliban's repeated refusal to give up bin Laden and renounce its ties to terrorism in the weeks after 9/11, the United States, along with NATO forces, launched a military campaign on October 7, 2001. The initial aerial campaign severely damaged al Qaeda training camps, and communication and command centers, and destroyed the Taliban's air defenses. In conjunction with the ground forces of the Northern Alliance, U.S. troops pushed Taliban fighters south and east into the heart of the country by early November. On November 12, Taliban forces fled the city of Kabul, which marked the beginning of the collapse of the Taliban regime. The Taliban surrendered Kandahar, their last stronghold, on December 7.

The United States moved quickly to establish a democratic government in Afghanistan. On December 5, 2001, negotiations in Bonn, Germany, resulted in the creation of an interim post-Taliban administration under Hamid Karzai. Over the next few years, the transition continued. On October 9, 2004, Karzai was elected president of Afghanistan in the country's first-ever presidential election, and one year later, in September 2005, the country elected representatives to parliament.

While attention shifted to Iraq in the wake of the 2003 invasion of that country, the military conflict continued in Afghanistan. The summer of 2002 saw a major resurgence in Taliban activity in the southeastern provinces. Escalation of fighting continued into 2006 and 2007.

Despite a record of overwhelming victories in battles against Taliban fighters, the coalition forces faced an increasing number of casualties as a result of suicide bombings, making 2007 the deadliest year for U.S. forces in Afghanistan since 2001; record numbers of Afghan civilians were also killed. Although NATO has managed to maintain its hold in most major cities, the Taliban had regained ground in the rural provinces, expanding from its traditional southern territory into the provinces along the Iranian border.[18] During this time, however, discussion of the Afghanistan War dipped below the political radar. In the run-up to the 2008 election, the Bush administration rarely mentioned Afghanistan. The leading Republican candidates ignored it as well, preferring to lump the war into the larger "war on terror." Democrats also relegated the conflict to second-tier status, referencing it only in passing to illustrate the cost of the Iraq War. In fact, in the six major debates held in 2007 among presidential candidates in the run up to the primaries, no question or candidate specifically addressed the conflict in Afghanistan.[19]

Readings of public support for the Afghanistan conflict are somewhat limited in temporal scope when compared with those for the other wars discussed in this book. Initial support for the conflict was extraordinarily high. As figures 2.4A and 24B show, from September 2001 through April 2002, between 80 percent and 90 percent of the public approved of the military action. After April 2002, only a smattering of questions was asked about the U.S. action. As the military's attention shifted to Iraq, it appears that pollsters followed suit. In fact, perhaps the initial measures of support for the conflict led some polling organizations to stop asking about Afghanistan. The polls that were taken after April 2002 demonstrate greatly diminished levels of public enthusiasm for the military effort. Still, public support for the Afghan war remained higher than that indicated by comparable figures for the Iraq War, the final conflict of the post–World War II era taken up in this book.

Iraq

In the wake of the invasion of Afghanistan, the Bush administration quickly turned its attention to Iraq. Following the 1991 Gulf War, the UN had mandated that all long-range missile programs, as well chemical, biological, and nuclear weapons programs, be halted, that all such weapons be

FIGURE 2.4A. Trends in support for the Afghanistan War, 2001–2.

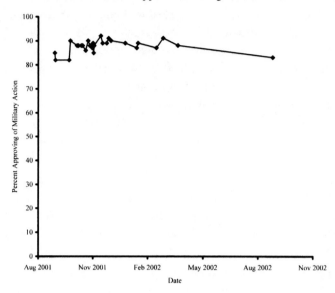

FIGURE 2.4B. Trends in support for the Afghanistan War, 2006–7.

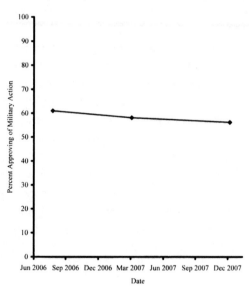

destroyed, and that the disarmament be verified by inspectors. The Iraqi government long resisted such demands, creating friction between Iraq and the United States throughout the Clinton administration. In 2002, however, the U.S. government began to increase pressure on Iraqi leader Saddam Hussein. In his January 2002 State of the Union address, President Bush put Iraq squarely at the center of the "Axis of Evil"—a group that also included Iran and North Korea. A few months later, in August 2002, Vice President Cheney publicly accused Saddam Hussein of developing weapons of mass destruction in order to dominate the Middle East and threaten the region's oil supplies.

In the fall of 2002, the Bush administration pushed Congress to authorize the use of military force in Iraq. In the weeks leading up to the congressional vote, the administration argued that Iraq was in possession of deadly weapons, including nuclear arms. Furthermore, several administration officials insinuated that Saddam Hussein had pursued collaborations with al Qaeda. In light of this push—and with the congressional midterm elections looming—in October 2002, both the House and Senate passed resolutions by wide margins authorizing the use of force, despite misgivings on the part of the Democratic leadership.

Events progressed quickly from there. In November 2002, the UN Security Council adopted a resolution that once again warned Iraq to fully account for and eliminate its weapons programs or "face serious consequences."[20] In January and February 2003, the United States began building its forces in the Persian Gulf. In his State of the Union address on January 28, 2003, President Bush clearly expressed the administration's rationale for war. "With nuclear arms or a full arsenal of chemical and biological weapons, Saddam Hussein could resume his ambitions of conquest in the Middle East and create deadly havoc in the region."[21] Secretary of State Colin Powell's February 5 presentation to the UN Security Council further signaled the administration's resolve.[22]

Unlike their positions during the buildup to the Gulf War in 1990, now many of the UN member states expressed concern about the case for war. At the same time that the United States began moving toward war, representatives from France, Germany, Russia, and China made the case that the inspection process should be allowed more time. French President Jacques Chirac took an outspoken stance against the war, declaring at a February 10 press conference that "nothing today justifies war" and that he had "no evidence that these weapons exist in Iraq."[23] The opposition of France and Russia to military action in Iraq made a UN resolution in support of the war impossible. On March 17, after meeting with leaders in the United Kingdom and Spain, President Bush ceased the effort to secure such a resolution. Later that evening, Bush gave Saddam Hussein an ultimatum—either flee Iraq within the next forty-eight hours and stand down, or face a U.S.-led attack.

On March 20, 2003, for the second time in little more than a decade, the United States invaded Iraq with a coalition of forces. Unlike the 1991 invasion, the goal this time was to topple Hussein and establish a new government in Iraq. The military operation proceeded swiftly. As in 1991, the Iraqi forces quickly crumbled, and on April 9, U.S. forces reached Baghdad. By April 14, nearly all the population centers in Iraq had been brought under American control. On May 1, 2003, after landing on the USS *Abraham Lincoln* in the copilot's seat of a military aircraft, Bush declared that major combat operations in Iraq were over. "In the battle of Iraq, the United States and our allies have prevailed," said Bush, while a banner declaring "Mission Accomplished" flew in the background.[24]

As it would happen, the initial military action was merely the tip of the iceberg. Soon after the invasion, in a pattern similar to the establishment of the Afghan government, the Coalition Provisional Authority was created as a transitional regime. The move toward democracy seemed to be proceeding smoothly. Opposition to the United States' presence soon emerged, however. The Iraqi resistance initially was limited to Baath Party loyalists but was later joined by religious fundamentalists and other Iraqis who began to oppose the occupation. The capture of Saddam Hussein on December 13, 2003, did not signal the end of hostilities as some had hoped. In fact, in the spring of 2004, resistance began once again to pick up, culminating in a series of battles in Fallujah late that year.

At that time, battle lines in the United States over the Iraq War were also beginning to solidify. As commander in chief, President Bush was strongly associated with support for the conflict. For much of this period, Republican Party elites followed his lead. The position of Democrats on this issue was less clear. A review of *Newsweek*'s coverage of Iraq from February 2002 through the 2004 presidential election demonstrates that Democrats lacked a clear agenda for how to proceed on the Iraq question.[25] For months after the initial invasion, there was limited dissent among Democrats. In the 2004 presidential campaign the notable dissenters on Iraq—Howard Dean and Wesley Clark—were quickly pushed aside by John Kerry, a senator who had voted to authorize war in Iraq and, in line with other prominent Democrats, never took a clear position against the war. In chapters 4 and 5, I address the implications of the partisan overtones of the Iraq War. For present purposes, however, what is important is that whereas Vietnam gradually became Nixon's war, Iraq was always Bush's battle.

In 2005, a number of seemingly positive developments appeared to signal a turn in the tide of the war. The January 31 election of the Iraqi transitional government, followed by a constitutional referendum in October and the election of the National Assembly in December, indicated progress toward a democratic government. Through it all, however, the insurgency continued. By 2006, it was apparent that progress toward political and economic stability in Iraq would be a rocky road. As of this writing, over five years after Bush's declaration of victory, U.S. troops still have a significant presence on the ground.

As the U.S. commitment in Iraq dragged on, social scientists and journalists had a clear window into the public's mind. The Iraq War has been the subject of more opinion polls than any other military action in U.S. history. In the five-year period from October 2002 until September 2007, academic and media organizations conducted almost eight hundred national-sample polls about the invasion.

The plethora of survey organizations involved in these efforts ensures a thickness to the data that did not exist for other wars. Making sense of this overwhelming mass of data, however, is a difficult task. In later chapters, I draw on specific surveys collected by myself and others to make particular points about the nature of public opinion concerning war. But to get a sense of the overall trends in support for war, we need somehow to reduce the sea of data into a more manageable form.

To present these data in a comprehensible way, I draw on work by Gary Jacobson, who has compiled a comprehensive set of published polling data concerning support for the Iraq War. These results can be found in figure 2.5. Figure 2.5 also contains a line indexing the overall trend in support for the war, compiling the disparate polls into a single estimate of war support at any one moment in time.[26]

In many ways, the pattern of public opinion on Iraq resembles the pattern of opinion on the Vietnam War, at least in the aggregate. High initial levels of support give way to mounting opposition. By mid-2004, the levels of support for war had flattened out, with a continuing slow decline, mirroring opinion on Vietnam after 1969. As I demonstrate in the chapters to follow, however, although the general trends of opinion on the two wars seem similar, there are some important differences across these conflicts as well, beginning with fundamental differences in the role played by partisan attachments in the two wars. Consistent with reaction to other wars in U.S. history, the public's reaction to the Iraq War, from the

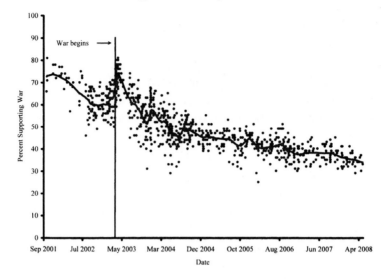

FIGURE 2.5. Trends in support for the Iraq War.

beginning of the intervention, mirrored basic divisions among the public about Bush's presidency.

The discussion of the similarities between the public's response to Vietnam and Iraq—and the brief allusion to the differences that exist in public opinion—underscores the importance of tracing opinion across a series of conflicts when studying opinion about war. The four wars considered here—Korea, Vietnam, Afghanistan, and Iraq—are very different wars in many respects. But there are many similarities as well. Korea and Vietnam were both cold war disputes that erupted into conflict in East Asia. Moreover, Vietnam and Afghanistan represent U.S. involvement in long-term, ongoing domestic civil conflicts. By examining the wars of the last fifty years together, we can learn a great deal about the origins and nature of support for international intervention up to the present day. To complete the picture, however, we also need to bring in the most important conflict of the twentieth century—a task I take up in the next chapter.

CHAPTER THREE

THE MYTHS AND MEANING OF PUBLIC OPINION AND WORLD WAR II

In June 2006, White House press secretary Tony Snow appeared on *CNN Late Edition with Wolf Blitzer.* Speaking about public opinion on the Iraq War, he said, "If someone had taken a poll in the Battle of the Bulge, I dare say people would have said, 'Wow, my goodness, what are we doing here?'"[1] Surely Snow was surprised to learn in the following days that, in fact, someone had taken a poll during the Ardennes offensive that represented Germany's last push of the war. From December 31, 1944, until January 4, 1945, the American Institute of Public Opinion (AIPO) asked, "If Hitler offered to make peace now and would give up all land he has conquered, should we try to work out a peace or should we go on fighting until the German army is completely defeated?" Contrary to Snow's speculation, 72 percent of the public expressed support for the stated U.S. policy of unconditional surrender; the American people wanted to continue fighting until victory was complete.[2]

Snow's ignorance of this poll is not unique. Aside from the work of a handful of historians, public opinion during the Second World War has gone largely unexamined. As a result, modern treatments of public opinion and war have almost completely ignored World War II.

OPINION POLLS IN THE 1930S AND 1940S: THE BIRTH OF SURVEY RESEARCH

Given the importance of World War II in American history, its relative neglect in the study of public opinion and war seems surprising. It is even more surprising given the richness of the public opinion data from the time. Indeed, as I mentioned in chapter 1, the mid-1930s saw the birth of modern techniques of public opinion research (Converse 1987; Smith 1987). More than 450 national-sample polls were conducted from 1935 to 1945, and these polls circulated widely in the political world. Roosevelt took great interest in the burgeoning field of survey research. The founders of the polling industry, Hadley Cantril, Harry Field, George Gallup, and Elmo Roper, provided the president with a wealth of information concerning the public's views on the issues of the day. Beginning in September 1939, FDR received results from polls that Elmo Roper conducted for *Fortune* magazine. Although FDR suspected George Gallup's AIPO of Republican leanings and was suspicious of its polling results, he eagerly sought the polling advice of Gallup's associate, Hadley Cantril, who was the founder and head of the Office of Public Opinion Research (OPOR). In researching his detailed history of public opinion during World War II, Steve Casey (2001) found original analysis conducted by Cantril in FDR's official files as well as in the president's personal files. Cantril himself described his relationship to the president in his memoir of his life as a pollster, *The Human Dimension: Experiences in Policy Research*: "I was [told] that the President would like any material available on public reaction to certain steps this country might take to help England. . . . More and more requests came from the White House as American involvement in the war increased and particularly, of course, after the Japanese attacked the United States at Pearl Harbor on December 7, 1941" (Cantril 1967, 35–38).

Cantril's account has been corroborated by several historians. From 1941 to 1945, many of the issues chosen for OPOR's surveys were selected at the suggestion of the White House, and Cantril's reports were among FDR's most important sources of information on public opinion (Steele 1974). In time, the OPOR polls were supplemented by polls conducted by the newly created survey division within the Office of War Information, which conducted polls for the U.S. government through the end of the war.[3]

Although survey research was in its infancy, pollsters covered many topics that would be familiar to modern researchers, such as support for presidential candidates, membership in different social groups, and general orientation with respect to the political controversies of the day. Most important, these surveys repeatedly asked a great number of questions concerning the Second World War (although for reasons that are not clear, such questions were almost exclusively focused on the European theater).

The existing studies that use these data are more than five decades old (Cantril 1944, 1948; Cantril and Strunk 1951; Field and Van Patten 1945; Smith 1947–48). Some researchers—most notably Page and Shapiro (1992)—have used the aggregate poll data to study patterns of stability and change in public opinion. But this work is the exception. For example, Erikson, MacKuen, and Stimson's (2002) groundbreaking study of macropolitical trends begins in the early 1950s. Furthermore, contemporary studies of individual-level behavior using poll data collected before 1952 are rare, consisting of a smattering of citations (Baum and Kernell 2001; Caldeira 1987; Schlozman and Verba 1979; Verba and Schlozman 1977; Weatherford and Sergeyev 2000).

One reason for this relative neglect arises from the potentially nonrepresentative nature of these polls.[4] Modern opinion polls are conducted using probability sampling to ensure that every citizen has a known probability of being interviewed. Polls in the United States before the 1950s, on the other hand, were conducted using quota-controlled sampling methods, in which pollsters sought to interview certain predetermined proportions of people from particular segments of the population.[5]

This practice created several problems. Apart from having to fulfill certain demographic quotas, interviewers were given discretion to select particular citizens to interview. Because interviewers preferred to work in safer areas and tended to survey approachable respondents, the "public" they interviewed often differed markedly from the public writ large.[6] The highly educated and professionals were more likely to be interviewed; as a result early opinion polls are not representative of the U.S. population.

The flaws of these early polls are well known. As a result, many political scientists have rejected out of hand polls conducted before 1950. For example, Converse concludes that the Gallup and Roper data "were collected by methods long since viewed as shoddy and unrepresentative" (1965, 331). Doug Rivers argues that quota sampling is "a methodology that failed" (quoted in Schafer 1999). Surveys conducted before the widespread adoption of probability sampling in 1949 have therefore largely been abandoned.

By recognizing and accounting for the limitations of the polls of the 1930s and 1940s, researchers can rescue these surveys from the dustbin of history. Although early opinion polls have substantial problems, the critical information those polls contain should not be neglected; in this book I take steps to account for these flaws.[7] This vast resource offers unique insights into the roots of public attitudes toward foreign policy.

Perhaps, though, such an enterprise is a fool's errand. Certainly every war is different in its own way, but in many circles World War II is viewed as an aberration of sorts, a uniquely popular war against a uniquely horrific enemy. World War II, writes Studs Terkel, was "a different kind of war. . . . It was one war that many who would have resisted 'your other wars' supported enthusiastically" (1984, 13). If, in fact, World War II was an exceptional event in American history, it would be difficult, if not impossible, to draw general lessons from public reaction to that conflict.

This common picture of World War II may, however, be based largely on myth. As historian C. C. Adams writes, World War II "has been converted over time from a complex, problematic event, full of nuance and debatable meaning, to a simple shining legend of the Good War. For many, including a majority of survivors from this era, the war years have become America's golden age" (1994, 2). In fact, the picture was far more complicated. Looking at the military experience, Adams notes, "Many soldiers didn't know what the war was about, and some resented their war-long terms of service. The majority of returning soldiers got no parades. . . . Wounded men repatriated to the U.S. were treated as though diseased, and people rushed to wash their hands after greeting them" (7).[8]

If our recollection of the military cause is in doubt, what about our recollection of the public's role? In the rest of this chapter, I examine the myths that have arisen around the public's reaction to World War II. First, I make the case that we can, in fact, draw more general lessons from the experience of the 1930s and 1940s. Second, and of equal importance, I show how these myths have influenced the study of public opinion and war in general. By embracing a misguided picture of opinion during the war, scholars have accepted an incomplete picture of public opinion during times of crisis. Revisiting and revising the myths surrounding World War II, with an eye toward general processes of public opinion formation, can therefore change our understanding of the nature of the public's preferences during these times. This revisionist account, in turn, sets the stage for the broader arguments I make in the chapters that follow about public support for war more generally.

Myth 1: World War II Was "the Good War"
There is a broad sense in popular accounts and some academic treatments of World War II that this conflict was the "Good War," in which the United States, shaken by the Japanese attack at Pearl Harbor, quickly rallied to

the cause of protecting democracy. Echoing this common understanding, Larson writes:

> In the Second World War—"the good war"—the public had an excellent cause. Of course Japan's attack on Pearl Harbor and Germany's declaration of war on the United States contributed greatly to support for U.S. entry into the war. But support also derived from the shared perception of important stakes and vast benefits of eliminating a grave threat to U.S. security and from optimism that the outcome would be a decisive victory and punishment of the Axis powers. . . . Further contributing to support for the war was a desire for punishment as a consequence of the Japanese sneak attack on Pearl Harbor, such atrocities as the Bataan Death March, reports of the Japanese torture of U.S. prisoners of war, and Germany's holocaust. (1996, 14–15)

Similarly, Darrell West (2003) writes, "the surprise Japanese attack on Pearl Harbor in 1941 changed public opinion. With the moral authority generated by a military attack, the American public shifted strongly in favor of war. . . . With a clear-cut enemy in Germany and Japan, and opponents who were easy to demonize given atrocities that they committed, the war was framed as a good war against evil opponents."

The implication of these statements is that the public rallied to war because the cause was just and the benefits clear. In this view, perhaps the public could again be mobilized to support a large-scale military effort if only a worthy cause could again be found. Thus the conventional wisdom regarding the virtue of World War II has at least indirectly influenced our perceptions of the possibility of support for "your other wars."

The explanations presented by these authors may seem plausible in retrospect, but as noted earlier, some historians have questioned these accounts. In fact, public opinion data from the 1940s call into question the rosy accounts of Larson and West. I take up this question further in the next chapter, but some examples illustrate this point. Several times during the war, Gallup asked the public if it had "a clear idea what the war is about." As late as March 1944, fewer than 60 percent said they did—a majority to be sure, but hardly a universal understanding of the "important stakes and vast benefits" of the war. Moreover, awareness of the extent of the Nazi atrocities was thin during the war years. In early 1943, a minority of Americans thought that Germany had set up death camps. And even when knowledge of the camps increased over the course of the war, a minority of respondents thought that the death toll at the camps would rise above 100,000.[9]

Furthermore, far from revulsion at the methods of the Axis powers, significant portions of Americans were themselves prepared to engage in mass killing throughout the war. The American people had little sympathy for the enemy leadership. In July 1942, OPOR asked, "When the war is over, how do you think we should treat the Nazi leaders?" Only 4 percent of respondents said that the United States should treat them fairly and give them a fair trial, as compared to 5 percent who wanted to torture the leaders, 11 percent who wanted to "treat them harshly," and 44 percent who thought the United States should "kill them."[10] This hostility extended to ordinary German citizens. When asked by OPOR in June 1942 what to do with Germany after the war, 13 percent wanted to "annihilate the people and the country" and another 20 percent wanted to extract "an eye for an eye" by treating Germany harshly.[11] Japan garnered similar levels of hostility. In the same survey, 15 percent wanted to annihilate the Japanese, and 14 percent wanted to treat Japan harshly. Even the prospect of victory did not tame the prevalence of vengeance. When asked in December 1944 what the United States should do with the Japanese people after the war, 13 percent said, "kill them all."

In short, contrary to popular belief but aptly summarized by Mueller, "the major reasons for supporting [World War II] were largely unappreciated while it was going on" (1973, 65). To explain continued support for the war, we must look elsewhere, to the political attachments and enmities found on the domestic scene.

Myth 2: Changes in the Media Environment Have Fundamentally Altered How the Public Experiences War

Even if the reasons for supporting World War II were not evident, it could be that the ways citizens experienced that war were different from the ways they experienced other wars. During the 1930s and 1940s, citizens learned about politics in a variety of ways. Residents of large metropolitan areas could select from among several daily newspapers. In 1940, the top ten most populated U.S. cities had anywhere from two to ten daily newspapers, and nine of the ten cities had at least three dailies—Cleveland being the exception, with only two newspapers. For instance, New Yorkers could read the *New York Herald Tribune*, the *New York Times*, the *New York Daily News*, the *New York Post*, the *New York Sun*, the *Brooklyn Eagle*, the *New York Daily Mirror*, the *New York World-Telegram*, *PM*, the *New York Journal-American*, and other papers targeted at more specialized ethnic and political groups. Residents of Chicago could choose from among the *Chicago Daily News*, the *Chicago Daily Times*, the *Chicago Herald*, the

American, and the *Chicago Tribune*. Even those who lived in rural areas had easy access to the print media. In fact, throughout this period, approximately 80 percent of Americans read a daily newspaper. In addition, radio played an increasingly important role in the daily lives of Americans. By 1940, over 80 percent of households in the United States had a radio, and with the beginning of the Second World War, more and more Americans turned to the airwaves for news about the European and Pacific conflicts. Citizens could even learn about political events while attending movies. Throughout this period, theaters regularly showed newsreels—short films consisting of several one- to two-minute stories about politics, world events, and entertainment—as part of the regular movie-going experience.

In the more than sixty years since the end of World War II, American military interventions have taken place in a vastly changed media environment. Television was just making inroads into American households during the Korean War, but by Vietnam, television news was ubiquitous. By the early 1960s, almost 90 percent of households had at least one television set (Prior 2007). The ability of journalists to transmit vivid images of the war's progress gave ordinary Americans a front-row seat to its conduct. Indeed, Michael Arlen (1982) has called Vietnam the first "living-room war."[12] By the time of the Gulf War, the development of satellite technology enabled television reporters to broadcast simultaneous images of the conflict.[13] The growth of the diversity of information available on the Internet since the early 1990s has only increased the accessibility and vividness of political news.

Moving from newsreels to YouTube and from the three network nightly newscasts to a proliferation of cable news shows has undoubtedly revolutionized the media environment. Several scholars have recently argued that the rise of these new media have changed the manner in which ordinary citizens learn about the political world as well. Kinder, for example, writes that "over the last half of the twentieth century, mass communications have transformed the landscape of American politics, vastly increasing the information about public affairs that is available to ordinary citizens. Through multiple channels . . . the volume of information relevant to politics circulating through American society is massive and increasing" (2003, 357). Similarly, Prior claims that "the differences between the media environments in 1935, 1970, and 2005 are impossible to miss. . . . It is difficult to imagine that differences as stark as these have no effect on politics" (2007, 2–3).

Some scholars—Prior included—have begun to examine the public's reaction to the new media landscape. For instance, Baum (2003) has demonstrated that the rise of "soft news"—entertainment programming that presents political information devoid of a public policy component—has changed the way many Americans learn about the political realm. For one, the proliferation of soft news programming since the 1980s has increased the likelihood that the public will be attentive to high-profile military involvement abroad. As a result, Baum claims, many more Americans were willing to express an opinion about U.S. actions during the Gulf War than had been willing to comment on U.S. involvement in Vietnam.

Unquestionably, technological innovations have reshaped the communication environment several times over since the 1930s, and these changes have indubitably altered the way citizens learn about political issues. But the question most relevant for the present study is whether these changes have fundamentally and inexorably altered the way citizens come to form and express their opinions about foreign policy, thereby rendering comparisons among the different wars of the twentieth century impossible. This question remains open. Here, I make the claim that the differences in the media environment between the World War II era and today may not be as large as some have presumed.

THE DEPICTION OF THE DEAD. Take, for example, the portrayal of casualties in World War II, compared to their depiction during the Vietnam and Iraq wars. Over the last seventy years, technology has made it possible to present immediate and direct images of combat. Moreover, in the last fifteen years, the proliferation of news outlets and individual bloggers on the Internet has made it more difficult for the government to fully control media depictions of war. Some commentators have therefore questioned how the public might have viewed the U.S. effort in the 1940s given a media environment similar to that during Vietnam or Iraq. As Victor Davis Hansen argued in an editorial in the New York Times, "CNN would have shown a very different Iwo Jima—bodies rotting on the beach and probably no coverage of the flag-raising from Mount Suribachi."[14]

Certainly censorship—and perhaps more importantly, media acceptance of that censorship—was prevalent during the Second World War. As Roeder writes in his systematic study of the portrayal of combat during World War II, "the U.S. government, with extensive support from other public and private organizations, made the most systematic and far-reaching effort in history to shape the visual experience of the citizenry" (1993, 2). It is, however, easy to exaggerate the changes from the 1940s to the 2000s. Even today, media depictions of the war dead are highly constrained by government policy. Early in the Iraqi conflict, the government banned pictures of coffins of the war dead being returned to U.S. soil. Since 2006, the military has required journalists to obtain a signed consent from a wounded soldier before his or her image can be published, and identifiable images of war dead are strictly prohibited.[15]

Perhaps more importantly, the true nature of the censorship during World War II has not been properly recognized by commentators such as Hansen. Military censors were most concerned with the portrayal of American troops and attempted to restrict any images that would paint the troops in a bad light. For instance, officials banned visual or written descriptions of atrocities committed by American GIs. When it came to describing the human costs of war, the military was more adaptable; the American public was never kept in the dark regarding the scope of American casualties. For the first twenty-one months of the war, the military did withhold all pictures of dead American soldiers. In 1943, however, fearing the public's war weariness, the Pentagon encouraged the media to increase the visibility of those soldiers killed in action. Roeder found that "by September 1943, concerns about public complacency led officials to release [from the Pentagon files] photographs that showed death, but not yet bloody death. During the next two years, as military successes magnified those concerns, government officials and media editors confronted Americans with increasingly vivid depictions of the war's impact" (1993, 1).[16] In short, although the government tried to manage the presentation of the war to the American people in the 1940s, just as during Vietnam and the Iraqi conflicts, the public had access to images of death in newsmagazines and on the movie screen.

In addition, the media regularly kept the American public well apprised of the scope of the human cost of the war. From the beginning of World War II, newspapers often reported war fatalities compiled by the Associated Press and the United Press Association from information provided by the government. Some newspapers supplemented these stories with lists of casualties from the local area.[17] For instance, on January 20, 1943, the *New York Times* published an article titled "Navy Reports 1,218 in Casualty List." The article went on to present casualty counts from recent months and gave the cumulative death toll from World War II—21,496 total casualties and 6,344 dead from December 7, 1941, to December 31, 1942. The article concluded with a list of the dead from New York City, along with information about the soldiers' next of kin.[18] Thus, despite the U.S. government's coordinated censorship activities during World War

II, the American public had ready access to the basic facts regarding the scope of the human costs of war.

MEDIA CHOICE AND INFLUENCE. The political implications of the extensive media choices in the modern era have parallels in earlier times. Certainly, today's citizen has a wide variety of media outlets from which she can select political news. Scholars have argued that some of these outlets—most notably Fox News—have clear partisan proclivities. A 2004 study of news viewership by the Pew Center for the People and the Press found that from 2000 to 2004, the percentage of Americans who watched the Fox News network increased from 17 percent to 25 percent. More importantly, the Pew study found that the Fox News audience took an increasingly conservative tilt over this time. In 2000, an equal proportion of Democrats and Republicans—18 percent of both groups—reported that they watched Fox. However, by 2004, 35 percent of Republicans and 21 percent of Democrats tuned in, a gap of 14 percent.[19] At the same time, Pew found that the public's evaluation of the credibility of various media outlets also polarized along party lines. Democrats in 2004 were about as trusting of ABC News, CBS News, and CNN as they were in 2000, but Republicans expressed far less trust in those outlets.[20] The rise of the Internet as an information source may only exacerbate this trend. Writing about the dissemination of political information on the Web, Cass Sunstein argues: "With a dramatic increase in options, and a greater power to customize, comes a corresponding increase in the range of actual choices, and those choices are likely, in many cases, to match demographic characteristics, preexisting political convictions, or both" (2007, 56).

Recent studies by Iyengar and Morin (2007) seem to bear out Sunstein's conjecture. Iyengar and Morin ran a series of experiments to see if partisans of different stripes sought out news from different media outlets when surfing the Web. They presented respondents with a set of stories drawn from an MSNBC news feed and randomly attributed these stories to one of four sources: CNN, Fox News, NPR, and the BBC. The researchers found that Republicans gravitated to stories that were attributed to Fox, whereas Democrats avoided Fox and split their attention between CNN and NPR (for similar findings, see Baum and Gussin 2008).[21]

The degree of media polarization in the modern era might, however, be overstated. Prior (2007), for instance, uses Nielsen data rather than survey self-report data and finds considerable overlap between the audiences for CNN and Fox. Some people may prefer Fox News to CNN, but a large number of citizens draw their news from both sources. Thus, although citizens may gravitate to particular news sources based on their political views, there is evidence against the extreme view of audience specialization. Media choice in the modern era, Prior argues, is better characterized as "limited selective exposure along partisan or ideological lines" (2007, 274).

Moreover, although today's technology may allow for faster dissemination of the news and provide a richer set of media options than was available in the 1940s, the modern era is not unique in offering such choices. The idea that people might choose to attend to media that conform to their preexisting predispositions through a process of "selective exposure" has a long pedigree in communication studies (Klapper 1960). Indeed, as Sunstein concedes, "long before the advent of the Internet, and in an era of a handful of television stations, people made self-conscious choices among newspapers and radio stations. In any era, many people want to be comforted rather than challenged. Magazines and newspapers, for example, often cater to people with definite interests on certain points of view" (2007, 56).

In the 1930s and 1940s there was a plethora of newspapers across the country—about two thousand in the mid-1930s, by one estimate (Prior 2007)—and major media markets often had several newspapers, as described earlier. Many of these papers wore their partisan leanings on their sleeves. Throughout the 1930s, a majority of newspapers took a decidedly antiadministration editorial tone. Winfield (1994) found that in 1932 FDR had the support of 41 percent of American daily newspapers, a level of support that dropped to 37 percent in 1936 and bottomed out at 25 percent in 1940.[22] Even so, in nearly every city, partisans could find papers that supported their views. Take the Chicago media market, for example. While the *Chicago Tribune* endorsed Willkie in 1940 and took a strident anti-FDR tone, the *Chicago Daily Times* backed FDR.[23]

Survey evidence from this time suggests that much like today, citizens were most likely to gravitate to media sources that shared their political predilections. Several times during the 1930s, Gallup asked respondents to assess the partisan leanings of the newspaper they most regularly read. For instance, a September 1936 poll asked, "Does the Newspaper which you read support Landon or Roosevelt for President?" A cross-tabulation of the results of this question by previous presidential vote demonstrates that respondents who voted against FDR in 1932 were far more likely to read Landon-leaning newspapers than were respondents who voted for FDR. The findings reflect the overall antiadministration balance of the press of the time: among those who voted for FDR, 41 percent read papers that favored Landon and 37 percent read papers that favored FDR, a gap of four percentage points. Turning to Hoover voters, however, I find that 59 percent read papers that favored Landon, compared to 14 percent who read papers that favored FDR—a gap of 45 percent.[24] Moreover, a remarkably similar pattern of results can be found in June 1938 with a slightly different question. Gallup asked respondents, "Does the newspaper you most regularly read support or oppose President Roosevelt?" In 1938, among FDR voters, 39 percent read a paper that opposed the president and 31 percent read a paper that supported him. Among those who voted against him in 1936, anti–FDR paper readership outnumbered pro–FDR paper readership by 56 percent to 13 percent.[25] Clearly, supporters and opponents of the president gathered their political information from very different media sources.[26]

Newspaper articles and editorial pages were not the only source of media diversity. During this time, citizens could also select from among various syndicated columnists to learn about the political world. In November 1939, Roper fielded a survey that asked respondents to list their favorite newspaper columnist.[27] With these data, it is possible to see if partisans gravitated to particular columnists as well as specific newspapers. I took the list of columnists prepared by Roper from this open-ended probe and coded the personalities into partisan groupings.[28] Among respondents who identified a favorite columnist, I found differences between those who said they would support a candidate from the Republican Party in 1940 and those who would support a Democratic candidate in that election. Twenty-four percent of Republican sympathizers listed a Republican-leaning columnist as their favorite, whereas 14 percent listed a Democratic-leaning columnist. The remaining 62 percent gave a columnist with no clear partisan leanings. Although Democratic sympathizers were no more likely than their Republican counterparts to list a Democratic-leaning columnist—15 percent said such a columnist was their favorite—they were much less likely to list a Republican-leaning columnist; only 13 percent listed a Republican columnist as their favorite, whereas the remaining 73 percent listed an unaffiliated columnist. Among those who read a column daily, this gap was slightly wider. Thirteen percent of Democratic sympathizers read a Democratic column, and another 13 percent read a Republican column. Among Republican leaners, on the other hand, 26 percent read a Republican columnist and 9 percent read a Democratic columnist.[29]

This evidence on the trends concerning media polarization, together with evidence on the presentation of information about the war dead, suggests that comparisons of the basic structure of public opinion from the 1930s and 2000s are appropriate. We find further support for making such comparisons in other areas of research on political behavior, where scholars have found similarities in patterns of public opinion across wide spans of time. For instance, consider levels of political information among the public. Even with the proliferation of new technologies and the increased availability of information about politics, levels of knowledge of basic political facts have remained stable from the 1950s to the present day (Delli Carpini and Keeter 1996; Prior 2007). As I demonstrate in the chapters that follow, the patterns of mass response to cues and information about foreign policy have remained remarkably consistent across time as well.

Myth 3: Pearl Harbor Suddenly and Fundamentally Turned an Isolationist Public into a Prowar Public

The conventional view of the American public in the early years of World War II is accurately captured by the term used as the subtitle of Folly's (2002) history of the United States during World War II— *The Awakening Giant*. Studies of World War II almost uniformly portray the American public as a stubbornly isolationist force from the mid-1930s through the end of 1941 (Casey 2001; Dallek 1995; Divine 1979; Heinrichs 1988, although see Braumoeller 2008 and Leigh 1976). Conventional wisdom tells us, however, that with the attack on Pearl Harbor on December 7, 1941, the inward focus of the United States ended suddenly. To use the words of Michigan senator Arthur Vandenberg, "That day ended isolationism."

The "awakening" of a slumbering American public at Pearl Harbor has had a pronounced influence on studies of American public opinion concerning foreign policy. Cyclical theories of U.S. diplomatic history, which posit that American attitudes toward foreign policy drift between long periods of generally interventionist postures and somewhat shorter periods of noninterventionist ones, are based on the notion that the American public underwent a dramatic shift from extreme isolationism before 1941 to extreme internationalism during World War II and the early cold war (Klingberg 1952, 1983). This belief has influenced even the work of scholars who focus exclusively on the modern era. For example, in his book *The Impact of Public Opinion on U.S. Foreign Policy since Vietnam*, Richard Sobel writes that "the bombing of Pearl Harbor was an event so large in the American psyche that it forever changed the public's perception of foreign policy" (2001, 44).

The conventional wisdom, then, is clear; December 7, 1941, was the turning point. With the declaration of war on America by Germany and Italy on December 11, 1941, the United States was firmly embroiled in the Second World War in both the European and Pacific theaters. Public opinion, in turn, shifted abruptly. Americans, regardless of their personal interests or political beliefs, shed their isolationist posture and quickly rallied behind the cause of war, or so the story goes.

At first glance, the empirical evidence seems to bear out this hypothesis. Polls taken from 1938 to late 1941 show that an overwhelming majority of the American public opposed direct U.S. involvement on the side of the Allies. For example, in a series of six Gallup polls taken in the spring and summer of 1940, no more than 10 percent of respondents said that the United States should "declare war on Germany [and Italy] and send our army and navy abroad to fight." Support for a declaration of war edged up over the next year, reaching 23 percent in June 1941.[30] Even then, however, the vast majority of Americans firmly opposed the war. Come December 1941, the public mood shifted dramatically. Although Japan's action and Germany's declaration of war may have guaranteed U.S. involvement in the war, the public quickly rallied behind the American war effort. In late December 1941, 87 percent of the public opposed ending the war "if Hitler offered peace now to all countries on the basis of not going farther, but of leaving matters as they are now." This high level of support held through the war. In a marked departure from modern conflicts, only once, in February 1944, did any organization ask whether the public thought World War II was a mistake. Specifically, in response to the question "Do you think you, yourself, will feel [in the years to come] it was a mistake for us to have entered this war?" only 14 percent thought they would feel the war was a mistake. In that same poll only 25 percent of those surveyed thought that "in the years to come, people will say it was a mistake for the U.S. to have entered this war," whereas in April 1944, only 21 percent thought that, after twenty years, "many people will look upon our going into the war against Germany as a mistake." The paucity of such questions is itself telling; pollsters saw no need to ask if respondents thought that it was a mistake to enter World War II because almost no one directly opposed the war.

Pollsters did, however, measure support for war in a more indirect manner. Gallup and OPOR regularly asked respondents a variety of questions concerning the public's commitment to the stated U.S. policy of unconditional surrender. The version asked in December 1941 was asked several times through mid-1943. After that time, OPOR asked a similar question: "If Hitler offered to discuss peace now, should the Allies accept this offer and discuss peace terms with Hitler?" The two survey organizations also asked similar questions in reference to the German army. The first version, fielded in 1942 and 1943, asked: "If the German Army overthrew Hitler and offered peace now to all countries on the basis of not going farther, but of leaving matters as they are now, would you favor or oppose such a peace?" The second version was asked throughout the war (including during the Battle of the Bulge, as discussed earlier) and read: "If the German army overthrew Hitler and then offered to stop the war and discuss peace terms with the Allies, would you favor or oppose accepting the offer of the German army?"

Figure 3.1 presents the level of support for the stated policy of unconditional surrender from December 1941 to April 1945. I present four trends in the graph. The dotted lines represent opposition to making peace with Hitler, while the solid lines present opposition to making peace with the German army. The solid squares represent the "status quo" form of the question, for which peace involves "leaving matters as they are now," and the diamonds involve the version of the question that merely asks whether the United States should "discuss peace terms."[31]

Some differences are readily apparent from the graphs. The public was always more willing to make peace with the German army than with Hitler. Moreover, the public was considerably more opposed to peace plans that involved preserving the current status quo. That said, the data show clear and consistent support for seeing the war through to the end. At no point did opposition to making peace with the German army fall below 50 percent. Moreover, the one noticeable dip in support—in the middle of 1944—is almost certainly an artifact of the design of these two surveys. Immediately before being asked the standard question about making peace with the German army, respondents were asked if they would be willing to make peace with Hitler. Question-wording experiments conducted early in the war indicate that asking the two questions in this particular sequence diminished support for unconditional surrender by over ten percentage points.[32] Correcting for this artifact indicates a steady level of support for the war.

Although the high levels of support for the war after U.S entry are readily apparent, the overall picture of public support may not be as clear as these results suggest. The events at Pearl Harbor certainly provide a breaking point in attitudes toward the war, but this breaking point is not the firm line that conventional wisdom would have us believe it was. Focusing only on the question of direct military involvement—support

FIGURE 3.1. Trends in opposition to making peace with Germans.

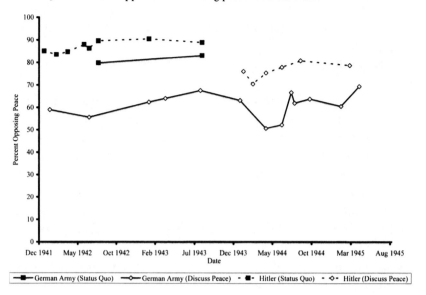

Percent Opposing Peace (y-axis)

Date (x-axis): Dec 1941, May 1942, Oct 1942, Feb 1943, Jul 1943, Dec 1943, May 1944, Oct 1944, Mar 1945, Aug 1945

Legend: ■ German Army (Status Quo) ◇ German Army (Discuss Peace) ■ Hitler (Status Quo) ◇ Hitler (Discuss Peace)

for a formal declaration of war—paints an incomplete picture of public sentiment in the months before Pearl Harbor and ignores important changes in public attitudes toward the conflict that occurred from 1940 to 1941.

Beginning in early 1940, Gallup and OPOR began asking, on a regular basis, two similar questions tapping support for entry into the war. The first question asked, "Which of these two things do you think is the more important for the United States to try to do? To keep out of war ourselves or to help England win, even at the risk of getting into the war?"[33] This question captures an important dimension of opinion concerning war because essentially it serves as a referendum on FDR's general policy of providing aid to England, from the Destroyers for Bases program, to the Lend-Lease proposal, to the use of U.S. warships to convoy aid to the English in 1941. As noted earlier, FDR was very interested in Cantril's survey results on this question and in fact told Cantril "he would appreciate it if this question could be asked periodically" (Cantril 1967, 35). The second question asked, "Which of these two things do you think is the more important? That this country keep out of war, or that Germany be defeated?"[34]

Figure 3.2 presents the level of support for entering the war, from 1940 to 1941. The points on the graph represent the percentage of the public who said that the United States should "help England" or "defeat Germany" at

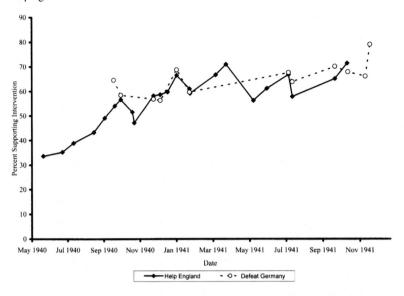

a given moment in time, as compared to those respondents who thought the United States should stay out or did not express an opinion.[35] When the question was first asked in May 1940, the majority of the public rejected the notion of directly aiding the Allied cause. This anti-intervention position remained the majority view through the summer of 1940. During the Republican convention of 1940, however, party leaders surprised their own members and nominated an internationalist candidate (and erstwhile Democrat), Wendell Willkie, for president. The importance of this selection and its effect on the shape of public opinion are discussed further in chapter 5. For now, what is important is that it seems that the change in message from Republican politicians, leading to a unified message on the war from both major party candidates, helped shift public opinion on the war more broadly.[36] In September 1940, although the public remained opposed to declaring war on Germany, a majority of Americans supported helping England even at the risk of becoming involved in the war.[37] This level of support dipped when Willkie began endorsing anti-interventionist policies as the 1940 campaign drew to a close (see chap. 5). But whatever the particular dynamic of opinion during the electoral season, after FDR's victory the support for helping England began again inching upward, albeit in fits and starts. Although there are some peaks and valleys in support for the Allied cause, in every poll conducted after November 1940 a majority of the public supported the policy of helping England and defeating Germany. Support rose to 70 percent for the first time in March 1941 and never dipped below 55 percent.

In addition, support for an activist position went beyond general expressions of support for England; the public endorsed taking specific actions that placed American troops at risk. In 1941, Gallup asked several times if "the U.S. Navy should be used to convoy ships carrying war materials to Britain" (see fig. 3.3). In April, 44 percent supported the convoys, but by May, a majority—57 percent to be exact—backed the policy. Support levels oscillated between 51 percent and 57 percent for most of the summer, before rising to 60 percent by the fall. Perhaps most important, the public was aware of the implications of these actions. In a June 1941 *Fortune* magazine poll, 81 percent agreed with the statement, "even though we are not actually fighting, we are now so much involved in the war that we are in it for all practical purposes."[38]

This is not to say that all members of the public were prepared to go to war if necessary to defend the interests of the United States (as defined by the Roosevelt administration). Pearl Harbor altered the structure of opinion on the war in one major, yet largely unappreciated, respect. Until December 7, 1941, support for helping England—and involvement in the war more generally—was an extremely partisan issue.[39] Consistent with the general argument of this book—developed more fully in the next two chapters—domestic political attachments greatly influenced attitudes on foreign policy. From 1939 onward, FDR's strategies increasingly reflected a policy of confrontation with the Germans, and his supporters among the public followed that lead. Consider the partisan gap on public opinion regarding the desirability of convoys in June 1941. Of those who expressed general support for FDR, 71 percent supported convoys, while only 33 percent of respondents who opposed FDR supported them.[40] The importance of political leadership is discussed in greater detail in chapter 5, but the point remains: the public was—on the whole—not as staunchly isolationist before U.S. entry into the war as conventional wisdom suggests. Moreover, a substantial segment of that public—those citizens who expressed support for the president—renounced isolationist tendencies long before Pearl Harbor.

Furthermore, the immediate reaction of the American public to Pearl Harbor was not to demand retribution against Japan, as many have assumed. In December 1941 the National Opinion Research Center (NORC) asked, "Which do you think we should consider our number-one

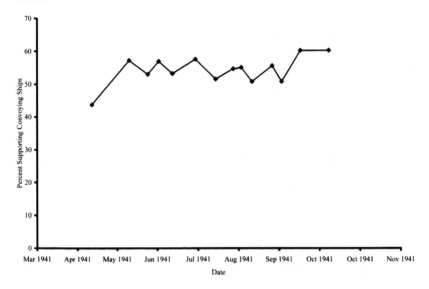

enemy—Japan or Germany?" The majority of the public—55 percent—replied Germany, while only 35 percent said Japan. Even on the West Coast, where reaction to the attack was most severe, citizens identified Germany as the number-one enemy by a margin of 50 percent to 45 percent.[41] During the following months this sentiment did not change. In a March 1942 OPOR poll, 43 percent of respondents said that Germany was the number-one enemy, as compared to 29 percent who said Japan, and Germany continued to outpoll Japan in a May 1942 OPOR poll by a nearly identical margin of 44 percent to 32 percent.[42]

In sum, the United States' entry into the war—and the public's reaction to that action—was the realization of long-term developments in political and military strategies on the part of partisan political actors. More than a year before Pearl Harbor, the public started preparing for war. Although public sentiment did indeed turn after the Japanese attack, that turn was neither as swift nor as sharp as conventional wisdom believes it to be. December 7, 1941, did not represent an abrupt break with an isolationist past. Rather it marked the realization of a policy that had been in the works for some time. Historians have long known that FDR was ready for the shift in American policy during the years before the United States became directly involved in the Second World War (Dallek 1995). The opinion poll data from this time make clear that large segments of the public—in particular those citizens who took their cues from FDR—were ready for U.S. involvement as well.[43]

Myth 4: The Public Reaction to World War II Was Unique

One of the more consistent themes in discussions of mass opinion about World War II is that public reaction to that war deviated from reaction to other wars. By now it should be apparent that this belief is highly questionable. World War II may be different in that it engendered continued high levels of support (for reasons discussed in chap. 5). Although the overall level of support for World War II remained high after 1942, public opinion still displayed the same divisions found on many political issues, including support for war more generally.

Consider, for example, one highly salient political cleavage in support for the use of force. One of the most consistent findings concerning public opinion about war is the existence of a gender gap (Eichenberg 2003). Studies of the Korean War (Modigliani 1972; Mueller 1973), the Vietnam War (Mueller 1973; Verba et al. 1967), and the 1991 Gulf War (Conover and Sapiro 1993) have all found that in general women are less supportive than men of the use of military force.

Analysis of the Roper, Gallup, and OPOR data demonstrates that opinion concerning involvement in World War II was also deeply divided along gender lines. Consider public opinion in August 1939. On the eve of World War II, Roper asked respondents their opinions of different courses of action the United States might take toward the impending conflict in Europe. I consider five of these measures in particular. The first three questions concern possible support for England and France in the event of war with Germany. Respondents were asked: "If England and France go to war against the dictator nations, should we: 1. Sell them food for cash, credit, or not at all? 2. Sell them war supplies for cash, credit, or not at all? 3. Send our army and navy abroad to help them immediately, or only if it is clear they are losing, or not at all?"

The two remaining questions tapped sentiment concerning U.S. involvement in war more generally. The first question asked, "Should we tend strictly to our business and go to war only to defend our own country from attack?" The second question asked, "Do you think there are any international questions affecting the U.S. so important to us in the long run that our government should take a stand on them now, even at the risk of our getting into war?"[44] The estimates of the differences between men and woman are presented in table 3.1.[45]

The size of the gender gap varies—and in some cases it is not sub-

TABLE 3.1 The gender gap on questions of intervention, August 1939

Topic	Gender gap (%)
Don't allow England/France to buy food	8
Don't allow England/France to buy war supplies	21
Don't send army and navy abroad to help England/France	6
U.S. should tend to its own business	5
No question so important that U.S. should risk war	12

Source: Author analysis of Roper Survey 7 (August 1939).
Note: Cell entries indicate the difference between the percentage of women choosing an isolationist response and the percentage of men choosing an isolationist response. Positive numbers indicate that women are more opposed to international involvement then are men.

stantively significant—but the gap is consistent in its presence across all five questions. Interestingly, the gap is largest—exceeding ten percentage points—when the term "war" is specifically mentioned. This result is consistent with Conover and Sapiro's (1993) findings concerning opinion on the 1991 Gulf War; the gender gap was strongest when the topic turned to specific questions of the use of force.

The differences found in August 1939 are typical of gender differences found in the period before the United States' entry into the war. Figure 3.4 revisits the "help England" series discussed earlier. The figure shows a general rise in support for more active U.S. engagement in the military conflict among both men and women. In every survey, however, men were more likely than women to want to help England—on average by over ten percentage points.[46] The magnitude of the gender gap is roughly equivalent to the size of the gaps found during the Korean and Vietnam wars (see Mueller 1973, table 5.5) and more recent conflicts (see Eichenberg 2003).

The gender gap persisted after the United States became directly involved in World War II. Although, as noted earlier, Pearl Harbor is often viewed as a great unifying force, not everyone reacted to the events of December 7, 1941, in the same way. In chapter 6, I explore the persistence of differences among immigrant ethnic groups during the war years. For present purposes, however, what is important is that the gender gap remained in place even after Pearl Harbor. In figure 3.5, I revisit the data from figure 3.1 and present trends in answers to whether the respondent would make peace with the German army, if offered.[47] In twelve out of thirteen polls from this period, men were more likely than women to support unconditional surrender, and the one poll in which women took the more

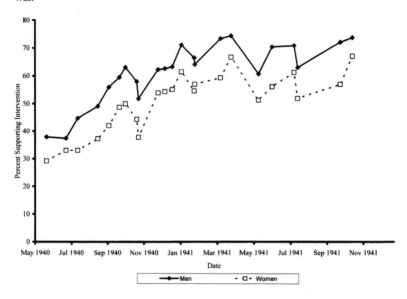

FIGURE 3.4. Gender gap in support for helping England over staying out of the war.

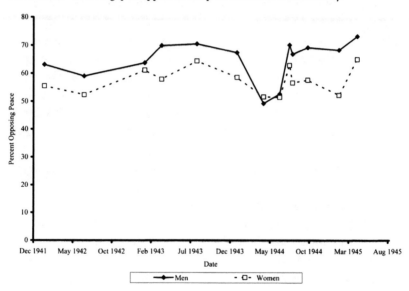

FIGURE 3.5. Gender gap in opposition to peace with the German army.

hawkish stance is the mid-1944 poll contaminated by the question-order effect discussed previously. On average, the gender gap is just over seven percentage points. Men were also more likely than women to subscribe to an internationalist posture after the war. Several times from 1942 to 1945, OPOR asked respondents if the United States should embrace the dominant orthodoxy in foreign policy that emerged after Pearl Harbor (Legro 2000) and take an active role in world affairs.[48] Figure 3.6 presents the trends, by gender, on this question. On all eight surveys, men were more likely to support an internationalist position by an average of twelve percentage points.

The prevalence of the gender gap on questions of war extends beyond the particular choices made by men and women on opinion surveys. Evidence suggests that, just as in the present day, men and women thought about the war in distinct ways. In July 1940, respondents to the OPOR survey were asked the "help England" question described earlier. Consistent with other surveys in this period, a large gender gap existed on this question: 45 percent of men but only 33 percent of women said that the United States should help England even if it meant involving the United States in war. But in addition to the standard closed-ended question, the respondents were also asked why they chose the position they did. This open-ended probe gives us a useful window into the respondents' thinking on this particular issue.

Research from opinion concerning other wars suggests that men and women differ in predictable ways in their thinking on questions that tap support for war. Using data from the Gulf War, Conover and Sapiro (1993) find that the roots of men's and women's thinking about war usually diverge even when the genders agree on the bottom line about the preferred course of action. Exploring these differences in the context of Vietnam, Schuman (1972) used data from the 1971 Detroit Area Study to examine the meaning of opposition to the war. Schuman asked respondents, "Was it a mistake to get involved in Vietnam?" Those who answered yes were then asked why they took the position they did. Schuman found that women, blacks, and older respondents were more likely to take what he called a "pragmatic isolationist" position than an ideologically driven dovish position. In particular, women were likely to have reservations about American involvement because they were uncomfortable with the deaths of American soldiers.

Analysis of the 1940 open-ended data reveals patterns of thinking consistent with Schuman's findings from the Vietnam era. Approximately equal proportions of men and women who opposed helping England were

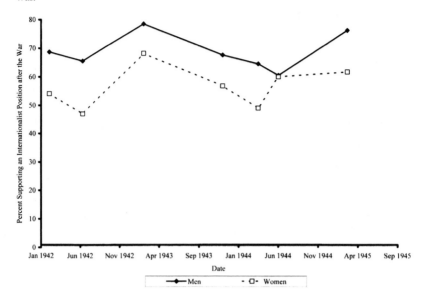

FIGURE 3.6. Gender gap on support for taking an internationalist position after the war.

unable to provide a rationale for their opinion (22 percent of men; 20 percent of women). In addition, identical percentages—18 percent for women and men—gave an isolationist answer as their top choice.[49] Beyond these similarities, however, significant differences emerged. The second most common response for both groups was "futility of war." More women than men chose that response category (13 percent vs. 9 percent). The third choice among men was "we are not prepared to risk a war" (8 percent). Among women, however, it was "don't want to send our boys over to be killed" (12 percent). Furthermore, breaking the open-ended responses into more general categories highlights the gender differences in the way that men and women thought about the war. I recoded OPOR's open-ended codes into five categories: (1) no answer, (2) principled isolationism, (3) war aversion, (4) anti-English sentiment, and (5) other reasons.[50] Consistent with Schuman's findings, women were slightly more likely to raise concerns relating to war aversion than were men. Specifically, 46 percent of women and 42 percent of men gave an answer that could be classified as war aversion. Thus, contrary to conventional wisdom, opinion concerning World War II was structured in much the same way as opinion concerning other wars. These similarities are found not only in familiar cleavages surrounding the direction of opinion, but also in the reasoning that underlies these opinions.

A closer examination of the opinion poll data from World War II indicates that, for the public, that war was in many ways a war like any other. At the same time, unlike other wars of the twentieth century, World War II engendered consistently high levels of support throughout nearly four years of U.S. involvement. As long as the study of public opinion and war sidesteps World War II, the reasons for the continued support for this war—or any other war—will remain a mystery. By examining the rich opinion data from this time, in combination with survey data collected during other wars more familiar to political scientists, we can revise faulty conclusions about the mass response to World War II and learn a great deal about public opinion toward war more generally. It is to this task that I turn in the next section of this book.

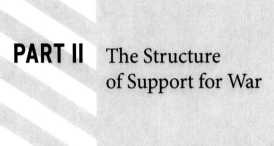

PART II The Structure
of Support for War

CHAPTER FOUR

THE CALCULATION OF COSTS: AN INNOCENT PUBLIC

Should the opinions of citizens in a democracy matter in decisions of war and peace? The answer to this critical question depends on the stock we place in the ability of the public to come to meaningful decisions regarding the conduct of foreign affairs. In recent years, a charitable view of the public's sophistication has emerged in the public opinion and foreign policy literature. There is a growing consensus that citizens, on the whole, hold foreign policy preferences that are sensible and that they adjust their preferences in response to world events that affect American interests (Holsti 1992, 2004; Jentleson 1992; Nincic 1988, 1992; Page and Shapiro 1992; although see Bartels 2003). Many scholars and policymakers argue that the events that occur during wartime—the successes and failures on the battlefield—determine whether the public will support military excursions. The public supports war, the story goes, if the benefits of action outweigh the costs of conflict; citizens, therefore, should have a place at the policy-making table.

In the next three chapters, I question these assumptions. I argue that although military events may shape public opinion, they do not do so in a straightforward and direct manner. It is not the direct influence of wartime events themselves that determine public opinion, as "event-response" theories of war-support claim. I argue that opinions concerning foreign policy, just like opinions about domestic politics, are structured by politically relevant predispositions. Hurwitz and Peffley (1987) convincingly demonstrate that an individual's foreign policy attitudes are structured by core values and abstract beliefs regarding appropriate general governmental strategies. Here, I focus on more basic predispositions, namely, ties to political and social groupings in American society. I find that attachments to and enmities toward politically relevant groups provide a baseline reaction toward a war, whereas the dynamics of elite conflict shape opinions among the public across time. Under this conception, the events of war are important but only acquire explanatory power indirectly. Partisan political actors, not the public, decide whether to lend support to an intervention depending on the costs of the conflict and the perceived success of the intervention. As I discuss in greater detail in the conclusion to chapter 5, the public appears "rational" only because it takes cues from elites who sensibly incorporate events into their decisions to support or oppose war. These claims are consistent with many existing understandings of public opinion and American politics, but they are at odds with leading work in the realm of public opinion and foreign policy.

In this chapter, I begin by describing the different theoretical positions on the determinants of support for war and present evidence from World War II and the ongoing Iraq War to question event-driven theories of war support. Although these conflicts differ in many critical respects, they also share important commonalities that allow us to speak to public opinion concerning war more generally.[1] In both wars, I find that significant segments of the public possessed little knowledge of the most basic facts of these conflicts. Thus, there is little evidence that citizens have the information needed to make cost-benefit calculations when deciding whether to support or oppose military action. Moreover, using data from survey experiments conducted during the Iraq War, I find that providing members of the public with correct information does not change opinions about the wisdom of intervention. I pay special attention here to information about military casualties to illustrate the shortcoming of the cost-benefit framework, in part because a concern with casualties has captured much scholarly and popular attention. The criticisms raised here, however, also apply to explanations involving other tangible costs (both human and monetary) and benefits (such as successful outcomes to wars). Throughout the chapter, I present more general evidence on these other quantities as well.

THE POWER OF EVENTS?

The conventional wisdom that has emerged over the last thirty years in the public opinion and foreign policy literature holds that the course of events in a given conflict directly determines public support for war. The most prominent line of argument in this vein is what Burk (1999) calls the "casualties hypothesis," the view that the American people will shy away from international involvement in the face of war deaths. This hypothesis grows out of Mueller's (1973) contention that public support for war is inversely related to the log of casualties. Some modifications have been made to this basic theory over time.[2] Gartner and Segura (1997, 2000), for instance, argue that casualty rates of military personnel in local communities are an important determinant of support for the war (see also Karol and Miguel 2007 on the relationship between casualties and presidential elections). Even so, the basic story advanced by Mueller remains a dominant view among both academics and policymakers (Burk 1999; Klarevas 2002; Gartner 2008; although see Kull and Destler 1999; Feaver and Gelpi 2004; Voeten and Brewer 2006).[3]

One thing that has changed in recent years is that scholars have moved beyond simply investigating the impact of casualties to examining the effects of other events that occur during the course of military conflict. Larson (1996) argues that the collective public decides whether to support a conflict based on a rational cost-benefit calculation. According to Larson (1996), the greater the perceived stakes, the clearer the objectives, and the higher the probability of success, the greater the level of public support for war.[4] Building on this argument, other authors contend that the ongoing success of a mission—whether the war will come to a victorious end—determines public support for conflict (Feaver and Gelpi 2004; Gelpi, Feaver, and Reifler 2005–6; Kull and Ramsay 2001). These theories differ in their particulars, yet all share the belief that "events" determine public support for war. Thus, even among scholars who consider factors beyond casualties, the basic logic underlying Mueller's argument remains the dominant position: the collective public is rational and will support war if, and only if, the events of war ensure that the costs of military action are outweighed by the perceived benefits of a successful outcome.

Although event-response theories of public support for war have made important contributions, they leave unanswered some essential questions. First, these theories presume that members of the public at least implicitly incorporate knowledge of political developments into their political judgments. An extensive line of research, however, finds great heterogeneity in levels of political knowledge among the public (Delli Carpini and Keeter 1996). Researchers have long understood that, on average, Americans know little about politics, yet Americans' knowledge levels are even lower when the focus turns to specific factual information. For instance, Gilens (2001) found that the public's knowledge of specific policy-relevant information is low, even among those respondents who have high levels of general political knowledge (see also Ansolabehere, Snowberg, and Snyder 2005; Wong 2007).

Second, much research on the relationship between casualties and support for war has examined differences in public support for intervention across wars, while setting aside the differences among individuals within particular conflicts (Klarevas 2002; Mueller 1973; Larson 1996; Jentleson 1992; Jentleson and Britton 1998). With some important exceptions (Gartner and Segura 2000; Gartner, Segura, and Wilkening 1997; Gelpi, Feaver, and Reifler 2005–6, and in the context of the "rally around the flag" phenomenon Baum 2002; Edwards and Swenson 1997), analysis has proceeded at the aggregate level.[5] Several existing theories therefore rest on untested notions of collective rationality. Larson, for instance, in his excellent overview of trends in public support for war, argues that the public will support war "if the aims are clear," but he does not describe the conditions under which individuals, much less the aggregate public, make such complex calculations. Thus, many existing theories of public support for military action fail to specify the mechanisms by which members of the public process information concerning the events of war and come to determine—both as individuals and collectives—whether to support or oppose a given military operation. Thus, while the existing aggregate-level work is indeed valuable, studies of collective opinion change provide an incomplete picture of public opinion. They should be supplemented by individual-level analysis that accounts for individual-level variation on relevant political dimensions (for an important step in this direction, see Page and Bouton 2006).[6]

This analysis leads to the final and most important point. Almost all the work described in the last few paragraphs sets aside the American political process. Treating the public as an undifferentiated whole—innocent of attachments to political parties and relevant social groups—leaves no room for the effect of domestic politics. Many researchers who study public opinion and war—even those scholars who conduct individual-level analysis—often talk about "the public" as if it were monolithic. But foreign policy is often as contentious and partisan as domestic politics.

Consider, for instance, the principal independent variable of both Kull and Ramsay (2001) and Feaver and Gelpi (2004): "war success." At the aggregate level, "perception of success" may have a clear meaning; it could vary over time in reaction to the events on the battlefield. But it is not clear how best to give meaning to the cross-sectional variation in individual perceptions of success. The literature on the effect of perceptions of the domestic economy on vote choice is instructive on this point. First, as Erikson (2004) notes (following Kramer 1983), because cross-sectional variation in perceptions of the economy represents variation in individual perceptions of a fixed quantity, cross-sectional variation in economic evaluations is in part random noise but is also in part determined by an individual's political predispositions. Similarly, we might expect that cross-sectional variation in evaluations of future military "success"—a quantity with a presumably objective answer—could in part also be random noise. But given the partisan nature of patterns of support for the Iraq conflict (Jacobson 2008), this variation is probably less random noise than it is the product of partisan projection effects (Lord, Ross, and Lepper 1979). That is, just as people use their political predispositions to assess the state of the economy in the domestic realm, they may use those same predispositions to assess the likelihood of success on the international stage. Such projection effects could undermine our ability to effectively assess the true relationship between the benefits of war—measured by the likelihood of a successful outcome—and support for that war. Indeed, recent research has demonstrated that economic perceptions may be determined by vote choice, rather than the converse (Wlezien, Franklin, and Twiggs 1997; Anderson, Mendes, and Tverdova 2004; Erikson 2004).[7] Similarly, just as the observed correlation between vote choice and economic perceptions is a result of voters bringing their economic assessments in line with their political judgments, the causal arrow between perceived success and war support could run from the latter to the former, rather than vice versa, as Gelpi, Feaver, and Reifler (2005–6) argue (for further discussion, see Berinsky and Druckman 2007 and chap. 5 of this volume).

A recent study by Gaines et al. (2007) illustrates the logic of this partisan misperception in the case of Iraq. Consistent with the argument made here, Gaines and his colleagues found that the facts of the war do not speak for themselves. The researchers examined the likelihood that ordinary citizens—in this case, college students—would deem a given number of casualties "large" or "small." They found that partisans differed greatly in how they mapped similar factual beliefs onto interpretations of casualty levels. Given the exact same estimate of troop deaths, Democrats were far more likely than Republicans to call the number of deaths "large." As Gaines et al. write, "Common standards for evaluating numbers of casualties do not exist. Respondents thus had wide latitude in interpreting the number of troops killed. The aggregate data suggest that both party allegiance and the strength of that partisanship influenced people's interpretation of their beliefs about troop casualties" (2007, 963).

When substituting "war success" for "casualties," the findings of Gaines et al. regarding the disconnect among facts, beliefs, and opinions are especially troubling for the Feaver, Gelpi, and Reifler studies. Measures of perceived success might not be precisely the same as measures of support for war, but both measures are shaped by the political predilections of survey respondents. As I demonstrate later, analysis of survey data concerning the current Iraq War suggests that, consistent with the findings of Gaines and his colleagues, Feaver, Gelpi, and Reifler's measure of perceived success is indeed best characterized as another measure of support for war, itself influenced by partisan elite discourse. More important, the general lesson here is clear. Theories of war and politics must account for the effects of the domestic political process.

MEDIATED REALITY: THE PRIMACY OF POLITICAL COMPETITION

In the early days of survey research, scholars argued that the public opinion concerning foreign policy was volatile and irrational—a fickle and changing "mood" in Almond's (1960) words (see also Converse 1964; Lippmann 1922; for a review, see Holsti 2004). The relative shortcoming of event-response theories, however, does not mean that we must retreat to these dismal conclusions regarding public opinion and foreign policy. Event-response theories, after all, are not the only explanation for the dynamics of public support for war. In this book, I examine two additional factors that shape public opinion on war: the influence of competition among political elites on the one hand and the power of group attachments on the other.

Theories of Elite Competition

Popular perceptions notwithstanding, politics has never stopped at the water's edge. Furthermore, in the United States, politics is steeped in partisan conflict. Partisanship influences the way in which citizens interpret ongoing events (Bartels 2002) and competing policies (Druckman 2001), and consequently it influences the political decisions they make. The leading proponent of an elite-driven opinion process in the context of foreign policy is Zaller (1992), who claims that elite discourse is the key to explaining war support (see also Brody 1991).[8] Zaller argues that the balance of persuasive messages carried in the political media determines the balance of opinion on a given policy controversy. For Zaller, the key is to examine how levels of political awareness condition responsiveness to political messages. Although many Americans are ignorant of political developments, "there is a small but important minority of the public that pays great attention to politics and is well informed about it" (1992, 16). Others, of course, lie between the two extremes. Zaller exploits variation in levels of information among the public to determine how exposure to and reception of political discourse affect the shape of public opinion. Individuals who are most politically knowledgeable are most likely to receive political messages and accept those messages that accord with their personal political predispositions. Among citizens who pay no attention to politics, we would expect to see small differences between individuals with discordant predispositions, regardless of the balance of elite discourse. If citizens do not hear political messages, they do not know when and if they should disagree. Among those individuals who pay close attention to politics, however, the balance of elite discourse is critical. If politicians with different values come to the same position on a political controversy, informed citizens will adopt that position. If, however, political elites disagree, the informed minority will mirror that split. The greater the volume of elite discourse favoring a particular policy position from elites of a particular political stripe, the more likely it is that the members of the public who share the political predispositions of those elites will adopt that position.

Of course not all citizens can map their personal preferences onto the world of politics. Take partisanship, for instance. Some citizens claim to be independent of the two parties. However, studies of partisan attachment find that setting aside those citizens who lean toward one of the parties greatly reduces the pool of political independents. Moreover, those "independents" who lean to one of the parties tend to vote and behave like committed partisans (Keith et al. 1992). At most, 10 percent of the general public and 5 percent of the voting public lack any partisan loyalties.

On the question of partisanship, another point bears mentioning here. Zaller's model—and my theoretical extension discussed below—presumes that political predispositions are exogenous and causally prior to political judgments on particular issues. It is plausible, however, that a citizen's position on specific issues could shape her basic predispositions, as well as the reverse. In fact, a number of scholars have argued that the measures of partisan identification I use throughout this book are profoundly influenced by how citizens line up on the controversies of the day (Fiorina 1981; Franklin and Jackson 1983; Jackson 1975). Yet the view advanced in this book is closer to the notion that partisanship is a fundamental trait, acquired early in life and largely immutable over the course of a lifetime (Campbell et al. 1960). My view is therefore concordant with that of Green, Palmquist, and Schickler, who argue that "partisan identities are early features of citizen self-conceptions. They do not merely come and go with election cycles and campaign ephemera" (2002, 4). In any event, even if attitudes toward war do influence partisan attachments, these changes are certainly small for even the most salient wars (Norrander and Wilcox 1993) and pale in comparison to the power that partisanship exerts as a basic perceptual screen.

Zaller (1992) makes his case in the context of the Vietnam War, arguing that the decline in support for that war was driven by a change in the balance of elite discourse across the 1960s. He found that in the early phase of the war, when political elites were almost uniform in their support for the U.S. policy in Vietnam, a monotonic relationship existed between political awareness and support for the war: those most attentive to elite discourse were most supportive of the current policy, regardless of their individual predispositions. Politically attentive hawks *and* politically attentive doves were more likely to support the war than their less engaged counterparts.[9] Zaller terms this phenomenon the "mainstream pattern" of political support. On the other hand, in the later phases of the Vietnam War, when the mainstream consensus dissolved into elite disagreement, a "polarization pattern" emerged. Here, the effect of political awareness on support for the war was conditional on an individual's political values. Citizens who were attentive to politics followed the path of those leaders who shared their political views. For the Vietnam War, greater awareness led to higher levels of support among hawks and higher levels of opposition among doves.[10]

Although Zaller's initial analysis focused on the Vietnam war, his story is not particular to Vietnam.[11] Zaller (1994) finds that patterns of convergence and polarization among the public followed the lead of elites during the buildup to the 1991 Gulf War. In the early fall of 1990, when both Republican and Democratic leaders supported Bush's buildup of U.S. troops in Saudi Arabia, highly engaged citizens supported military action, regardless of their party identification. When congressional Democrats began to raise objections to possible military action in the wake of the 1990 election, however, mass opinion soon followed suit. On the eve of the war, large differences over the wisdom of military intervention emerged between highly attentive Democrats and Republicans.[12] Reaching farther back in history, Belknap and Campbell (1951) argue that a similar pattern of opinion convergence and polarization existed during the Korean War. They find that differences between Republican and Democratic identifiers were greatest among those respondents with high levels of political information. Although a reanalysis of this data indicates that the degree of polarization was substantively small and statistically insignificant, the findings are suggestive.

Theories of elite competition account for some of the shortcomings of event-driven theories of support for war; they explicitly bring politics into the study of public opinion, allowing us to see how individuals with different political predilections interpret events and react to different forms of elite discourse. Furthermore, as I discuss in the conclusion to chapter 5, such theories allow events an indirect role in shaping public opinion. Politicians who care about their future careers and think—rightly or wrongly—that the public cares about events may incorporate information about military successes and failures into their positions on war. Elites then communicate their evaluations to their supporters in the public through the media and other channels.[13] Thus, partisan political actors, not ordinary citizens, balance costs and benefits when deciding to lend support to military action. The public may appear "rational," but only by following elites who share their basic political predilections.

The Elite Cue Theory

At the same time, Zaller's explanation is incomplete. Zaller claims that the dynamics of opinion are driven exclusively by the net balance of partisan messages gleaned by individuals through political discourse. For Zaller, opposition to a conflict emerges only as a result of a clear message in elite rhetoric. It is the aggregation of oppositional messages among political leaders that leads to mass opposition. Yet it is not clear if the mere content of elite messages is the only path to political influence. Certainly, there are cases in which political actors on both sides of a controversy provide persuasive messages, leading to polarized opinions among the public. But even in the absence of discourse on one side of a given controversy, individuals may have the information they need to come to a judgment regarding the fit between the policy options on the table and their political predispositions. Here the literature on cue taking and heuristics is instructive. Several studies have demonstrated that poorly informed citizens can make decisions that emulate the behavior of well-informed citizens by following the cues of politicians who share their political views (see Lupia 1994; Popkin 1991; Sniderman, Brody, and Tetlock 1991). We would therefore expect that citizens use the position of a prominent elite as a reference point and decide whether to support or oppose a policy based on that position, even in the absence of explicitly contradictory messages. Under some circumstances, elite consensus on only one side of the partisan divide can therefore lead to attitude polarization when the opposition is silent.

In effect, citizens delegate the difficult process of arriving at an opinion on a complicated policy matter to trusted political experts. Presidents can serve as such cue givers, especially in the realm of foreign policy (Meernik and Ault 2001). Such reasoning is particularly likely during those times when the partisan climate is especially polarized. For instance, if I am a Democrat in 2004, I need only know that George Bush supports a policy initiative to recognize that I should oppose such a course of action (unless Democratic politicians also clearly support that position).

Moreover, the balance of partisan discourse itself can serve as a cue both to committed partisans and to the small percentage of the public without partisan attachments. For instance, unified opposition to a course of action can signal that an intervention is a poor idea; unified support can signal that an intervention is wise because all partisan political actors are able to set aside their differences to pursue a common goal. Similarly, the support of international institutions—such as the United Nations or allied foreign governments—may serve as a cue that intervention is justified. Thus the finding that support for intervention increases when multilateral actions are proposed (Kull and Ramsay 2001) may better reflect a process of cue taking rather than support for such interventions on their face.

Use of these cues, however, requires that citizens have knowledge of the positions of relevant political actors.[14] Here is where Zaller's information-based theory can be brought into accord with cue-taking theories.[15] As an individual's level of political information increases, his awareness of the positions of particular elites—and the distinctiveness of those positions relative to other political actors—increases. Thus a pattern of opinion polarization could occur even in the absence of vocal opposition, provided a strong cue-giver takes a clear position on that policy. As I show in the next chapter, this alternative mechanism of elite influence I have developed—what I call the elite cue theory—can explain the pattern of opinion in World War II, when both FDR and his Republican opponents took distinct positions. Moreover, unlike Zaller's original formulation, the theory can also explain the polarized pattern of opinion surrounding the war in Iraq, a situation in which Bush took a strong prowar position but Democratic Party leaders failed to express strong support or opposition. Although I do not directly test the elite cue theory against Zaller's Reception-Acceptance-Sampling (RAS) theory in this book, and the two theories are quite similar, the elite cue theory seems to provide a more comprehensive explanation of the opinion formation process. The RAS model explains Republican support for the Iraq War, but it cannot explain the divergence of opinion on the Iraq War in the absence of clear antiwar messages from Democratic politicians in the early years of the war. The elite cue theory, on the other hand, argues that the political rhetoric of Republican elites caused opinion polarization for *both* Republican and Democratic identifiers.[16]

Groups

Political elites are not the only source of individual-level structure in war-based attitudes that are grounded in domestic politics. Recent research in the field of public opinion has demonstrated the continuing power of stereotypes and other group-centered attitudes or heuristics in shaping political understanding and behavior (Berinsky and Mendelberg 2005; Gilens 1999; Hurwitz and Peffley 1998; Kinder and Sanders 1996; Mendelberg 2001; Sears, Sidanius, and Bobo 2000; Sniderman and Piazza 1993; Valentino, Hutchings, and White 2002). This literature stems from Converse's insight, worked out in his seminal work on belief systems, that the public's beliefs are mostly structured by the social groupings of society (Converse 1964). Presaging later work on cues and heuristics (Popkin 1991; Sniderman, Brody, and Tetlock 1991), Converse (1964) noted that reference group cues could serve as the foundation of "ideology by proxy," creating meaningful patterns in the attitudes and behaviors of ordinary citizens. Groups as cognitive constructs can play a significant role in shaping public opinion.

Much work in the domestic realm has born out Converse's predictions. For present purposes, it is important to note that membership in and attitudes toward particular groups can affect individuals' baseline reaction to a given conflict. In chapter 6, I discuss in greater detail the tendency of a person's attitudes toward domestic groups to structure his opinion on key foreign policy issues. For instance, as I show later, during the 1930s and 1940s enmity and attachment to different ethnic groups led to consistent differences in support for military action in the European theater and beyond.

EXPECTATIONS

Given this review of the relevant literature, my expectations regarding the relative role of events, elites, and groups in structuring opinion concerning war are clear. Consistent with recent work on U.S. public opinion, I expect that events will have little direct effect on the public's day-to-day judgments regarding the wisdom of war. This is not to say that events never play a direct role in structuring opinion; certainly cataclysmic events, such as Pearl Harbor or the attacks of 9/11, can directly influence public opinion. But the events that many scholars of public opinion and war have examined—casualties and other mission indicators—are more ephemeral and are often interpreted through a partisan lens. As a result, knowledge of wartime events will not be widespread, and such events will play only an indirect role in determining public support for war. Furthermore, correcting misperceptions of these events will have little effect on war support.

Conversely, I expect that attachments to groups and patterns of elite discourse—the stated positions of leading Democratic and Republican politicians—will play a large role in determining public support for war.[17] Individuals will use their attitudes toward domestic groups and the positions of prominent elites as reference points, providing structure and guidance to opinions concerning war. Moreover, contrary to Zaller, I expect to find divergence even without politicians taking clear positions on both sides of a controversy. The presence of a prominent war-supporting cue giver can lead to a polarization of opinion as long as his opponents across the partisan aisle do not cross party lines to support war (and vice versa). Although citizens, in this view, do not rationally balance the costs and benefits of military action, neither do they blindly follow the messages disseminated by political elites and carried through political discourse. Rather, they use preexisting group loyalties and enmities at the same time that they account for patterns of political leadership and partisan conflict in order to come to reasonable decisions that accord with their predispositions.

To date, not much work in political science has focused on the power of groups in structuring foreign policy attitudes. I return to this theme in chapter 6. For the remainder of this chapter and the next, I focus on the relative explanatory power of events and elites. Event-response theories, such as the casualties hypothesis (and its extensions), and the elite cue theory, which places the primary mechanism in the hands of partisan political actors, provide very different explanations for the dynamics of public support for war. These theories also carry very different normative implications; whether partisan political actors lead or follow opinion concerning war is a question with profound consequences for the practice of democracy. It has been difficult to assess the relative validity of the two approaches, however, because scholars have focused on the cold war and post–cold war American experiences, namely, war failures and short-term military excursions (Sobel 2001). Consider, for instance, the Korean and Vietnam wars. Both the elite cue theory and the event-response theory predict that public support would decline as the conflicts unfolded. In the first view, as divisions among elites widened over time during both the Korean and Vietnamese conflicts, public opinion became polarized, thereby decreasing overall support for war. At the same time, because most scholars have used cumulative casualties as a measure of the war's cost (Larson 1996; although see Gartner, Segura, and Wilkening 1997; Gartner and Segura 1998), and because cumulative casualties—as Gartner, Segura, and Wilkerning (1997) note—are collinear with time, the casualties hypothesis predicts a secular decline in support for war over time. Thus, for both theories of public support, time is correlated with the explanatory variables of interest: real-world events and how those events are discussed by elites. To distinguish the accuracy of these two theories, we need to look to new evidence.

WARTIME EVENTS AND THE AMERICAN PUBLIC: EMPIRICAL EVIDENCE

In the rest of this chapter, I investigate the ability of the public to integrate ongoing military developments into their judgments on war. I find that, on average, knowledge of the basic facts of war is scarce and—previewing the argument in chapter 5—the facts people think they know are influenced by their partisan political attachments; Republicans and Democrats hold in their heads very different pictures of the "world out there."

I first present data from World War II suggesting that explanations that look to battlefield events cannot account for public opinion during the war years. As World War II continued, cumulative U.S. casualties increased, but support for the war did not falter. Moreover, explanations that draw on other wartime events are not well supported by the data. Second, I present additional evidence from two survey experiments concerning opinion on the war in Iraq. These experiments demonstrate that citizens do not adjust their attitudes toward war in response to explicit information about wartime events, as event-response theories suggest they should. These data lay the groundwork for the next two chapters. Although World War II and the Iraq War are different in many ways, in both wars the determinants of public opinion can be found at the intersection of elite discourse and the ethnic and political attachments of members of the public.

World War II

Contrary to the expectations of the casualties hypothesis, support for World War II, over the almost four years of U.S. involvement in the conflict, did not wane, even as war deaths mounted, particularly after the spring of 1944.[18] Campbell et al. (1965) use a number of questions to measure support for the government's stated military aims and demonstrate that significant majorities of the public supported the war. As noted in chapter 3, more direct measures of support for the conflict, although confined to a limited time period, paint a similar picture. A majority of the public always supported the stated U.S. policy of unconditional surrender, and variation in such support over time was orthogonal to both monthly and cumulative casualty counts, which rose greatly over this period (see fig. 3.1). In addition, no more than a handful of respondents said they thought that they would view U.S. involvement in the war as a mistake in the years to come.

Furthermore, as we will see later with the Iraq War, large segments of the public were ignorant of the human costs of the war, even though information concerning war deaths was readily available, as detailed in chapter 3. An October 1945 Gallup survey asked, "How many American soldiers, sailors, and airmen were killed in the war—just your best guess?" The median response of 500,000 was higher than the correct number (approximately 300,000 soldiers died). Moreover, as with Iraq, there was wide variation in answers to the question. Twenty-eight percent of respondents guessed that the war dead stood at over one million, and 15 percent guessed that fewer than 200,000 died.

Other explanations that find the roots of continued support of the American public in wartime events are also problematic, as noted in chapter 3. There is a broad sense in popular accounts and some academic treatments of World War II that this conflict was the "good war," in which the benefits of intervention were clear. According to this account, the United States, shaken by the Japanese attack at Pearl Harbor, quickly rallied to the cause of protecting democracy. Recall Larson's argument, presented in the last chapter. Larson argued that support for the war derived from a desire for retribution against the atrocities committed by the Axis powers and "the shared perception of important stakes and vast benefits of eliminating a grave threat to U.S. security" (1996, 14–15).

Larson's explanations may seem plausible in retrospect, but public opinion data from the 1940s do not provide support for such accounts. Knowledge of the atrocities discussed by Larson, such as the Holocaust, was thin during the war, perhaps in part because the Office of War Information (OWI) sought to downplay information about the plight of European Jews (Leff 2005).[19] In January 1943, only 47 percent of the population thought that Germany was engaged in the mass destruction of Europe's Jewish population.[20] Even when belief in the existence of concentration camps became widespread in late 1944—when 76 percent of the public believed that "the Germans have murdered many people in concentration camps"—less than half of respondents thought that the toll at the camps would rise above 100,000. Furthermore, at several points in time, Gallup and Hadley Cantril's Office of Public Opinion Research (OPOR) asked the public if they had "a clear idea what the war is about." In March 1942, almost four months after the attack on Pearl Harbor, only 43 percent of Americans felt they had such an idea. By July, that figure rose to 62 percent, but for the rest of the war, the percentage of Americans who agreed with the statement fluctuated in the 65–70 percent range, rising to 72 percent in January 1944 but falling below 60 percent in March 1944. Thus, although a majority of Americans could identify a war aim, a sizable minority could not. Certainly, the specific context of the Second World War helped engender high levels of support for the war. Support for the U.S. effort at the time, however, was not as self-evident as it appears in retrospect. Thus, the existing accounts that root continued public support in ongoing wartime events do not hold up under a scrutiny of the evidence.

The War in Iraq

The data from World War II suggest that the primacy given to events as explanations for U.S. support for war is unwarranted. Those data, however, are admittedly merely suggestive. To explore more directly the role of events in shaping opinion, I turn to the modern stage of the war in Iraq, around which I have designed experiments to measure the influence of events on the shape of public opinion concerning war.

Two facts about the Iraq War are particularly relevant for present purposes. First, dissemination of information regarding wartime events—especially the ongoing count of war dead—has been present in the news. For instance, I used Lexis-Nexis to perform a search of Associated Press articles of June 23–August 2, 2004, that mentioned Iraq (this period begins a month before the survey described in the next section). Of the 82 separate stories in this time period, 57 used the term "casualty." Of these articles, 10 gave the cumulative casualty count. These counts were all correct. Thus, although casualty information was not necessarily prevalent, it was accurate. We can therefore surmise that any misreporting in levels of war deaths by citizens is the result of faulty perceptions of reports of war deaths on the part of citizens, not faulty reports of the number of deaths by the media.[21] Second, as discussed in chapter 2, the positions of prominent cue givers regarding support for war were clear. Iraq was very much Bush's war. The question, then, is this: given the presence of relevant information in media, which factor better explains variation in support for the war: casualties, as the event-response theory would suggest, or elite positions on the wisdom of that conflict, as the elite cue theory contends?

THE IRAQ WAR CASUALTY SURVEY. To answer this question, I conducted an experimental survey in the summer of 2004. The Iraq War Casualty Survey, conducted from July 23 to August 2, 2004, by Knowledge Networks, asked a nationally representative sample of respondents: "Please give your best guess to this next question, even if you are not sure of the correct answer. As you know, the United States is currently involved in a war in Iraq. Do you happen to know how many soldiers of the U.S. military have been killed in Iraq since the fighting began in March 2003?"[22]

At first glance, it appears that the public is informed about the level of troop deaths in Iraq. The mean estimate of deaths in the sample was 952 deaths, while the median response was 900 deaths.[23] Both of these figures are extraordinarily close to the true casualty count, which rose from 901 to 915 over the span of the survey. The accuracy of the median respondent, however, obscures large variation in the casualty estimates. Respondents gave answers ranging from 0 deaths to 130,000 deaths. Even setting aside the extreme responses (casualty guesses under 10 and over 10,000), the standard deviation of the casualty estimate was 802.[24]

A simple tabulation of the estimates illuminates the pattern of responses to the casualty question. I scored those respondents who estimated the number of war deaths to be between 801 and 1,015 (the true estimate +/− 100 deaths) as "correct." Those who gave an estimate of 800 or lower were scored as "underestimators," whereas those who guessed higher than 1,015 are considered "overestimators."[25] The modal response (47 percent) is a correct answer. Nearly as many respondents (42 percent), however, underestimated the number of war deaths (11 percent overestimated the number of deaths).

This pattern of knowledge of casualties found in the survey extends to knowledge of the rate of American deaths in Iraq from around the same time. The Pew Research Center conducted a survey in September 2004 that asked respondents, "What's your impression about what's happened in Iraq over the past month? Has the number of American military casualties been higher, lower, or about the same as in other recent months?" Although a plurality of 46 percent gave the correct answer of "higher," a majority of respondents gave an incorrect answer. These knowledge levels certainly compare favorably to knowledge of other political facts, such as the percentage of the budget devoted to foreign aid (Gilens 2001). The Iraq War Casualty Survey demonstrates, however, that even in a relatively high salience environment, great variation exists in correct knowledge about events on the ground in Iraq. These results call into question the external validity of studies, such as Gartner (2008), that investigate the effect of presenting information about casualty levels and rates, in a real or hypothetical situation. Even if the stark presentation of such knowledge can alter opinions in the context of an experiment, the salience of that knowledge in the general public may be too low to meaningfully structure the opinions of the majority of the public.[26]

More important for present purposes, the variation in knowledge of casualties is not random; elite cues play a significant role in biasing the recall of knowledge. I examined the determinants of perceived level of casualties using measures of political engagement and partisan political leanings.[27] Specifically, I modeled responses to the three-category casualty estimate scale (underestimator/correct/overestimator) as a function of the respondents' partisanship to capture the effect of elite cues and account for partisan bias (see Bartels 2002).[28] I also included as independent variables the amount of attention the respondent pays to news about Iraq, the amount of time the respondent watches Fox News (following Kull, Ramsey, and Lewis 2003–4), and the respondent's general political knowledge, education, and gender.[29]

I generated predicted probabilities that a "typical" member of the public would choose a particular response category, given his or her partisanship.[30] These results are presented in table 4.1. As expected, compared to strong Republicans, strong Democrats are less likely to underestimate and are slightly more likely to overestimate casualty levels.[31] By way of comparison, the effect of partisanship on the probability of underestimating casualty levels is roughly equal to the effect of moving from low information to high information. In short, perceptions of war deaths are influenced not only by information and engagement with political news, but also by the individual's political predispositions.[32]

This finding is consistent with the Pew data on casualty rates described earlier. Among independents, 47 percent correctly stated that casualty rates were higher in the current month than in the previous month.[33] Democrats were even more likely to say that casualties were higher—54 percent gave the correct answer—and Republicans were less likely to say that casualties were increasing—only 36 percent gave the correct answer.[34]

These findings of partisan misperceptions also square well with those of Kull, Ramsey, and Lewis (2003–4), who found in a series of polls during 2003 that although both Democrats and Republicans correctly perceived the Bush administration's position on the war, Republicans (and in

TABLE 4.1 Effect of partisanship and information on predicted probability of estimating correct casualty level

Independent variable	Probability of underestimating (%)	Probability of giving correct answer (%)	Probability of overestimating (%)
Partisanship			
Strong Republican	48	44	8
Strong Democrat	35	54	12
Difference between groups	−13	+10	+4
Information			
Low information	51	31	18
High information	36	56	7
Difference between groups	−15	+25	−11

particular, supporters of George Bush) were more likely than Democrats to misperceive the truth concerning the presence of weapons of mass destruction in Iraq. The authors found similar gaps when they replicated their analysis using similar questions in 2004 and 2006. For instance, in March 2006, the authors found that 60 percent of Republicans, but only 23 percent of Democrats, believed that Iraq had a weapons of mass destruction (WMD) program or actual WMD. In the same poll, 63 percent of Republicans believed that Iraq either had been directly involved in 9/11 or provided support to al Qaeda, compared with 35 percent of Democrats who held such beliefs (Kull 2006).[35] All together, these studies suggest that when viewing events in Iraq—be they casualty counts, casualty rates, or alliances between the Iraqi government and terrorist organizations— respondents use their partisan leanings as a filter.

Having demonstrated that the respondents' perceptions of events in the Iraq War are influenced by partisanship, I next moved to the more important question of whether the casualty estimates had any influence on opinions concerning war. I measured attitudes toward the Iraq War with two common measures of war support. The first question asked, "Do you think the U.S. made the right decision or the wrong decision in using military force against Iraq?" The second question asked, "All in all, considering the costs to the United States versus the benefits to the United States, do you think the current war with Iraq has been worth fighting, or not?"[36]

I modeled the answers to these questions as a function of the respondents' casualty estimates and their partisanship.[37] I included partisanship to provide a point of comparison for the effect of elite cues. I return to partisan differences in the next chapter, but what is important for present purposes is that I found that a respondent's estimate of war deaths has a substantively small and statistically insignificant effect on that person's war support.[38] The effect of moving from a casualty estimate of 10 deaths to 10,000 deaths is to reduce the probability of stating that the United States made the right decision by 6 percent and to reduce the probability of saying that the costs were worth the benefits by 2 percent. By comparison, the effect of moving from a strong attachment to the Republican Party to a strong attachment to the Democratic Party is to reduce support by 70 percent on the "correct decision" question and by 66 percent on the "worth fighting" question.

These results extend beyond this one study. Using a broader range of data sets, Cobb (2007) comes to the same conclusion: perceptions of casualty counts are largely unrelated to support for the Iraq War. Moreover, these results are actually consistent with results reported in Mueller (1973). Mueller notes that during World War II, Korea, and Vietnam, certain polls asked respondents to estimate the number of war dead. Mueller found that there was no tendency for high or low estimators to support or oppose the war (1973, 62–63).[39] Even Gartner (2008), who demonstrates that respondents who are told that "most military leaders believe, and evidence suggests that the cost in American lives is likely to get worse before it gets better" are significantly more likely to oppose war compared with respondents who are told that "both the administration and military leaders believe and evidence suggests that the worst is behind us," identifies an effect that pales in comparison to the effect of partisanship. Although Gartner uses variables on different scales and does not present the substantive effects of key variables, a back-of-the-envelope calculation indicates that the "casualty forecast" treatment has anywhere from one-quarter to one-eighth the power of partisanship, depending on the model specification.[40]

I was also able to test more directly the influence of casualty information on perception of war. Embedded in the Iraq War survey was an experiment in which one-half of those respondents who were asked to estimate how many soldiers died in Iraq were then told, "Many people don't know the answer to this question, but according to the latest estimates, 901 soldiers have been killed in Iraq since the fighting began in March 2003."[41] In other words, one-half of the respondents who were asked to estimate the number of American deaths were given a "treatment" of correct information before answering the questions concerning support for the Iraq

War. This experimental design allowed me to compare levels of support for the war between two comparable groups: (1) the respondents in the "estimate war deaths" condition who underestimated casualties (for example, those who said that there were fewer than 800 casualties) but were not told the correct number of war deaths; and (2) the respondents in the "corrected" condition who underestimated war deaths but were then told the number of U.S. soldiers who died.[42] I made a similar comparison for respondents who overestimated casualties. This comparison is a powerful one because the "correct information" treatment was randomly assigned. The only difference between the "estimate" group and the "corrected" group is that respondents in the "corrected" condition were subsequently told the true casualty rates.[43] Thus, by comparing these two groups, I was able to assess the effect of introducing the correct information on support for war on individuals who are similarly misinformed about casualty rates.

The results of these analyses are presented in table 4.2.[44] There are no reliably significant differences between the respondents in the two conditions in either a substantive or a statistical sense.[45] Furthermore, the direction of the treatment effect is in the incorrect direction for both the "worth fighting" and the "right decision" questions—respondents who are told that the number of war deaths is larger than they had believed were *more* supportive of the war (although the difference is small and statistically insignificant by a wide margin).[46] Among overestimators, the effect of the treatment was in the expected direction for the "worth fighting" question only and is statistically insignificant.[47] Casualties, it seems, have little effect on levels of support for the war.

THE HUMAN AND MONETARY COSTS OF WAR. One of the best-known findings from the survey research literature is that seemingly minor alterations in the wording of particular questions can result in large differences in the answers respondents give to surveys. Recent advances in theories of the survey response have enabled researchers to predict when opinion changes will occur.

Conventional theories of public opinion treated responses to survey questions as the product of individuals' attempts to reveal their fixed preference on a given policy issue. In the last twenty years, however, a more fluid view of the survey response has emerged, based in part on theories of preference construction developed in cognitive psychology (see, for example, Fischoff 1991; Slovic 1995). This view, advanced most forcibly by

TABLE 4.2 Experimental effect of casualty information on
support for the Iraq War

Among casualty underestimators

Did the U.S. make the right decision in using military force against Iraq?	U.S. made right decision (%)
Estimate war deaths condition	52
Corrected information condition	56

Note: N = 252; $\chi^2(1)$ = 0.40; Pr = 0.53.

Has the current war in Iraq been worth fighting?	Worth fighting (%)
Estimate war deaths condition	42
Corrected information condition	47

Note: N = 253; $\chi^2(1)$ = 0.71; Pr = 0.40.

Among casualty overestimators

Did the U.S. make the right decision in using military force against Iraq?	U.S. made right decision (%)
Estimate war deaths condition	58
Corrected information condition	58

Note: N = 57; $\chi^2(1)$ = 0.00; Pr = 0.95.

Has the current war in Iraq been worth fighting?	Worth fighting (%)
Estimate war deaths condition	42
Corrected information condition	48

Note: N = 57; $\chi^2(1)$ = 0.26; Pr = 0.61.

Zaller and Feldman (1992), argues that "individuals do not typically possess 'true attitudes' on issues, as conventional theorizing assumes, but a series of partially independent and often inconsistent ones" (Zaller 1992, 93; see also Chong 1993, 1996; Feldman 1989; Iyengar and Kinder 1987; Tourangeau, Rips, and Rasinski 2000; Zaller and Feldman 1992). According to this line of public opinion research, a survey response is not necessarily a revealed preference. Answers to survey questions are therefore, in part, determined by the balance of arguments made salient by survey questions. Bringing additional pieces of information—to use Zaller's terminology, "considerations"—to mind alters the base of information that individuals use to come to particular decisions. From this point of view, highlighting negative information—such as the human and monetary costs of war— should cause individuals to focus on the downside of war. In the aggregate, questions that contain information about casualties and the costs of war should therefore yield lower levels of support for war than questions that omit such information.

Somewhat surprisingly, in two separate experiments I did not find this predicted pattern of results. The design of the 2004 Iraq War Casualty Survey experiment allowed me to directly test for the effect of introducing casualty information on support for war. The Iraq War Casualty Survey was part of a larger experiment. Up to this point, I have described only one-half of the design. I asked one-half of the respondents to my survey to estimate the number of casualties in Iraq, as described earlier. The other half of the respondents were not asked to provide such an estimate, which permits a further experimental test. The respondents who did not provide casualty estimates were randomly assigned to one of two experimental conditions. In the "control" condition of the experiment, respondents were neither asked nor given any information concerning the casualty rates in Iraq; they were simply asked their levels of support for the conflict. In the "information only" condition, respondents were not asked to provide an estimate of war deaths, but they were told the correct casualty rates. I found no statistically significant difference in the answers to the war-support questions between these two conditions. Making salient a negative consideration—the scope of the human cost of war—and providing specific information about that cost did not change the aggregate shape of opinion on the war.

In the fall of 2005, I collected additional data to assess the effects of event-specific information on opinions concerning the Iraq War. Respondents to an omnibus survey were randomly assigned to one of six conditions: a "baseline" condition, a "standard survey question" condition, or one of four information conditions.[48]

> Form 1 (baseline): "All in all, do you think the war with Iraq was worth fighting, or not?"
>
> Form 2: (standard survey): "All in all, considering the costs to the United States versus the benefits to the United States, do you think the war with Iraq was worth fighting, or not?"
>
> Form 3: "As you may know, since the war in Iraq began in March 2003, many American soldiers have been killed. All in all, considering the costs to the United States versus the benefits to the United States, do you think the war with Iraq was worth fighting, or not?"
>
> Form 4: "As you may know, since the war in Iraq began in March 2003, almost 2,000 American soldiers have been killed. All in all, considering the costs to the United States versus the benefits to the United States, do you think the war with Iraq was worth fighting, or not?"
>
> Form 5: "As you may know, since the war in Iraq began in March 2003, the U.S. has spent a large amount of money on operations in Iraq. All in all, considering the costs to the United States versus the benefits to the United States, do you think the war with Iraq was worth fighting, or not?"
>
> Form 6: "As you may know, since the war in Iraq began in March 2003, the U.S. has spent almost 200 billion dollars on operations in Iraq. All in all, considering the costs to the United States versus the benefits to the United States, do you think the war with Iraq was worth fighting, or not?"

The first (baseline) condition presented a neutral stimulus; respondents were simply asked whether or not they support the war. In the second (standard survey question) condition, respondents were explicitly asked to consider the costs and benefits of the Iraqi invasion, following the convention of poll questions asked by the *Washington Post* and Gallup, among others. Respondents in the other four conditions were asked forms of the questions that highlighted specific information about the human and financial costs of the Iraq War, in either general (forms 3 and 5) or specific (forms 4 and 6) terms.[49]

Given the vast amounts of research on question-wording effects, we would expect to find large differences, across conditions, based on the types of information presented in the question. This is not the case, however. In fact, as table 4.3 demonstrates, there are almost no differences on levels of support across conditions.[50]

Why, in the face of strong negative information, did these treatments have no effect? As the Iraq War survey demonstrates, the lack of an effect

TABLE 4.3 Experimental effect of war information on support for the Iraq War, autumn 2005

Has the current war in Iraq been worth fighting?

Experimental condition	U.S. made right decision (%)
Baseline	40
Standard survey	42
Many soldiers died	43
2,000 soldiers died	41
U.S. spent a lot of money	40
U.S. spent $200 billion	37

Note: N = 1,168; χ^2 (10) = 9.48; Pr = 0.49. Entries indicate the percentage of respondents in a given condition who supported the Iraq War.

does not result because respondents had already incorporated accurate casualty and cost information into their judgments. As the 2004 Iraq War survey demonstrates, many respondents did not know the correct casualty figures. Rather, as I discuss in the next chapter, we failed to find substantive differences among the conditions because respondents had already made up their minds on Iraq. Citizens discounted new information in favor of more important considerations—their attachments to particular political leaders.

CHAPTER FIVE

PARTISAN STRUCTURE OF WAR SUPPORT: EVENTS, ELITES, AND THE PUBLIC

War is in the air and the Senate is abuzz. The president of the United States has asked Congress to give him the authority to use military force in a country where mere years before U.S. troops were involved in military action. Leaders from both parties line up to argue their case as debate proceeds in the Senate.

Although properly respectful of the gravity of their decision, members of the president's party make the case that war is necessary. Says one, "It is the threat to regional peace and security that justifies [the use of force]. . . . I will support the resolution, of which I am an original cosponsor, and I urge my colleagues to support it as well." On the Senate floor, another member of his party makes a long and impassioned case for intervention:

> While I know some of my colleagues believe strongly that the administration has not articulated forcefully, consistently and clearly the mission and goals of this use of force, and I still have some unanswered questions about the administration's military plans . . . I believe there is little alternative for us but to intervene. . . . I hope and pray that we do not suffer any American casualties in [this intervention] and that innocent civilian casualties on both sides are kept to a minimum, but I fear that if we do not act now thousands will lose their lives in the coming months and years. . . . I believe that it is our duty to act. In this case we cannot shirk our responsibility to act. We cannot stand idly by. That's why I intend to support the president's decision.

Across the partisan aisle, a different message emerges. Members of the opposition party caution against the intervention. "Americans are going to be killed," warns one senator. "They are going to come home in body bags, and they will be killed in a war that Congress has not declared." Adds his colleague, "I am afraid we may be starting something we can't get out of; I am afraid we might be there for years and years and years." "I believe we are coming close to starting World War III," concludes a third senator.

The division between Democrats and Republicans at the elite level is echoed in the opinions of the public. When asked if they support the use of ground troops, a *Washington Post* poll finds that 61 percent of those citizens who identify with the president's party support military action, compared to just 40 percent of those citizens who identify with the opposing party. This gap persists even after the intervention begins. Two months after U.S. forces engage the enemy, the *Washington Post* asks, "Considering everything, do you think the United States did the right thing in getting involved in a military conflict . . . or do you think it was a mistake?" Once again, the public divides along partisan lines. Of citizens who identify with the president's party, 66 percent say that military action was "the right thing." Conversely, even though the initial mission appears to be a success, citizens who identify with the party of opposition remain skeptical of intervention—only 46 percent believe that the United States "did the right thing."

This narrative should sound familiar to those who followed the events related to the U.S. invasion of Iraq in March 2003. This story, however, is not about Iraq; it is about U.S. involvement in Kosovo in the spring of 1999.[1] Here the Republicans are the party of opposition—at both the mass and the elite level— whereas the Democrats are the party of support. The senators who warned of the dangers of long-term involvement are, respectively, Robert Bennett (R-UT), Don Nickles (R-OK), and Ted Stevens (R-AK)—all senators who supported the resolution authorizing the use of force in Iraq in October 2002. The senators urging intervention were Carl Levin (D-MI) and Paul Wellstone (D-MN), both of whom voted against authorizing intervention in Iraq. Admittedly, the two conflicts were different in several ways. But given circumstances that are similar in a number of other respects, party leaders took very different positions on the wisdom of intervention in Kosovo and Iraq, reversing positions—and even rhetoric—between the two conflicts. When these party elites shifted their positions, the public followed suit. The nature of partisan political conflict, it seems, plays a central role in determining support for war at both the elite and mass levels.

In this chapter, I draw on the elite cue theory presented in chapter 4 and demonstrate that patterns of conflict among partisan political actors shape mass opinion on war. The nature of the debate among political elites concerning the salience and meaning of wartime events determines if the public will rally to war. I present evidence from World War II, Vietnam, and the war in Iraq—cases that span sixty-five years of American history—to come to this common conclusion. Although these conflicts differ in many respects, the public reacted to elite positions in similar ways. When elites come to a common interpretation of political reality, the public gives them great latitude to wage war. But when prominent political actors take divergent stands on the wisdom of intervention, the public divides as well.

WORLD WAR II

As discussed in the last chapter, unfolding wartime events alone cannot explain the high levels of public support for World War II. Contrary to the expectations of the casualties hypothesis, support for the war effort did not wane over time, even as deaths mounted. Certainly Pearl Harbor contributed to an initial rally among the public to the cause of war in the Pacific, but rallies tend to be ephemeral (Brody 1991; Parker 1995). Pearl Harbor cannot explain the high levels of support for the European theater efforts, especially in the uncertain times before D-day. Furthermore, as noted in chapter 4, knowledge of the wartime atrocities, which might have fueled the war effort, was slim. What then can explain continued public support for the war? Surely something else was at work. The key, I argue, is that it was not the direct influence of events that determined support for World War II, but rather the patterns of elite conflict during the 1930s and 1940s.

The picture of elite discourse concerning World War II is clear. Legro's (2000) study of political rhetoric in the 1930s and 1940s indicates that from 1938 through the end of 1941, support among elites for some form of U.S. involvement in World War II generally increased over time. The gap between FDR and his critics on the necessity and wisdom of U.S involvement in the Second World War remained large, however. For instance, Legro (2000) finds that FDR's critics—as represented by the editorial page of the *Chicago Tribune*, a paper that can be seen as the mouthpiece of the isolationist wing of the Republican Party—moved in an internationalist direction through 1941. Yet FDR's position consistently outpaced that of his critics. Beginning in 1939, FDR moved in a strongly internationalist direction, but it was not until 1942 that the *Tribune* expressed any support for military commitments abroad. Conversely, from 1942 on, "the collective orthodoxy embraced the necessity of international cooperation and multilateralism" (Legro 2000, 261).

Additional evidence on the nature of elite discourse comes from an analysis of the *Congressional Record* (see Appendix C for coding details). Figure 5.1 presents the month-by-month proportion of prowar to antiwar statements expressed by members of Congress from 1938 to 1945, broken down by party. The figure also includes a trend line for the proportions for each party.[2] As the figure demonstrates, for almost the entire period, Democrats in Congress offered a message that was consistently more prowar in tone than that of their colleagues across the aisle. Moreover, among Democrats in the pre–Pearl Harbor period, the prowar stance reached a majority position by late 1940. Although Republicans softened their antiwar stance even before Pearl Harbor—reflecting the general internationalist trend in rhetoric found by Legro—they lagged behind Democrats.[3] After Pearl Harbor, however, both parties expressed a strong prowar message.

In sum, analysis of elite rhetoric, including the *Congressional Record* analysis presented in figure 5.1, demonstrates that before Pearl Harbor, FDR took a strong prowar stance. Over time, Democrats in Congress expressed increased support for his position. Although FDR's critics—both in Congress and in the press—also moved in an internationalist direction from 1938 until 1941, the gap between these two parties remained large. Thus, with the notable exception of the 1940 presidential election discussed later in the chapter, elite discourse split along the lines of partisan support for or against FDR before Pearl Harbor but presented a largely united front after the United States entered the war. This line of argument is not intended to minimize the importance of Pearl Harbor in shaping opinion on the war. Given the ephemeral nature of rally effects (Brody 1991), however, it is clear that greater attention needs to be paid to how support for the war was sustained through the nearly four years of U.S. involvement. The elite cue theory suggests that we look at the interaction between individuals' attention to elite discourse and their political predispositions to see how changes in the balance of political messages resonated with the public. In particular, we should see the polarization pattern of support before the United States' entry into the war, and—following the balance of elite discourse—the mainstream pattern from 1942 onward, as elites remained in agreement about the wisdom of war.[4]

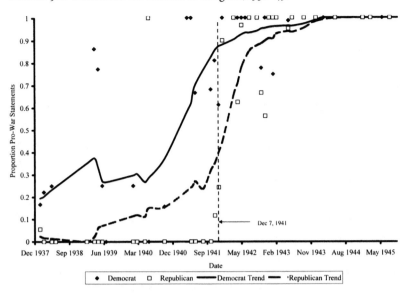

FIGURE 5.1. Parties and war rhetoric in Congress, 1938–45.

To test these expectations, we must focus on the expressed preferences of supporters and opponents of the president. Although there are several predispositions relevant to the study of war, in this period support for FDR is the most appropriate one, given the president's role in pushing the United States to aid England and the prevalence of isolationist tendencies among his opponents in the Republican Party. We would expect that from 1939 until 1941, supporters of FDR who are attentive to politics should be more likely to adopt FDR's position than similar individuals who do not follow politics. Specifically, these respondents should be more likely to state that the United States would be willing to risk war to aid the Allied countries, if not enter the war immediately. Opponents of FDR, on the other hand, should be less likely to support aiding the Allies as their levels of attention to elite discourse increase (with the exception of the 1940 presidential campaign). With the United States' entry into the war in December 1941, however, discourse unified behind the president's position; both Democratic and Republican politicians supported the war. The mainstream pattern of support for the war should therefore emerge during this time. Regardless of an individual's political predispositions, a citizen with higher levels of political information should express greater support for the administration's policies than would a citizen with less information.

Data and Analysis

I draw on a series of polls conducted by Gallup, OPOR, and Roper from 1939 to 1944 to examine the dynamics of war support (for a discussion of these data, see Appendix C). The first set of these polls was conducted during the period before Pearl Harbor. Specifically, I examined polls conducted by Gallup in November 1939, June 1941, and August 1941, as well as a poll conducted by OPOR in January 1941. The second set of polls was conducted in the period after the United States entered the war. These polls include surveys conducted by Gallup in August 1943, OPOR in June 1942 and June 1944, and Roper in March 1943. In line with the elite cue theory, my expectation was that public opinion, measured in 1939 and 1941, would exhibit the polarization pattern, whereas opinion measured in the polls conducted after the United States' entry into the war would exhibit the mainstream pattern.[5] In a later section, I also draw on an AIPO poll from October 1940 that demonstrates that when elite rhetoric concerning the wisdom of intervention briefly shifted during the 1940 presidential campaign, the dynamics of public opinion shifted as well.

To determine whether the mainstream pattern or the polarization pattern better characterized public opinion, we need individual-level measurements of three quantities: support for the war, political predispositions, and levels of political information (which, following Zaller, proxies attentiveness to elite discourse). The opinion polls collected by Gallup, Roper, and OPOR contain measures of all the necessary quantities, albeit inconsistently. First, consider the primary independent variables: predispositions and information. We have several measures available that tap support for the president. I use two of these measures: (1) the candidate for whom the respondent voted in the last election; and (2) the respondent's approval or disapproval of FDR.[6] Both of these measures have their strengths and weaknesses. The respondent's vote in the last election is an exogenous measure of his support for Roosevelt. It is possible, however, that people who found FDR persuasive in the past—in particular during his landslide 1936 reelection campaign—would no longer support him at the time of the survey. The approval measure, on the other hand, captures precisely the contemporaneous support for the president I seek to tap, but introduces potential endogeneity concerns; respondents could express support for the president *because* of his position on the war. Thus, where possible, I use both measures in concert to create a predisposition measure that parses the strong supporters of FDR from the strong opponents of FDR. I label those individuals who voted for FDR in the last election and currently support him as "pro-FDR." Respondents who voted against FDR and currently disapprove of his performance are "anti-FDR."[7] Respondents who fall into neither camp are the comparison category. Measurement of the second independent variable, political information, is clear-cut. A number of polls from 1939 to 1945 asked items that assessed attentiveness to ongoing political controversies. Other surveys asked questions concerning political leaders, geography, or knowledge of current events that are similar in form to measures of political information used today (Delli Carpini and Keeter 1996; Zaller 1992).[8]

Finally, turning to the dependent variable—support for the war—I find that different strategies need to be adopted for different periods of the conflict. Before the United States entered World War II, pollsters often asked if the country should become involved in the war and attempted to gauge the conditions under which the public would be willing to risk entry into war. Measuring support for the war after Pearl Harbor is a less straightforward task, however. As noted in chapter 3, unlike pollsters during the Vietnam, Korean, and Iraq wars, survey researchers during World War II never regularly asked respondents if becoming involved in the military conflict was a "mistake." To tap into support for the war, we must measure war support in an indirect manner. There are a number of items appropriate to such an analytic strategy. As discussed in chapter 3, pollsters measured support for the U.S. diplomatic and military aims, both contemporaneously and in the future. These questions can be used to measure underlying support for the military and governmental objectives of the war effort. For instance, several organizations asked respondents if the United States should adopt an internationalist posture and take an active role in world affairs after the war, thereby embracing the dominant orthodoxy in foreign policy that emerged after Pearl Harbor (Legro 2000). Admittedly, these questions are not perfect measures of support for war. Fortunately, more direct measures of support for the war effort exist. As detailed in chapter 3, several polls during this time asked if the United States should make peace with Germany under current conditions. All told, then, the existing opinion poll data contain the measures necessary to conduct repeated individual-level analysis over time and to trace the individual-level processes of opinion formation and change.

For each poll, I modeled opinion on the war—various indicators of support for administration policy—as a function of (1) pro/anti FDR predisposition, (2) information levels,[9] (3) interactions between FDR predispositions and the information term, and (4) a series of demographic variables to control for biases arising from sampling concerns. (See Appendix C and Berinsky 2006 for further discussion.)[10] Instead of presenting the coefficients from my analysis, I present graphs of the predicted effects of information and partisanship on respondents' support for war (the full coefficients used to generate the figures are presented in Appendix C).[11]

Figures 5.2A–E demonstrate that, as predicted by the elite cue theory, the polarization pattern characterizes opinion from 1939 through the middle of 1941, outside of the 1940 presidential campaign period (as discussed later).[12] Figure 5.2A presents analysis of a question in November 1939 that asked whether respondents "approve the changes which Congress made in the Neutrality Act which permits nations at war to buy arms and airplanes in this country." The figure demonstrates that as information levels increase, opponents of FDR are much less likely to support changing the law. The difference between the high- and low-information opponents of FDR is significant.[13] High- and medium-information supporters of FDR, on the other hand, are more likely to support the change than are low-information FDR supporters. In figure 5.2B, I present the results of a similar analysis using data from a January 1941 poll. As information levels increase, supporters of the president are more likely to endorse the administration's position that it is more important to help England than it is to stay out of the war. By contrast, opponents of FDR are equally likely to express an antiadministration position, regardless of their information levels.[14] The polarization pattern of opinion continued through the middle of 1941. Figures 5.2C and 5.2D demonstrate this pattern on two questions relating to the war. The first asks whether the respondent would support a peace plan that would allow Germany to keep the land it had occupied through the spring of 1941. The second question more directly concerns U.S. involvement in the war, asking if "the U.S. Navy should be used to convoy ships carrying war materials to Britain." Although the polarization pattern is more pronounced on the question about the peace plan, opinion is still significantly polarized along lines of support for FDR in the case of the use of convoys. Furthermore, as figure 5.2E demonstrates, this pattern of polarization continues to characterize opinion on the question of convoys one month later.

Consistent with expectations, the pattern of public support for military action changed greatly after the United States entered the war. The surveys used here cover various times during the war and encompass data from several survey organizations, but the results are virtually identical. In line with the expectations of the elite cue theory, as discourse moved from a two-sided to a one-sided flow in 1941, the public followed suit. Citizens who approved of FDR's performance as president remained more supportive of the stated war aims of the U.S. government than were opponents

FIGURE 5.2A. Evidence of polarization pattern, Gallup, November 1939: Approve of changes to the neutrality law.

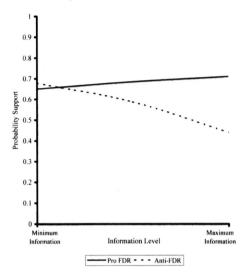

FIGURE 5.2B. Evidence of polarization pattern, OPOR, January 1941: More important to help England than stay out of the war.

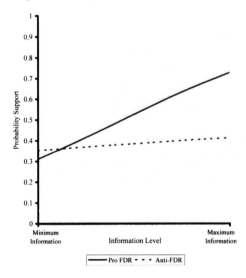

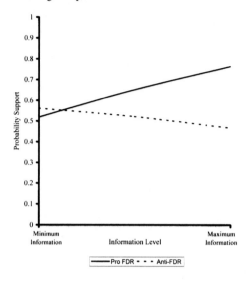

FIGURE 5.2C. Evidence of polarization pattern, Gallup, June 1941: Let Germany keep land in exchange for peace.

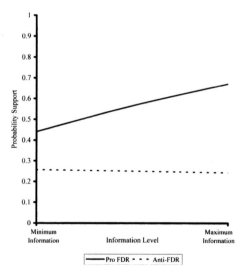

FIGURE 5.2D. Evidence of polarization pattern, Gallup, June 1941: Use the U.S. Navy to convoy ships to England?

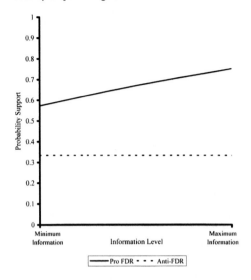

FIGURE 5.2E. Evidence of polarization pattern, Gallup, August 1941: Use the U.S. Navy to convoy ships to England?

of FDR even after Pearl Harbor. The size of the differences between these two groups diminished greatly after 1941, however. More important, measured in a variety of ways—whether the United States should send its army abroad, whether the United States should take an active role in world affairs after the war, and, most critically, whether the United States should make peace with Germany if Hitler were overthrown—individuals more attuned to elite discourse were more supportive of an active U.S. role, regardless of their predispositions regarding FDR (see figs. 5.3A–E). To be precise, unlike the pre-1942 data just analyzed, the effect of information does not distinguish between supporters and opponents of the president.

The shift in the dynamics of opinion is not simply the result of a change in general sentiment toward administration policies during wartime. On domestic issues, the public remained divided, in line with elite positions on the issues. In a 1944 Roper poll, I find the expected polarization pattern regarding support for the position that the next administration should "work with businessmen" rather than "take care of the people" (see fig. 5.4).

Election of 1940

To this point, I have presented evidence that citizens who opposed FDR changed their behavior with the onset of the Second World War. I argue that this change is the direct result of a change in patterns of elite conflict,

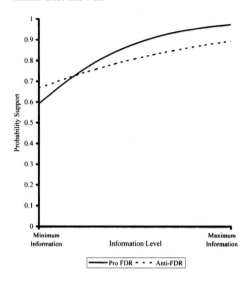

FIGURE 5.3A. Evidence of mainstream pattern, OPOR, June 1942: Take an active part in world affairs after the war.

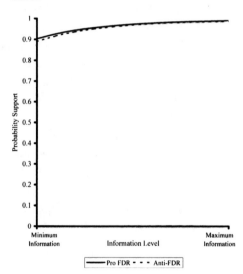

FIGURE 5.3B. Evidence of mainstream pattern, OPOR, June 1942: Do not make peace with Hitler.

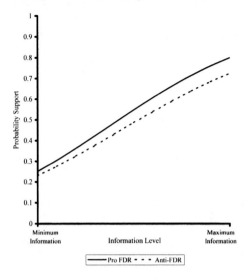

FIGURE 5.3C. Evidence of mainstream pattern, Roper, March 1943: United States should take active role in international organization after war.

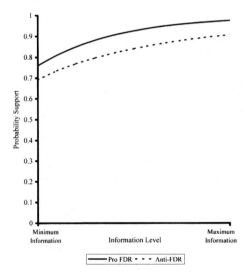

FIGURE 5.3D. Evidence of mainstream pattern, Gallup, August 1943: Oppose peace with Germany even if Hitler were overthrown.

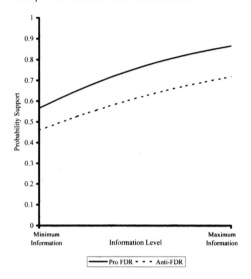

FIGURE 5.3E. Evidence of mainstream pattern, OPOR. January 1944: Oppose peace with Germany even if Hitler were overthrown.

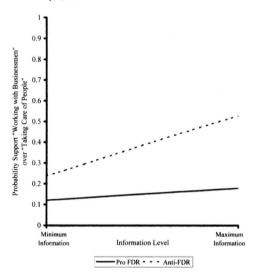

FIGURE 5.4. Distinctiveness of domestic policy, February 1944.

but it could also be that individuals changed their behavior for other reasons. For instance, perhaps after 1941 the interests of the opponents of FDR changed. More problematic for my position, it could be that the events of late 1941 themselves directly transformed how individuals processed information concerning the war—that is, it could be that Pearl Harbor changed beliefs about how effective isolationist positions were likely to be for U.S. interests. Under this view, those individuals who were most politically informed would be able to make the same calculations as partisan political actors, mirroring the opinions of those elites but not taking their cue from elite positions. The observed mainstream pattern might therefore be the result of simultaneous movement in the interests of the opponents of FDR and not a result of elite influence.

Although I do not have direct evidence that shifts in elite discourse led to changes in the dynamics of opinion in late 1941, I do have indirect evidence from a survey taken around the 1940 election. I find that when the messages of partisan political actors regarding the wisdom on intervention shifted—although briefly—the dynamics of public opinion shifted as well.

The 1940 election was surprising in that the foreign policy positions of the major party candidates resembled a one-sided flow. At their convention that summer, the Republicans did not nominate an isolationist like Ohio's Robert Taft or Michigan's Arthur Vandenberg. Instead, in what historian David Kennedy (1999) terms an "astonishing surprise," the Republicans nominated an erstwhile Democrat, Wendell Willkie, for the ticket. In this presidential contest, unlike that of 1936, no significant conflict over domestic issues occurred between the two major party candidates; although Willkie had clashed with the Roosevelt administration on economic issues, he refrained from endorsing laissez-faire economic policy and gave his blessing to most of the New Deal social legislation. The gap between FDR and his Republican opponent was even smaller on foreign policy. As Kennedy notes, "Willkie was an unshakable internationalist. He had publicly criticized Nazi aggression and had spoken out eloquently in favor of repealing the arms embargo and in support of aid to Britain" (1999, 456). Willkie went so far as to say that he was "in agreement with many of the basic international objectives of this administration at the present time" (Casey 2001, 27).[15] Thus, for most of the fall of 1940, a single message emanated from both campaigns regarding the wisdom of involvement in the Second World War.[16] Furthermore, surveys from the time suggest that the politically informed segment of the public recognized Willkie's divergence from the Republican orthodoxy of the period. In an October 1940 Roper survey, nearly four times as many respondents thought that Willkie would favor selling naval vessels to Britain (42 percent) than said that he would not (12 percent) (Cantril and Strunk 1951, 982).[17]

The 1940 election therefore provides an interlude during which the normally two-sided discourse surrounding war became one-sided in a highly salient context. Although Willkie's nomination was not purely exogenous to the political environment, his candidacy introduced a significant change in the political rhetoric of FDR's most prominent opponent. We can therefore examine opinion data to see if the data is best characterized by the polarization pattern, as it was in August 1939 and January 1941, or if the brief but powerful change in discourse from a highly prominent and visible political actor led to a corresponding change in the dynamics of mass opinion along levels of political engagement. The October 1940 Gallup poll provides an opportunity to do so because it contains two questions relating to war that are extremely similar in tone and form to those presented in figures 5.2A–E: (1) Should we help England if the British would lose without our aid? and (2) should we send airplanes to England? These questions do not perfectly replicate the items examined in figures 5.2A–E, but they are highly similar in spirit to those questions. In addition—and unlike other polls from the election season—this poll contains the information measures necessary to conduct analysis parallel to that presented in figures 5.2A–E and 5.3A–E.[18] As figures 5.5A–B demonstrate, opinion on these questions follows the mainstream pattern, therefore bolstering the position of the primacy of elite cues. In sum, the 1940 campaign briefly created a more unified and engaged public in a time when political polarization was the rule. Thus it is not simply that the events at Pearl Harbor alone changed the dynamics of opinion; with a salient shift in elite rhetoric occurring more than one year before the United States formally entered the war, the dynamics of opinion on the question of aiding the Allied cause changed as well.

THE WAR IN IRAQ

In the previous chapter, I presented experimental evidence indicating that manipulating information about the costs of military action did not alter support for the Iraq War. Partisan differences on support for war, however, were stark in my 2004 survey—the gap between Democrats and Republicans on measures of war support was almost fifty percentage points (growing to seventy percentage points when the attitudes of strong identifiers are compared). These results square well with other polling on support for the war. Jacobson's data on support for the war, broken down by partisanship, are presented in figure 5.6. Jacobson (2008) finds that large gaps between Democrats and Republicans existed even before the war began in March 2003. In January 2003, for instance, Republicans were

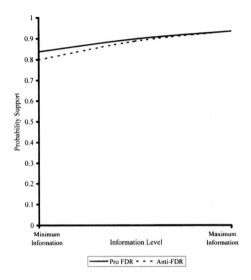

FIGURE 5.5A. Evidence of mainstream pattern, Gallup, October 1940: Help England if British lose war without aid?

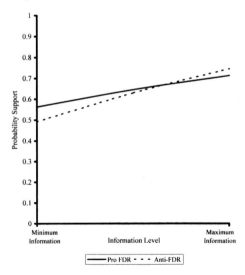

FIGURE 5.5B. Evidence of mainstream pattern, Gallup, October 1940: Send airplanes to England?

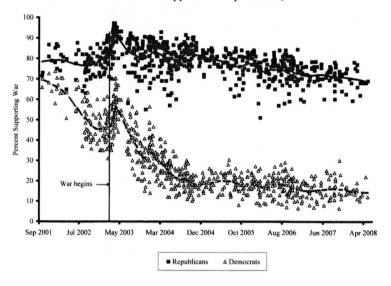

FIGURE 5.6. Partisan trends in support for Iraq War, 2003–8.

over 30 percent more likely to support the war than were Democrats. The commencement of hostilities slightly narrowed the partisan divide, but by April 2003 that gap began to grow even larger, exceeding sixty percentage points in the last quarter of 2004 and holding fairly steady through 2006. Only the decreased enthusiasm for the war among Republicans prevented this gap from growing larger.

Such results should not be surprising. Although event-response theories cannot explain differences across individuals in support for war, models that account for the influence of partisan cues strongly predict patterns of war support. Recall that the elite cue theory hypothesizes that members of the public will look to prominent political actors as guides for their positions on the war. In the context of Iraq, the Bush administration's clear stance on the war—and the general unity of the Republican Party for much of this time—has provided such a guide. Although Democratic leaders had not taken a consistent and strong antiwar stance at the time of the Iraq War Casualty Survey in the summer of 2004, both Republicans and Democrats who were attentive to politics could use the strong support of the war by George Bush and Republican Party leaders as a cue to influence their own positions on the war, even absent the types of persuasive antiwar messages from the Democrats that Zaller's model requires.

Not only is the gap between partisans on Iraq large, but as predicted by the elite cue theory, support for the Iraq conflict follows the same type of polarization pattern found in the World War II era. The persistence of partisan differences in support for war—so evident from the over-time trends presented in figure 5.6—is also reflected in cross-sectional analysis of public opinion. As noted previously, to determine whether the mainstream or polarization pattern better characterizes public opinion, we need individual-level measures of three quantities: support for the war, political predispositions, and levels of political information. The Iraq War Casualty Survey contains all of these quantities. Following Zaller (1992, 1994), I modeled the measures of support for war as a function of partisanship, information, the interaction between information and partisanship, and several control variables. Figures 5.7A–B present the results of an analysis of the effects of political information levels on support for the war.[19] The figures demonstrate that, as a modal respondent's attention to political discourse increases, he adopts diametrically opposed positions on the war, depending on whether he is a Democrat or a Republican. Although there is a gap between Democrats and Republicans at the lowest information levels, this gap grows as information levels increase, indicating that differences in elite positions are reflected in individuals' positions on war.

It is also interesting to note that, consistent with the criticism raised of Feaver, Gelpi, and Reifler in the last chapter, the "success" question—like other measures of support for the war—is heavily influenced by partisanship. Recall that I argued in chapter 4 that estimates of "likely success" are themselves prone to partisan subjectivity. In the Iraq War survey, I asked Feaver, Gelpi, and Reifler's success question. Democrats were less likely than Republicans to take a sanguine view of the war effort; 85 percent of Republicans but only 51 percent of Democrats thought that the United States was very or somewhat likely to succeed in Iraq. These results are comparable to the partisan differences found with somewhat different forms of the "success" question asked by other survey organizations. In October 2004, PIPA asked, "How confident are you that the U.S. intervention in Iraq will succeed? Please answer on a scale of 0 to 10, with 0 being not at all confident and 10 being extremely confident." The mean score among Republicans was 7.0 but only 3.3 among Democrats. Similarly, in December 2005, the *Washington Post* asked, "All told, do you think the United States will win or lose the war in Iraq?" Eighty-nine percent of Republicans but only 35 percent of Democrats thought that the United States would win. When a slightly different form of the question was asked—"All told, do you think the United States is winning or losing the war in Iraq?"—a similar partisan breakdown emerged: 82 percent of Republicans and 29 percent of Democrats believed the United States was winning. These partisan differences have persisted across the span of the war. Since March

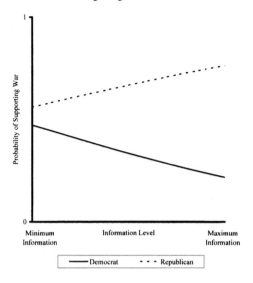

FIGURE 5.7A. Patterns of polarization in Iraq War attitudes, August 2004: Current war in Iraq has been worth fighting.

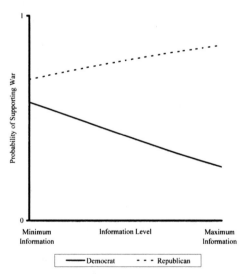

FIGURE 5.7B. Patterns of polarization in Iraq War attitudes, August 2004: United States made the right decision in using military force against Iraq.

2003 the Pew Center for the People and the Press has regularly asked its respondents, "How well is the U.S. military effort in Iraq going?" In figure 5.8, I present a graph of the percentage of respondents who said "very well" or "fairly well," broken down by partisanship.[20] Although both Democrats and Republicans expressed more pessimistic assessments of the situation in Iraq in the wake the 2006 election (see the later discussion), the most striking feature of the graph is the distinctiveness of the two groups: from late April 2003 until October 2007, Democrats were on average 42 percent less optimistic than their Republican counterparts.

Furthermore, the patterns of partisan difference described here are not particular to the Iraq War. In June 1999, with Bill Clinton leading the charge on U.S. intervention in Kosovo, the *Washington Post* asked, "As of now, which side do you think won the Kosovo conflict: Serbia, or the United States and its European allies?" Consistent with the patterns of support for war described in the introduction to this chapter, 60 percent of Democrats but only 41 percent of Republicans thought the United States won.

Equally important for present purposes, the assessment of success exhibits the same polarization pattern as opinion questions on war support. Returning to the Iraq War survey, analysis demonstrates that as political information increases among Republicans, the estimates of perceived success increase slightly (see fig. 5.9). Among Democrats, however, increasing political information decreases the estimates of success greatly, mirroring the political divisions found on questions tapping war support. This pattern of polarization extends to similar analysis conducted using the Pew data on respondents' estimates of how well the war in Iraq is going. In January 2004, July 2005, January 2006, and August 2006, the gap between Democrats and Republicans in their estimates of war success was highest among those who pay the most attention to current events (see figs. 5.10A–D). In short, consistent with the discussion in the previous chapter, individuals seem to arrive at their assessments of the benefits of war through the same processes they use to arrive at their judgments of support for war.[21]

Afghanistan and Iraq: A Tale of Two Wars

The distinctiveness of the Iraq War is even clearer when it is considered alongside another contemporary conflict—the military action in Afghanistan that began in 2001. As noted in chapter 2, unlike Iraq War, the invasion of Afghanistan had strong bipartisan support among politicians from the beginning of the conflict. As a result, popular support for the war was high; from September 2001 through April 2002, between 80 percent and

FIGURE 5.8. Partisan trends in estimates of Iraq War success, 2003–7.

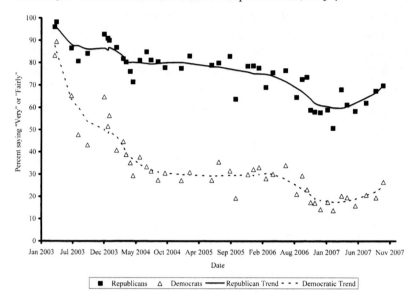

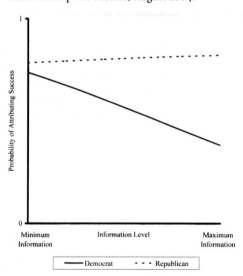

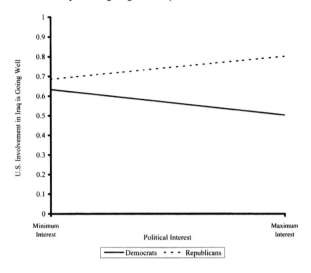

FIGURE 5.10A. Patterns of polarization in estimates of how well the Iraq War is going, January 2004.

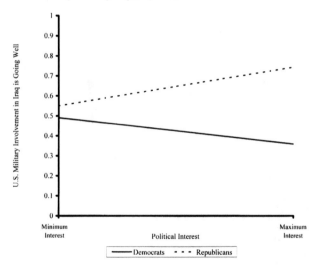

FIGURE 5.10B. Patterns of polarization in estimates of how well the Iraq War is going, July 2005.

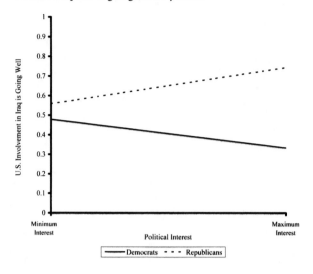

FIGURE 5.10C. Patterns of polarization in estimates of how well the Iraq War is going, January 2006.

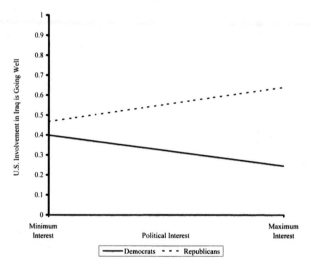

FIGURE 5.10D. Patterns of polarization in estimates of how well the Iraq War is going, August 2006.

90 percent approved of the military action (Jacobson 2008). Even with the large partisan divisions on Iraq evident at the mass level by the fall of 2004, we would expect to see results closer to the mainstream pattern of opinion on Afghanistan.

Although, as noted in chapter 2, most pollsters stopped asking about support for the Afghan conflict in early 2002, data exist that allow for a comparison of the nature of support for interventions in Afghanistan and Iraq.[22] Specifically, the 2004 National Elections Study (NES) contains nearly identical measures of support for both conflicts. Analysis parallel to that conducted for the Iraq War Casualty Survey is presented in figures 5.11A–B. As expected—and in contrast to opinion on Iraq—increased levels of political information increased the probability that respondents would say that Afghanistan was worth the costs for both Democrats and Republicans. Interestingly, although higher levels of information led to increased support for the Afghanistan action regardless of a respondent's political affiliation, a large difference exists in levels of support for the war across all levels of political information.[23] This result suggests that, at least by 2004, the partisan divide had established a baseline reaction to Bush's actions, reflected in the wide partisan differences in support for both conflicts, a difference that is also mirrored in experimental evidence described later.[24]

All told, these results corroborate elite-centered views of war support. As discussed in the previous chapter, perceptions of war deaths are influenced by the respondents' partisan attachments. Furthermore, as also discussed in the previous chapter, the perceptions of war deaths do not influence attitudes toward war, and correcting respondents' misconceptions has little effect on support for war. Analyses presented in this chapter show that whatever inconsistent effects arise from presenting correct information pale in comparison to the effects of partisanship. The identification of the Iraq War with the Bush administration allows partisans who pay attention to politics to quickly ascertain their stance on the war. The evidence of increased polarization over time, even among those individuals who pay little attention to politics, may explain in part the sharp divergence in war support between Republicans and Democrats from the time of the war's immediate aftermath in May 2003 and the 2004 survey. As Iraq increasingly became portrayed as "Bush's war," even the least politically engaged partisans could use the position of President Bush and the leaders of the Republican Party as a cue to find their own opinion on the war. This withdrawal of support among Democrats in large part accounted for the initial decline in support for the war (see Jacobson 2008).

The analysis presented here suggests that patterns of elite conflict play a

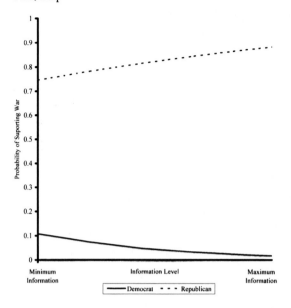

FIGURE 5.11A. Opinions on attitudes toward war, 2004 NES, Iraq.

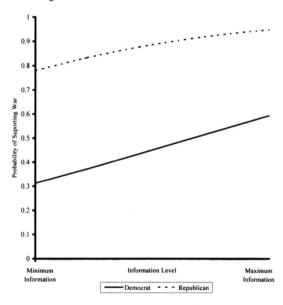

FIGURE 5.11B. Opinions on attitudes toward War, 2004 NES, Afghanistan.

critical role in determining patterns of war support, as the elite cue theory predicts. What the future holds for Iraq remains to be seen. However, the individual-level perspective advanced here can shed some light on the dynamics of aggregate public opinion. Jacobson (2008) demonstrates that from April 2004 until the eve of the 2006 election, collective support for the war did not decline monotonically but rather oscillated between 40 and 50 percent (see fig. 2.5 for the presentation of these data). The splintering of the Republican consensus on Iraq in the wake of the 2006 election may, however, provide another important demonstration of the power of elite rhetoric. The fading of unity on the wisdom of involvement among prominent Republican politicians should lead to the withdrawal of support among some Republican identifiers. Indeed, preliminary survey data collected by Jacobson (2008) suggest that Republican support for the war—which fluctuated between 75 and 85 percent from November 2003 to November 2006—dropped below 70 percent for the first time in the wake of the 2006 election (see fig. 5.6). Although Democratic support remained steady (and low) through 2007, Republican support continued to drop. A reconsideration of the wisdom of the war by its most ardent supporters in government may, then, lead to a collapse in support for military action among the public as well.

VIETNAM

Up to this point, I have argued that elite positions play a large role in shaping public opinion on war, but the reach of this conclusion may not extend past the two conflicts discussed here. At first blush, Vietnam and Korea appear to be troubling counterexamples for my theory of elite competition. In both wars, the management of the conflict changed parties during the course of the war, from Democratic to Republican presidents. How can elite cues function under these circumstances? Do they lose their power? Do cue takers shift sides en masse?

Previous analysis suggests that even in an environment in which control of the presidency switches parties, partisan cues can play a sensible role in structuring opinion. As noted previously, although Belknap and Campbell (1951) found that opinion concerning the Korean War showed some hints of the polarization pattern before the 1952 election, Eisenhower never embraced the war after his election and quickly saw an end to the conflict.

Vietnam presents a different case. As noted in chapter 2, Vietnam is an outlier among the wars of the last sixty-five years in that, during Johnson's time as president, polarization occurred within the Democratic Party, not between the parties. The first real hints of opposition within Congress came through hearings conducted by Senator William Fulbright—a Democrat—in 1966. This debate grew and spilled into the 1968 campaign, splintering the Democratic Party into rival factions in the primaries and beyond. At the same time, messages from the Republican side did not change appreciably.

In the late 1960s, however, the dynamics of elite cues *did* change. The 1968 presidential campaign pitted Richard Nixon against Johnson's vice president, Hubert Humphrey. Analysis of campaign rhetoric by Page and Brody (1972) found little difference in the public statements of the major party candidates. The public accurately perceived the minimal difference between the parties; on average, the public could not distinguish the positions of the candidates on escalation/de-escalation questions (see further discussion in chap. 8). After 1968, however, Vietnam became Nixon's war, both in fact and in the public mind. In the 1972 election, Nixon and McGovern took distinct positions on the war, and large segments of the public accurately perceived these differences (Aldrich et al. 2006).[25]

In developing the model of attitude formation and change described earlier, Zaller (1992) drew heavily on data concerning opinion during the Vietnam War. Unlike the analysis just presented, however, Zaller did not use partisanship as his mediating variable. Instead, to capture the shifts in elite rhetoric that occurred in the mid- to late 1960s, Zaller used as his central consideration a "hawk–dove" measure. This variable almost certainly captures the division within the Democratic Party, and indeed, Zaller finds that the polarization in public opinion concerning the war increased steadily from 1964 to 1968. Zaller used as his dependent variable a measure of continuing support for the official U.S. government policy in Vietnam.[26] Over time, better-informed hawks were more supportive of the war than poorly informed hawks. The same pattern was found among doves in 1964, consistent with a mainstream pattern. By 1966—and especially by 1968—this dynamic had changed. Information levels were no longer monotonically related to support for the war; instead a polarization pattern of opinion emerged.

Given the shifting nature of the divisions within the Democratic Party during this period, Zaller's work cannot speak to the link between the partisan leaders and ordinary citizens. To assess the importance of party identification, I performed an analysis similar to that of Zaller's by using partisanship in place of his constructed hawk–dove measure.[27] The patterns of public opinion are presented in figures 5.12A–D and differ appreciably from Zaller's original results.[28] As expected, the data demonstrate

FIGURE 5.12A.   Vietnam analysis: Opposition to de-escalation, 1964.

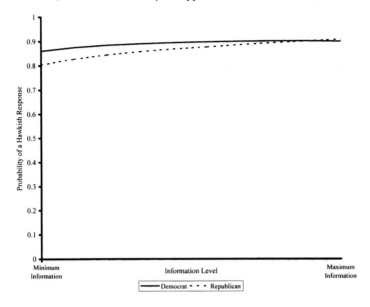

FIGURE 5.12B.   Vietnam analysis: Opposition to de-escalation, 1966.

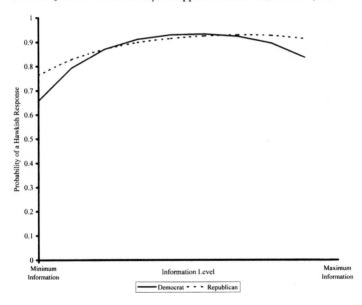

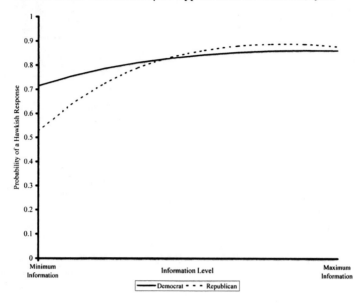

FIGURE 5.12C. Vietnam analysis: Opposition to de-escalation, 1968.

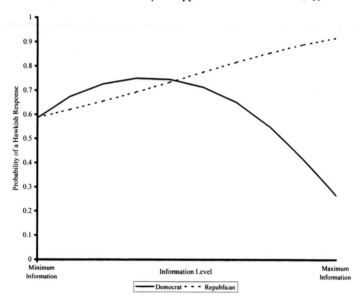

FIGURE 5.12D. Vietnam analysis: Opposition to de-escalation, 1970.

a lack of polarization along party lines through 1968. In line with the elite cue theory, however, by 1970 polarization emerged across party lines, with high-information Democrats most opposed to the war.[29]

Moreover, I find a nearly identical pattern of opinion expression when using a measure of war support that extends through 1972, a time when the image of Vietnam as "Nixon's war" had solidified. From 1964 to 1972, the NES asked respondents, "Do you think we did the right thing in getting into the fighting in Vietnam, or should we have stayed out?" The "mistake" question can serve as a measure of broad support or opposition to the war effort. As Mueller argues, "the question always asks for the respondent's general opinion on the wisdom of the war venture itself, and thus it seems to be a sound measure of a sort of general support for the war" (1973, 43). Analysis of this question is presented in figures 5.13A–E. As the figures show, consistent with the effects of partisanship on the escalation question, the dynamics of opinion on the mistake question changed after 1968. Although some differences existed between high-information partisans in 1966, reflecting the split within the Democratic Party on the wisdom of intervention in Vietnam, opinion before 1969 largely exhibits the mainstream pattern. During Nixon's presidency, however, the polarization pattern is dominant. The aftermath of the 1968 election therefore represents a breaking point for the effects of partisanship.

The implications of the shift in the party of the president in 1968 can also be seen in aggregate measures of support for the war. As figure 2.2 demonstrates, between 1964 and 1968 there was a large drop in war support, but after 1968 support for the war remained fairly stable, with a slight but steady drop in support over time. Figure 5.14 demonstrates that this drop occurred entirely because Nixon lost the support of Democrats. The partisan differences shown in figure 5.14 may seem small, but they are small only if we use the unprecedented size of the partisan differences over the Iraq War as our baseline. Looking at the longer time trends, the importance of the 1968 election becomes clear. When Johnson held the office of the presidency, Democrats were more supportive of the war than were Republicans. Only when the office passed to Nixon did their levels of support drop below that of Republicans.

Together these analyses suggest that although the split within the Democratic Party along hawk–dove lines influenced opinion about the Vietnam War in the late 1960s, partisanship also played an important role in shaping opinion concerning the war. The split within the Democratic Party on the wisdom of the war certainly led to a decline in overall support for the conflict during Johnson's presidency. The election of Nixon,

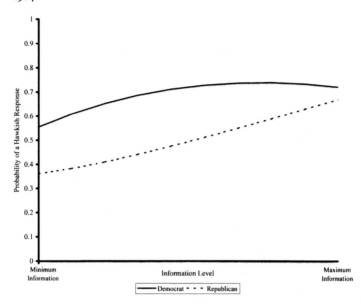

FIGURE 5.13A. Vietnam analysis: United States did not make a mistake, 1964.

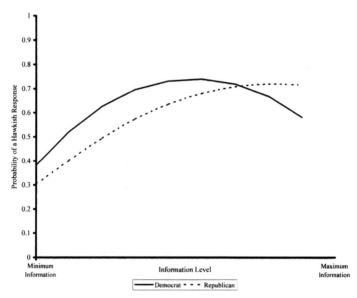

FIGURE 5.13B. Vietnam analysis: United States did not make a mistake, 1966.

FIGURE 5.13C. Vietnam analysis: United States did not make a mistake, 1968.

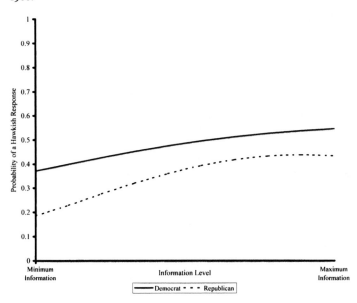

FIGURE 5.13D. Vietnam analysis: United States did not make a mistake, 1970.

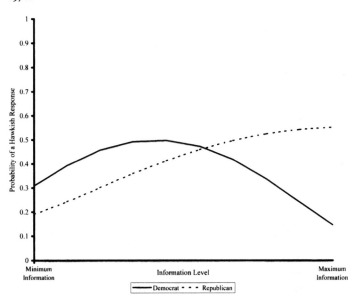

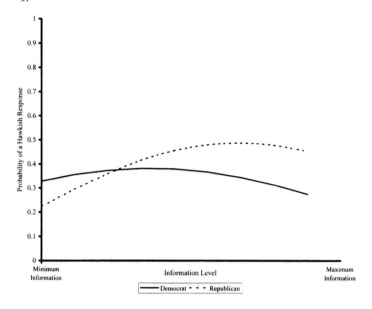

FIGURE 5.13E. Vietnam analysis: United States did not make a mistake, 1972.

however, added a partisan flavor to opinion dynamics after 1968, leading to a further decline in support for that conflict.

KOREAN INTERVENTION EXPERIMENT

Although the observational data from World War II, Vietnam, and Iraq support the primacy of the elite cue theory advanced here, I conducted a survey experiment in June 2006 to further explore the determinants of public support for military intervention.[30] In this experiment, I presented respondents with a hypothetical military intervention in South Korea but varied the particulars of the scenario in ways that relate to the context of the intervention, the probable costs of the mission, and elite cues about the wisdom of intervention.[31] After presenting the scenario, I gauged the respondents' support for military action. To be precise, I ran a fully crossed between-subjects experiment with three treatment dimensions.[32] These dimensions were as follows:

1. Situational factor: cost in causalities. Mueller's theory predicts that as deaths rise, support for war declines. In my experiment, respondents received a low-casualty estimate (300–500 dead) or a high-casualty estimate (2,500–3,500 dead) for the mission. These

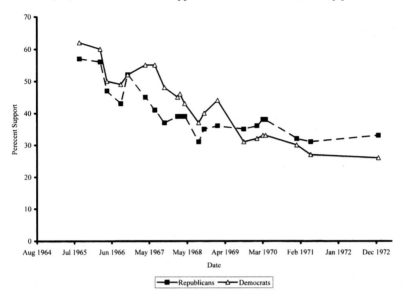

FIGURE 5.14. Partisan trends in support for the Vietnam War, Gallup poll.

estimates were based on the reported estimates of American war deaths before military action in recent conflicts.[33]

2. Context of intervention: principal policy objective. In chapter 4, I briefly discussed Jentleson's (1992) arguments concerning the importance of the "principle policy objective" of a given intervention. Jentleson claims that support for war will vary as a function of the frame of goals for a military mission. He finds that missions with a foreign policy restraint goal are more popular than those with an internal policy change goal. Respondents were therefore presented with either a foreign policy restraint scenario (defend South Korea against an invasion by North Korea) or an internal policy change scenario (stabilize a democratic government in South Korea).[34]

3. Elite discourse: party positions. The elite cue theory predicts that elite consensus behind war leads to increased support for war, whereas dissent leads to polarized opinion. To account for the most relevant partisan cues, respondents were told the positions of the two parties in Congress regarding the wisdom of intervention. Specifically, respondents were presented with one of four partisan cues: (a) Democratic support/Republican support; (b) Democratic support/Republican opposition; (c) Democratic opposition/Republican support; and (d) Democratic opposition/Republican opposition.

The full text of the experimental treatments is presented in Appendix C. To give a feel for the nature of the treatment, compare the control condition for internal policy change:

> There's a lot of talk these days about American military and economic policies abroad. We'd like to get your thoughts on these issues by exploring an imaginary situation. Say that American troops are called upon to stabilize a democratic government in South Korea. . . . What do you think? Should the U.S. military become involved or stay out?

to the condition in which the casualty estimate is low and Congress gives its unified support to the intervention:

> There's a lot of talk these days about American military and economic policies abroad. We'd like to get your thoughts on these issues by exploring an imaginary situation. Say that American troops are called upon to stabilize a democratic government in South Korea. Non-partisan experts estimate that from 300–500 troops would be killed in this military action. Both Democratic and Republican Party leaders support this mission because it is consistent with their national security goals. . . . What do you think? Should the U.S. military become involved or stay out?[35]

Although the details of these scenarios are admittedly sparse, the relevant cues referenced by the different theories are clearly provided.[36] Respondents are told the positions of the leaders of the major political parties and are given estimates of the number of Americans dead resulting from the military action.[37] Thus, the fully crossed design of this experiment allowed me to test the independent and conditional effects of the three experimental dimensions.[38]

On the basis of the observational and experimental data presented in this chapter, I expected that elite cues would be a more powerful and consistent determinant of war support than situational factors. The results of the experiment are presented in table 5.1. Given the large number of conditions in the design, I present the results of the experiment as a set of first differences, providing the estimated effect of a treatment for a partisan subgroup relative to the control condition. Because each respondent was presented with an intervention scenario, I use the internal policy change control condition as the baseline. Each cell in table 5.1 can therefore be read as the effect of a given treatment on a person of a particular political stripe.[39]

One of the most striking results of the experiment is not conveyed by table 5.1. Perhaps reflecting the large divide over the use of military force

TABLE 5.1 Korea experiment, 2006

Casualty treatment

Party affiliation	Low casualty estimate (%)	High casualty estimate (%)
Independents	+10	+2
Republicans	−8	−12**
Democrats	+5	+0

PPO treatment (relative to internal policy change PPO)

Party affiliation	Foreign policy restraint PPO (%)
Independents	+11*
Republicans	+4*
Democrats	+11**

Partisan cues treatment

Party affiliation	Unified opposition (%)	Unified support (%)	D support/ R oppose (%)	R support/ D oppose (%)
Independents	−4	+0	−4	−2
Republicans	−7*	+13**	−1	+13**
Democrats	−14**	+4	−2	−5*

Note: PPO, principle policy objective. The estimate in each cell is the predicted change in the probability of supporting war for an average respondent in a given experimental condition relative to the control condition.
* Different from the control condition at the .10 level.
** Different from the control condition at the .05 level.

by the Bush administration, the partisan divide over even a hypothetical intervention is extremely large. My analysis of the data indicates that across all conditions, Republicans are 22 percent more likely to support intervention than are Democrats.[40] Furthermore, also reflecting the current divide over Iraq, independents are far closer to Democrats than to

Republicans in their positions on the use of force. These findings are consistent with public opinion data concerning other hypothetical military actions. For instance, an October 2007 Zogby poll found that 52 percent of the public would support a U.S. military strike to prevent Iran from building a nuclear weapon. Although the partisan divisions were more muted than those on Iraq, similar divisions emerged; 71 percent of Republicans supported a strike, compared to 41 percent of Democrats and 44 percent of independents.[41] Together, these results show that the ability to gain currency on questions of support for war with experiments may be constrained by the current political environment. Even with successful randomization, it is impossible to divorce completely experimental investigations of public opinion concerning hypothetical wars from the current war in Iraq.

That said, given the power of randomized experiments to illuminate causal paths, it is certainly possible to learn something about the determinants of support for war from these experiments. As predicted, differences in the casualty estimates fail to meaningfully change the levels of support for war. The differences in support for military action between conditions with low-casualty estimates and those with high-casualty estimates are statistically insignificant regardless of the respondents' partisan attachments. Among Republican respondents, the mere mention of casualties decreases support for intervention.[42] In any case, the effect of casualty levels on support for war is essentially the same for both the high-casualty and the low-casualty conditions. The bottom line on the question of casualties is simple: any shift in support based on casualties is small—on the order of five percentage points—and statistically unreliable.

There does, however, appear to be some support for Jentleson's contention concerning the importance of the context of a given action. The policy objective of a mission seems to affect baseline support for military action—at least for some respondents. Respondents are more likely to support a mission designed to repel an attack than they are to support one designed to foster a democratic regime.[43] What is interesting is that this effect is considerably smaller for Republicans than it is for respondents of other partisan stripes. Thus, I again find that partisanship conditions the impact of other important variables. Moreover, returning to the theme of the last chapter, I find that the context of the mission does not significantly affect the respondents' willingness to accept casualties. I conducted additional analysis in which I allowed the effect of the casualty estimates to vary across the two types of missions. I found that these interactions were statistically and substantively insignificant.[44] If anything, and contrary to expectations, it appears that respondents were slightly more sensitive to casualties when the intervention was attributed to a foreign policy restraint goal rather than to an internal policy restraint goal.[45]

Finally, I turn to the effect of the partisan cues. As expected, the cues have little effect on support for war in either a substantive or a statistical sense for political independents. The expression of opposition—especially by Republicans—depressed support for intervention, but this effect was not statistically significant. On the other hand, respondents with partisan attachment do respond to the cues. Both Democrats and Republicans react to unified political opposition to war by lowering their levels of support, as predicted. Unified opposition, it seems, is an informative cue for *all* respondents, regardless of their personal political attachments. This effect, however, is much larger for Democrats than it is for Republicans.[46] Furthermore, Republican partisans appear to support war only if led by Republican members of Congress. Republican support in Congress—regardless of the stance of the Democratic leaders—leads to increased support for action. In fact, this effect is larger than for either of the situational factors. For Democratic identifiers, on the other hand, the support of Democrats in Congress has no significant effect on support for intervention. Democrats, though, seem to respond negatively, but only marginally, to Republican support when coupled with Democratic opposition. Much as Democrats reacted to Bush's support for the Iraq War by rejecting that war, as the elite cue-taking theory predicts, Republican support for the hypothetical intervention leads to mass opposition on the part of Democratic identifiers.

The inability of cues from Democratic politicians to increase support for war does not square with theoretic expectations, but these results are consistent with other recent experimental evidence concerning support for interventions, both invented and real. Howell and Kriner (2008) find that support for military action from Democratic members of Congress does not increase the support for interventions among Democratic identifiers in Iraq, nor does it change support for hypothetical action in Eritrea (in response to sponsorship of terrorists by the government) or Liberia (in response to human rights atrocities). Again it appears that political reality has intruded on experimental evidence. Given the current divide between Democrats and Republicans on the Iraq War, even with a proper experimental design, it may be impossible to detect the full power of the relevant political cues. That said, the evidence presented here demonstrates that even in such an environment, partisan cues can be powerful determinants of support for war.

CONCLUSION

The results presented in the last two chapters challenge the view that the events on the battlefield are sufficient to explain the dynamics of public reaction to war and suggest that—just as in domestic politics—patterns of elite agreement and disagreement play a critical role in shaping popular responses to war.[47] In four seemingly diverse cases involving actual and hypothetical conflicts, the structure of opinion on war looks remarkably similar. Although the influence of partisanship may have reached its apex during the war in Iraq, the importance of basic political attachments has long extended beyond the water's edge. The elite cue theory advanced here demonstrates how prominent cue-givers can provide structure to the foreign policy opinions of the public. This evidence is an indictment not just of the casualties hypothesis—which has been criticized by other authors (Burk 1999; Klarevas 2002; Kull and Ramsay 2001; Feaver and Gelpi 2004; Gelpi, Feaver, and Reifler 2005–6)—but also more generally of event-response theories positing that individuals make decisions regarding the wisdom of war through a cost-benefit calculation. After all, even in the wake of a successful victory over Iraq in 1991, Democrats remained 20 to 30 percent less supportive than Republicans of the Gulf War (Jacobson 2008). Moving to the evidence at hand, as the discussion of the survey data from World War II in the last chapter demonstrates, even in a highly charged climate a large proportion of citizens did not have a clear idea of what the war was about and were ignorant of the Nazi atrocities. Only in retrospect do these facts seem to justify U.S. involvement. During times of war, individual-level knowledge of central facts of war is weak. Finally, as the 2004 Iraq War experiment and the work of Gaines et al. (2007) demonstrate, the most basic interpretation of these facts is heavily colored by partisan attachments. In the battle between facts and partisanship, partisanship always wins.

This is not to say that wartime events are meaningless for the study of public opinion and war. The patterns of political consensus during World War II implicitly beg the question of why, unlike the case in other conflicts in American history, elite discourse did not shift during the course of the war, even in the face of mounting costs and the uncertain outcome of the military effort in 1942 and 1943. More generally, the World War II experience raises the puzzle of how it is that political leaders come to decide whether to support a military intervention. Here, the public opinion literature has largely been silent. Zaller (2003) argues that during Vietnam, Kennedy and Johnson followed political strategies based on their reading of "latent public opinion"—where they thought the balance of public sentiment would lie in the future. Certainly this type of elite response to electoral incentives is plausible. But even in this case, the estimation of latent opinion is a somewhat mysterious and uncertain process. Politicians who care about their future careers might want to base their decisions on more tangible evidence. Here, perhaps, is a role for the direct effects of military events. There is little evidence that the public makes the complex calculations described by Larson (1996) and other authors who posit that the public collectively balances costs and benefits when deciding whether to lend support to military action. It is reasonable to think, however, that political leaders—those actors with the most at stake in a given controversy—would make such calculations. In this conception, the events of war are important but acquire most of their explanatory power indirectly. Partisan political actors, not the public, decide whether to lend support to an administration's policy, depending on the costs of the conflict and the perceived success of the intervention (Levy 1989). In the aggregate, the public may appear "rational," but only because it takes cues from elites who sensibly incorporate diplomatic actions and events on the battlefield into their decisions to support or oppose war. Thus the phenomenon, commonly seen as driven by the cognitive processes of the collective public, can be recast as an elite-level phenomenon. Providing evidence for this view, Gartner, Segura, and Barratt (2004) find that variation in state-level casualties affected the positions of incumbent senators and their challengers during the Vietnam War. But as the World War II case indicates, casualties do not necessarily define the flow of elite discourse. By refocusing the discussion of the effects of events from the mass level to the elite level, we can better explain the causes and consequences of convergence and divergence in elite discourse.

Work in this vein has important implications for the study of international relations more generally. Reiter and Stam (2002) argue that democracies are hesitant to enter war and only become involved in wars they are likely to win. If a democracy is caught in a difficult and protracted war, it is likely to give in and accept a draw. Reiter and Stam attribute this process to the sensitivity of the democratic public to casualties. If, however, it is the dynamics of elite conflict, rather than mere casualties, that determines public support for war, then to properly understand the decision to wage war we need to understand how domestic politics and partisan divisions structure the way that ordinary citizens come to understand real-world events. To date, even the best work in international relations on public opinion concerning war has failed to account for the effects of partisan and other societal cleavages on levels of support for war. In these models, the public is an undifferentiated mass, reacting in a uniform manner to changes in the course of war. It is important to consider the nature of domestic opposition not only as a signal to opposing leaders on the international stage (Schultz 1998) but also as an independent force that can shape the public's preferences over military engagement. By accounting for heterogeneous responses to the tides of war and by explicitly allowing a role for elite mediation of foreign events, we can better understand how citizens in democracies can guide and constrain the government's ability to wage war. Surely political elites have the agency and flexibility to interpret the meaning of ambiguous wartime events. Thus it is not simply a direct reaction to casualties or victories on the battlefield that causes support for war to wax or wane. The analyses presented here indicate that it is how the war experience gets filtered through domestic politics that matters most. As the Kosovo example that began this chapter demonstrates, rhetoric is a malleable tool, easily altered to serve the particular interests of the majority party.

Locating the limits of popular support for war in politicians' decisions rather than in the decisions of ordinary citizens has critical implications for the functioning of democracy. The experience with World War II demonstrates the central role that partisan political actors play in influencing the preferences of the public. In fact, the partisan differences that remained—albeit in a greatly diminished state—after Pearl Harbor demonstrate the continued influence of "normal" partisan politics, even in times of unifying crises. The fact that World War II—unlike Vietnam and Korea—was ultimately successful should not obscure the potential hazards that could occur when patterns of political conflict among government actors structure the opinions of the public. Under comparable circumstances of elite harmony, perhaps different ends—a conflict with a costly and disastrous conclusion—could emerge from similar means.

CHAPTER SIX

ETHNIC GROUPS: ATTACHMENTS, ENMITIES, AND SUPPORT FOR WAR

Although partisanship is a critical mediator of wartime opinion, it is not the only predisposition relevant to public opinion about foreign policy. A tremendous body of research has demonstrated that attachments and enmities to salient social groupings in society shape political understanding and behavior on domestic issues. In this chapter, I argue that beliefs about those groups to which individuals feel loyalty or hostility also structure their attitudes in the realm of foreign policy. The effects of group loyalties differ from the effects of partisanship because long-standing group attachments lead to sizable, but stable, differences in opinion on war. As I demonstrate in this chapter, these differences are resistant to alternations in political messages and persist even in the face of massive changes within the political environment, such as the attack at Pearl Harbor in 1941. Furthermore, in contrast to the partisan elite cueing discussed in the last chapter, elite leadership cannot explain the association between ethnicity and opinion on war. Group attachments therefore allow individuals to form their own opinions independent of partisan political leadership. In these ways, group-based differences provide a bedrock structure to public opinion.

I draw primarily on data from World War II—a time when internal ethnic divisions were a highly visible part of the social sphere in the United States. Although the power of groups was especially strong in World War II, group-based differences can provide structure to citizens' understanding of foreign policy more generally. Thus, as in earlier chapters, to demonstrate the generality of the group-based perspective, I look to other cases involving group-based thinking—namely, sanctions on South Africa in the mid-1980s—to demonstrate that feelings toward domestic groups can structure opinion on foreign policy more generally.

GROUPS AND POLITICAL THINKING

Converse's (1964) landmark work on belief systems is primarily remembered for its dismal conclusions regarding the possibility of ideological thinking among members of the public.[1] Converse, however, did not merely document the shortcomings of the citizenry; he also considered the ways that individuals could come to reasoned political decisions, even in the absence of an overarching guiding ideology. Converse concluded that two factors might organize public opinion. The first was the existence of narrow-issue publics—groups of citizens with relatively crystallized opinions in given issue areas (see Hutchings 2003 for an elaboration of this insight). The second—and the one more relevant for present purposes—is the power of groups.

Drawing on contemporary theories of "reference groups," Converse claimed that visible groups in a society provide structure to individual political judgments. Specifically, he argued that citizens could "evaluate parties and candidates in terms of their expected favorable or unfavorable treatment of different social groupings in society" (1964, 216) and mentioned race, religion, and nationality as clear referents on the political scene in the 1950s (see also Campbell et al. 1960; Hyman and Singer 1968). According to Converse, ordinary individuals could situate themselves on the stage of mass politics through the use of these group reference points, thereby coming to meaningful political decisions.

Converse placed a great deal of weight on the power of groups because groups were relatively simple concepts, requiring a lower threshold of sophistication than needed to employ abstract concepts, such as ideology. As Converse argued, to make use of group-based reasoning, citizens need only "be endowed with some cognitions of the group and with some interstitial 'linking' information indicating why a given party or policy is relevant to the group" (1964, 236–37). The first part of this equation is fairly straightforward. Groups that are prominent within a society are more likely to be recognized by individual members of the public. The second portion, the linking information, varies from issue to issue. Sometimes, the connection between a group and a policy is ephemeral. In other situations, however, "the cues presented to citizens concerning links between the group and party or policy are so gross that they penetrate rapidly even to the less informed" (238). As discussed later in further detail, high-profile foreign policy issues—such as matters of war and peace—involving other nations may be a class of situations for which these links are clear. Under such circumstances, even casual observers of the political scene can understand complex political events. Presaging later work on cues and heuristics (see Popkin 1991; Sniderman, Brody, and Tetlock 1991; and, in the domain of race, Dawson 1994), Converse (1964) concluded that reference group cues could serve as the foundation of "ideology by proxy," creating meaningful patterns in the attitudes and behaviors of ordinary citizens.

Evidence from open-ended questions on likes and dislikes of political parties demonstrated the centrality of group thinking in the belief systems of the general public. Coding the statements in these questions, Converse assigned respondents to one of five "levels of conceptualization." Although few respondents thought about politics in ideological terms, a large plurality of respondents (42 percent) were classified in the "group interest" category.[2] These were respondents who had a clear image of politics as an arena of group concerns and used this understanding of group relations to come to political judgments.[3] For example, one respondent disliked the Democratic Party because "it's trying to help the Negros too much." Similarly, another respondent said that she did not favor the Democrats because "they were hard on the farmers. . . . [Truman] said he was going to do things for the farmers and he backed out" (Campbell et al. 1960).

The reference group theories Converse and his colleagues drew on have, to a certain degree, fallen by the wayside in favor of other group-based theories, such as social identity theory (Tajfel and Turner 1979; Tajfel 1981) and realistic group conflict theory (Bobo 1983; Campbell et al. 1965; Sherif 1966). Converse's central insight remains important, however; groups as cognitive constructs can play a significant role in structuring public opinion. To a large degree, ordinary citizens interpret politics through the lens of social groups (Walsh 2004; see also Hale 2004).

Much work since Converse has underscored the cognitive power of groups in influencing political behavior. Kinder, Adams, and Gronke (1989) found that individuals come to understand the national economy through the prism of groups to which they belong. They found that the largest predictor of judgments of change in national economic well-being was change in the economic well-being of respondents' own group's. Other work has found that liked or disliked population groups can anchor political reasoning. Brady and Sniderman concluded that individuals arrive at political understanding—"an impressively accurate map of politics" (1985, 94)—by referencing their political affect toward politically strategic groups.

Similarly, Mutz (1998) argues that group influence is sociotropic. When making political decisions, citizens rely primarily on their perceptions of large-scale collectives—including groups—that exist beyond the realm of personal experience. For instance, Mutz and Mondak (1997) found that group-based economic perceptions affected the presidential vote in 1984. This influence was not a function of the types of factors typically examined in modern group-based theories of political choice, such as group membership, group identification, or forms of group comparison. Instead, citizens used groups as cognitive reference points.

Thus, setting aside a strict adherence to reference group theory, we see that the central finding relevant here is that both in-groups—the collection of individuals of which a citizen is a part—and out-groups—those groups to which a citizen does not belong but toward which she feels enmity or affection—can be important reference points in political understanding and choice. Put simply, citizens can use their affect toward groups to comprehend and guide complex political decisions.[4]

When Do Groups Matter?

To argue that "groups matter," however, is not sufficient; we also need to know which groups matter and when they will matter. Certainly membership in or hostility toward politically relevant groups can provide a reference point for political choice, but given the broad constellation of groups in American society, what are the factors that determine which groups will guide political cognition and decision-making?

First, consider the effects of group membership. As Kinder, Adams, and Gronke (1989) note, people may use groups as reference points for understanding that may, in turn, influence political choice. Sometimes group membership is a more powerful force than at other times. Here is where Converse's "interstitial" information can play a key role. As Conover (1988) notes, the framing of an issue by media and political leaders may invoke "group cues" that heighten the influence of one's own group in political thinking (see also Price 1989). It is the political environment that makes groups salient to political decision-making.

When considering affect toward other groups, it is important to recognize that variation also exists in the nature and power of that affect. One line of work suggests that it is not the particular group that matters for political decision-making as much as it is feelings toward groups in general. Kinder (2003) has explicated the concept of ethnocentrism—a coherent ideology concerning group relations in which one's own ethnic identity is regarded as superior to all others. Kinder has shown that ethnocentrism—measured as subscription to stereotypes concerning a wide range of groups—affects opinion in a variety of domains, from immigration to attitudes concerning 9/11 (Kam and Kinder 2007; Kinder 2003). Moreover, he has shown that the power of ethnocentrism extends to the realm of foreign policy. Kinder and D'Ambrosio, for instance, demonstrate that opinions about the first Gulf War were influenced by ethnocentrism (reported in Kinder 2003).[5]

Beyond generalized sentiment concerning other groups, affect toward specific groups may play an important role as well. Conover's (1988) notion of group cues applies not just to group membership (in-groups) but also to cognition concerning other groups (out-groups). After all, when specific issues cue particular groups, they activate not just relevant group memberships, but attachments and enmities to those groups as well. Thus, when considering the place of out-groups in political cognition, it is critical to consider the larger political context surrounding an issue. Some groups are more prominent than others in political discourse on particular issues; attitudes toward these groups can play a key role in the individual decision-making process.

GROUPS AND FOREIGN POLICY

Although much research on domestic public opinion has examined the role of groups, little work on this subject has been done in the realm of foreign affairs. In the immediate post–World War II years, scholars looked for a link between group affiliations and attitudes toward international involvement (Rieselbach 1960; Russett 1960). These authors examined the relationship between ethnic affiliation and isolationism by using both aggregate congressional voting records and individual-level public opinion data, but found little evidence for such a connection. These studies may have prematurely closed the door to work on the role of groups in foreign policy. Kinder's work on ethnocentrism finds that groups—considered broadly—matter in the development of public opinion concerning foreign policy. It is a small step to argue that in the realm of foreign relations, beliefs regarding specific groups should play a powerful role as well.

South African Sanctions
Ordinary individuals may come to understand complex foreign policies in part by using the lens of group attachments and dislikes forged in the domestic political arena. To demonstrate the generality of this relationship across time, I first take up a modern example, examining attitudes in

the mid-1980s concerning trade sanctions against South Africa. This case demonstrates that in foreign policy, as in domestic policy, groups matter. Although issues of trade are unlike issues of war in many ways, both involve complicated subjects removed from the everyday lives of ordinary Americans. In issues of foreign economic policy—as, I show later, in issues of war—individuals rely on attachments to and dislike of domestic political groups to reach political decisions.

From the early 1960s through the early 1980s, U.S. policy toward South Africa was driven largely by economic concerns.[6] The resources and markets of South Africa made it an attractive trading partner for the United States. At the same time, the policy of apartheid in South Africa, enacted in 1948—by which blacks were separated from whites and denied voting rights—created a tension between economic interests and moral considerations. Beginning in the 1960s, the General Assembly of the United Nations began passing motions condemning South Africa and in the mid-1970s approved the International Convention on the Suppression and Punishment of the Crime of Apartheid. This convention provided a legal framework within which nations could apply sanctions to press the South African government to change its racial politics.

By the mid-1980s, the tension between economic and moral concerns began to tip toward the side of morality. Concern over South Africa among political actors had led to a series of mass protests in the United States. The Reagan administration, however, was especially hostile to the notion of enacting sanctions, referring to the incumbent South African Botha administration as "an ally and a friend." The Reagan administration's stance led to a series of conflicts between Reagan and the Democrats in Congress. In 1985, spurred by the Congressional Black Caucus, the House passed a bill calling for sanctions on South Africa, including broad restrictions on trade and the divestment of economic interests of U.S. companies. The Senate followed shortly thereafter. This effort was preempted by an executive order imposing more limited economic sanctions. At the time Reagan signed the order, he stated that he opposed sanctions but had issued the order to forestall the harsher sanctions envisioned by Congress. But the next year, over Reagan's veto, Congress passed the Comprehensive Anti-Apartheid Act of 1986, which prohibited U.S. trade and other economic relations with South Africa.

The South Africa sanctions issue meets Converse's conditions for facilitating group-based cognition. Given the clear racial component of the South Africa issues and the obvious parallels to the U.S. experience with slavery, the links between the relevant domestic group—blacks—and the international issue are apparent. Moreover, the centrality of race in the contemporary American political scene (Kinder and Sanders 1996; Carmines and Stimson 1989) ensured that attitudes about blacks as a domestic group were well developed at this time.[7]

Previous research supports the prevalence of group-based thinking on the South Africa question. Hill (1993) examined data from the 1988 National Elections Study (NES) and found that Americans used their general racial posture—measured by the racial resentment scale (Kinder and Sanders 1996)—to come to judgments concerning sanctions.[8] Here I turn to a similar data set, the 1986 National Elections Study, to assess the impact of groups.

To measure attitudes on the desirability of sanctions, I draw on the same NES question about South Africa used by Hill (1993).[9] This question was asked in a fully filtered form. Respondents were first asked if they had an opinion on U.S. policy toward South Africa. Almost half of those asked said they did not have an opinion. Respondents who indicated that they had an opinion were then asked about their support for sanctions.[10] To measure group membership, I use the respondents' race, scored as a dummy variable for black respondents. To measure affect toward the relevant out-group, African Americans, I use a respondent's feeling thermometer scores for "blacks," which is exogenous to my issue of interest— sanctions toward South Africa.[11]

To explicate the substantive effects of the group variables, I first present differences for the variables of interest in table 6.1.[12] I find that in-group membership and feeling toward the relevant domestic group are highly significant in both a statistical and substantive sense. The first row of the table gives the effect of race for the modal respondent on the probability that he would support sanctions, given that he has offered an opinion to the question asked. Here, the minimum value is nonblack, and the maximum value is black. The next row presents the effect of a move from the minimum (observed) value to the maximum value of the feeling thermometer.

Table 6.1 demonstrates that both group-based variables strongly predict opinions on the proper direction of U.S. foreign policy. As expected, blacks were 18 percent more likely than whites to support sanctions against South Africa. The effect of attitudes toward blacks is even stronger. Those most cool toward blacks are 47 percent less likely to support sanctions than those individuals most warm toward blacks. Thus, given a political context in which the linkages between attitudes toward domestic groups and foreign policy issues are clear, domestic ethnic-group divisions can

Variable	Minimum value (%)	Maximum value (%)	Effect (%)
Black	45	63	18
Feeling thermometer toward blacks	20	67	47

Note: The table shows the effect of moving from minimum value to maximum value on the probability of supporting sanctions (conditioned on answering the sanctions question). All values have been set to the mean except for categorical variables, which have been set to their mode.

structure opinions in the realm of foreign policy (see also Page and Bouton 2006 on the link between Jewish identity and support for Israel).

GROUP ATTITUDES AND PUBLIC OPINION CONCERNING WORLD WAR II

Group-based thinking extends directly to public opinion about war. The World War II era is an especially fruitful area for research.[13] Throughout the 1930s and 1940s, many members of different European ethnic groups maintained distinct identities and links to their mother country. Consequently a great deal of ethnic hostility existed in the United States. The immigration experiences of the late nineteenth and early twentieth centuries solidified opinions about particular ethnic groups—most notably Jews and Italians—independent of wartime opinion. Furthermore, the nature of the wartime experience brought to the forefront important information linking the domestic and international realms. The war was, after all, a *world* war, fought with and against countries that had provided generations of immigrants to America. Linking domestic identity to international affairs was therefore a fairly straightforward task. Little research, however, has been conducted on the relationship between groups and opinion toward the war.[14]

To the extent that such work exists, prevailing wisdom seems to be that ethnic-group membership shaped opinion before the United States' entry into the conflict but dissipated as a factor after Pearl Harbor. Tracing the tension between group ethnic identities and a unified national identity, Gleason (1981) finds that ethnic groups retained nationalistic identities throughout the 1930s and into 1940. For instance, during this time the German-American Bund was politically active, and the Italian American press maintained a pro-Fascist orientation. Indeed, "until the summer of 1940, there was no question that Italian-Americans in general were solidly behind Mussolini" (1981, 349). Gleason, however, argues that the act of going to war altered the link between ethnic identity and attitudes toward the war. As he writes, "the practical effect of wartime experience was assimilative in the sense that it enhanced national unity and a common sense of national belongingness" (516). Similarly, Perlmutter argues, "wars, revolutions, and national liberation movements abroad always galvanize American ethnic and racial groups. . . . during World War II [but before the United States' entry], more than 200 organizations, not including small local or state societies, engaged in a wide variety of activities on behalf of their ancestral homelands" (1966, 64–65). But, Perlmutter claims, once the United States entered the conflict, domestic ethnics repudiated the ties to their mother countries and pledged their full allegiance to America. These speculations, however, remain just that—mere speculations. The role of group identity and ethnic enmity in structuring opinion about World War II deserves closer examination.

To assess the strength of beliefs toward ethnic groups in structuring opinion, we must collect reactions toward other groups in society and membership in particular ethnic groups. The available data are limited, however. Information about feelings toward relevant domestic groups was only sporadically collected during the 1930s and 1940s. On the question of group membership, we have a different problem. Both OPOR and NORC measured information concerning the respondents' parents' place of birth and sometimes the respondents' own place of birth. Thus we can identify those respondents who are first- and second-generation immigrants, but we cannot measure how close those respondents felt to their own groups. Yet even with these indirect measures, it is possible to draw on reference group theory and learn a great deal about how ethnic loyalties and dislikes structured opinion on the war.[15]

GROUP MEMBERSHIP AND FOREIGN POLICY

We can begin to look at the effect of group membership on foreign policy by using the parental lineage information discussed previously to isolate the ethnic lineage of the respondents. Specifically, we can see if both parents were born in the United States or if at least one parent was born in an Axis country, an Allied country, or another foreign country.[16] These questions, of course, are not ideal measures of group attachment. First, they only allow us to identify and measure second-generation effects.[17] We cannot trace the precise ethnic lineages of the respondents. Second, the measures do not assess how close a respondent felt toward her own group. Thus, we cannot consider theories of group relations aside from reference group theory. But although these measures might not be perfect, they are the only information we have to work with. Analyses using these measures can illuminate important issues of public support for war. In fact, given the same information, the U.S. government performed similar analysis using opinion polls collected by the Survey Division of the Office of War Information.[18]

I began by examining the effect of ethnic-group membership on opinion before the United States became involved in the war, using a series of polls conducted by OPOR in the first quarter of 1941. I organized the items concerning war into three groups. The first group involves questions relating to political comprehension. These questions are especially interesting because they allow us to determine how group attachments affected the way in which individuals understood developments pertaining to the war. The second group is composed of questions that ask about support for direct U.S. involvement in the European war. The final group of questions encompasses items relating to war outside of the European theater.

I modeled the respondents' answers as a function of their ethnicity and their background characteristics, to control for any factors—such as region of residence—that might be correlated with both ethnic background and opinion concerning the war.[19] I present the predicted probability of holding an interventionist attitude for "average" respondents who differ only in their ethnic background. Specifically, the tables present the predicted opinion for three groups: (1) the respondents whose parents were both born in the United States, (2) the respondents with at least one parent from an Allied country, and (3) the respondents with at least one parent from an Axis country.[20]

Table 6.2 presents the effect of ethnic-group membership on the three classes of variables.[21] Turning first to the political understanding questions, we see that individuals with ethnic ties to the Axis countries were less likely than members of other groups to think that England would win the war, and tended to attribute less sinister motives to Germany and Italy. Conversely, individuals with ethnic ties to the Allied countries were more likely to take a positive view of the Allied war effort and were slightly more likely to take a dismal view of the prospect of a world under Axis rule. In some cases, these differences were extremely large. For instance, the gap between Allied and Axis ethnics on questions of whether Italy and Germany would start a war was 33 percent in the March 12, 1941, survey and 28 percent in the March 28, 1941, survey.

Turning next to questions concerning actions in Europe, we see that table 6.2 demonstrates that the effect of ethnic-group membership extends

TABLE 6.2 The power of ethnic attachments, before the United States' entry into World War II

Political understanding

Question	Date	U.S.-born parents (%)	Allied parents (%)	Axis parent (%)
England is winning the war	January 28, 1941	30	38	21
England will win the war if no other countries enter	March 12, 1941	58	68	42
If England loses, Germany and Italy will start a war	March 12, 1941	61	70	37
If Germany wins, I will be as free as I am now	March 12, 1941	36	38	53
If Germany wins, they will control trade	March 12, 1941	58	61	44
England will win the war	March 28, 1941	83	91	68
Italy and Germany will start a war within 10 years	March 28, 1941	67	71	43

European theater

Question	Date	U.S.-born parents (%)	Allied parents (%)	Axis parent (%)
Help England rather than stay out	January 28, 1941	56	74	30
	March 12, 1941	62	70	30
	March 28, 1941	74	79	47
Defeat Germany rather than stay out	January 28, 1941	52	61	36
Willing to fight in Europe if U.S. gets involved?	March 12, 1941	46	53	32
Vote to go to war?	January 28, 1941	10	14	5
Favor war if convoy is sunk?	January 28, 1941	17	20	12

(continued)

TABLE 6.2 The power of ethnic attachments, before the United States' entry into World War II (*continued*)

Proximate questions

Question	Date	U.S.-born parents (%)	Allied parents (%)	Axis parent (%)
Should the U.S. fight preemptive wars?	March 12, 1941	51	58	33
U.S. should risk war to keep Japan down	March 28, 1941	56	63	50
Defend Latin America if attacked by European power?	March 28, 1941	75	77	68

Note: The table entries represent the predicted probabilities of agreeing with the given statements for each ethnic group. The model respondent is a rural resident of the Midwest, a housewife, a student, or retired person, who is of "average" class and has some high school education. The results do not change significantly if other model respondent profiles are used.

beyond the realm of political understanding into the domain of political choice, especially for those respondents who descend from parents born in Axis countries. The "European theater" questions concern the trade-off between helping England and staying out of the war, the trade-off between defeating Germany and staying out of the war, the willingness of individuals to fight in Europe if the United States became involved, and support for going to war.

The "help England" question is especially significant because it essentially serves as a referendum on FDR's war policy. As noted in chapter 3, although support for isolationism may have died at Pearl Harbor, its death throes began almost a year earlier. Aggregate support for helping England had increased over the course of 1940, and by January 1941 more respondents wanted to help England than wanted to take a course of action ensuring that the United States would stay out of the war. Clearly, the American public on the whole was mobilizing for U.S. involvement in the European theater. But not all Americans felt the same way; important variation existed on the basis of ethnic-group membership.

Each time the "help England" question was asked, respondents whose parents had been born in Axis countries were far less likely to support the Allied cause. The average difference between respondents with native-born parents and those with at least one parent born in an Axis country was 28 percent. With regard to questions concerning involvement in the war in Europe that did not directly ask about England, the gap between respondents with at least one parent born in an Axis country and those whose parents were born in the United States was smaller but still sizable.

The effect of having parents born in an Allied country was considerably smaller across the board on the "help England" questions. On average, having an Allied parent increased interventionist sentiment by ten points, less than half the size of the Axis parent effect. In addition, the substantive effect of Allied heritage also shrank over time. The diminishing effect of Allied heritage, however, is not the result of diminished support among those citizens whose parents were born in Allied countries. Rather, during this time, support for the war among those with parents born in the United States increased greatly. On the other questions concerning the European theater, the effect of the Allied parent variable is smaller still.[22] Even on these questions, though, the net effect of the ethnic heritage measures is a huge gap in opinion between those of Allied and those of Axis descent.

Turning finally to the proximate questions—whether the United States should fight preemptive wars, whether the United States should risk war to contain Japan, and whether the United States should defend Latin America if it were attacked by European powers—the effects of the ethnic background variables were in the same direction as before, but the effects are diminished in size, as the work of Converse and Conover suggests. When the "interstitial" information is more obscure—as it is on these issues—the group membership effects shrink. On all three of the proximate questions, the Allied parent variable effect is small. Although the effects remain powerful in the Axis parent case, and influence even attitudes toward war with Japan, the differences in opinion between the Axis group and the native group are smaller than those found on the other questions.

Clearly, depending on the nature of political context, the power of some ethnic ties is stronger than others. Attachment to Axis countries through one's parents structures a variety of war-related attitudes. The Allied parent variable, on the other hand, is less powerful, more limited in scope, and seems to diminish in strength with time. It appears that, over the course of the first quarter of 1941, descendants of U.S. citizens came to think more like the children of parents born in the Allied countries, whereas the children of parents born in Axis countries retained a distinct opinion on the war.

Unlike the effects of partisan attachment discussed in the last chapter, the effect of group membership does not depend on the respondents' level of political sophistication.[23] This result suggests that group membership structures opinion on the war, independent of political attentiveness. Citizens do not merely take cues from leaders when engaging in group-based cognition; they have agency to arrive at political judgments themselves, using their social attachments as a guide.[24] For *all* members of ethnic groups, group connections play an important role in political cognition and choice.

Post–United States' Entry

Polls taken after the United States became involved in the Second World War demonstrate continued divisions of opinion along ethnic lines. I followed the same analytic strategy as I had with the prewar data. Because much more data exist for the 1942–45 era, I present time-trend graphs of the predicted views of the different ethnic groups. This analysis indicates that the conventional wisdom that views Pearl Harbor as a grand unifying event is incorrect. As noted in the previous chapter, the types of questions asked by pollsters changed once the United States became directly involved in World War II. The prewar differences on questions of understanding and choice largely persisted, however, and at times were quite large.[25]

One line of questions concerns understanding of the war. The first asks, "Do you think Russia can be trusted to cooperate with us after the war is over?" The second asks, "Can England be depended upon to co-operate with us after the war?" The final question was, "Which of these two statements do you think is closer to the truth? (1) England is now fighting mainly to keep her power and wealth. (2) England is now fighting mainly to preserve democracy against the spread of dictatorship." These differences are presented in figures 6.1–6.3. The points on the graphs represent the predicted position of the three groups—those with at least one parent born in an Allied country, those with at least one parent born in an Axis country, and those with both parents born in the United States—while the lines represent the trends of these points.[26] The graphs are scaled from 0 to 1 to show the full range of possible responses.

Differences exist among the groups on questions of trust.[27] Among all ethnic groups, some movement occurs over time in sentiment toward Russia, indicating that factors other than group membership provide structure to opinion (fig. 6.1). These trends are consistent with Page and Shapiro's (1992) conception of "parallel publics"—the notion that subgroups of the population may hold distinct opinions but still change those opinions in parallel over time. Even in the face of short-term fluctuations, however, the differences between the ethnic groups endure. Those respondents descendant from Axis countries are less trusting of Russia (fig. 6.1) and England (fig. 6.2) until the very end of the war. Citizens descended from Allied countries, on the other hand, take a more positive view of the Allies than

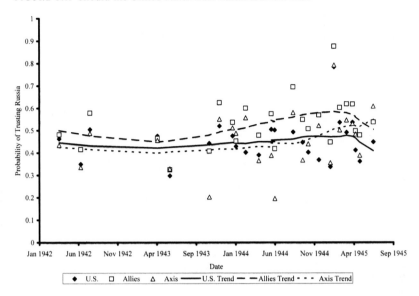

FIGURE 6.1. Should the United States trust Russia after the war?

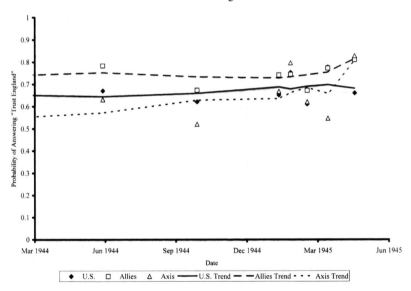

FIGURE 6.2. Should the United States trust England after the war?

FIGURE 6.3. England is fighting only to preserve democracy.

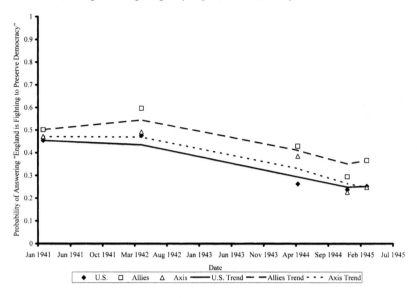

do respondents with two native-born parents on the trust questions and are more sanguine about England's motives (fig. 6.3).

Another line of questions probes attitudes on opinion toward the war. The central item of interest is whether the respondent would be willing to make peace with the German army.[28] As noted in chapter 3, this question serves as a referendum on support for the stated U.S. policy of unconditional surrender. Figure 6.4 demonstrates fairly consistent trends across the war years. Although there is some movement in opinion over time, sentiment on this question largely remains stable from 1942 to 1945. What is most distinctive is the behavior of the Axis group. In the first year of American involvement, respondents with at least one parent born in an Axis country were about twenty points less supportive of war than were those with native-born parents. This gap closed over time but remained on the order of 10–15 percentage points through the end of the war. Respondents with at least one parent born in an Allied country, on the other hand, held opinions that were largely indistinguishable from those whose parents had been born in the United States, mirroring the general shape of opinion that crystallized in early 1941.[29]

These differences among ethnic groups extend to the question of how severe a peace treaty should be relative to the Treaty of Versailles. Throughout the war years, both Allied ethnics and native U.S. respondents recommended a punitive resolution to the war. As figure 6.5 demonstrates,

FIGURE 6.4. Oppose peace with the German army.

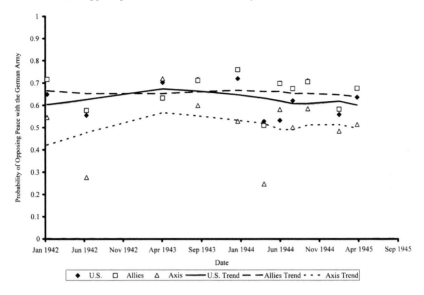

by the end of 1943, a ten-point gap opened between these groups and those respondents with at least one parent born in an Axis country. This gap persisted through the end of the war.[30] On balance, the data presented here suggest that long-standing ethnic divisions can resist even large-scale unifying events such as war.

ATTITUDES TOWARD DOMESTIC GROUPS: THE STRUCTURE OF WAR SUPPORT

Having established the power of membership in particular ethnic groups in structuring public opinion about war, I next turn to questions concerning the effect of sentiment toward other groups.[31] The role of affect toward out-groups in society is a potentially powerful factor in structuring support for war because large segments of the population may hold strong views about those groups, regardless of their size in society. One survey particularly well suited to the examination of the role of attitudes toward other groups in society is the poll conducted by Roper for *Fortune* magazine in August 1939, described briefly in chapter 3. Recall that Roper asked respondents their opinions about a variety of courses of action the United States might take toward the conflict in Europe. Respondents were also asked a series of questions about their feelings toward particular domestic ethnic groups.[32] Specifically, Roper asked, "Of the people now in

FIGURE 6.5. Make peace treaty more severe than last war?

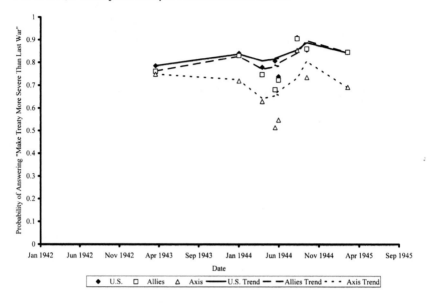

the U.S. who were born in foreign countries, which nationality would you say has made the best citizens? Which the worst?" A total of 44 percent of the sample identified at least one nationality that made the worst citizens, whereas 49 percent named at least one group that constituted the best citizens. These numbers are especially high given that the item was phrased as an open-ended question; respondents were required to produce their own ethnic labels for the interviewer. Table 6.3 presents the distribution of answers to these questions.

Somewhat surprisingly, given the persecution of German nationals during World War I, a plurality of respondents said that Germans made the best citizens, followed closely by the English. On the question of which nationality made the worst citizens, a large proportion of respondents—22 percent—identified Italians (with another 1 percent identifying Sicilians).[33] No other ethnic group approaches this figure. In fact, respondents named Italians as the worst citizens almost four times as often as they named any other group. This pattern of aversion can be found in every geographic region and among every subgroup of the population.[34] Even respondents with relatively little contact with Italian immigrants expressed dislike for Italians. For instance, over one-quarter of the residents of the west-central states said that Italians made the worst citizens, when less than 1 percent of the population of that region were first- or second-generation Italian

TABLE 6.3 Distribution of ethnic-group attachments and enmities, August 1939

Of the people now in the U.S. who were born in foreign countries, which nationality would you say has made the best citizens? Which the worst?

	Percent
Best	
1. Germans	13
2. English	10
3. Irish	6
4. Scandinavians	5
5. Swedes	4
Other group	13
Don't know/good and bad in all groups	51
Worst	
1. Italians	22
2. Jews	6
3. Germans	4
4. Japanese	2
5. Sicilians	1
Other group	8
Don't know/good and bad in all groups	56

Source: Author analysis of Roper Survey 7 (August 1939).

Americans.[35] These results are especially striking in light of the fact that the Roper sample is certainly an overeducated sample relative to the population.[36] Given the strong relationship between tolerance and education levels, we might expect that the true levels of ethnic dislike would run even higher in the population at large.[37] The high levels of hostility toward Italians should not, however, obscure the significant levels of dislike of other groups. Nontrivial portions of the population also mentioned Jews and Germans as the "worst" groups. Clearly in the late 1930s, enmity toward certain ethnic groups ran high in the American population.

What is especially important about these results is the fact that these enmities were almost certainly forged on the domestic stage, independent of the international events of the mid- to late 1930s. Admittedly, I cannot rule out the possibility that attitudes about war shaped feelings toward domestic groups; the existing data do not allow me to empirically sort out the direction of causality. Indeed the fairly low prevalence of anti-Japanese sentiment in 1939 indicates that the World War II experience influenced affect toward and treatment of Japanese Americans in the 1940s, as I discuss later in the chapter. I can, however, establish the exogeneity of attitudes toward two key groups—Italians and Jews—by relying on historical accounts of their immigrant experience.

Anti-Italian sentiment had a long tradition in America before the beginning of World War II.[38] During the 1880s, European immigration to America shifted from the traditional regions of northern and western Europe to the less familiar regions of southern and eastern Europe. Although immigrants from almost every country in Europe experienced discrimination at one point or another, Italians were prominent victims (Alba 1985; Higham 2002). Stereotypes for Italians ranged from the physical—references to their "low foreheads" and "dark skin"—to the psychological—references to their "dangerous social tendencies" and their "proclivity for crime" (Alba 1985; Higham 2002). I. W. Howerth (1894) expressed a common perception, writing, "Of our immigrants the most refractory are undoubtedly the Italians . . . the opinion has become current that individually and collectively they are a very dangerous people. And thus it is that the adjectives lazy, filthy, cruel, ferocious, bloodthirsty, and the like, are supposed to be particularly applicable to this class of immigrants. No epithet is too insulting to apply to the 'Dago.'" This portrayal of Italians continued through the 1930s. *Life* magazine, for example, intending to compliment baseball star Joe DiMaggio, wrote, "Although he learned Italian first, Joe, now 24, speaks English without an accent, and is otherwise well adapted to most U.S. mores. Instead of olive oil or smelly bear grease he keeps his hair slick with water. He never reeks of garlic and prefers chicken chow mein to spaghetti."[39]

Jews also engendered a great deal of hostility in America. From the middle of the nineteenth century, Jews were widely seen as "avaricious social climbers who pushed themselves where they were not wanted" (Alba 1985). During the 1890s, it was widely feared that Jews would unduly influence the U.S. economy; by the 1900s this fear had subsided, but the anti-Semitic notions of Jews as a greedy and vulgar race persisted throughout World War II (Higham 2002). Clearly, dislike of these particular ethnic groups emerged independent of the war.[40]

For present purposes, more important than the absolute levels of fondness or enmity toward foreign groups is the political power of these feelings. As noted previously, groups "enter into political thinking most strongly on issues where the group cues are explicit and salient" (Conover 1988, 61). Given the salience of the impending war, we would expect that citizens could easily map their feelings toward ethnic groups onto the international scene. That is, the linking information that lies at the heart of group-based cognition was widely available. This was the case not only for Germans—the primary aggressors in the brewing conflict—but for Italians as well. Casey (2001) performed a quantitative content analysis of FDR's speeches during 1937–41 to determine whom FDR labeled "the enemy." By 1941, the target of U.S. alarm was clearly Hitler and Nazism. In the second half of 1941, 110 of the 145 references FDR made to an "enemy" mentioned the Nazi regime. But FDR had not always focused on the Nazis. In the second half of 1939, 2 of the 8 references made by FDR to "the enemy" were aimed at Mussolini and the Fascist government of Italy. Additionally, during the first half of 1940, there were no specific references made to Hitler, whereas 9 out of 25 references were made to Mussolini and/or the Fascist Italian government.[41] Thus, not only the German government but the Italian government featured prominently as enemies of the United States in the political rhetoric of the time. By highlighting the Italian government in his rhetoric, FDR facilitated the linking of attitudes toward domestic Italians—which were stable and, on balance, highly negative—to the gathering international crisis. In short, given our theoretical expectations, feelings toward German and Italian domestic groups should structure opinion on the conflict at hand.

To assess the effect of these likes and dislikes of particular groups on opinion toward the war, I estimated a series of models using the same five dependent variables from the Roper study that I examined for the gender analysis in chapter 3. Recall that three of these questions concern possible support for England and France in the event of war with Germany, and the final two items tapped more general sentiment concerning the United States' involvement in war.

In predicting the answers to these items, I included measures for whether respondents expressed support for Germans, Italians, and English as the "best" citizens, and whether they considered Germans and Italians the "worst" citizens.[42] I expected that among those expressing sympathy for the English and antipathy toward Italians and Germans I would find increased support for the war, whereas among those voicing sympathy for Germans and Italians I would find decreased support for aggressive U.S. action. I also included a measure to tap feeling toward Jews.[43] Although the full extent of the Holocaust may not have been widely known (see chap. 2), I expected that, given the clear anti-Semitic rhetoric of the Nazis, dislike of Jews would lead to different judgments than dislike of Italians or Germans; the expression of anti-Jewish sentiment should lead to the manifestation of an isolationist, rather than an internationalist position. The measure I used specifically taps feeling toward American Jews.[44] Respondents scored high on this variable if they expressed a nontolerant position.[45]

I ran the analysis using each of the five dependent variables.[46] In table 6.4, to ease the interpretation of these results, I present the first differences—the increase or decrease in the predicted probability of giving an anti-intervention response—resulting from labeling a particular group the "best" or the "worst" compared with not labeling a group in this way.[47] As the table demonstrates, the respondents' reactions to particular ethnic groups structure opinions toward the war in important ways. Although the size of the effects varies somewhat, the results of judgments of groups on attitudes toward the war are largely consistent across the different measures. Respondents who prefer immigrants from England are more likely to support action on the part of the United States vis-à-vis the Axis countries. In all five cases, these respondents give more interventionist responses, and the difference is substantively large in four of the cases. Conversely, expressing warmth toward ethnic Italians increases the probability of expressing support for anti-interventionist policies. This effect is moderately large on several of the items and has the correct sign in four of the five cases. The effect of liking Germans has a somewhat inconsistent effect. Sometimes expressing attachment to citizens from Germany increases the probability of giving an anti-interventionist response, sometimes it decreases the likelihood of such an answer, and other times it has no effect. Turning to the "dislike" questions, I find that the claim that immigrants from Axis nations make the worst citizens predisposes respondents to support interventionist policies. The "German worst" variable affects the pro-intervention direction in all five cases and is substantively large on the question of sending the U.S. armed forces abroad. Moreover, expressing dislike for Italians decreases anti-interventionist sentiment on all the items.[48] These patterns in favor of intervention are not driven by the simple dislike of groups that are "different." Respondents who express nontolerant attitudes toward Jews are more likely to express anti-interventionist sentiment on all five questions. Thus, specific attachments and (especially) resentments toward particular groups—not simply general resentment—structure opinion toward the war. To use the terminology of Campbell and LeVine (1961), opinion is not determined just by universal ethnocentrism; instead, it is also ordered by specific stereotypes. *Domestic* loyalties and animosities determine, in part, where individuals stand on foreign policy issues.

TABLE 6.4 Group attachments and enmities and support for isolationist positions, August 1939

Preferences	U.S. should tend to its own business (%)	No question is so important that U.S. should risk war (%)	Don't allow England/France to buy food (%)	Don't allow England/France to buy war supplies (%)	Don't send U.S. Army and Navy abroad to help England/France (%)
English best	–7	–5	–2	–5	–13
Germans best	+0	–3	+0	+2	+6
Italians best	+2	–2	+2	+5	+6
Germans worst	–1	–2	–2	–3	–11
Italians worst	–1	–2	–2	–6	–5
Restrict rights of Jews in America[a]	+1	+5	+3	+3	+3

Source: Author analysis of Roper Survey 7 (August 1939).

Note: Cell entries indicate the effect of giving a particular response to the likes/dislikes question on the probability of choosing an isolationist response. The model respondent is a female, lower-middle-class resident of New England, living on a rural farm, who is a housewife, a student, or retired person who expresses tolerance for Jews and states no like or dislike of any particular ethnic group. The results do not change significantly if other model respondent profiles are used.

[a] Those who would restrict the right of Jews in America have rejected the statement, "In the United States the Jews have the same standing as any other people, and they should be treated in all ways exactly as any other Americans."

THE JAPANESE INTERNMENT

To this point, I have explored the ways in which opinions about domestic groups can shape the foreign policy opinions of the public. Under certain circumstances, however, changes in the international arena can also shape animosities toward ethnic groups. As noted earlier, on the eve of World War II dislike of the Japanese was outstripped by dislike of Italians, Jews, and Germans. But after the attack on Pearl Harbor, the patterns of hostility shifted greatly.

One of the largest stains on the U.S. commitment to equality and freedom was the forced internment of Japanese Americans during the Second World War. Two months after the attack at Pearl Harbor, FDR signed Executive Order 9066, which authorized the removal of over 100,000 Japanese Americans—the majority of whom were citizens—from the West Coast of the United States to "relocation centers" far from their homes. In retrospect, the unfairness of this action is clear. The Civil Liberties Act of

1988, which granted reparations to those interned during World War II, established that "a grave injustice was done to both citizens and resident aliens of Japanese ancestry by the evacuation, relocation, and internment of civilians during World War II."

When the internment policy was first implemented, however, public support for the program was extremely high. In March 1942, NORC asked a number of questions relating to the treatment of Japanese Americans. Although the individual-level data have been lost to time, even the uncorrected marginal estimates of public sentiment are illuminating. The survey revealed that an overwhelming majority of Americans thought that the United States "was doing the right thing in moving Japanese aliens (those who are not citizens) away from the Pacific coast." Ninety-three percent of respondents agreed with this statement, and only 1 percent disagreed. Support for the U.S. internment policy dropped when the focus shifted to "Japanese who were born in this country and are United States citizens," but 59 percent of respondents still supported internment of Japanese American citizens. Thus although Americans took the legal status of Japanese Americans into consideration when assessing proper U.S. policy, they were willing to send their fellow citizens to internment camps. This anti-Japanese stand included support for punitive treatment of all detainees; two-thirds of respondents thought that civilians of Japanese descent "should be kept under strict guard as prisoners of war" (Cantril and Strunck 1951, 380).

The internment of U.S. residents of Japanese descent was viewed by many Americans as a permanent policy, at least in the early part of the war. In December 1942, Gallup asked, "Do you think the Japanese who were moved inland from the Pacific coast should be allowed to return to the Pacific coast when the war is over?" Only 33 percent of respondents thought that the Japanese should be allowed to move back, whereas 48 percent were opposed. Gallup then asked respondents who were opposed to repatriating Japanese Americans from the internment camps, "what should be done with the Japanese?" Among opponents of repatriation, 56 percent wanted to "send [Japanese Americans] back to Japan," 14 percent wanted to "put them out of this country," 11 percent wished to "leave them where they are—under control," and 8 percent favored some form of genocide, arguing that the United States should "kill them, get rid of them, destroy them."

Even toward the end of the war, a majority of Americans remained hostile to Japanese Americans. In September 1944, NORC asked, "After the war, do you think Japanese living in the United States should have as good a chance as white people to get any kind of job, or do you think white people should have the first chance at any job?" Sixty-four percent said that the United States should give jobs to white people first, 14 percent said that the Japanese should have as good a chance as anyone, and 10 percent said Japanese should get jobs "if they were loyal citizens." As was the case in the early war period, citizenship was a clear consideration for survey respondents. In April 1945, NORC asked a question about jobs that distinguished between citizens and noncitizens. Forty percent of respondents believed that non-Japanese should get jobs ahead of Japanese citizens, compared to 56 percent who supported such a policy for "Japanese now living in the United States who are not American citizens." The close of the war did not end suspicion of the Japanese. In May 1946, two-thirds of NORC respondents thought that "the Japanese who lived in this country" spied for the Japanese government, and as many respondents thought that Japanese Americans destroyed American war materials (31 percent) as thought they did not (32 percent).

In sum, although the internment of the Japanese during World War II may seem in retrospect to be a dismal chapter in U.S. history, in the heat of war Americans freely sacrificed the basic liberties of their fellow citizens. The surrender of civil liberties in time of threat is a familiar pattern. Although the policy toward Japanese Americans in the 1940s is exceptional in some respects, the internment experience is by no means unique. In the next chapter, I show that the dynamics of civil liberties judgments exhibited by the American public during World War II follow patterns consistent with public opinion on civil liberties more generally, both during other times of war and during times of peace.

PART III Public Opinion and War:
Back to the Water's Edge

CHAPTER SEVEN

CIVIL LIBERTIES AND WAR

The trade-off between security and civil liberties is always difficult to navigate in a democratic society. During times of national crisis, liberty does not always prevail, as the discussion of the internment of Japanese Americans during World War II in the last chapter illustrates. The subversion of basic rights is not, however, merely the stuff of history. In the days and weeks after 9/11, some worried that the government's offensive against terrorist activity might undermine the democratic foundations of American society. Elisa Massimino, the director of the Washington office of the Lawyers Committee for Human Rights, cautioned that the Patriot Act would lead America down a troubling road: "These kinds of provisions, once they infect a country's justice system, are incredibly hard to cure."[1] The public's role in this debate was uncertain. Would citizens willingly cede their basic liberties to government authorities for the promise of protection from unknown threats? Would they offer up the rights of minority groups as sacrifices for that cause as they had in the 1940s?

In late 2001, a number of scholars and media organizations conducted in-depth investigations of America's commitment to civil liberties and political tolerance to answer just these questions. The overall tenor of these findings provided mixed support for critics such as Massimino. On the whole, public support for the protection of civil liberties was lower than it had been before the attacks.[2] On the other hand, aggregate support for measures designed to preserve civil liberties remained strong. For instance, Davis and Silver (2004) found that a majority of the public took a proliberty position on two-thirds of questions involving the trade-off between security and civil liberties, ranging from a slim majority of 53 percent who thought that the government should not be permitted to "arrest and detain a non-citizen indefinitely if that person is suspected of belonging to a terrorist organization" to a near-unanimous support level of 92 percent who believed that people who participate in nonviolent protests against the U.S. government "have the right to meet in public and express unpopular views as long as they are not violating the law."[3] Although U.S. citizens may indeed have been willing to accept greater restrictions on some liberties after 9/11, residual support for protecting civil liberties remained fairly strong even in the wake of that devastating terrorist attack.

Not all citizens were so accepting of these basic liberties, however. As I discuss in more detail later, the overall picture of support for civil liberties may have been one of moderation, but that support was tempered by fear and trust. Some citizens held steadfast in their support for liberties. Others—those who perceived a heightened sense of threat but trusted the government—were willing to grant the government a wide berth in navigating the war on terror.

These patterns of opinion should be familiar to scholars of American politics. In this chapter, I show that civil liberties judgments during wartime differ in their depth and scope—not in their structure—from civil liberties judgments during peacetime. Civil liberties judgments in times of war are no different from calculations made during times of "normal politics." Thus, as in earlier chapters, we can understand the nature of public opinion during war by looking to the same kinds of processes that motivate judgments concerning domestic politics. At times, partisan attachments provide citizens with a guide for navigating trade-offs between security and liberty. But partisanship does not always provide such a roadmap. A more consistent influence on how citizens make these critical trade-offs is perception of threat, whether the source of that threat be domestic or international in nature. Any change in how individuals reason about civil liberties during war is the result of public reaction to a change in the magnitude of perceived threat, not a shift in the underlying dynamics of opinion as attention moves from the realm of domestic politics to the international stage. Breaking somewhat from the theme of the last section of this book, however, I find that the conditions of war might introduce a new consideration into the mix. In particular, I make the novel argument that differences among individuals in support for war—as distinct from differences in perceptions of threat—shape how members of the public judge the validity of restrictions on civil liberties. Perhaps most troubling for the prospects of an open democratic society, supporters of a war are the most enthusiastic about suppressing the speech of others, especially their opponents.

This chapter begins with a discussion of the formation of civil liberties judgments in peacetime. I first argue that the findings of the political tolerance literature—which concerns the rights of marginal groups—can inform our understanding of how the public reasons about support for civil liberties more generally. In both cases, the perception of a threat—whether it be from a particular group in society or from an undifferentiated and ambiguous menace—reduces support for protecting civil liberties. I then draw on a diverse set of public opinion data from the last half century to demonstrate the consistency in patterns of support for liberties across times of war and times of peace. I first use data, collected over the last thirty years on support for restrictions on the liberties of particular groups, to show that any threat—even one ostensibly unrelated to the target of a particular civil liberties judgment—leads individuals to restrict the rights of others. Moreover, I find direct parallels between the public's reactions to the attacks on the Pentagon and the World Trade Center and the structure of civil liberties judgments during peacetime. As was the case in the months after 9/11, those individuals who trust the government are more willing to cede their liberties to political authorities when threatened than those individuals who do not trust politicians in Washington. Having established the general principles that structure public opinion concerning civil liberties, I examine sixty years of survey data concerning trade-offs between liberty and security during wartime. Although they were measured at different moments in U.S. history and in somewhat different ways, I demonstrate that these same factors—namely, threat and, in some cases, the group attachments and enmities discussed in the previous section of this book—structured civil liberties judgments during World War II, Vietnam, and the present day.[4]

CIVIL LIBERTIES AND POLITICAL TOLERANCE

Before examining specific trends in support for civil liberties during times of war, we must place these decisions in the larger context of the study of tolerance for political dissent. Explaining popular support for the protection of civil liberties is a central concern in the study of political behavior. Democratic society, after all, rests on the willingness of its citizens to resist encroachments on basic liberties. When they consider them in the abstract, Americans have long expressed broad support for civil liberties. As far back as 1938, 92 percent of respondents said that they "believe in freedom of speech." Forty years later, McClosky and Brill (1983) found that 90 percent of Americans supported "free speech for all, no matter what their view might be" (see also McClosky 1964; Prothro and Grigg 1960). But, as noted earlier, civil liberties are rarely contemplated in the abstract. In practice, as Gibson and Bingham (1985) observe, support for civil liberties must be weighed against support for other values and beliefs (see also Sniderman et al. 1996).

Scholars who study public support for civil liberties generally follow one of two research traditions. Some scholars choose to study questions that concern the proper scope of government restrictions on basic civil liberties for a society as a whole—the types of questions that were asked in the wake of 9/11. A second set of scholars instead studies "political tolerance"—the extension of fundamental rights to particular groups in society. Researchers in the first tradition essentially ask, "What should we let the government do to us (as a society as a whole)?" Scholars of political tolerance instead ask, "What should we let the government do to others?" Interestingly, the study of general societal restrictions is by far the less developed of the two traditions. Although the proper measurement of political tolerance—the extension of civil liberties to groups that express ideas in opposition to one's own—has been the subject of voluminous debate in political science, public opinion scholars have only recently studied support for general restrictions in a comprehensive way.

This bifurcation in the literature has obscured some important insights. Although almost all scholars have studied judgments about one's own rights and the rights of others as distinct processes, the two traditions in large part address different sides of the same coin. Both literatures address the treatment of the same general freedoms, such as free speech and free association. Moreover, many scholars in both traditions look to similar explanatory factors, for example, the prevailing political climate and demographic variables such as education. Of course, some important differences exist between the two types of questions. The discussion in the last chapter of the treatment of Japanese Americans demonstrates that affect toward disliked groups can play a large role in determining levels of political tolerance. As Sniderman, Brody, and Tetlock (1991) have shown, however, respondents' judgments about the rights of particular groups are at least as reflective of "principled" support for general democratic norms as they are about affect toward those particular groups.[5] Put another way, following Chong (1993), there are two classes of considerations on civil liberties issues: (1) considerations of principles and rights and (2) considerations about the people and groups involved in the issue, including considerations about how the issue might affect oneself. The general trade-off questions and the tolerance items differ in the balance of these relevant ideas, but both give us a window into general judgments regarding civil liberties. In fact, empirically the two types of items appear to be highly related. For instance, Skitka, Bauman, and Mullen (2004), using a composite measure of support for civil liberties, find that questions about the liberties of minority groups and a measure asking if the Bush administration has gone too far in restricting civil liberties to fight terrorism scaled on the same dimension (see also the discussion of the Pew studies later in the chapter).[6]

Civil Liberties: Us and Them

Making these parallels between societal and group-specific measures of commitment to civil liberties is valuable because we can draw on the larger body of theoretical and empirical work on liberties from the political tolerance tradition to learn about how people come to accept restrictions on their own rights. Seminal studies of public support for civil liberties in the 1950s by Stouffer (1955) examined respondents' willingness to grant free speech to particular groups that lay outside of mainstream society at that time, namely, socialists, atheists, and Communists. Stouffer found strong support for restricting the rights of these groups. Researchers who studied public willingness to extend liberties to these same groups in the early 1970s found remarkable increases in tolerance. Some authors attributed these trends to changes in society that created a political climate more accepting of dissent (Davis 1975; Nunn, Crockett, and Williams 1978).

These increases, however, turned out to be largely illusory. Sullivan, Pierson, and Marcus (1982) demonstrated that although Americans were, on the whole, more tolerant in the 1970s of the particular groups that Stouffer investigated in the 1950s, this increase in tolerance did not extend to other controversial groups in society. When Sullivan and his colleagues measured an individual's willingness to extend free speech to groups that an individual said she disliked, they found levels of political intolerance comparable to those found by Stouffer. Sullivan, Pierson, and Marcus therefore concluded that any apparent increase in tolerance was a result of an increase in the likeability of socialists, atheists, and Communists, not an increase in general support for civil liberties.[7] Sullivan, Pierson, and Marcus instead proposed measuring tolerance using their "least-liked" strategy, in which a researcher first asks which groups a respondent dislikes and then assesses tolerance toward those groups. This measurement strategy has been widely adopted in the study of tolerance (see, however, Gibson 1992).

In these studies, the primacy of threat is clear. One of the strongest findings in the tolerance literature is that perceptions of conditions of threat increase support for restrictions on civil liberties (Marcus et al. 1995; Sullivan, Pierson, and Marcus 1982). For instance, looking in the 1950s, Stouffer found that respondents who believed that American Communists were a danger to the United States were more likely to support restrictions on civil liberties than those who believed that Communists posed no danger.[8] Sullivan, Pierson, and Marcus (1982) extended this analysis and found that respondents were most intolerant of those groups they found normatively threatening—groups that were viewed as "violent," "dangerous," or "untrustworthy."[9] Although these authors focused on threats from particular groups, more recent work has examined a broader conception of threat. Marcus et al. (1995) found that those respondents who feel threatened by many groups from across the ideological spectrum—individuals high on "threat predisposition"—were most willing to restrict the civil liberties of any and all marginal groups. In fact, the effect of general threat was even stronger than that of threat from the least-liked group (see also Feldman and Stenner 1997; Stenner 2005).[10]

Paralleling the conclusions of the tolerance literature, research in the post-9/11 era has found that the correlates of tolerance are analogous to the predictors of a general commitment to civil liberties. Davis and Silver (2004) and Huddy et al. (2005) both found that individuals who were concerned about the possibility of future terrorist attacks were most willing to sacrifice their liberties.[11] Threats from particular targets may be significant predictors of intolerance, in times of peace as in times of war. It is, however, the perception of threat—whether it be the threat from a disliked group or an undifferentiated threat to the society as a whole—that leads to support for restrictions on one's own civil liberties *and* the rights of particular groups.[12]

In the rest of this chapter, I explore the relationship between threat and support for civil liberties using a variety of measures of both concepts. In part, this strategy is a function of the limitations of the available data; when studying the attitudes of citizens in earlier times, I am by necessity constrained by the choices and interests of other scholars. This measurement strategy is also an advantage, however. In a variety of settings—on both the domestic and international stages—I demonstrate that citizens react to threats by ceding to the government those rights that protect the basic liberties of themselves and other citizens.

THE POLITICS OF FEAR

Much of the research on civil liberties has examined the effect of threats from specific groups on levels of political tolerance. During times of war, however, societal groups only indirectly trigger responses of fear. For my purposes, it is important to demonstrate that fear and threat independent of particular groups can structure judgments concerning civil liberties. Therefore, to lay the groundwork for the analysis that follows later in this chapter, I begin with an example far removed from war, namely, the relationship between a generalized threat from crime and the civil liberties of marginal groups. For the last thirty years, the General Social Survey (GSS) has asked respondents about their willingness to extend rights to five diverse targets from across the political spectrum, namely, racists, militarists, atheists, homosexuals, and Communists.[13] Following convention, I constructed an intolerance score by measuring the percentage of time a respondent supported restricting the civil liberties of a particular group in a particular realm.[14]

The GSS questions concerning perceptions of threat are more limited. Over the last thirty years the GSS has fairly consistently asked one item relating to fear of crime: "Is there any area right around here—that is, within a mile—where you would be afraid to walk alone at night?"[15] This item is less than ideal for a number of reasons. First, the item is phrased in a generic way with few response options; it does not allow us to discriminate among respondents in terms of their levels of threat. Furthermore, the item asks about personal threat, which, as several scholars have noted, exerts a less powerful influence on political tolerance than a societal threat (see Davis 2007 for a review).[16] At the same time, the particular limitation of this item allows for a strong test of the effects of threat on civil liberties judgments. The GSS item does not refer to any of the groups included in the civil liberties battery and is therefore conceptually orthogonal to those judgments. A finding that perceptions of a generalized feeling of threat influence civil liberties judgments here—with a somewhat poorly specified and operationalized concept of threat—provides strong evidence of some relationship between general fear and civil liberties.

Controlling for factors plausibly associated with both levels of intolerance and threat, I predicted an individual's intolerance score as a function of the threat variable.[17] As expected, I found that those respondents who feel threatened in their neighborhoods are more willing to tolerate restrictions on civil liberties than those who are not.[18] This effect is not particularly large—threatened respondents are the equivalent of 3 points (on a 100-point scale) less tolerant than other respondents—but the difference is statistically significant.[19]

The relationship between threat and intolerance is even stronger when I use a more precise measure of threat. In 2000, respondents were asked how afraid they were of nuclear war.[20] This measure taps the preferred concept of sociotropic threat—the threat to the nation as a whole, as opposed to a particular threat to the respondent—and allows a greater gradation of levels of threat in the response.[21] Substituting the nuclear war question for the "fear of neighborhood" question in the analysis indicates that respondents who think war is more of a threat today scored 13 points lower on the 100-point tolerance scale than those who thought it was less of a threat.[22]

Most important, the GSS data allow us to investigate directly the proposition that general threat—rather than the particular fear of war or foreign attack—determines, in part, the civil liberties judgments of individuals. Davis and Silver (2004) explore the relationship between threat and trust in government and find that those individuals who trusted the federal government were willing to give up their liberties after 9/11. Citizens' levels of trust in government, however, also moderated the impact of the perceived threat of another attack. Fear of terrorism had no effect on civil liberties judgments for respondents who expressed low levels of trust. On the other hand, among respondents who placed a great deal of trust in the government, greater concern about another attack was associated with much lower support for civil liberties (Davis and Silver 2004).[23] Davis and Silver's work is unique on this score; although it may not be surprising that those individuals who place the most trust in the government are the most willing to allow the government to restrict liberties, to my knowledge no other scholars have explored the effect of political trust on civil liberties judgments. There is, however, no reason to believe that the cause of that fear should be particular to the terrorist attacks of 9/11. Citizens should cede authority to a trusted actor when they are fearful, no matter the source of that fear.

In 1987, in addition to the civil liberties item and the threat question, the GSS asked respondents how much they trusted the government.[24] Analysis of the relationship among trust, fear, and civil liberties indicates that in a very different context, using very different measures, the same pattern found by Davis and Silver unfolds. Among those respondents who trust the government, the effect of feeling threatened in one's neighborhood increases support for restrictions by 9 percent of the tolerance scale. On the other hand, among those who do not trust the government, being fearful of one's neighborhood increases support for restrictions by 4 percent of the scale, a statistically significant difference.[25]

Certainly threat is not the only reason that people support restriction on civil liberties. But it is clear that the effects of threat and trust are part of a more general process that extends beyond simply the case of a large attack, such as 9/11. Thus in the realm of civil liberties, as in other aspects of war, it seems that public opinion follows patterns familiar from the ebb and flow of normal domestic politics.

CIVIL LIBERTIES AFTER SEPTEMBER 11

Having established the importance of perceptions of threat, I now return to the central area of concern: support for civil liberties during wartime. As discussed previously, the public's judgments concerning civil liberties were somewhat in flux in the wake of 9/11. Overall support for civil liberties was lower than it had been before the attacks. But that picture is a single snapshot (although see Davis 2007).[26] To further explore civil liberties in the wake of 9/11, I turn to a series of polls taken by the Pew Center for the People and the Press.[27] The Pew Center has asked several questions concerning civil liberties over the last ten years. Three of these items were asked repeatedly and allow us to trace opinion change over time. The first question is roughly analogous to Davis and Silver's general civil liberties item and reads, "In order to curb terrorism in this country, do you think it will be necessary for the average person to give up some civil liberties, or not?" This question provides an especially valuable source of trend data because it was asked by Pew twice before September 11, in both March 1996 and June 1997. The other Pew questions concerning civil liberties followed a similar theme but were worded in slightly different ways. Specifically, Pew asked a second item in 2001 and 2002, which read, "What concerns you more right now? That the government will fail to enact strong, new anti-terrorism laws, or that the government will enact new anti-terrorism laws which excessively restrict the average person's civil liberties?" A third item was asked beginning in 2004 and read, "What concerns you more about the government's anti-terrorism policies, that they have not gone far enough to adequately protect the country or that they have gone too far in restricting the average person's civil liberties?"

The over-time trends for the trade-off questions are presented in figure 7.1. Before the attacks of September 11, a significant majority believed that it would not be necessary to sacrifice civil liberties to curb terrorism.

In the immediate wake of the attack, support for that position dropped sharply.[28]

The September 2001 Pew survey also asked about support for a number of other measures relating to restrictions on civil liberties.[29] Although these items differed in form from the Davis and Silver trade-off questions, they provide a similar picture of the depth of support for civil liberties. Several policies proposed to restrict civil liberties engendered high support. For instance, 70 percent of respondents favored a requirement that citizens carry a national identity card to be shown to a police officer on request. But respondents did not extend a blank check to the government. Only 26 percent favored allowing the U.S. government to monitor personal telephone calls and e-mails. Furthermore, a majority of 57 percent of respondents opposed "allowing the U.S. government to take legal immigrants from unfriendly countries to internment camps during times of tension or crisis" (although, echoing opinion on the internment of Japanese during World War II, 29 percent supported this position and 14 percent said they did not know where they stood on the matter). Thus, the effect of the terrorist attack on support for civil liberties was clear. For whatever reason—the increased salience of threat, the unified elite positions in the immediate wake of the attack, or some combination of the two—September 11 changed the way the country as a whole thought about civil liberties. Backing for restrictions on liberties—both in the abstract and in particular circumstances—rose in the wake of the attack, relative to support during the peaceful times three years earlier.

Following the immediate aftermath of September 11, however, the tide quickly turned. Support for civil liberties climbed significantly, reaching a majority position by August 2003, and by 2004 nearing the highs found in the late 1990s. The quick recovery in support for civil liberties was mirrored in other polls taken at that time (see Huddy, Khatib, and Capelos 2002). Further poll data suggest that support for civil liberties has climbed even further since that time, as figure 7.1 demonstrates.[30]

Not everyone, however, was so quick to embrace the pro–civil liberties position. Consistent with the existing research just described, cross-sectional analysis of the Pew data indicates that the effects of threat persisted long after 9/11. Pew measured threat using both sociotropic and personal threat questions on surveys from 2001 to 2004 (see further discussion in chap. 8). In line with the earlier findings , sociotropic threat had a larger effect than personal threat on every survey. Regardless of the measurement strategy, those respondents most threatened by the possibility of a future attack were most supportive of restricting civil liberties, even

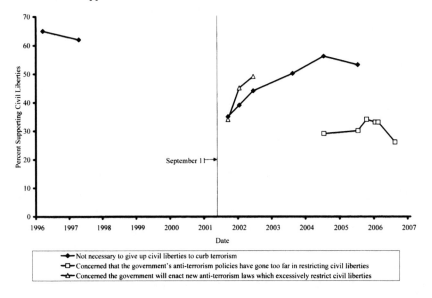

FIGURE 7.1. Support for civil liberties, 1996–2006.

Percent Supporting Civil Liberties

September 11 ⟶

Date

➤ Not necessary to give up civil liberties to curb terrorism
➤ Concerned that the government's anti-terrorism policies have gone too far in restricting civil liberties
➤ Concerned the government will enact new anti-terrorism laws which excessively restrict civil liberties

controlling for the demographic and political determinants of support for liberties.[31]

The Emergence of Partisanship

The continued effect of generalized threat on opinion was not the only evidence that the familiar forces of domestic politics shaped the dynamics of civil liberties after 2001. Partisanship has largely been ignored in the tolerance literature, but it is a predisposition that, as demonstrated in chapter 5, is critical for understanding the structure of opinion during wartime.[32] Davis (2007) found that partisanship did not play a role in determining support for civil liberties in the immediate aftermath of 9/11, arguing that a sense of patriotism in late 2001 was instrumental in causing Democrats and independents to accept conservative positions. This condition, however, was temporary. As blind patriotism faded over time, partisanship emerged as an important fault line on civil liberties.

Pew did not measure party identification in its September 2001 survey, so it is not possible to confirm independently the lack of partisan divisions in the immediate wake of the attack. Pew, however, measured respondents' partisanship in every other survey represented in figure 7.1. We can therefore explore trends in the degree of polarization along party lines in civil liberties judgments. Before September 11, the available evidence suggests that Democrats and Republicans came to similar judgments regarding the civil liberties/security trade-off. Republicans were, in fact, slightly less supportive of civil liberties restrictions, although this difference was small and statistically insignificant. Figure 7.2, however, presents a picture of a growing partisan gap from 2002 onward, in line with developments on other issues associated with the Bush administration (Jacobson 2008). In January 2002, relatively small differences emerged between Democrats and Republicans. These differences have increased tremendously over time. Aggregate support for civil liberties grew as 9/11 receded into the past, but partisan identifiers rejected the security position of that trade-off at different rates.

At the same time, as the data from the late 1990s suggest, the emergence of the partisan gap on civil liberties judgments does not represent a return to equilibrium. The gap between Democrats and Republicans instead represents the emergence of a new fault line mirroring political debate on issues of both war and peace more generally (Jacobson 2008). In fact, by 2006, the civil liberties trade-off question exhibited the same pattern of partisan polarization found in measures of support for the Iraq War discussed in chapter 5 (see fig. 7.3). As citizens' level of interest in politics increased, the gap between Democrats and Republicans grew larger. The Pew data therefore lead to an important conclusion. The events of September 11 had an immediate impact on the trade-off between security and civil liberties, but public opinion quickly exhibited the contours of normal politics not only in levels of support for civil liberties but also in partisan divisions that mirror the politics of the day. As was the case with support for war, the partisan loyalties of respondents played a large role in structuring their political judgments concerning civil liberties.

Civil Liberties and War

Partisanship and perceived threat are both important determinants of support for basic liberties. Attitudes toward war, however, might also shape the ways in which the public views restrictions on civil liberties, even accounting for perceptions of threat from external forces. Those individuals who rally to a military cause might see restrictions on domestic liberties as a logical extension of the overall war effort, as Bush's actions and rhetoric advocating a large-scale war on terror would imply. Furthermore, just as trust in government leads some individuals to willingly cede power to the state in the presence of fear, general support for the policies of government in the international realm could lead to an increased willingness to submit to the authority of government in the domestic realm. The available data do not permit a detailed analysis of what drives the relationship between

FIGURE 7.2. Partisan gap in support for civil liberties, 1996–2006.

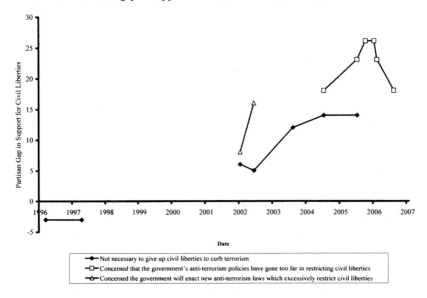

FIGURE 7.3. Partisan polarization in support for civil liberties, January 2006.

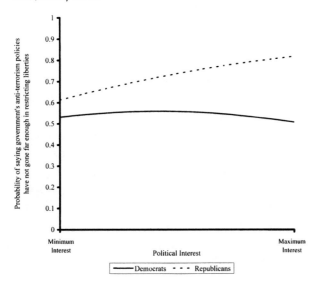

war support and judgments concerning civil liberties. Yet whatever the reason, given the potential threat to democracy caused by attempts to stifle dissent, the link between support for war and support for civil liberties is a crucial area of concern.

From 2001 to 2006 Pew used different questions to gauge respondents' willingness to engage in aggressive foreign action. In the wake of September 11, Pew asked, "Do you favor or oppose taking military action, including the use of ground troops, to retaliate against whoever is responsible for the terrorist attacks?"[33] Between 9/11 and the United States' invasion of Iraq in 2003, Pew asked respondents if they would support an invasion. After March 2003, Pew asked respondents a common version of the retrospective support question on Iraq, "Do you think the U.S. made the right decision or the wrong decision in using military force against Iraq?" Although these different items registered different levels of support, in all cases those respondents most supportive of military action—real or hypothetical, retrospective or prospective—were most willing to support restrictions on civil liberties, even controlling for those factors we know to influence both attitudes toward liberties and support for war, such as partisanship and perceptions of threat (see Huddy et al. 2005).[34] Figure 7.4 presents the effect of an increase in support for restricting liberties associated with a move from opposition to support for military action on six questions asked in the September 2001 survey.[35] Two of the items are taken from the over-time trends presented in figure 7.1. On the question of whether a respondent would be willing to trade civil liberties for security, supporters of military action were 13 percent more likely to advance restricting civil liberties than were opponents. On the question of whether the respondent was concerned that the government would unnecessarily enact new strong anti-terrorism laws, supporters of retaliation were 17 percent more likely to support enacting such anti-terrorism laws. Similar differences exist on the other civil liberties questions, ranging from 6 percent in support of a national identification card to 20 percent in support of allowing the government to monitor phone and e-mail conversations. These effects persisted even after the mean levels of support for civil liberties increased from 2002 to 2006 and a partisan gap opened on the question of the desirability of these restrictions (see fig. 7.5).

SUPPORT FOR THE VIETNAM WAR AND CIVIL LIBERTIES

The results concerning the relationship between support for war and support for restrictions on civil liberties in the present day are strong and

FIGURE 7.4. Relationship between support for retaliation for 9/11 and support for restricting civil liberties, September 2001.

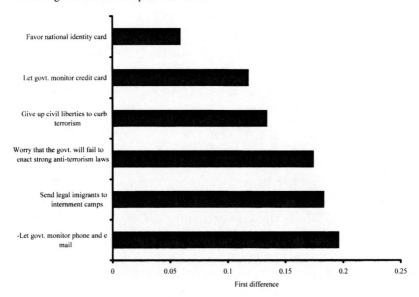

FIGURE 7.5. Relationship between support for the Iraq War and negative civil liberties judgments, 2001–6.

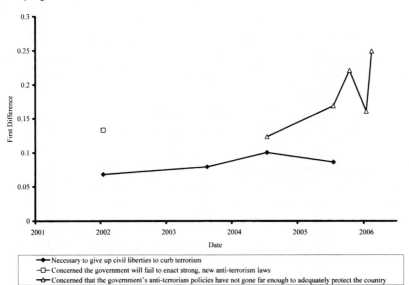

robust. It is possible, however, that these results are particular to the present political climate. In the immediate wake of 9/11, the link between a desire for an aggressive military response and the adoption of measures designed to ensure security could have resulted from a sudden shift in elite rhetoric or the existence of a salient threat to the United States. Over time, however, the political climate changed greatly. As figure 7.2 demonstrates, from 2002 onward, a large gap opened between Democrats and Republicans on questions of adopting restrictions on civil liberties, just as it did on questions of support for aggressive military action throughout the world (Jacobson 2008; see chap. 5). I can account for the extreme polarization along partisan lines in judgments concerning both military action and civil liberties judgments by controlling for partisan attachments in my statistical analyses. Perhaps, however, even measures of partisanship cannot fully capture the polarizing effect of the current political climate on both support for war and support for restrictions on civil liberties. To test the generality of these findings, it would be useful to examine the nature of this relationship in a less politically polarized time.

Such a task is easier said than done. There exists little individual-level survey data concerning civil liberties judgments during times of war. Potentially fruitful times, such as the Korean War era, are entirely devoid of data.[36] Fortunately, however, some relevant data exist from the Vietnam era. Louis Harris and Associates asked in November 1965 and May 1967 a pertinent question about free speech and dissent: "Do you think people have the right to conduct peaceful demonstration against the war in Vietnam, or do you feel people don't have that right?"[37] This question is phrased in a less general manner than the items analyzed from the present day, reflecting the era in which it was asked. As Erskine notes in a review of polling questions on civil liberties, "the semantics of the late 1960's in particular turned from simple freedom to speak to the right to protest and organize protests" (1970, 483). As a result, the question is not an ideal indicator of civil liberties judgments.[38] The Harris surveys are valuable in two respects, however. First, both of these surveys contain rich measures of support for the Vietnam War; it is therefore possible to create reliable scales of attitudes toward the war.[39] Second, and more important for present purposes, the polls were conducted at times that allow us to gauge the effect of war support on civil liberties judgments in political contexts that differ significantly from the present day. The 1965 poll was carried out at a time when support for the war was high among both Democrats and Republicans. The 1967 poll was conducted at the time of the emergence of the cleavage within the Democratic Party that lead to the decline in support for the Vietnam War, but before the emergence of partisan polarization on the war (see chap. 5 for discussion). Republicans were somewhat more supportive of protecting civil liberties than Democrats, but, reflecting the relative positions of the two parties on the war, the gap between the two parties was small.[40] These polls therefore enable us to gauge whether attitudes toward war are correlated with attitudes concerning civil liberties at a very different time in history.

The majority of respondents on both Harris surveys supported the rights of the protesters. In November 1965, 58 percent of respondents agreed that individuals should have the right to conduct peaceful demonstrations, and in May 1967, 61 percent took the pro–civil liberties side. As in the present day, however, this support was tempered among those most supportive of war. Figure 7.6 presents the relationship between levels of war support and the probability of advocating a restriction on the right of protest. Although the surveys were conducted in different political contexts and use somewhat different indices of war support, the results are the same; supporters of the Vietnam War were the most enthusiastic about restricting the liberties of its opponents. In 1965, a shift from the most extreme antiwar position to the most extreme prowar position increased the probability of supporting restrictions on civil liberties by 18 percent; in 1967 a comparable movement on the war-support scale increased support for restrictions by 25 percent. In sum, although the measures of commitment to civil liberties may not be as deep or broad as the measures found in the present day, in both cases the conclusion regarding the link between support for military action and commitment to tolerance is the same. Supporters of war are the most eager to restrict the liberties of others in society.

CIVIL LIBERTIES DURING WORLD WAR II

Finally, I turn to World War II. Following the themes of previous chapters, I find that World War II was not a unique moment in American history from the standpoint of public opinion concerning civil liberties. The public reacted in ways similar to that of their counterparts during the Vietnam era and the present day, and—more important for the argument in this book—public opinion regarding civil liberties was largely structured in ways consistent with patterns found in the domestic arena.

Comparable over-time data on support for civil liberties are thin for the World War II era. Gallup and OPOR, however, asked several items that directly tapped support for free speech. The first question concerned support

FIGURE 7.6. Support for the Vietnam War and civil liberties judgments.

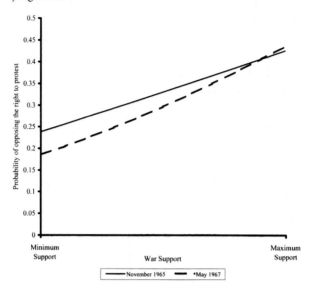

for the rights of Fascists and Communists; a second item asked about the rights of "radicals." Both of these questions were first asked in 1938, before open hostilities began, and were then asked at several points during the war.[41] These questions, of course, are problematic in some respects. Most important, both are affected by the concerns of comparability raised by the work of Sullivan, Pierson, and Marcus (1982). Public sentiment toward Communists and radicals undoubtedly changed during the course of the war, as the United States developed an alliance with Russia (albeit one of convenience). Before the war began, large segments of the population viewed Communists as a threat to America—a threat even greater than Fascists. For instance, when Gallup asked in 1939, "Which do you think is the greater danger to America—the Communists living in this country or the Nazis living in this country?" 33 percent of respondents replied that Communists posed the greater threat, compared to the 28 percent who said Nazis. Although Gallup did not define the term "radicals," the word's historical association with the Communist Party undoubtedly colored respondents' answers to the second civil liberties item. When Germany attacked Russia in June 1941, the meaning of the target groups changed. Communists—and perhaps "radicals"—might not have been worthy of embrace, but these groups were de facto allies of the United States in 1941 and formal allies by 1942.

It is possible, however, to account indirectly for the effect of changes in the sentiment toward the particular groups targeted by the civil liberties question. As noted in chapter 6, a common question asked during World War II was, "Do you think Russia can be trusted to cooperate with us when the war is over?" If we assume that individuals who did not trust Russia had greater negative affect toward radicals and felt greater threat than those who did trust the Soviet Union, then this question can be used as a rough proxy for negative sentiment toward "radicals."[42] We can therefore examine trends in tolerance among both the full sample and the subset of respondents who said they would not trust Russia after the war.

In figure 7.7 I present the trend data for the two free speech items, and two other items relating to civil liberties that are phrased in a more general manner—support for unconditional free speech and the belief that "people should be allowed to speak on any subject."[43] The measures on the two questions that mention target groups in June 1938 provide a baseline of support for the rights of all three groups before the war.[44] As the figure demonstrates, even before active fighting began, only a minority supported free speech for any of the marginal groups. Consistent with opinion data from the present day, however, the introduction of a salient international threat diminished support for civil liberties even further. The interesting point here is that support for civil liberties declined *before* the United States was attacked at Pearl Harbor. Thus, the onset of the climate of threat did not seem to occur in the immediate wake of Pearl Harbor, as some might expect, but rather during the early days of the war in 1940 and 1941. As figure 7.7 demonstrates, Gallup's question about Fascists and Communists shows a decline in support for extending civil liberties—to marginal groups in particular—after 1940.[45] Thus the data suggest that it was the gathering storm of war, not the attack at Pearl Harbor, that increased support for general restrictions on civil liberties.

Unfortunately no data exist to trace support for free speech for Fascists and Communists after the United States began active combat. OPOR did, however, repeat the Gallup question concerning free speech for radicals several times from 1942 to 1945. In July 1942, support for free speech stood 8 percent below the baseline reading of 1938. The trend data on the item concerning Fascists and Communist suggest that support for free speech may have dropped even further in the intermediate years, but without polling results it is impossible to say for sure. In any case, from July 1942 until the end of the war, support for civil liberties recovered—even among those respondents who did not trust Russia—exceeding the baseline readings

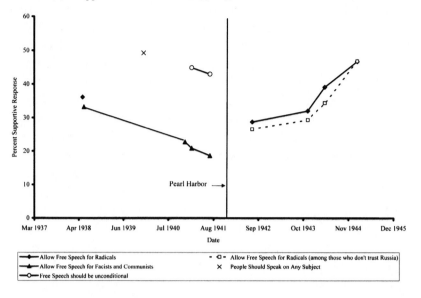

FIGURE 7.7. Support for civil liberties, 1938–45.

from 1938. Thus, although the period of "threat" began before the United States entered the war, support for civil liberties, following the pattern observed in the present day, seems to have recovered quickly from that initial threat.

The individual-level determinants of civil liberties judgments are also similar in many respects to those found both during times of peace and in the crisis of the first decade of the twenty-first century. For instance, the effect of threat follows a familiar pattern. Although there are no consistent individual-level indicators of threat, two surveys taken a year apart before the United States' entry into the war asked, "Do you think that Axis will attack us if Britain is defeated?" Although this measure does not tap the "worry" dimension of the current questions, it can serve as a rough, albeit imperfect, proxy for sociotropic threat. In July 1940, among those respondents who expressed an opinion, 62 percent believed the Axis would attack the United States. By July 1941 this figure had risen to 73 percent. More important, as in the present day, those respondents who felt threatened by the Axis were more supportive of restricting civil liberties than were respondents who did not feel threatened. In July 1940 respondents who believed the Axis countries would attack the United States were 4 percent more likely to support free speech restrictions than were respondents who did not feel so threatened. In July 1941, feelings of threat reduced support for free speech by 8 percent.[46] On the other hand, as during the Vietnam

War, partisanship did not have the impact on civil liberties judgments it does in the present day. Although supporters of FDR were less supportive of protecting civil liberties than were his opponents during the war years, these differences were small. Furthermore, much of the partisan difference can be accounted for by controlling for education level—a factor that was associated with both increased support for civil liberties and the tendency to vote for Republican candidates in this era. Moreover, the unification of opinion behind the war after the United States' entry in 1941 did not alter the partisan balance of opinion on civil liberties. Interestingly, then, it appears that support for civil liberties judgments did not follow the paths of partisan polarization that infected opinion about the war.

Returning to familiar patterns, however, I find that the relationship between support for war and restrictions on civil liberties in the period before the United States' entry into the war also mirrored that of the post 9/11 era. Figure 7.8 presents the effect of war support on intolerance for four polls taken from November 1940 to July 1941. In all cases, those most supportive of increased U.S. involvement were more supportive of restricting speech. This relationship holds both for questions that relate to tolerance toward specific groups and for more general questions relating to free speech.

Once the United States entered the war, not only did support for free speech increase, but contrary to the findings from the present day, the effect of war support on levels of free speech seems to have faded as well. As was the case in chapters 4 and 5, I am limited in my analysis of the effects of war support by the nature of the data. But, as before, I use support for the stated policy of unconditional surrender as a measure of war support. In the early period of the war, as expected, opposition to making peace with the German army was positively related to opposition to free speech. Over time, however, the relationship between the two quantities diminished. These results are presented in figure 7.9. In April 1942, the association between the two variables was reduced by half, and by early 1945 it had reversed direction. One complication with this analysis is that I am limited in the over-time analysis to a single imperfect measure of war support. For the April 1944 survey, I was able to examine the "refusal to make peace with Hitler" version of the unconditional surrender question in addition to the "German army" form of the question. Using the "Hitler" form of the question increases the positive relationship between war support and civil liberties restrictions. Those least supportive of allowing Hitler to unconditionally surrender are 8 percent more likely to support restricting the free speech of radicals, an effect much larger than the

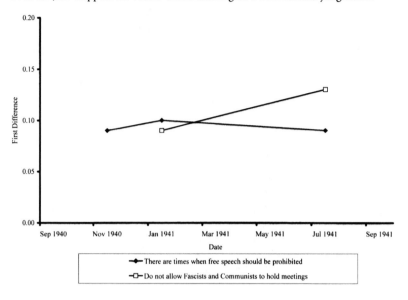

FIGURE 7.8. Support for World War II and negative civil liberties judgments.

There are times when free speech should be prohibited
Do not allow Fascists and Communists to hold meetings

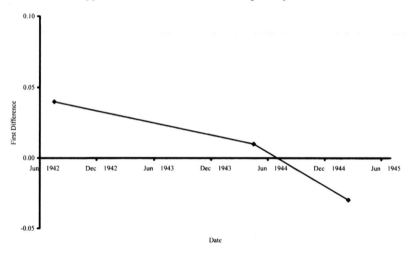

FIGURE 7.9. Support for World War II and allowing free speech for radicals.

effect reported in figure 7.9 for the same time period. This result does not, however, change my interpretation of the over-time change in the effect of war support presented in figure 7.9. During World War II, unlike the present day, an overall rise in support for civil liberties coincided with a reduction in the difference between those most supportive of stated U.S. war aims and the rest of the population.

CONCLUSION

In a democratic society, conditions of war inevitably lead to worries about civil liberties. As the analyses presented in this chapter demonstrate, such fears may be well-founded. War can diminish support for civil liberties both directly and indirectly. As in the domestic realm, the environment of fear and threat created by a state of crisis leads some citizens to support greater restrictions on certain basic democratic rights. Moreover, supporters of military action are generally most willing to suppress civil liberties.

War, however, does not inevitably threaten the foundations of democracy. Support for civil liberties may dip with the onset of conflict, but in the aggregate, support for such liberties seems to recover quickly. Moreover, the emergence of familiar domestic cleavages may in practice limit the scope of restrictions on liberties. Such a process can be seen in the post-9/11 era. While Republicans embraced both the general spirit and the particular provisions of the Patriot Act, over time Democrats came to reject these measures. As long as the opposition party maintains an independent position, the government may not be able to run roughshod over individual rights. Moreover, even in times of partisan consensus there may be checks on the power of government. During World War II, for instance, the effect of support for aggressive military action on civil liberties judgments was large initially but faded over time. In sum, for good and—as the case of the treatment of Japanese Americans during World War II demonstrates—for bad, civil liberties during times of war often follow the familiar patterns of civil liberties during times of peace. In both cases, perceptions of threat and attachments to political groups determine the scope of restrictions citizens are willing to bear.

CHAPTER EIGHT

ELECTIONS DURING WARTIME

Twenty months after the U.S.-led invasion of Iraq, citizens marched to the polls to cast their votes for president. From the beginning of the 2004 campaign, the Iraq War cast a long shadow over the election. Bush predicated his electoral strategy on embracing the role of commander in chief, and although he attempted to tie himself more closely to 9/11 and the larger war on terror than to Iraq, he could not distance his administration from the war that had begun under his watch. On the Democratic side, John Kerry won the presidential nomination in large part because his military experiences during the Vietnam War made him—at least in theory—an attractive candidate to the American public during a wartime election. Accordingly, media organizations focused much of their election coverage and analysis on the Iraq conflict. For instance, two weeks before the election, Edward Epstein wrote, "George W. Bush is the latest President to learn that wars tend to turn elections into referendums on the presidents who wage them and that Americans like a winner, not a president or his party's chosen successor who seem bogged down in an unwinnable conflict."[1] Moreover, the public seemed to respond to this coverage: in a poll released the night before the election, ABC News reported that the Iraq War was the most important issue on voters' minds, just slightly ahead of the economy and terrorism.

Although, in the immediate aftermath of the election, political commentators and journalists largely focused on the power of a cultural divide and associated "morals issues," the academic studies that emerged in the following months seemed to confirm the early predictions of the pundits.

Contrary to the "culture war" explanation reported widely in the media, many political scientists argued that beliefs about the Iraq War had a much greater impact on vote choice than did moral issues. For instance, Klinkner found that "whether or not a voter thought the Iraq war was worth it had a 57 percentage point difference in the probability of voting for Bush. In comparison, whether or not a voter supported gay marriage had only a 14 percentage point difference in the probability of voting for Bush" (2006, 288). Thus, voters' evaluations of the war in Iraq played a role even greater than their opinions on "cultural" or religious issues in their choice of presidential candidates.

Or so it seemed. In this chapter I take the stance of the contrarian and show that the causal assumptions underlying this conclusion fall wide of the mark. I argue that the typical analysis of the impact of war on the vote leads to misleading results. Indeed, such studies lead to counterintuitive findings that do not comport with cross-election trends. For instance, analyses of election study polls from 1952 and 1968 indicate that Democrats were not penalized for the Korean and Vietnam wars, even though, in both cases, the incumbent president withdrew from the race. The reason for these puzzling findings is straightforward. In chapter 5, I demonstrated that citizens differ in their support for wars because leaders they trust differ in their support for those wars, not the reverse. Given the partisan roots of opinion concerning war, it is extremely difficult—if not impossible—to uncover the effects of war by studying presidential contests in isolation through the use of the cross-sectional data employed by many scholars. As I show in this chapter, although cross-sectional analysis of opinion polls may measure the degree of polarization by the major-party candidates on issues related to the conduct of war, it cannot uncover the effect of the war on candidate choice because wars are judged through the lens of basic partisan predispositions.

This is not to say that wars cannot shape electoral outcomes. In the second half of the chapter, I shift gears and explore how war *does* affect elections. I argue that war influences elections in much the way that other domestic issues do. Although elections during wartime might, on their face, appear different from elections during times of peace, the underlying structure of choice is rooted in the same normal ebb and flow of domestic politics. Specifically, I conduct an in-depth analysis of the wartime elections of the 1940s and the 2000s to show that war impacts elections through two causal paths.

First, war, much like the economy, can function as a performance issue for leaders. When times are bad, incumbent politicians pay a price at the polls. Just as leaders may be punished for poor economic performance in the domestic realm, incumbent politicians can be hurt by bad news coming from abroad, even if those politicians seeking election are not directly responsible for the problems facing the nation.

Second, as in the realm of civil liberties, the state of fear and threat brought about by war can change the dynamics of political choice and the way in which citizens evaluate their leaders. Foreign crises may cause members of the electorate to place a high value on leadership, thereby benefiting the party in power. Thus although leaders do not seem to be directly rewarded for successful military incursions, the very condition of war may advantage those incumbents. As I show later in this chapter, both FDR and Bush, it seems, benefited from the conditions of crisis that began under their respective watches.

I close the chapter with a discussion of the British general election of 1945. The victory of the Labour Party over Churchill and the Conservatives underscores the central themes of this book. Even in the wake of a nation-saving military victory, a popular incumbent could not escape the tides of domestic politics.

SUPPORT FOR WAR AND ELECTORAL CHOICE

My analysis begins with a close look at the 2004 election. As noted earlier, much of the existing analysis confirms the critical importance of the Iraq War to the outcome of the 2004 election. Klinkner (2006), for one, claimed that the issue of the Iraq War was more than four times as important as that of gay marriage in determining a voter's preferred candidate. Similarly, Jacobson found that "relative support for Bush and Kerry varied dramatically according to whether or not voters approved of the war, believed it was part of the war on terrorism, had made the United States safer, and thought it was going well" (2008, 192–93). Adding to the chorus, Gelpi, Reifler, and Feaver (2007) concluded that retrospective judgments about the "rightness" of war were powerful predictors of vote choice in the 2004 election. Similar conclusions have been reached by Abramson et al. (2007), Hillygus and Shields (2005), and Weisberg and Christenson (2007). All told, a number of authors have used cross-sectional survey data to argue that the Iraq War was a critical issue in the 2004 election.

The apparent importance of the Iraq War as a campaign issue seems to increase when the 2004 election is placed in historical perspective. A comparison of the effect of war support on presidential votes across different wartime elections implies that Iraq is a uniquely powerful war. Table 8.1

TABLE 8.1 Estimated effect of opposition to war on the vote for the incumbent candidate

	Retrospective performance (%)	Prospective policy (%)	
		Withdrawal vs. status quo	Escalation/de-escalation scale
Korean War			
1952 NES	−8[a]**	−4[b]	—
Vietnam War			
1968 NES	−7[a]	−12[c]**	+18[d]**
1972 NES	−20[a]**	—	−51[d]**
Iraq War			
2004 CBS News	−56[e]**	—	—
2004 NES	−56[f]**	—	—
2004 PEW	−52[g]**	−33[h]**	—
2004 ABC News	−67[i]**	−34[j]**	—

Sources: Author analysis of opinion surveys; see online appendix for details

Note: A dash indicates that a question was not included in a given survey.

[a] "Do you think we did the right thing in getting into the fighting in (Korea two years ago / Vietnam) or should we have stayed out?"

[b] "Which of the following things do you think it would be best for us to do now in Korea? Pull out of Korea entirely, keep on trying to get a peaceful settlement, or take a stronger stand and bomb Manchuria and China?"

[c] "Which of the following do you think we should do now in Vietnam? Pull out of Vietnam entirely, keep our soldiers in Vietnam but try to end the fighting, or take a stronger stand even if it means invading?"

[d] "There is much talk about 'hawks' and 'doves' in connection with Vietnam, and considerable disagreement as to what action the United States should take in Vietnam. Some people think we should do everything necessary to win a complete military victory, no matter what results. Some people think we should withdraw completely from Vietnam right now, no matter what results. And, of course, other people have opinions somewhere between these two extreme positions. Suppose the people who support an immediate withdrawal are at one end of this scale at point number 1. And suppose the people who support a complete military victory are at the other end of the scale at point number 7. At what point on the scale would you place yourself?"

[e] "Do you think we did the right thing in taking military action against Iraq or should we have stayed out?"

[f] "Taking everything into account, do you think the war in Iraq has been worth the cost or not?"

[g] "Do you think the U.S. made the right decision or the wrong decision in using military force against Iraq?"

[h] "Do you think the U.S. should keep military troops in Iraq until the situation has stabilized, or do you think the U.S. should bring its troops home as soon as possible?"

[i] "All in all, considering the costs to the United States versus the benefits to the United States, do you think the war with Iraq was worth fighting, or not?"

[j] "Do you think the United States should keep its military forces in Iraq until civil order is restored there, even if that means continued U.S. military casualties, or do you think the United States should withdraw its military forces from Iraq in order to avoid further U.S. military casualties, even if that means civil order is not restored there?"

* $p < .10$; ** $p < .05$.

presents the relationship between opposition to war and vote choice for each of the post–World War II presidential elections held during times of war: 1952 (Korea), 1968 (Vietnam), 1972 (Vietnam), and 2004 (Iraq).[2] The entries in the table essentially replicate Klinkner's analysis of the 2004 election and represent the apparent effect of voters' opposition to a war on the probability that they will vote for the incumbent candidate.[3] The size of this effect is estimated by comparing the respondent who is most supportive of the war to the respondent who is most opposed to that war, while controlling for partisanship, race, gender, region of residence, education, and income.[4] Negative probabilities indicate that citizens who disapprove of current war policy are less likely to vote for the incumbent's party. I separate out those questions that ask about retrospective performance — items that ask if a given war was "worth the cost" or the "right thing" to do — from those items that tap prospective policy — whether the United States should "pull out" of a given conflict or "do everything necessary to win a complete military victory." Because several questions use somewhat different wording to tap the same concerns, I present all available polls and the full text of the questions in the table.[5]

Considering first those questions that ask about retrospective approval, we see the table shows that the gap between a war's supporters and its opponents was nearly three times as large in 2004 as it was in any previous election.[6] Moving to the prospective questions, we see that the same pattern appears. Although comparisons are rendered difficult by the lack of consistent wording among the questions, the gap in the 2004 election between respondents who supported withdrawal and those who wished to maintain current levels of military effort seems much larger than in any other election.

Another way to measure the effect of attitudes toward war on the election outcome is to assess what Achen (1982) calls the "level importance statistic" — the actual influence of an independent variable on a dependent variable in a particular sample. This quantity is simply the product of the mean of a given variable and its corresponding regression coefficient.[7] The level importance measure allows us to account not only for differences in the potential impact of different wars but also for differences in the actual levels of support for various conflicts at the time of the relevant election. Such a measure should be familiar to election scholars; Miller and Shanks (1996) compute a statistic similar in spirit to Achen's measure to assess what portion of the aggregate results of a given election can be attributed to a particular issue.

The results of this analysis for the retrospective evaluation questions are presented in figure 8.1. Although there is some variation in the esti-

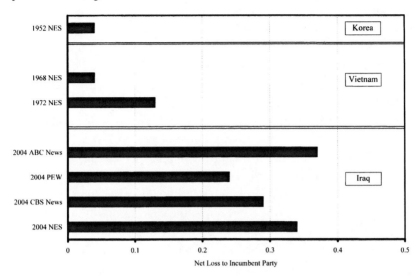

FIGURE 8.1. Estimated net contribution of retrospective evaluations of war on presidential voting.

mate of the apparent effect of the Iraq War, the comparison of the effects across the different wars is the same as that uncovered in table 8.1. In both 1952 and 1968, the war seemed to have cost the Democratic Party about 5 percent of the two-party vote, a figure smaller than the 13 percent loss experienced by the Republican Party and arising from the Vietnam War in 1972, and much smaller than the 31 percent loss arising from the Iraq War in 2004.[8] All told, then, the analysis seems to indicate that 2004 was indeed a historic election.

The Effect of War Revisited

Perhaps, though, the story here is not as straightforward as it appears at first glance. On closer examination, the results presented in table 8.1 and figure 8.1 are somewhat puzzling. For instance, consider the elections held during the Vietnam and Iraq wars. Both the 1968 and 2004 presidential contests took place in the shadows of extended foreign wars. In both years, the original justification for the conflict—the attack on American forces in the Gulf of Tonkin in Vietnam and the need to prevent Saddam Hussein from deploying weapons of mass destruction in the case of Iraq—were highly contested by the time of the election. In spite of this, the cross-sectional analysis paints a very different picture of the effects of opposition to the war for the two elections. The effect of retrospective opposition to the Vietnam War on the vote in 1968 appears to be the smallest of any election in figure 8.1—approximately one-seventh of the total effect of retrospective evaluations of war, as gauged by a similarly worded question asked by ABC News about Iraq in 2004—and not statistically significant. If these results are to be believed, Bush paid a price for his position on the war, whereas Humphrey was inexplicably able to shrug off the very issue that drove Lyndon Johnson from office only six months earlier.

Of course there are several reasons why these conflicts could exhibit different dynamics. One potential difference between the two elections is the mere fact that Humphrey ran on Johnson's record, whereas Bush ran on his own. Analysis of data from the 1968 NES demonstrates, however, that Humphrey was unable to shake the public's perception of his strong ties to the Johnson administration. In 1968, the NES asked respondents to evaluate twelve political figures on a "feeling thermometer scale" in the postelection poll. As Boyd (1972) notes, the correlations of respondents' feelings about Humphrey and Johnson were higher than for any other pair of political figures—higher even than the pairing of Humphrey and his own vice presidential candidate, Edmund Muskie.[9] More important, Johnson and Humphrey were also tightly linked in the public mind on the question of policy concerning Vietnam. Page and Brody (1972) compare the public's placement of Humphrey, Johnson, and Nixon, using the seven-point NES escalation/de-escalation scale described in table 8.1. Page and Brody found that the public placed all three candidates quite close together.[10] Johnson and Humphrey, however, were especially close. Analysis of the 1968 data shows that Humphrey's and Johnson's positions were correlated at 0.72, nearly four times as large as the 0.19 correlation between Johnson and Nixon.[11] Figure 8.2 charts the distribution of placements for Nixon, Johnson, and Humphrey, graphically demonstrating the strong link between Humphrey and the president. In short, Humphrey and Johnson were viewed in the public's mind as nearly interchangeable candidates, which makes the small effect of the war on Humphrey's vote in 1968 even more puzzling.[12]

A close comparison of elections held during Vietnam raises further questions about the individual-level analysis presented in table 8.1. In both 1968 and 1972, the incumbent party was hurt by retrospective evaluations of the war. Opponents of the war were less likely to vote for Humphrey, the Democrat, in 1968 and were less likely to vote for Nixon, the incumbent Republican president, in 1972 (although this effect was not statistically significant in 1968). Interestingly, the relationship between war disapproval and the vote seems to be nearly three times as large in 1972 as it was in 1968. Moreover, the relationship between the seven-point escalation/de-

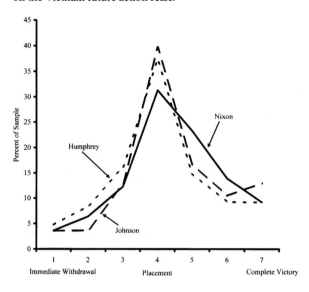

escalation scale and the vote increased greatly from 1968 to 1972, seemingly
providing further support for the assertion that the Vietnam War was an
even more important issue in 1972 than it was in 1968. But such a conclusion seems at odds with a reasoned interpretation of the election results.
Nixon's margin of victory over McGovern in 1972 was much larger than his
margin over his opponents in 1968. But if we believe the individual-level
results, Vietnam should have been a greater drag on his vote in 1972. In
1972, after all, it was Nixon who was hurt by those who disapproved of the
war, not his Democratic opponent. Moreover the increased importance
of the escalation/de-escalation scale in the 1972 election does not square
with the election results. Indeed, from 1968 to 1972 the country as a whole
moved in a more dovish direction; according to the NES data, the percentage of people who took a position on the de-escalation side of the future
policy scale increased from 30 percent to 45 percent over that time.

All told, the individual-level analysis does not lead to a plausible or
coherent story about the effect of war on different elections. Bush seems
to have suffered a tremendous penalty for initiating the Iraq War—on
the order of 25 to 30 percentage points—yet he was elected to a second
term, albeit in a close vote. By contrast, although Stevenson lost handily
to Eisenhower, he seemed to bear little cost for the intervention in Korea
begun by the incumbent president of his own party. The Vietnam-era elections are puzzling as well. In 1968 Johnson withdrew from the race after

the New Hampshire primary in March, but the individual-level analysis indicates that the war barely affected the public's electoral calculus. In 1972, by contrast, the war appears to have cost Nixon 15 percent of the vote, in an election in which he stormed to a 23-point victory over George McGovern. In short, when considered in the context of the history of presidential elections during wartime, the individual-level analysis of the impact of war on electoral outcomes is perplexing at best.

Aggregate Analysis: Predicting Election Outcomes

The puzzle deepens further if we move to the aggregate level and expand the scope of analysis to include elections held during times of peace as well as those held during times of war. Over the last thirty years, a cottage industry has grown up around statistical models designed to predict presidential election results.[13] These models typically use aggregate measures of economic and political fundamentals, such as presidential approval and ideological positioning, to determine likely vote share. Almost all forecasting models predict election outcomes at least in part as a function of indicators of economic performance—such as changes in the gross domestic product (GDP) or real disposable income (RDI).[14] The most appropriate indicator of economic performance is a matter of heated debate. Bartels and Zaller (2001), however, test a variety of measures and find that the variable that best explains electoral outcomes is a measure of change in RDI, weighted by a factor that discounts past change in disposable income at an exponential rate—a measure first advanced by Hibbs (2000). Of course there are many factors that can affect the outcome of an election, but this measure provides a baseline to see how particular electoral outcomes differ from what we would predict based on economic performance alone.

In figure 8.3, I present the relationship between weighted change in RDI and the vote for the presidential candidate of the incumbent's party for the elections from 1952 to 2004.[15] The most striking feature of this figure is the disconnect between this analysis and the individual-level analysis presented in figure 8.1. Although that earlier analysis indicated that opinion on war exerted the greatest influence in the 2004 contest, Bush's vote total in that election falls almost precisely on the regression line, indicating that economic factors alone may explain the electoral outcome.[16] By contrast—and again at variance with the individual-level analysis in figure 8.1—the incumbent's party did much worse in the 1952 and 1968 elections than one would expect on the basis of economic performance.[17] In other words, the conditions of war should have hurt the incumbent's party the

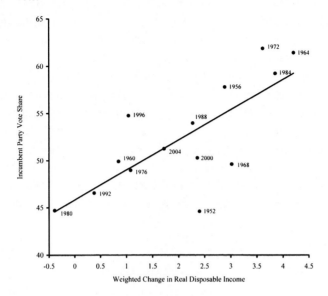

FIGURE 8.3. Weighted change in real disposable income as a predictor of the incumbent party vote share of the two-party vote.

most in these two elections (given the discrepancy between the predicted electoral performance and the actual electoral performance).

The anomalous nature of the wartime elections of 1952 and 1968 is not simply a function of the particular specification employed here. Using a variety of measures of economic performance and other political variables, several scholars have documented the unique character of those contests. For instance, Rosenstone (1983) argues for the inclusion of a measure of support for the war for the 1952 and 1968 elections in his voting model to account for the underperformance of the incumbent party in those contests. [18] Bartels and Zaller (2001) find that a simple dummy variable for the war years of 1952 and 1968 improves the accuracy of vote predictions, regardless of which economic indicator they use to model the outcome of the election.[19] Thus it is clear from the aggregate analysis of electoral outcomes that the elections of 1952 and 1968 are different from the other elections in the post–World War II period. In both cases, the incumbent's party did much worse than the measures of economic performance indicated they should.

These results, taken together with those presented in the preceding section, leave us with a muddled picture. For those cases in which the aggregate-level analysis shows that the incumbent party was more hurt relative to baseline economic performance—1952 and 1968—the individual-level analysis shows little or no effect of war. And for the election in which the individual-level analysis indicates that the war should have most hurt the president's party—namely, 2004—the outcome is almost exactly predicted by economic performance. Although the argument could be made that Bush did suffer a penalty for Iraq but it was balanced by a gain in public approval for his performance after 9/11, it is difficult to advance a consistent account that plausibly explains the divergence of the individual-level and aggregate analyses across all the postwar elections. Put another way, one might be able to tell a reasonable story about the magnitude of the regression coefficients on war support in any given election—as scholars such as Klinkner (2006) have done—but the combined analysis of individual elections does not fit neatly together. All told, the individual-level analysis in table 8.1 and figure 8.1 makes little intuitive sense.

ELITE POSITIONING AND ELECTORAL OUTCOMES

How then can we make sense of these seemingly anomalous findings? Although no previous scholar has compared the individual-level and aggregate-level analysis for the entire post–World War II election series as I have above, the 1968 presidential election has attracted some attention.[20] This election poses a puzzle not simply for scholars who study war and public opinion, but for those interested in investigating the impact of issues on the vote decision more generally. As Page and Brody note, "despite the unusually high salience of the Vietnam war in 1968, the conventional wisdom about American electoral politics remained true: policy preferences had little effect on the major-party vote (1972, 993–94).[21] In essence, Page and Brody identify the same problem underscored by the multi-election analysis presented in figure 8.1: opinion about the Vietnam War did not affect vote choice in 1968, when by all rights it should have played a large role.

Page and Brody's solution to this conundrum was to look at the position of the candidates on the conduct of war. As noted earlier, the average citizen saw almost no difference between the positions of Nixon and Humphrey on the war.[22] This ambiguity in the public mind reflected the rhetoric of Nixon and Humphrey. Page and Brody analyzed the campaign speeches of the two candidates and concluded that there was indeed actually little difference between Nixon's and Humphrey's stated positions on Vietnam policy. As they note, both candidates advocated "war as usual, with a rather gradual de-escalation of American effort if and when certain conditions were met. Members of the public were entirely justified in seeing Nixon and Humphrey as standing close together near the center of the Vietnam policy scale" (Page and Brody 1972, 985).

As discussed in chapter 5, the positions of Humphrey and Nixon were fairly representative of their respective parties. The split over Vietnam emerged first within the Democratic Party, becoming a partisan issue only after the 1968 election. It is therefore not surprising that the predicted effect of war would pale in comparison to other factors in the context of the 1968 election. In the absence of any difference between the candidates on the issue of Vietnam, the *estimate* of the effect of the war on the vote would be small regardless of the true effect of the war on the election.

This difficulty in interpreting cross-sectional coefficients as causal effects is akin to the problems involved in estimating the effect of the economy on electoral outcomes. Kramer's (1983) critique of the economic voting literature argues that the correlation between vote choice and economic perceptions is a result of voters bringing their economic assessments into line with their political judgments. Similarly, the causal arrow between a vote for president and support for war may run from the former to the latter, rather than vice versa. Indeed, the elite cue theory described in chapter 4 and explicated in chapter 5 provides strong support for this conjecture. In situations in which political leaders provide clear cues concerning the wisdom of foreign entanglements, their supporters among the public follow suit. In war, as with the economy, people take their cues from political leaders, judging policy and performance through the lens of their preexisting political predispositions.[23] Page and Brody's (1972) analysis of the 1968 election, therefore, provides a key insight for analysis of the relationship between wartime opinion and election outcomes more generally. When the candidates agree on the future course of a war—as Humphrey and Nixon did in 1968—the apparent effect of war on the vote will be small. On the other hand, when they disagree—as Nixon and McGovern did in 1972—the estimated effect of opinion about war on the vote will be large, not because evaluations of war determine vote choice but because individuals' partisan leanings shape opinion about war.[24] Moreover, merely controlling for other factors that are related to attitudes about war and to electoral choice—such as partisanship—cannot solve this problem. In fact, as Achen (1986) aptly demonstrates, the use of control variables may only exacerbate the difficulty. This dynamic is not unique to attitudes about war. In fact, the discussion here should cast doubt on any analysis that uses attitudes on polarized issues to explain vote choice.

This perspective can illuminate the pattern of individual-level findings shown in figure 8.1. By 1972, what had changed about Vietnam was not the true effect of the war on the election. In fact, figure 8.3 shows that Nixon did *better* than would be predicted by the performance of the economy. Instead, what changed was the partisan structure of war support. It was not until after Nixon ascended to the presidency that a split emerged between Republicans and Democrats at the mass and elite levels (see chap. 5). The increase in the magnitude of the relationship of attitudes toward the war and vote choice between 1968 and 1972 is a direct result of the polarizing effect of Nixon's presidency on attitudes toward the war.

In Iraq, we can see an extreme realization of the types of changes that occurred from 1968 to 1972 over the Vietnam War. The unique circumstances of Bush's presidency—beginning with his contested win in the 2000 election—led to a partisan polarization of the electorate across a variety of issues, most notably the Iraq War. As Jacobson (2008) notes, Bush was "a divider, not a uniter." Iraq in 2004 appears to be a much more important issue in the election than Vietnam was in 1968, not because it exerted a larger electoral impact but because the public was much more polarized along partisan lines in 2004 than it was in 1968, even though the mean levels of support for the two wars were not radically different.

Although they may not measure the effect of the war on election outcomes, the cross-sectional analyses presented in table 8.1 seem to measure the degree of polarization on the war issue by the major parties' candidates. In elections with little or no elite polarization—the contests of 1952 and 1968—the individual-level analysis shows little effect of war on the vote. By contrast, in those cases in which one candidate took a position distinct from that of the other candidate—the elections of 1972 and 2004—war appears to have had a large effect on candidate choice.[25]

Retrospective Evaluations

At the same time, it is important to recognize that, under certain circumstances, war may play a role in determining *collective* electoral choice. Just as a downturn in the economy can hurt an incumbent, even if members of his party continue to support him, a lack of war success may hurt a sitting president. Given the importance of partisanship and elite leadership on opinions of war, however, any effects of war will be apparent only at the aggregate level. As figure 8.3 demonstrates, it appears that the Democratic candidates were hurt by war in 1952 and 1968 simply because they shared the same political party as the incumbent president. Just as with economic voting models (Erikson 2004; Kramer 1983), only over-time analysis of voting trends can control for the impact of partisan influence on policy evaluations in any single election. Thus, although Gelpi, Reifler, and Feaver's (2007) cross-sectional perspective on the effects of war success may be flawed—as discussed in chapter 4—their over-time perspective, which can incorporate changes in the central tendencies of media and political figures, can be informative. Success—or more precisely, the absence of success—can matter in elections.

Once we recognize the importance of candidate positioning for vote choice, the role of independent voters can be better understood. True independents—those individuals who do not lean toward either of the two major political parties—represent only a small portion of the citizenry and an even smaller portion of the voting public (Keith et al. 1992). At key times, however, the 5 percent of the electorate that does not hold partisan attachments may play a decisive role in elections. If these voters choose to punish the incumbent administration, they may prove decisive; independents who cast votes retrospectively may tip the scales against incumbent administrations, even in the face of straight partisan voting by the vast majority of the electorate.

This somewhat pessimistic discussion of the locus of electoral control is important because it can affect the lessons we take away from particular election outcomes. Just because voters collectively act to punish incumbents for past failings does not mean that they behave rationally, even in the aggregate. The particular retrospective framework advanced by Achen and Bartels (2002) is especially enlightening. In these authors' view, citizens are not logical or calculating but rather tend to focus on short-term developments divorced from any larger meaning. They find that citizens punish leaders for bad news, whatever its source. Bad economic times could be shown to cause citizens to vote against incumbents. But Achen and Bartels also find that floods and shark attacks lead the electorate to punish those in power. From this perspective, any retrospective effect of war on election outcomes should not be taken as a sign of a deep rationality. Once the media provides the signal that a war is not progressing well—especially if they are indexing the judgments of politicians—the electorate can just as easily turn against the incumbent as they would in the wake of an uptick in shark attacks or a spell of bad weather.

PATTERNS OF INFLUENCE: ELITE LEADERSHIP AND ELECTORAL ADVANTAGE

The analysis of voting patterns over the last fifty years presented in figure 8.2 indicates that presidents may suffer consequences at the polls for wars that do not go well, but might they also gain electoral support for successful military efforts? From Achen and Bartels' (2002) perspective, leaders should not expect to be rewarded for such endeavors; in their view, after all, voters are blindly vindictive, only punishing incumbents for poor performance. But not all scholars agree with this position. Whether or not incumbents are rewarded for success remains an open question. There is, in fact, a large body of work in international relations that explicitly argues that leaders in democracies can gain from international interventions. Diversionary war theory holds that leaders may respond to unfavorable domestic circumstances by pursuing interventions abroad (Lebow 1981; Rosecrance 1963). Presidents, in essence, may distract the public from "bad times" with a "good war."[26] The empirical foundation for this theory is, however, weak. For instance, although Chiozza and Goemans (2004) find that winning a war can extend the tenure of political leaders in some regimes, victory has no effect on the electoral fortunes of leaders in democracies.[27] In a similar vein, Gaubatz (1999) argues that democratic leaders are, in fact, less likely to go to war in the period just before an election than they are at the beginning of their term of office. One reason for the thin record of support for diversionary war theory may be found in the same balance of domestic political forces discussed in chapter 4. As Schultz (2001) notes, politicians who oppose military interventions that turn out to be successful can pay a price at the polls.

The behavior of both the in-party and the out-party matters, however. Arena (2008), for instance, finds that the electoral gain for the incumbent party from a successful war is predicated on the behavior of the domestic political opposition. Incumbents can gain at the polls only when they initiate wars that are ultimately successful *and* when the political opposition expresses resistance to that conflict. Given the strategic incentives for political leaders from both sides of the aisle, it is not surprising that this set of circumstances almost never occurs. Under some circumstances, the opposition may miscalculate and take this course of action. But as Schultz (2001) notes, the out-party must "choose its battles wisely"—by contesting the wisdom of only those wars they expect will not play well with the domestic audience. The empirical record suggests that politicians do a fairly good job at making such calculations. Arena finds that the out-party did not oppose or even criticize any war that ended in victory in any election since World War II in the United States, the United Kingdom, Israel, or India. Thus, in line with the expectation of Achen and Bartels, it seems there is little direct gain to incumbents to be had from favorable performance in war.

This is not to say that incumbency is without its advantages. After all, the long literature on rally effects in the approval ratings of politicians suggests otherwise. It could be, however, that the dynamics of war, rather than the particular circumstances of a given war, create situations that benefit incumbents. In the previous chapter I discussed how war can create conditions of threat and fear in a society that lead individuals to cede authority to the state. Merolla, Ramos, and Zechmeister (2007) demonstrate that conditions of crisis such as war may also change the dynamics of elections. Specifically, Merolla and her colleagues argue that crises heighten the persistence and effects of charismatic political leadership. Using experimental data, they find that during these times, "citizens focus attention on strong leaders, projecting additional leadership qualities onto likely candidates and perceiving differences in candidates' leadership capabilities in starker terms" (2007, 1). Moreover, they find that citizens place greater weight on leadership traits in their voting decisions during crises. This dynamic is not simply an effect of war in and of itself. It is the persistence of a crisis—be it of domestic or foreign origin—that stimulates the salience of leadership judgments.[28] When a crisis is externally provoked, incumbent leaders are the most likely beneficiaries of the heightened perceptions of charisma, regardless of their personal characteristics (Merolla, Ramos, and Zechmeister 2007). Of course, there may be exceptions to this pattern. The 2004 election in Spain, for instance, does not seem to follow these dynamics.[29] But the theory seems to provide a plausible baseline for electoral behavior. Thus, although leaders may be punished for events outside of their control—as Achen and Bartels (2002) aptly note—incumbent leaders may also achieve an electoral gain in response to crises both because the public views incumbents as better leaders during such times and because those with leadership qualities have a larger impact on vote choice than they would at other times.

George W. Bush and the War on Terror

To explore the relationship between threat and vote choice, I turn to the 2000 to 2004 election cycle. The dynamics of choice across these elections appear to bear out the findings of Merolla, Ramos, and Zechmeister (2007) in the context of the "war on terror." It is apparent that the three elections were held under very different circumstances. Figure 8.4 presents over-time public opinion data for two questions directly related to levels of perceived threat in the public at large: (1) the percentage of respondents who said they were "very worried" about a future terrorist attack and (2) the percentage who said they believed a terrorist attack was "very likely."

FIGURE 8.4. Trends in fear of terrorism, 2001–7.

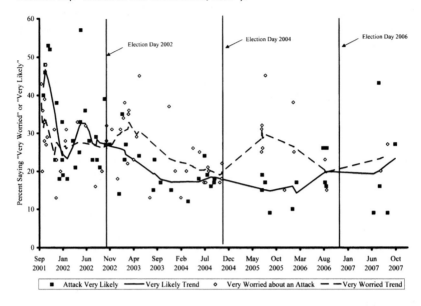

I present both the individual data points and a smoothed trend line for these two series.[30] Although the two questions do not move in lockstep, some common trends can be found.[31] The percentage of people who were "very worried" and thought that another attack was "very likely" began to decline soon after the initial spike around September 11, whereas levels of fear remained fairly high through the end of 2002. The 2002 election, therefore, took place in an environment of elevated threat (compared to the 2000 presidential election). The "very likely" series continued its downward trend through 2003 and 2004. The "very worried" series followed suit beginning in mid-2003. Thus, levels of threat were much lower in 2004 than they were in 2002. Although levels of threat trended upward in mid-2005—perhaps reflecting elevated coverage of terrorism in the wake of the London bombing in July of that year—by the fall of 2006, the "very worried" series tended to its lowest levels of the time series, and the "very likely" series continued to stand below its 2002 level.[32]

To determine whether individual-level reactions to different levels of threat conformed to the expectations of Merolla, Ramos, and Zechmeister (2007), I examine data concerning support for President Bush from the National Elections Study from 2000 to 2004. These studies were part of a panel design, so it is possible to look at the same individuals over the entire election series. Figure 8.5 presents the mean respondent evaluation of

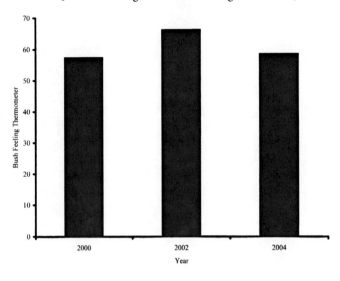

FIGURE 8.5. Bush's feeling thermometer ratings, 2000–2004.

Bush, as reflected in his feeling thermometer scores.[33] As expected, positive evaluations of Bush rose from 2000 to 2002, before dropping off in 2004. Admittedly, the differences here are small, but in close elections such small differences can have a large impact on the electoral outcome. The source of this surge and decline can be found in perceptions of Bush's abilities, as Merolla, Ramos, and Zechmeister would predict. Figure 8.6 demonstrates that ratings of Bush's leadership indeed rose from 2000 to 2002 before declining in 2004, as perceptions of threat receded.[34] Moreover, as Merolla, Ramos, and Zechmeister also predict, much of the rally to Bush can be explained by the dynamics of leadership. Figure 8.7 presents the regression coefficient for leadership evaluations on feeling thermometer scores, when controlling for the partisanship and demographic characteristics of the respondents.[35] The figure demonstrates that, as predicted, the relationship between the two quantities strengthened from 2000 to 2002 and remained steady through 2004.[36] Together these results suggest that the increased levels of threat in 2002 gave Bush—and, by extension, Bush's party—an electoral boost. Although the effect of leadership on Bush's feeling thermometer levels was the same in 2004 as in 2002, the mean level of leadership declined over time, to levels similar to those found in 2000, thereby accounting for some dissipation of the rally.[37] Although similar data do not exist for 2006, figure 8.4 suggests that a further decline in levels of threat after 2004 may have continued the dissipation of Bush's rally.

FIGURE 8.6. Bush's leadership ratings, 2000–2004.

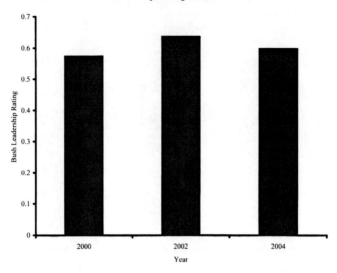

FIGURE 8.7. Relationship between Bush's leadership and Bush's feeling thermometer, 2000–2004.

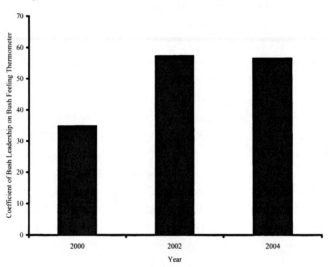

ELECTIONS DURING WORLD WAR II

The dynamics of threat and leadership seem to account for the rally to Bush in post-9/11 America, both in the laboratory (Merolla, Ramos, and Zechmeister 2007; Merolla and Zechmeister 2009) and in the observational data reported here. These dynamics may also account for rallies to FDR during the World War II period. Although the polls from this time do not contain the leadership measures necessary to fully explore the causal claims advanced by Merolla, Ramos, and Zechmeister, available survey data suggest that even before the United States' entry into the war, the change in the climate of threat caused by war aided FDR's political fortunes. If the polls are to be believed, the mere threat of war returned FDR to office for an unprecedented length of tenure.

Just after the outbreak of the Second World War, in September 1939, Gallup twice asked if respondents would vote for FDR for an unprecedented and controversial third term under two different conditions: (1) if the war were ongoing and (2) if the war were over (see table 8.2). In both cases, the polls indicated that FDR would receive a majority of support if war continued through the 1940 election and would lose decisively if the war ended.[38] More crucially, FDR's shifting fortunes depending on the possible resolution of the war were the sole result of defections from FDR; almost no supporters of the Republican candidate switched their vote between the two scenarios.

Polling data collected four years later demonstrate a similar pattern of support for FDR in the 1944 presidential contest. Before the 1944 election, a variety of polling organizations repeated an exercise analogous to Gallup's. In early 1944, both Gallup and OPOR asked a question similar in form to the one asked in 1939, with the additional scenario of electoral choice under the condition that "the end of war was clearly in sight" (OPOR) or the war "might be over in a few weeks or months" (Gallup). As in 1939, the end of the war appeared to translate into electoral defeat for FDR (see table 8.3). These results are not limited to the early electoral season. Beginning in 1943 and continuing through the end of 1944, Roper asked respondents about their voting intentions six times (see table 8.3). In every case, the polls predicted that FDR would win the election if the war continued and would lose handily if the war were over in both the European and the Pacific theaters. In the event that only the war in Europe were over, the race between FDR and his (sometimes unnamed) Republican opponent would be tight. Although it is not possible to directly attribute these results to an increase in the public's attribution of leadership qualities to FDR, it is

TABLE 8.2 War scenarios and percent vote for FDR in the 1940 election

Vote FDR to a third term?

	September 18, 1939	September 26, 1939
War ongoing	53	55
War over	45	47

Sources: Author analysis of AIPO 169 and AIPO 170.

clear that the war changed how respondents thought about the presidential elections in 1940 and 1944—or, at the very least—how they thought they might think about their choices in those contests.

What is especially interesting from a historical perspective is that FDR himself appears to have known about these dynamics. Casey (2001) reports that Cantril kept the president informed of the close relationship between the fortunes of war and FDR's reelection campaign in 1944. Cantril specifically warned FDR that if the American people became convinced that that the war would be over before Election Day, they would vote against the Democratic candidate. According to Casey, the White House asked Cantril to keep the data away from both Gallup and the press. Furthermore, FDR went on a public relations offensive to make the case, mainly through White House spokespeople, that the war would not be over before 1945 (Casey 2001). Setting aside the fact that Gallup himself conducted similar polls—reported in table 8.3—not to mention that this same information was regularly published in *Fortune* magazine throughout the fall of 1944, it seems that the polls may have changed FDR's electoral strategy.

That said, the results presented in tables 8.2 and 8.3 should be taken with a grain of salt. After all, these surveys asked respondents to assess their likely behavior in a hypothetical situation. Whether they would have actually voted that way in the event of peace is a matter of conjecture. The face validity of these results is, however, bolstered by two additional pieces of evidence.

First, a survey experiment conducted by Gallup provides evidence that the results do not merely reflect respondents' attempts to adjust their vote choice to changing hypothetical situations. Pollsters typically asked each respondent how they would behave across a variety of different scenarios. Research on the question-answering process suggests that respondents who were first asked if they would vote for FDR in the event of an ongoing

TABLE 8.3 War scenarios and percent vote for FDR in the 1944 election

Gallup and OPOR

Vote for FDR if . . .	March 1944 (OPOR)	April 1944 (Gallup)
War ongoing	56	54
End of war clearly in sight	47	48
War over	37	38

Roper

Vote for FDR if . . .	March 1943	February 1944	April 1944	June 1944
War ongoing	65	57	55	54
European war over	—	53	51	49
European and Pacific war over	33	44	44	41

Vote for FDR if . . .	Early October 1944	Late October 1944
Vote were today	50	49
Germany surrendered	45	43

Sources: Author analysis of OPOR 23 (March 1944), AIPO 316 (April 1944), Roper 34 (March 1943), Roper 38 (February 1944), Roper 39 (April 1944), Roper 40 (June 1944), Roper 43 (October 1944), and Roper 44 (October 1944).

Note: The dash indicates that the "European war over" option was not given in the March 1943 Roper survey.

war might see no other choice but to adjust their likelihood downward in the event of a termination of hostilities. In effect, the within-subject design used by the pollsters may have determined the pattern of results found in tables 8.2 and 8.3. In 1943, however, Gallup ran an experiment in which interviewers randomly asked one-half of the sample if they would support FDR if the war were ongoing and the other half how they would vote if the "war was over soon." We can compare the effect of this between-subjects design to the within-subject design employed in the surveys reported in tables 8.2 and 8.3. As table 8.4 demonstrates, the estimate of the effect—about six percentage points—is roughly the same for the comparable question asked by Gallup one year earlier.

The second piece of evidence concerns the face validity of the results presented in tables 8.2 and 8.3. The Roper October 1944 surveys had, in addition to the hypothetical war scenario, an item that essentially serves as a four-point scale measuring support for FDR.[39] A cross-tabulation of the two questions demonstrates that the ongoing war held weak identifiers in FDR's camp; in both surveys it was those respondents with loosely held beliefs who shifted their votes among the different scenarios. Specifically, although Dewey and FDR held their strong supporters at roughly equal rates under the two scenarios, weak FDR supporters were much more likely to change their votes under the scenario in which the war was over than were weak Dewey supporters (see table 8.5).

THE BRITISH GENERAL ELECTION OF 1945

All told, the evidence suggests that FDR's reelection efforts were helped by the ongoing hostilities in the European and Pacific theaters. Perhaps, then, we can learn more by looking across the Atlantic to the election held in England in the wake of V-E day—one in which Churchill, the victorious British prime minister, was unceremoniously dumped from office.

The 1945 British general election was highly unusual in that it was the first contest to be held in England in almost ten years. In 1935, the Conservative Party had lost a large number of seats but still held nearly twice as many seats as all other parties in Parliament combined. The outbreak of World War II interrupted the normal election cycle. In September 1939, all major parties in the House of Commons agreed to an electoral truce; according to this policy, in place of a by-election, the party whose member had vacated a seat had the right to nominate a candidate without opposition from the other parties who were part of the agreement (Pelling 1967). In essence, World War II froze the political landscape in the United Kingdom.

With the end of the war, this six-year period of political stability ended. On May 23, 1945, Churchill announced the termination of the coalition government and plans for the dissolution of Parliament in June, to be followed by a general election in July. After a hard-fought but swift campaign, the election results were announced on July 26, 1945. The Labour Party easily won, with 393 seats to the Conservative Party's 213. Churchill

TABLE 8.4 Estimate of the effect of war on the vote for FDR in the 1944 election

Comparison	%
Between-subject (May 1943)	
War ongoing	58
War over soon	52
Within-subject (April 1944)	
War ongoing	54
End of war clearly in sight	48

Sources: Author analysis of AIPO 295 (May 1943) and AIPO 316 (April 1944).
Note: The between-subject comparison represents questions asked on different forms; the within-subject comparison, questions asked sequentially.

TABLE 8.5 War scenarios and the strength of FDR support, October 1944

	FDR should be president (%)	FDR better than Dewey (%)	Dewey better than FDR (%)	Electing FDR would be bad (%)
Early October				
If vote were today	96	91	5	2
If Germany surrendered	91	80	3	1
Late October				
If vote were today	97	91	3	1
If Germany surrendered	92	77	3	1

Sources: Author analysis of Roper Survey 43 (October 1944) and Roper Survey 44 (October 1944).
Note: Cell entries indicate the percentage of persons who would vote for FDR.

retained his seat in Parliament but lost his office; that same day, Churchill resigned as prime minister, and the Labour Party formed a new government under the leadership of Clement Attlee.[40] Ironically—but consistent with the expectations of Arena (2008) and Achen and Bartels (2002)—the reward for winning the Second World War was a quick route to the exit door.

Why did the Conservatives lose the 1945 election? Different scholars have arrived at distinct answers to this question. Ball (2003) argues that the Conservative campaign was poorly planned and failed to take into account the public's concern for domestic issues. Cole (1948) argues that Churchill's behavior during the campaign ensured his defeat. Most famously, on June 4,

Churchill broadcast a speech to the nation in which he argued that the socialist government promised by the Labour Party could not afford to allow public dissent and would require "some sort of Gestapo" (as quoted in Jenkins 2001, 792). This level of partisan belligerence, according to Jenkins (2001), undermined Churchill's hard-earned place as leader of the English nation. Atlee himself attributed his party's win to Churchill's strategic mistakes and the effectiveness of Labour's radio-based campaign. As Franklin and Ladner (1995) note, these accounts of the election outcome share the proposition that Labour's "surprise" win came about because of the nature of the campaign. Furthermore, if we are to believe the data presented earlier concerning FDR's electoral prospects for a third term, perhaps we can believe that the war was the only thing that could have kept Churchill in power.

A closer examination of the survey data from this election, however, illustrates many of the themes of this book. The outcome of the British general election of 1945 had little to do with the war. Instead, it reflected the return to the politics of peacetime, which focused on the longstanding cleavages in British society over domestic issues.

The Conservative loss in the election may have been shocking, but it should not have been a surprise; the turning fortunes of the party were apparent in polls taken by the British Institute of Public Opinion (BIPO) more than two years earlier. As figure 8.8 demonstrates, in June 1943 Labour held an eight-point lead over the Conservatives in the polls.[41] Although Labour's lead over the Conservatives fluctuated during the next two years, rising to 20 points in February 1945, and declining to 6 points on the eve of the election, in every survey—nine polls in all—Labour held a significant lead over the Conservatives.

What might have surprised commentators about the election results was the overwhelming support for Churchill in the same polls. Between June 1943 and May 1945, the BIPO asked fourteen times whether the public approved of the prime minister. These readings ranged from 81 percent to 93 percent approval, with an average approval rating of 88 percent.

These warm feelings for Churchill did not, however, extend to his party, which is apparent not only in the aggregate results reported in figure 8.8 but also in individual-level analysis of the polls. The June 1943 poll is the only existing individual-level survey that contains measures of both approval of Churchill and support for the Labour Party. Although, not surprisingly, support for the Labour Party was higher among those respondents who disapproved of Churchill than among those who approved, the differences between the two groups were not large. Labour had the support

FIGURE 8.8. British political preferences, BIPO polls, 1943–45.

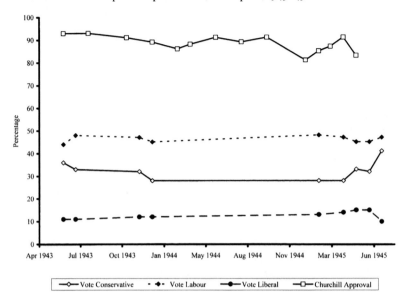

of 42 percent of citizens who disapproved of Churchill, compared with 37 percent of those who approved of the prime minister. Moreover, Labour received a plurality of all votes among those respondents who *approved* of Churchill; even in this group, the Labour Party led the Conservative Party by a margin of 37 percent to 27 percent.

The disjuncture between Conservative Party support and Churchill approval lies in the presence or absence of class-based cleavages. The parties, after all, typically divided over social welfare concerns. In the June 1943 poll, the Conservatives led Labour 50 percent to 11 percent among those of "above average" income levels. Among those with less-than-average income, Labour led the Conservatives by a margin of 43 percent to 21 percent. BIPO polling suggests that, if anything, this class-based cleavage widened by Election Day. In the first postelection polls, conducted in July 1945, among respondents with above-average income, Conservative led Labour 69 percent to 10 percent. Among lower-income respondents, Labour led 50 percent to 22 percent. By contrast, there were almost no class-based differences on measures of Churchill approval. According to the June 1943 poll, Churchill's approval level stood above 90 percent for *all* income groups (see table 8.6). In fact, across all four polls from June 1943 to March 1944 for which individual-level data exist, the average difference between the two groups was only four percentage points.

The 1945 election was decided, therefore, not on personality but on the

TABLE 8.6 Class cleavages on Churchill approval and Conservative Party support

Income	Approval rating (%)			
	Churchill approval			
	June 1943	November 1943	January 1944	March 1944
Above average	96	92	96	88
Less than average	92	89	89	86
	Conservative Party support			
	June 1943		July 1945	
Above average	50		69	
Less than average	21		22	

Sources: Author analysis of BIPO 99 (June 1943), BIPO 103 (November 1943), BIPO 105 (January 1944), BIPO 107 (March 1944), and BIPO 123 (July 1945).

resurgence of class-based politics, after a period in which the interparty compromise of 1939 obscured large changes in the partisan identities of the citizens of the United Kingdom. Franklin and Ladner (1995) argue that from 1935 until 1945, a new generation of voters—those who had been socialized into Labour affiliation—came into the electorate, sweeping the Conservatives from power.[42] The English people may have loved Churchill, but his copartisans could not escape the realities of the new political landscape.

One puzzle remains. If figure 8.8 is to be believed, it appears that— contrary to the implications of the research of Arena (2008) and Achen and Bartels (2002)—the Conservatives may have achieved an electoral gain from winning the war in June 1945, a fact obscured by the Conservative loss in the election. Conservative Party support, after all, rose almost ten points in the last month of the campaign. It is important not to read too much into this apparent rally, however. For one, this gain came at the expense of the Liberal Party, not the more electorally potent Labour Party; Labour support remained steady across this entire period. In addition, an alternative explanation for the jump in Conservative support might have some currency. Table 8.6 demonstrates that from June 1943 to July 1945, lower-class support for the Conservative Party remained steady, but upper-class support increased by almost 20 percent. The jump in support for Conservatives among high-income respondents is, in fact, greater than the increase in support for Labour among low-income respondents. Perhaps the end of the electoral campaign facilitated a rally to the Conservatives from their core supporters, as citizens began to tie their votes more firmly to their political predilections (Gelman and King 1993). In any case, these polls suggest that in the United Kingdom—apparently unlike the United States—the war and its termination did not alter the base of the ruling party's electoral support.

Of course analysis of the English data is not fully comparable to that of the American data reported elsewhere in this chapter. For one, we need to account for the special issues arising from the parliamentary system of government in the United Kingdom. If Churchill's electoral fortunes were not tied to those of his party, would he have lost the election? From one perspective, it seems almost unimaginable. How, after all, could a politician with an approval rating of over 80 percent lose at the polls? Nevertheless, as with the question about the vote for FDR during war discussed in the last section, this is a hypothetical question that cannot be answered. For one, approval ratings are not interchangeable with margins of electoral victory. For instance, FDR's approval rating during this same period in the United States exceeded his electoral support by a substantial margin. In addition, Churchill's support lay on different foundations than that of his party. If the British people had been forced to balance the prime minister and his party, there is no telling what choice they would have made.

What the data do clearly show is that whatever the personal gain to a politician from war, even the strongest and most respected candidate cannot escape the vagaries of domestic politics. Whether Churchill's tenure came to an end because—like FDR—the electorate was ready to vote him out with the cessation of hostilities or—more likely—because the end of the electoral truce of 1939 revealed a change in the electoral landscape, success at war did not translate into success at the polls. Domestic political concerns again reigned supreme.[43]

CONCLUSION

The analysis in this chapter underscores several lessons. Although the study of elections during wartime is an important topic, to date much of the literature has followed an ill-advised path. When a set of candidates takes more polarized positions on war, their supporters among the public will follow suit—either because they listen to their preferred candidate or because they take cues from the candidate they distrust. Analysis of survey data will make it appear that positions on war shape vote choice, but in fact the reverse is true. Instead of focusing on single elections, we need to extend our focus across time. There, the impact of war will become clear.

The impact of war may be multifaceted. Incumbents can bear a high price for leading the country into war, as Lyndon Johnson and his vice president and successor Herbert Humphrey found in 1968. But the news is not always so grim. Fear can change the dynamics of particular elections, as the 2000–2004 election cycle clearly demonstrates and the 1940 and 1944 elections imply. As Churchill's fate in the 1945 British general election also demonstrates, however, even the most successful wartime leaders cannot escape domestic concerns.

CHAPTER NINE

CONCLUSIONS

As the Iraq War entered its sixth year in March 2008, public opposition to the war ran high. A CBS poll taken on the anniversary of the war found that 41 percent of Americans thought that the United States should never have gotten involved in Iraq, and only 36 percent of respondents thought that the United States did the right thing in going to war.[1] The Bush administration, however, seemed to take this news in stride, as illustrated by this exchange between Vice President Dick Cheney and ABC chief White House correspondent Martha Raddatz:

> RADDATZ: Two-thirds of the Americans say [the Iraq War is] not worth fighting.
> CHENEY: So?
> RADDATZ: So? You're—not, you don't care what the American people think?
> CHENEY: No, I think you cannot be blown off course by the fluctuation in public opinion polls.[2]

Cheney might have seemed out of step with public opinion, but his position was fully consistent with the one adopted by Republican partisans. Although it is true that only about a third of all Americans thought the United States did the right thing in invading Iraq, a large majority of Republicans—68 percent to be exact—continued to support the war (in contrast to the 12 percent of Democrats who supported the military action). As I have argued in this book, examining support for war without allowing for the influence of politically relevant domestic divisions—both among politicians and members of the public—is a flawed undertaking. To understand opinion about foreign policy, we must first understand how people reason about politics more generally.

Surprisingly, this simple observation has not taken root in the analysis of public opinion and foreign policy. Since the 1950s, the consideration of public opinion about war has largely proceeded apart from the consideration of public opinion about domestic politics. In this book, I have made the argument that we cannot fully understand the public's place in matters of war unless we integrate the two fields of study.

My position is not simply an academic exercise. Finding the public's proper role in making the decision to wage war is a critical matter. In a democratic country, of course, citizens are the ultimate arbiters of government. Although citizens may not dictate the specific direction of government action in every policy area, no course of action can be sustained without the support of the public. Cheney's comment aside, with the rise of opinion polls over the last century, politicians in the United States have cast a careful eye on public reaction when planning military interventions abroad. In fact, the Bush administration's commitment to the "Strategy for Victory" provides evidence of the continued relevance of public opinion.

In the early days of opinion polling, however, the wisdom of involving the public in matters of war was in question. Political scientists believed that the public was ill informed about foreign policy issues. Furthermore, in those few instances in which citizens actually paid attention to foreign affairs, scholars argued that citizens' preferences were volatile and guided by irrational impulses. In more recent years, a more generous view of the capabilities of the public has emerged. As noted in chapter 4, there is a growing consensus that the mass public, on the whole, holds sensible preferences about foreign policy, and that they adjust their preferences according to changes in world events that reflect on American interests. Public opinion concerning foreign policy more generally and in the realm of war in particular is, to use Page and Shapiro's (1992) characterization, "rational" (see also Page and Bouton 2006).

Neither of these viewpoints is quite correct. By drawing on the vast literature detailing the determinants and bases of domestic public opinion, we can come to a more evenhanded conclusion. In the preceding pages, I have taken issue with the stance of the revisionists—who give the public too much credit—without retreating to the dismal conclusions of the traditionalists—who place too little confidence is the capacities of the ordinary citizens. I have made the case that we can best understand public opinion in times of war by looking to the same attachments, enmities, and emotions that structure opinion toward domestic issues. Specifically, I considered the expression of mass support for war, support for the protection of civil liberties, and elections held during times of war. In examining these different facets of the relationship between ordinary citizens and political leaders, I have argued that the study of domestic politics and international affairs must proceed from a common foundation.

SUMMARY

I began this book with an overview of the major conflicts in U.S. history since the 1930s, and the public's reaction to those wars, paying special attention to public opinion during the Second World War. Specifically, in chapter 3 I addressed some of the myths that have arisen concerning the public's reaction to World War II and discussed the relevance of the polls conducted during that time to our understanding of public opinion during wartime more generally. Undoubtedly, World War II was an exceptional event in world history, and—following the attack by the Japanese armed forces at Pearl Harbor and Hitler's declaration of war in December 1941—it engendered unprecedented levels of public support through the four years of the war. Many of the reasons that have been cited for its popularity, however—such as the atrocities of the Nazi regime and the desire for vengeance after Pearl Harbor—did not seem to play a large role in shaping opinion. Along similar lines, generations of scholars have misinterpreted the meaning and importance of the events of December 7, 1941, in critical ways. The bombing of Pearl Harbor has been commonly thought of as the precise moment of the United States' conversion from isolationism to interventionism. In fact, as I showed in chapter 3, poll data demonstrate that the public had been moving in that direction for some time. Although the public never supported declaring war on the Axis powers, by early 1941 almost 70 percent of the public supported helping England, even at the risk of being drawn into the war. Pearl Harbor did, however, have the effect of creating a broad consensus on an issue that had been, up to that point, highly partisan—first among elites and then among the public. Evidence suggests that FDR—and those citizens who supported FDR—had been preparing for war long before December 7. Pearl Harbor did change opinion, but it did so by galvanizing those politicians and members of the public who were not inclined to support FDR on the war—or any other policy. As I further demonstrate in the rest of the book, the high levels of support for World War II seem to have depended on the unusual durability of elite consensus on the correctness of war.

In part 2 of the book I explored the roots of public support for war. I argued that a key to understanding public opinion concerning foreign policy is to look to the affections and animosities that structure thinking about familiar domestic issues. I began this discussion in chapter 4 by reconsidering the widely held view that ordinary citizens have views on foreign policy that adjust in response to specific changes in external circumstances. For instance, some scholars have suggested that public support for war decreases as a direct response to mounting casualties. Others argue that that the public comes to its opinion by way of a cost-benefit analysis. These theories rely on the assumption of a well-informed rational public—one willing and able to make complex judgments, incorporate new information, and determine the likelihood of military success. In chapter 4, I question each of these beliefs. For one, existing accounts of public support for military action fail to specify the mechanism by which members of the public process information concerning the events of war. I presented evidence from surveys conducted during World War II and the war in Iraq that demonstrated the limited power of events to explain the public's views on war. For instance, I used experimental evidence to demonstrate that providing citizens with relevant information about the financial and human costs of the Iraqi intervention did not alter the levels of support for that conflict. The tides of war cannot directly explain why citizens rally to some military actions while rejecting others.

What, then, does determine public opinion on war? In the remainder of part 2 I argued that we should look to the factors that shape opinions on domestic policies—the attachments and enmities forged on the domestic political stage. In particular, partisan politics and group attachments drive the public's decision to support or oppose military conflicts.

In chapter 5, I made the case that those political elites with a stake in the outcome of policy decisions have the power to mold the meaning of ambiguous events on the battlefield. Patterns of agreement and disagreement in the interpretation of these events by political actors with partisan and career aspirations shape public opinion more than the events themselves. Partisan politics therefore has the potential to shape public opinion by framing conflicts, interpreting events, and defining such vague variables as "war success." Citizens support wars championed by politicians they trust and rebuff conflicts associated with politicians they reject.

This "elite cue" theory—advanced in chapter 4 and explicated in chapter 5—can explain patterns of support for a variety of conflicts that, on their face, appear to be quite different, including World War II, Vietnam, and the Iraq War. For instance, I found that in the 1930s and 1940s, those citizens who paid close attention to politics were most likely to express views in line with the parties they generally supported. Through 1941, Democrats followed the lead of FDR in calling for increased aid to England in its fight against the Axis powers. This level of support reached its apex among those respondents who were best informed about politics and could discern the differences between the positions of the two parties. Among Republicans, on the other hand, increased attention to politics led to increased rejection of FDR's policies, in line with the positions of Republican leaders. With the onset of the United States' involvement in the war, the behavior of Democrats did not change. Increased attention to politics still led to an increase in support for war. After Republican party elites rallied to the cause of war, however, Republican partisans in the electorate changed their opinions dramatically. At the mass level, Republicans and Democrats responded in similar ways from 1942 until the end of the war.

The balance of partisan rhetoric is not, however, the only factor that determines mass levels of support for war. In chapter 6, I discussed how both identification with and hostility toward groups in society can have a powerful influence on a person's opinions concerning foreign policy. In particular, attachments and enmities that arise solely from domestic considerations can shape these opinions. During World War II, ethnic and racial ties were especially important, because large segments of the U.S. population could trace their (relatively recent) ancestry to one or more of the countries involved in the war. I demonstrated that throughout the war, respondents who descended from parents born in Axis countries were more opposed to continuing the U.S. military effort and held a more negative view of the Allied powers than did those respondents whose parents were born in the United States or in Allied countries. These differences persisted even after the United States entered the conflict. I also found that dislike of particular ethnic groups shaped opinion on the war. These enmities, forged on the domestic stage prior to and independent of the international events of the mid-to-late 1930s, led some respondents to offer or withhold support for the war. In general, negative feelings toward members of Axis countries were associated with interventionist attitudes, whereas negative feelings toward Jews were correlated with a more anti-interventionist attitude.

Of course, the specific nature of group-specific cues may vary from conflict to conflict. Although immigrants may show some loyalty to their home country, as Axis ethnics did during World War II, in other cases expatriates may feel hostility toward their former homeland or a particular political regime. Cuban Americans demonstrate just such a phenomenon.[3] It is therefore important to pay attention to the cues in the broader political context. In any case, the general point remains; group-based judgments grounded in the complexities of domestic politics can structure political thinking about foreign affairs.

In part 3 of the book, I explored how the public's experiences during wartime shape normal democratic processes outside of support for ongoing conflicts. I began in chapter 7 with a discussion of civil liberties during wartime. Once again, I argued that studies of domestic public opinion can powerfully inform our study of opinion during times of crisis. During World War II, the internment of Japanese Americans was a telling illustration of the public's willingness to sacrifice the rights of *others* during wartime. Yet similar feelings are present during peacetime as well. A deep body of literature concerning the determinants of political tolerance finds that individuals are most willing to restrict the liberties of those groups from which they feel threatened. I find that similar processes are at play when people make judgments about their *own* rights. In general, attacks on America or the onset of war initially increases citizens' willingness to limit civil liberties. Although partisan cues sometimes play a role in determining the scope of restrictions individuals are willing to bear, it is the individual's perception of threat and his level of trust in the government that seem to have the largest effects. These dynamics are most obvious in the present day. General support for civil liberties dropped sharply following the 9/11 attacks but rebounded soon after, reaching pre-9/11 levels by 2004. Meanwhile, those respondents who were most fearful of another attack remained supportive of restricting civil liberties. Similar patterns of support for civil liberties were also found during World War II, however. Even before the beginning of the conflict, a significant portion of the public was willing to restrict the rights of marginal groups. As tensions rose in Europe—well before the United States entered the war—support for civil liberties decreased.

Chapter 8 considered the effect of war on presidential elections over the last sixty-five years. The war in Iraq is commonly assumed to have played a critical role in the 2004 election. Some scholars have interpreted the correlation between vote choice and support for the war as evidence of a causal relationship. Exploring a larger set of presidential elections, using both cross-sectional and aggregate data, I demonstrated, however, that the research used to support this conclusion is contradictory and counterintuitive. Instead, consistent with the argument about the primacy of partisan attachments advanced in chapter 5, I found that the causal arrow most likely points in the opposite direction; voters' partisan predispositions determine their support for the war more than the reverse.

This is not to say that the conditions of war do not shape election outcomes. Continuing the theme of this book, I argue that war may affect elections through two causal paths, both of which are rooted in the normal ebb and flow of domestic politics. First, incumbent politicians (or their party) can be hurt by bad news related to the war, even if they are not responsible for the war, in much the same way that economic woes, floods, or even shark attacks can shape election outcomes. Second, the circumstances of war often lead the public to feel a heightened sense of fear and threat. These conditions may lead them to place a higher value on leadership, thereby increasing support for incumbent politicians. This effect can be seen in the four-term tenure of FDR, which seems to have been made possible, in a large part, by the public's reluctance to change leaders with the war looming. The primacy of incumbency is apparent also in the electoral success of Republican incumbents in the 2002–4 election cycle. Around 2002, when perceptions of threat were high, the public seems to have rallied around Bush and Republicans in Congress.

LESSONS LEARNED

Where then, does this leave us? Throughout this book I have emphasized two themes. Most important, I have made the case that the study of public opinion about war—and public opinion about foreign policy more generally—must be integrated with the study of domestic public opinion.[4] The separation of the study of public opinion and foreign policy from the rest of the field of public opinion has hindered the progress of both scholars of international relations and scholars of American politics.

Scholars in the field of foreign policy have trod a path that public opinion researchers have long thought to be a dead end. The picture of the average citizen in the public opinion and foreign policy literature—one who calculates the costs and benefits of military action and comes to a reasoned judgment concerning the wisdom of military intervention— would be unrecognizable to students of American politics. It is true that citizens may, in the collective, act in ways that seem to be rational reactions to changing events. And the study of collective opinion on war has yielded some important insights into public opinion. But focusing only on the aggregate level paints an incomplete picture of the behavior of individuals in a democracy. Perhaps some citizens can and do make the types of complex calculations described by scholars in the rationalist tradition: carefully considering the prospects of victory and balancing the costs of a mission against the benefits of a successful outcome. In a world in which people are preoccupied with the concerns of their day-to-day lives, however, other individuals may simply perform the mental equivalent of flipping a coin when deciding whether to support a war. When we try to explain support for war by focusing on aggregate opinion, we ignore the latter group, while implicitly privileging the former group in our account of support for war. As Converse explains, "the process of aggregation drives out noise . . . the drawing of means hides a sea of noise [in public opinion] as aggregation always does. The signal extracted from this noise is very recognizable because it is undoubtedly shaped in large measure by the small minority of the electorate that is nearly as well informed about these matters as are our elite informants" (1990, 378–82).

Converse's dismal conclusion is not, however, the final word on this matter. Just because the rationalist account of public support for war overstates the ability of the public to come to reasoned decisions over matters of war and peace does not mean that public opinion lacks structure or coherence. As shown in chapter 5, a large portion of the citizenry judge the wisdom of war by following cues provided by trusted politicians. Members of the public may support or oppose war because they follow leaders who share their general political views or reject the positions of leaders whose interests do not accord with their own. Such decisions may not meet exacting standards of good citizenship, but they are certainly "rational" in the context of a representative democracy. In complex situations, where the stakes may be unclear and the outcome uncertain, it makes sense for citizens to adopt the positions of politicians who share their basic political orientations.

Admittedly, however, this process of cue taking may be problematic. For one, the possibilities for true popular control of the government could be thwarted. Perhaps Page and Shapiro (1992) overstate the case when they argue that government officials can sometimes "conceal or misrepresent reality without being challenged." But in the realm of foreign affairs, where events take place far from the personal purview of the average citizen, politicians have a great deal of flexibility in interpreting the meaning of events on the ground. Sometimes, these politicians can lead the public down a virtuous path. But other times, as Page and Shapiro demonstrate in their discussions of the Vietnam War and the "missile gap" controversy in 1960, the public can be misled or even induced to act against its interests. Locating the limits of popular support for war in decisions of politicians rather than in the decisions of ordinary citizens has critical implications for the functioning of democracy. If Larson is correct, then a calculating public can restrain its leaders from pursuing a path of folly. But if I am correct and politicians, rather than ordinary citizens, must put a stop to war, perhaps such bulwarks lie on shaky ground.

Scholars of American politics also have much to gain by paying closer attention to public opinion concerning foreign policy. Expanding our scope of inquiry into the foreign realm can open new windows into the domestic political process. Although times of war do not fundamentally change citizens' decision-making processes, they do offer conditions that can illuminate our understanding of public opinion more generally. For instance, rarely in the domestic arena do the two major parties switch sides on a given issue. Take the realm of economic policy. For several generations, the Democratic Party has been more likely than the Republican Party to champion policies that advance the interests of lower-income Americans. True, the intensity of these positions has waxed and waned over time, but the relative location of the two major parties on the central economic cleavage of American society has remained fairly constant. Moreover, in domestic politics there is rarely anything truly new under the sun. Although novel issues that cut across party lines sometimes emerge on the political scene—women's equality and abortion rights in the 1970s, for instance—these issues are often incorporated into existing political cleavages, as Stimson (2004) has shown. In the rare cases when parties do shift position on major issues, the process of conversion may take years. Moreover, the reverberations of these changes may take even longer to shape the political system. Carmines and Stimson's (1989) discussion of the evolution of the politics of race is a case in point. From the mid-1940s until the early 1960s, Senate and House Republicans took consistently more liberal voting positions on bills concerning racial policy than did Democrats. Beginning in the early 1970s, however, Democratic politicians became the voice of racial liberalism. This shift is noteworthy not simply because changes of this sort are rare but also because it took almost ten years for the parties to sort out their positions on this issue.[5]

In the realm of foreign policy, however, politicians often have wider room to maneuver, and political positions are often more malleable. Electoral shifts can change the partisan orientation of the leaders of wartime efforts, as Nixon's embrace of the Vietnam conflict after his victory in the 1968 election demonstrated. But circumstances outside of specific electoral wins and losses can also alter the shape of elite politics. In chapter 5, I compared the 1999 NATO intervention in Kosovo to the 2003 invasion of Iraq. In the span of four years, different presidents of different parties invoked almost exactly the same rhetoric to rally their supporters to war. Although the circumstances surrounding the Clinton-led incursion into Kosovo were very different from the Bush administration's invasion of Iraq, many of the justifications for the two actions were similar. Several prominent politicians who voted on both resolutions changed their positions across the different conflicts, and some—such as Robert Bennett—switched sides in dramatic fashion. The public's reaction to this shift in debate was to follow those leaders who share its political predispositions. Democratic identifiers supported the intervention in Kosovo but opposed the Iraq action. Republicans took the opposite position in both wars.

The Kosovo/Iraq pairing is not even the most dramatic reversal discussed in this book. After the 1940 Republican convention, Wendell Willkie broke from the Republican establishment in supporting FDR's wartime strategy early in the presidential campaign. He reversed himself suddenly, however, in the campaign's final days, charging FDR with leading the nation down a path to certain war. Throughout it all, Republican partisans followed suit. Given this salient shift in elite rhetoric, the dynamics of opinion on the question of aiding the Allied cause changed as well. Although we would predict these patterns of change from theories of opinion on domestic politics, we rarely get a chance to explore the political implications of such shifts, given the overriding stability in the relative positions of the parties in the domestic realm.

Studying basic processes of political choice during times of crisis can also open new windows into the nature of public opinion on matters removed from support for war. Take, for instance, the study of civil liberties. Scholars have long known that individuals are more willing to accept restrictions on public support for liberties when they themselves feel threatened. But because these scholars have conducted their investigations during times of peace, they have primarily examined threats arising from particular groups in society. As a result, public opinion researchers have focused mainly on political intolerance—support for limitations on the rights of others in society. By expanding our scope of investigation to include times of national threat, however, we can see how people respond to threat vis-à-vis their *own* rights and liberties. In chapter 7, I found that the processes that shape individuals' judgments about these rights are, in fact, largely the same as those that shape judgments about the rights of marginal groups in society. The ubiquity of the power of threat in shaping how citizens view the legitimacy of restriction not only on others but on themselves as well has far-reaching implications for the practice of democracy.

A HISTORICAL APPROACH

In this book I have also sought to make a larger point about the study of the public and war. Although at one level each war is unique, all the wars examined in this book share certain characteristics that make it possible to draw more general lessons about the public's response to war. To fully understand public opinion about war, we need to extend our scope of inquiry across a broad span of time, reaching back to the Second World War.

When considering the relationship between government and its citizens, politicians and pundits—not just scholars—have largely focused on developments during the cold war and post–cold war periods in isolation, one war at a time. As a result, the analysis of the relationship between government and the public during wartime has largely overlooked the largest and most important international conflict in U.S. history—World War II—and has failed to draw general lessons by ignoring similarities among the public's reactions to different conflicts in American history.

Many commentators see World War II as a conflict unique in scope and power. In contrast to this view, I have shown that the contours of public opinion during the 1930s and 1940s fit patterns that are similar to other conflicts over the last fifty years. Ethnic identity may have played a greater role in structuring support for World War II than at other times in U.S. history, but largely because the ethnic divisions in American society were more prominent at that time, and those dimensions were tied to salient allies and adversaries in that conflict. In most ways, at least with respect to the reaction of the American public, World War II seems to be a war like any other. Throughout the 1930s and 1940s, the shifts in the balance of cues from partisan actors led to corresponding shifts in the preferences of the public. This pattern was true regardless of whether those shifts were brief—as was the case during Willkie's campaign for president in 1940—or more enduring—when FDR obtained the support of his Republican opponents after the United States' entry into the war. In World War II, as in other wars, the patterns of agreement and disagreement among partisan political actors played a critical role in shaping popular responses to war.

In fact, what this book has shown is that if any conflict in U.S. history is unique, it is the current war in Iraq. In chapter 2, the comparison of aggregate trends in popular support across wars may make it appear at first glance that Iraq has much in common with Vietnam. But a look below the surface reveals that, although party loyalties shaped the public's experiences of both wars, Iraq represents the extreme realization of the power of partisanship.

In April 2004, support for the Iraq War dropped to 25 percent among Democrats. This level of support equaled the lowest level of support for the Vietnam War among those who identified with the party out of power—the 26 percent of Democrats who supported Vietnam in January 1973.[6] At the point in 1973, however, where out-party support for the Vietnam War reached its nadir, overall support for the war stood at 29 percent. By comparison, in April 2004, nearly 50 percent of the public still backed the Iraq War. The impact of partisanship can explain the different levels of enthusiasm for the two wars. Support for Iraq remained relatively high because of the extraordinarily high levels of enthusiasm for the war effort among members of the GOP; over 75 percent of Republicans expressed support for the war at the time of the April survey. Partisan differences are always important, but as Jacobson (2008) convincingly demonstrates in his comparison of the post–World War II conflicts—Korea, Vietnam, the Gulf War, and the 1999 Kosovo intervention—the magnitude of the partisan differences over the Iraq War is unparalleled in the history of opinion polling. Even the basic facts of the war—the presence of weapons of mass destruction, the number of casualties, and the published conclusions of the 9/11 commission—have been contested by Republican partisans. From the early days of the war, among both politicians and the public, the Iraq War has been a Republican war.

At the same time, it is important to recognize that although the magnitude of the partisan differences over the Iraq War is massive, the dynamics of opinion concerning the Iraq War are in many ways familiar. Those partisans in the electorate who are aligned with the president are more likely to support war, as was the case both during the early 1970s and in the years before Pearl Harbor. Furthermore, as in previous wars, the gap in levels of support between Democratic and Republican citizens is largest among those who pay closer attention to politics. What makes Iraq unique are the scale and scope of the partisan differences, not the way in which ordinary citizens come to judgments on the wisdom of war.

The analysis presented in this book, however, raises another question. How did this unprecedented chasm between the positions of the two groups of identifiers arise? Again, we can find an answer in the particulars of the domestic political scene. The magnitude of the partisan gap is not a function of the war per se but rather an outgrowth of changes in the larger political environment. Trends in partisan polarization may have been exacerbated by the saliency of the war and the battle between the Bush administration and its critics, but polarization is by no means a product of the war. Differences between Democrats and Republican, after all, have existed since the beginning of the Bush administration and extend to many domestic issues as well. In 2004, for instance, Democrats and Republicans differed greatly on a number of social issues. On the question of abortion, according to the NES, 26 percent of Republicans agreed with the statement "By law, a woman should always be able to obtain an abortion as a matter of personal choice," compared with 46 percent of Democrats who supported that position. On the question of capital punishment, 85 percent of Republicans favored the death penalty for persons convicted of murder, whereas only 52 percent of Democrats favored that position. These differences also manifest in traditional cleavages over questions of economic policy. In 2004, 62 percent of Republicans favored allowing the investment of Social Security funds in the stock market, but only 28 percent of Democrats favored pursuing such a policy. Among those who placed themselves on a scale measuring support for tasking the U.S. government with seeing to it that "every person has a job and a good standard of living," versus letting "each person get ahead on their own," 61 percent of Republicans but only 26 percent of Democrats supported a policy of self-reliance. These differences extend back before the Iraq War to the early days of the Bush administration. In 2002, 62 percent of Republicans and 32 percent of Democrats took comparable positions on the "standard of living" scale.[7] Clearly, the American public is extremely divided over a wide variety of issues and has been for the entire Bush presidency (see Jacobson 2008 for more data and further discussion).

Moreover, the degree of partisan polarization today seems to be larger than that found at any other time since the advent of organized survey research.[8] Let us use, as an indicator, beliefs about the incumbent president. Although partisans have always expressed greater support for leaders of their own party than for presidents of the opposition party, these differences have reached historic levels in recent years. The gap in Bush's approval ratings between Republicans and Democrats in the first quarter of his administration—well before the beginning of the Iraq War—was 57 percent, a difference larger than for any previous president. In part, this gap may be a result of the disputed nature of the 2000 election; just before his inauguration, 90 percent of Republicans and only 20 percent of Democrats believed that Bush had won the election legitimately. But the partisan gap found in Bush's "honeymoon period" is itself reflective of long-term trends. From the 1950s through the 1970s, the gap between Democrats and Republicans in their support for newly inaugurated presidents was on the order of 20–30 percent (the exception being Lyndon Johnson, who had only a ten-point gap when he ascended to the office in the wake of the assassination of Kennedy). In the 1980s, this gap rose to the range of 30–40 percent, reaching 50 percent with Clinton's first term in 1993 (Jacobson 2008).

The public has almost certainly not charted its own path to partisan rancor. The analysis in chapter 5 demonstrates that on questions of support for war, political leaders guide the choices of the public. The same is true in times of peace. As Hetherington (2001) has shown, when political leaders diverge, the public follows suit. The reason the public is so divided over political matters today is because the party leaders stand so far apart on critical issues. In figure 9.1, I present data concerning the relative positions of the two parties in Congress from 1877 to the present, based on the voting records of their members.[9] In the graph, higher numbers indicate greater levels of polarization between the parties. Looking at the Iraq War from the perspective of this longer time span is especially illuminating. The Korean and Vietnam wars took place during the trough of partisan polarization. Since that time, there has been a steady rise, culminating in the high polarization scores during the Kosovo intervention and the Iraq War.

Much ink has been spilled on the question of partisan polarization and the ways it has shaped domestic politics, but there has not been a similar discussion in the public opinion and foreign policy literature. In part this lack of attention could be the result of the fact that from the 1950s through the early 1980s—the focus of a great deal of the extant literature—the parties stood relatively close together (see fig. 9.1). Although polarization levels rose during the Gulf War in the early 1990s, they still stood far below those found in the present day. The Iraq War has taken place in a greatly changed political climate. With polarization among elites at an all-time high, it could be that the factors that sustained support for war among the general public are a thing of the past. Without a real shift in the way politics is conducted in this country, it may not be possible to sustain a large-scale mobilization for war, such as that seen during World War II.

Still, it is important to recognize that the climate may change in the future, as it has in the past. Today—as in previous political eras—reactions to foreign conflicts are forged in the crucible of domestic politics. Looking for differences along partisan lines in support for the Iraq War is like looking for a haystack on top of a needle, but that is a function, not a cause, of the current political environment. If the enterprise of opinion polling had

FIGURE 9.1. Polarization between parties in the House of Representatives, 1877–2005.

begun earlier, allowing us to conduct surveys during World War I — a time of similarly extreme partisan polarization (see fig. 9.1) — perhaps scholars would have noticed the change begun during World War II and continuing through the wars in Korea and Vietnam. In fact, the partisan rancor among politicians concerning possible American involvement in the League of Nations after World War I demonstrates the central role that partisanship has long played in discussions of war and peace. If we continue to ignore the impact of domestic politics on support for foreign policy during times of crisis, these changes will continue to go unnoticed. To fully understand opinion during times of war, we need to integrate the study of domestic politics and the study of international matters. A greater sensitivity to changes in the larger political context can allow us to better understand public opinion about both specific conflicts and war more generally.

DESCRIPTION OF DATA AND WEIGHTING

Modern opinion polls are conducted using probability sampling to ensure that every citizen has an equal chance of being interviewed. Polls in the United States before the 1950s, however, were conducted using quota-controlled sampling methods in which pollsters sought to interview certain predetermined proportions of people from particular segments of the population (see Berinsky 2006 for a description of the quota-sampling practices). Although some pollsters used quotas in seeking a descriptively representative group of citizens (Roper 1940), others designed quotas to produce sample proportions that differed systematically from the population. George Gallup was most interested in predicting elections, so he drew samples to represent each population segment in proportion to the votes it usually cast in elections. Because southerners, African Americans, and women turned out at low rates during this period, these groups were deliberately underrepresented in opinion polls. For example, the 1940 census found that 50 percent of the U.S. population was female, 10 percent was African American, and 31 percent lived in the South. By contrast, a December 1940 Gallup poll included only 34 percent women, 3 percent African Americans, and 13 percent southerners.[1] Thus, the Gallup data that scholars use to represent the voice of the public, in fact, come from a skewed sample of that public.

The practice of quota sampling also introduced unintended distortions. Apart from having to fulfill certain demographic quotas, interviewers were given much discretion to select particular citizens to interview. Because interviewers preferred to work in safer areas and tended to survey approachable respondents, the "public" they interviewed often differed markedly from the public writ large. For example, the 1940 census indicated that about 10 percent of the population had at least some college education, whereas almost 30 percent of a typical 1940 Gallup sample had attended college. Similarly, polls conducted by Gallup and Roper tended to include more "professionals" than identified by the census. The skew in these variables is not surprising, given that education and occupation were not quota categories. It is likely that the highly educated and professionals were more willing to be interviewed; as a result, they comprise a disproportionately large share of these samples.

For the purpose of interpreting frequencies on variables of interest, the central problem is that many of the survey samples do not represent certain groups in proportion to their population share. However, although the quota-controlled sample data were collected in ways that appear from a modern vantage point to be haphazard, the data collection process introduced *predictable* deviations between the characteristics of the sample and that of the population. I can therefore employ methods designed to account for these measurable differences to make reasonable inferences about the U.S. population.

A WEIGHTING SOLUTION

The quota-controlled sampling procedures introduced a unit nonresponse problem—certain classes of individuals were either willingly or inadvertently underrepresented in the samples. When we have detailed information about the characteristics of nonrespondents, we can employ selection bias techniques to account for the differences between the sample and the population (Achen 1986; Breen 1996; Heckman 1979). But when we only have information about the population relative to the sample—auxiliary information taken from the census—we typically apply weighting adjustments to reduce the bias in survey estimates that nonresponse can cause (Holt and Elliot 1991; Lohr 1999; Kalton and Flores-Cervantes 2003).[2]

I employ a model-based poststratification weighting scheme.[3] Under the model-based approach to sampling—which provides the foundation for my weighting strategy—I consider the values of the variables of interest to be random variables. Model-based approaches therefore involve employing a model of the joint probability distribution of the population variables (Thompson 2002). It is necessary to take a model-based approach to draw inferences from quota samples because, as Lohr (1999) notes, we do not know the probability with which individuals were sampled. Through the use of weights, I can have greater confidence that the inferences I draw about public opinion more accurately reflect underlying public sentiment.

Although the use of weights to adjust for nonresponse is common, there is controversy about the best way to implement weighting (Lohr 1999). In a preliminary analysis, therefore, I implemented four solutions recommended by the survey weighting literature (see Bethlehem 2002; Deville and Sarndal 1992; Deville, Sarndal, and Sautory 1993; Kalton and Flores-Cervantes 2003; Little 1993; Gelman 2005; Gelman and Carlin 2002). These methods were cell weighting, raking, regression estimation, and a regression modeling approach advanced by Gelman (2005). Each of these techniques has its own strengths and weaknesses, and I used all four methods to gauge their robustness. In the end, I found that all the methods gave roughly equivalent answers (see Berinsky 2006 for details). I prefer cell weighting because it is simple to employ and requires minimal assumptions. When possible, the aggregate opinion results presented in this book are weighted through use of the cell-weighting method. In some cases I used raking methods. In any case researchers employing different weighting methods will come to similar pictures regarding the shape of public opinion from this era—conclusions that are sometimes different than those reached using the raw survey marginals.

Cell weighting is a simple way to bring the sample proportion in line with auxiliary information—namely, census estimates of the population proportion. I stratify the sample into a number of cells (J), on the basis of the characteristics of the population deemed important (the matrix of X variables). If the distribution of demographic variables in the sample differs from the distribution in the population, poststratification weights are used to combine the separate cell estimates into a population estimate by giving extra weight to groups underrepresented in the sample and less weight to those overrepresented. Using cell weighting to adjust for nonresponse requires us to assume that the respondents within a given cell represent the nonrespondents within that cell. That is, I must assume that the data are missing at random (MAR) (Little and Rubin 2002; I discuss possible violations of this assumption later in the appendix). Under poststratification, the estimate of the population mean for our quantity of interest (for instance, support for FDR) is

$$\hat{\theta} = \sum_{j=1}^{J} \frac{N_j}{N} \hat{\theta}_j$$

where N_j refers to the population size in each poststratification cell j, N is the total population size, $\hat{\theta}$ is the weighted estimate of the mean, and $\hat{\theta}_j$ is the sample mean for poststratification cell j (Lohr 1999).

A well-known practical limitation of cell weighting is that as the number of stratification variables increases, the number of weighting cells becomes larger. With fewer cases in each cell, the aggregate estimates derived from the weighting estimator are less stable. Still, cell weighting has advantages. First, as Lohr (1999) notes, cell weighting requires minimal assumptions beyond the one that the data are MAR (an assumption common to all forms of weighting). For instance, as Kalton and Flores-Cervantes (2003) note, unlike other methods, cell weighting requires no assumptions regarding the structure of response probabilities across cells. In addition, cell weighting allows the researcher to take advantage of information concerning the joint distribution of weighting variables—information I have from census data.

In some cases (discussed later), however, I do not have the information concerning the joint distribution of census variables necessary to implement cell weighting. In those cases, I use a raking procedure. Raking—also known as iterative proportional fitting (Little and Wu 1991) or rim weighting (Sharot 1986)—allows researchers to incorporate auxiliary information on several dimensions. Raking matches cell counts to the *marginal* distributions of the variables used in the weighting scheme. For example, say we wish to weight by gender and a three-category age variable. Picture a three-by-two table, with age representing the rows and gender representing the columns. We have the marginal totals for each age group, as well as the proportion of men and women in the sample. The raking algorithm works by first matching the rows to the marginal distribution (in this case age) and then the columns (gender). This process is repeated until both the rows and columns match their marginal distributions.[4]

Although raking may be a less desirable procedure for the 1930s and 1940s survey data, the use of the different methods in the different circumstances should not affect the results reported in this book. As noted earlier, in previous work I have found that the estimates from the raking and cell-weighting methods are very similar (see Berinsky 2006 for further discussion).

WHAT TO WEIGHT ON? THE ART OF SELECTING WEIGHTING VARIABLES

Poststratification weighting rests on a firm statistical foundation but in practice requires a series of data-analytic choices. All weighting methods, after all, rely on auxiliary information to arrive at valid inferences. Kalton and Flores-Cervantes (2003) report that it is important to choose auxiliary variables that predict the response probabilities of the different cells. To make the case that our methods capture and correct for differences between the survey samples and the population, I discuss how auxiliary information from the census can be used to correct the problems introduced by quota sampling.

The distortions introduced by quota sampling can be divided into two types: nonrepresentative strata size and nonrandom selection within strata. Nonrepresentative strata-size distortions arise through the instructions the central survey offices of the polling firms give to the field staff; for example, by setting the quota of female respondents below its true population proportion, the pollsters deliberately skew their samples. By contrast, nonrandom selection within strata distortions is a result of interviewer discretion in respondent selection. This discretion ensures that the citizens who were interviewed differed in systematic ways from citizens who were not. Although these distortions arise through different processes, both can be addressed with a common solution. By employing auxiliary information about the population, I can correct for the known differences between the sample and the population.

The use of auxiliary information is an especially powerful way to correct for nonrepresentative strata-size distortions. There is no reason to suspect that the members of deliberately underrepresented groups—such as women and southerners—who were interviewed were systematically different from the members of those groups who were not interviewed (conditioning on the interviewer-induced differences that I address later). After all, the sample imbalance exists because the pollsters deliberately drew nonrepresentative samples based on these characteristics. Thus, using the cases of those members of the underrepresented groups who were interviewed to represent those respondents who were not interviewed is appropriate. I can simply use the observable characteristics of the respondents to reweight the data.

Auxiliary information can also be used to correct for distortions arising from nonrandom selection within strata. The latitude given to interviewers in selecting their subjects ensured that the probability of being interviewed depended on respondent characteristics that interviewers found attractive. Thus, within quota categories, those citizens who were interviewed were not necessarily representative of the population in that category, potentially violating the MAR assumption. Correcting for nonrandom selection within strata is difficult because I do not have information on the people who were not interviewed. I do, however, sometimes have important information that can be employed in analysis—namely, the education level of the respondent. Although interviewers did not explicitly select respondents on the basis of their schooling, education is the best proxy the surveys have for the "observables" that made an interviewer more likely to pick one individual from a given demographic group than another individual. The key is that education (1) is a powerful predictor of who is a desirable interview subject, (2) affects politically relevant variables, (3) was *not* used as a quota control, but (4) was often measured by survey organizations. Therefore, by utilizing auxiliary information on education levels, I can account for at least some of the problems introduced by nonrandom selection within strata. Although education measures were not included in every survey in this period, a respondent's occupation can serve a similar purpose. For the same reason that interviewers gravitated to highly educated respondents, they tended to interview professionals at the expense of laborers and other members of the working class. In addition, occupation, like education, was not used as an explicit quota variable. Similarly, interviewers often collected information on telephone access, another marker of high social status in the 1930s and 1940s that was not subject to quotas. Thus, even when education is not available, I can correct for nonrandom selection within strata with auxiliary information on occupation or telephone ownership.

The use of auxiliary data—particularly on education, occupation, and phone access—to account for differences between the sample and the population is imperfect. It is possible that the low-education respondents selected by interviewers were not fully representative of the population of low-education citizens. Thus, controlling for education does not completely solve the problem of nonrandom selection within strata because the use of weights may multiply the influence of respondents who are "unusual." Education, however, captures many of the important interviewer-induced differences between respondents and nonrespondents. Although quota-controlled sampling procedures (as they were practiced in the 1930s and 1940s) reduced the probability that certain individuals—women, southerners, nonprofessionals, and those with low education—would be interviewed, no individuals were excluded from the sampling scheme. In almost all of the surveys, every individual therefore had some probability—no matter how low—of being included in the survey samples of this era.[5] By using auxiliary information on education and occupation, I can take advantage of the residue of interviewer-induced distortions to correct at least some of the problems caused by nonrandom selection within strata. Controlling for some of the problem through the use of proxy variables, such as education, is preferable to completely ignoring the problem. In essence, by conditioning on the variables that affect the probability that a given individual would be interviewed, I can better fulfill the conditions required by the MAR assumption. Without detailed information on nonrespondents, this strategy is the best solution available to modern researchers.

In sum, the use of auxiliary information can mitigate the deficiencies of quota-controlled sampling procedures. Thus, in aggregate analysis, I weight the data on education levels, occupation, phone access, and those quota category variables—such as gender and region—that can be matched to census data. If education levels were available, I created cell weights using education, gender, region, and (if available) race.[6] If the survey did not contain a measure of education, I created cell weights using a dummy variable for "professional" occupation, gender, region, and (if available) race. If neither education nor a reliable occupation variable was available, I created raking weights based on the marginals of gender, region, phone access, and race (when available). The necessary population counts for the 1940 census are available from the Integrated Public Use Microdata Series (Ruggles et al. 2004) and aggregate census records of phone access. Even when weighting makes only a modest difference in conclusions, it nonetheless provides more confidence that our estimates are not attributable to problematic sample design.

IRAQ WAR CASUALTY SURVEY ANALYSIS

I present here the full question wording for the items and treatments used in the Iraq War Casualty Survey. I also report the analyses used to generate the predicted probabilities presented in the text and tables in chapter 4.

SURVEY QUESTION WORDING

Independent Variables — Media Use

Information Scale — items are recoded into an additive scale, rescaled to the 0–1 interval

1. Which party has the most members in the House of Representatives in Washington . . . the Democrats or the Republicans?
   A. Democrats
   B. Republican
2. Whose responsibility is it to decide if a law is constitutional or not . . . the President, Congress, or the Supreme Court?
   A. The President
   B. Congress
   C. The Supreme Court
3. Whose responsibility is it to nominate judges to Federal Courts . . . the President, Congress, or the Supreme Court?
   A. The President
   B. Congress
   C. The Supreme Court

4. How closely are you following the news about the situation in Iraq now?

    A. Very closely

    B. Somewhat closely

    C. Not very closely

    D. Not closely at all.

Do you ever watch Fox News?

    A. Yes

    B. No

Note: Partisanship is measured using the standard NES branching seven-point scale, rescaled to the 0–1 interval, with Strong Democrats as 1 and Strong Republicans as 0.

Experimental Treatments (Respondents are randomly assigned to one of four conditions)

CONDITION 1 — NO INTRODUCTORY QUESTIONS ASKED

CONDITION 2 — CASUALTY GUESS ONLY

Please give your best guess to this next question, even if you are not sure of the correct answer. As you know, the United States is currently involved in a war in Iraq. Do you happen to know how many soldiers of the U.S. military have been killed in Iraq since the fighting began in March 2003?

    Enter number: _____

    [If don't know (DK) or no answer, probe:] What is your best guess?

    [If DK or no answer again, probe a second time:] Even if you are not sure, I'd like you to give me your best guess.

    [If DK or no answer to the second probe, record the answer as given.]

[CONDITION 3 — CORRECT INFORMATION ONLY]

As you know, the United States is currently involved in a war in Iraq. You might be interested to know that since the fighting began in March 2003, 901 soldiers have been killed in Iraq. [The casualty count was updated once to 915 in the course of the experiment.]

[CONDITION 4 — BOTH QUESTIONS ASKED:]

    1. Please give your best guess to this next question, even if you are not sure of the correct answer. As you know, the United States is currently involved in a war in Iraq. Do you happen to know how

many soldiers of the U.S. military have been killed in Iraq since the fighting began in March 2003?

Enter number: _____
[If DK or no answer, probe:] What is your best guess?
[If DK or no answer again, probe a second time:] Even if you are not sure, I'd like you to give me your best guess.
[If DK or no answer to the second probe, record the answer as given.]

2. Many people don't know the answer to this question, but according to the latest estimates, 915 soldiers have been killed in Iraq since the fighting began in March 2003.

Dependent Variables
1. Do you think the U.S. made the right decision or the wrong decision in using military force against Iraq?
    A. Right
    B. Wrong
1a. Do you feel strongly or not strongly that the U.S. made the [right/wrong] decision?
    A. Strongly
    B. Not strongly
2. All in all, considering the costs to the United States versus the benefits to the United States, do you think the current war with Iraq has been worth fighting, or not?
    A. Worth fighting
    B. Not worth fighting
2a. Do you feel strongly or not strongly that the war in Iraq [has/has not] been worth fighting?
    A. Strongly
    B. Not strongly
These dependent variables are each separately recoded as a four-point scale, with support for the war as 4 and opposition to the war as 1.

CODING RULES

Information is measured by the number of correct answers to three multiple-choice questions concerning the roles of the different branches of the U.S. government (see Mondak 2001). Attention paid to Iraq is measured on a four-point scale ranging from "very closely" to "not at all closely." Education is measured on a four-point scale (less than high school/high school graduate/some college/college graduate). Partisanship is measured using the standard seven-point National Elections Study scale. Here, as elsewhere, all variables have been rescaled to a 0 (minimum) to 1 (maximum) interval.

TABLE B.1 Multinomial logit analysis of determinants of estimates of war deaths

Variable	Correct answer vs. underestimate		Correct answer vs. overestimate	
	Coefficient	(SE)	Coefficient	(SE)
Constant	1.67	(0.45)**	−0.08	(0.70)
Information	−0.94	(0.31)**	−1.44	(0.48)**
Education	0.10	(0.09)	0.06	(0.15)
Gender	0.03	(0.18)	−0.02	(0.29)
Follows Iraq news	−2.06	(0.38)**	−1.33	(0.61)**
Watches Fox News	−0.14	(0.53)	0.42	(0.85)
Party identification	−0.51	(0.26)**	0.11	(0.43)

Source: Analysis of Iraq War Casualty Survey.
Note: N = 621; LL = −544.58.
* p < .10; ** p < .05.

TABLE B.2 Probit analysis of the effects of casualty estimates on support for the Iraq War

Variable	U.S.-made correct decision		War has been worth fighting	
	Coefficient	(SE)	Coefficient	(SE)
Constant	1.69	(0.36)	1.23	(0.35)
Log (casualties)	−0.05	(0.11)	−0.01	(0.11)
Party identification	−2.09	(0.17)**	−1.95	(0.17)**
N	609		610	
LL	−335.76		−343.31	

* = p <.10; ** p <.05.

CONGRESSIONAL RECORD CONTENT ANALYSIS

To measure the balance of elite rhetoric for the period between 1938 and 1945, I coded the text of the *Congressional Record*. To collect relevant entries, I had my research assistants consult the *Record*'s index for each year from 1938 to 1945 and gather all entries given under the headings "war" and "World War Two."[1] Excluding all entries referring to either the appendix or to particular bills, we assessed the internationalist tone of every speech and remark made on the floor of Congress.[2]

Creating the relevant codes was not a straightforward task. The meaning of any particular statement within the *Congressional Record* is entirely dependent on the context in which it was presented. Consider the hypothetical example of a congressman arguing that the United States ought to send weapons and other supplies to the Allies but not send American troops; the argument would have been strongly interventionist in 1939, moderately interventionist in most of 1941, and isolationist in 1942 or thereafter. Additionally, there is the issue of coding speeches in which a congressman argues that it had been a mistake to aid the Allies initially, but that having done so, the United States was now committed and must therefore undertake other interventionist policies in order to win the war. To avoid confusion, we coded each statement on the basis of two criteria: tone and position. For both criteria, we used the same three-category coding scheme: internationalist, isolationist, and indifference.

The *tonal* code refers to the overall theme or message of the speech. If the statement conveys sympathy for the Allies or antipathy for the Axis, then it is coded as interventionist, even if it does not advocate helping the Allies. If the tone implies little difference between the Allies and the Axis,[3] then the tone is coded as isolationist. If the tone seems genuinely indifferent, it is coded as neutral. If a statement advocates helping the Allies (independent of the form that help might actually take), the statement is coded as pro-interventionist; alternatively, if it advocates keeping out of the conflict or suggests an ambivalent stance toward the allies, it is coded as pro-isolationist. Thus, statements referring to the moral worth or suffering of British friends, the evil and mendacity of Hitler/Germany, or the greatness and importance of democracy (to name just a few) are coded as pro-interventionist *even if they do not advocate military aid.* Similarly, statements that malign allied propaganda, draw moral equivalence between the belligerents, or stress the primacy of American security are coded pro-isolationist *even if they do not expressly advocate neutrality.*

The *positional* code refers to the actual policy position taken in the speech regarding the bill, measure, or other specific issue at hand. For example, if the speaker advocates extending additional lend-lease aid to the Allies, or increasing America's own defense preparation, then that remark is coded as interventionist. If the speaker argues against aiding the Allies, the remark is coded as isolationist. The remarks suggesting indifference are coded as neutral. For instance, in the debate about the amendment of the Neutrality Act allowing for greater aid to the Allies, speeches supporting the amendments are coded as pro-interventionist, whereas those opposing the amendments are coded as pro-isolationist. This measure helps to illustrate how the debate was viewed at the time.

Given that content analysis of a text is somewhat subjective, and given that we had multiple researchers coding different years, it was necessary to take steps to ensure inter-coder consistency. Each coder went through a two-hour training session in which sample passages were coded and discussed. To measure the degree of consistency, we gave each coder the same several pages from the *Record* as a sample to code independently, in order to compare their respective results and ensure their consistency. Furthermore, in a few instances we had one coder independently recode randomly chosen selections from another coder's assigned year, without having first seen that other coder's results, in order to ensure consistency. We found that, in these tests, inter-coder consistency was approximately 90 percent.

In figure 5.1, I present the proportion of prowar to antiwar statements of members of Congress from 1938 to 1945, broken down by party. In addition to the raw data points, I present smoothed data series. I created these series using a lowess smoother, employing Cleveland's tricube weighting function, with a bandwidth of 20 percent of the data. In figure 5.1, I present the tonal data, but the results from the two coding systems yielded results that were highly similar; the positional data graph looks nearly identical to figure 5.1.

WORLD WAR II ANALYSIS

Although the World War II data were collected using quota-sampling methods, it is possible to draw inferences about the U.S. population from this data through methods that account for bias in the sampling procedures. In Appendix B, I outlined a strategy to estimate aggregate statistics, such as population means, from the survey data using poststratification weights. In chapter 5 I am interested in estimating more complex relationships among the variables available in the data through individual-level regression analysis. Whether or not to include weights in regression analysis is a source of ongoing controversy in the survey research literature.[4] Several authors caution against the use of weights in this manner (see Lohr 1999, 362–65, for a review). This admonition is especially pertinent here because my weights are poststratification weights, not sampling weights. Winship and Radbill (1994) note that when weights are solely a function of observed independent variables that can be included in a regression model—as is the case with my data—unweighted ordinary least squares (OLS) will yield unbiased parameter estimates. Thus, the most straightforward method of dealing with the potential bias created by quota sampling is simply to include the weighting variables as independent variables in the regression model (Gelman 2005; Gelman and Carlin 2002).[5] In this case, the problem is similar to omitted variable bias: the oversampling of certain types of respondents—namely, highly educated white males—may mask the true relationship among other predictors if these variables are not controlled for. In this way, the individual and aggregate analyses are closely related, in that in order to get aggregate estimates, I average over the proportions of different types of respondents present in the population. Just as the cell-weighting and regression estimation methods incorporate information about the joint distribution of the sample, introducing the quota variables—and relevant interaction terms—as independent variables allows me to control for the sample imbalances introduced by the quota-sampling methods of the time (see Berinsky 2006 for further discussion).

Although it is possible to control for the bias in the coefficient estimates, compiling accurate measures of uncertainty is a complicated process. Standard tests of statistical significance assume that the data are drawn through probability sampling. Quota samples, however, rely on interviewer discretion for respondent selection, thereby diverging from strict random sampling. Thus, as Gschwend notes, "it is neither clear according to statistical theory how to compute a standard deviation, nor how to estimate standard errors" (2005, 89).

In the analyses in this book, I follow the convention of other scholars who have analyzed the data (Baum and Kernell 2001; Schlozman and Verba 1979; Verba and Schlozman 1977; Weatherford and Sereyev 2000) and present standard errors for the estimated coefficients. In effect, I analyze the data as though they were generated through probability sampling. My confidence in the validity of the results does not rely on the statistical tests alone, however. The convergence of the results in the same period (pre-December 1941 versus post-December 1941) for both the information analyses in chapter 5 and the group-based analyses in chapter 6 speaks to the robustness of my results, given that the polls were conducted by different organizations that implemented quota sampling in different ways (see Berinsky 2006 for discussion of the different quota-sampling methods).

Tests of statistical significance on the individual coefficients are not sufficient to address the hypotheses evaluated in chapter 5. My central argument is that supporters and opponents of FDR came to different conclusions regarding the United States' entry into the war as their information levels increased before December 1941. After Pearl Harbor, however, the effect of information on support for the war should be the same for both supporters and opponents of the president. I performed two sets of tests to assess my level of confidence in the analyses supporting this argument. I first performed a likelihood-ratio test to assess whether the information interactions were equivalent for supporters and opponents of FDR. Second, I used CLARIFY (2000) to put confidence bounds on the behavior of supporters and opponents of FDR at endpoints of the information scale. This analysis allowed me to test whether, as I claim, high-information supporters of FDR behaved differently than low-information supporters, and furthermore, whether these two groups behaved differently than their corresponding numbers among FDR's opponents.

In almost all cases, both sets of tests confirmed my conclusions. However, I briefly discuss cases in which both tests did not yield the expected results. In two instances of the demonstration of the mainstream effect, I find that the null hypothesis of the equality of interactive terms is rejected, contrary to expectation. These two analyses are those using the October 1940 AIPO poll and the March 1943 Roper poll. Although the coefficients are statically different in magnitude, the effect of information is in the same direction for both groups; higher levels of political information lead to higher levels of support for war. Thus, the substantive conclusion of the analysis is the expected one; the elite cue theory is supported.[6] The only test that is potentially problematic is the test for the equality of interactive terms in the January 1941 AIPO analysis. I cannot reject the null hypothesis that the coefficients are equal. Yet the predicted probabilities of supporting England yield statically distinct results for supporters and opponents of FDR, as expected. Moreover, these results are almost identical to those found in an analysis performed on another data set collected by OPOR at the exact same time. This convergence across independent data sets further bolsters the robustness of this result.

The full results of the analysis are available in the online appendix (http://www.press.uchicago.edu/books/berinsky/). There I present several pieces of information about the analysis. For each poll, I present (1) the variable(s) used to measure FDR predispositions, (2) the items used to create the information scales, with complete question wording, (3) the wording of the dependent variable(s) that measure war support, (4) the full results of the statistical analysis, and (5) the tests of significance—both the likelihood-ratio tests and the predicted probability tests for each of the analyses. To give readers a flavor of the analysis, I present here the full results for two of the analyses. In all the analyses (both here and in the online appendix), information levels are rescaled to a 0–1 interval, in which 0 represents the lowest level of information/engagement and 1 represents the highest level of information/engagement. All other variables are broken into a series of dummy variables, with the corresponding dummy indicators listed in the tables.

SURVEY QUESTION WORDING—WORLD WAR II ANALYSIS

All information measures are additive scales, rescaled to the 0–1 interval.

AIPO 176—November 1939
FDR PREDISPOSITIONS
I use a combination of the respondent's vote in the 1936 election and approval of FDR

INFORMATION SCALE
1. Have you heard of the Townsend Plan for Old Age Pensions? (Yes is scored as 1, else 0.)

2. Do you recall how much per month each person is supposed to receive under the Townsend Plan? (Correct answer—$200—is scored as 1, else 0.)

DEPENDENT VARIABLE
Do you approve of the change which Congress made in the Neutrality Act which permits nations at war to buy arms and airplanes in this country?

AIPO 243—July/August 1941
FDR PREDISPOSITIONS
I use a combination of the respondent's vote in the 1940 election and approval of FDR.

INFORMATION SCALE
1. Do you happen to know who General de Gaulle is? (Correct answer—"He is with the Free French" "A Free French General," "Leader of Free French Forces," "French General who is fighting against Germans"—is scored as 1, else 0.)
2. Do you happen to know about where Dakar is? (Correct answer— West Africa, Northwest Africa, West Coast of Africa, across from Brazil, Africa near South America, French West Africa—scored 1, else 0.)

DEPENDENT VARIABLE
Do you think the United States Navy should be used to guard (convoy) ships carrying war materials to Britain?

TABLE C.1 Support for the Neutrality Act, November 1939

Do you approve of the change which Congress made in the Neutrality Act which permits nations at war to buy arms and airplanes in this country?

Variable	Yes vs. don't know		No vs. don't know	
	Coefficient	(SE)	Coefficient	(SE)
Constant	2.73	(0.61)**	1.11	(0.66)*
Support FDR	0.14	(0.43)	−0.11	(0.49)
Oppose FDR	2.22	(0.86)*	2.51	(0.89)**
Information	0.38	(0.45)	0.87	(0.48)
Info × support FDR	0.13	(0.60)	−0.42	(0.66)
Info × oppose FDR	−3.08	(0.98)**	−3.00	(1.00)**
Male	0.92	(0.22)**	−0.31	(0.24)
Economic class				
Upper class	0.91	(0.97)	0.58	(0.68)
Middle class	0.71	(0.22)**	0.35	(0.23)
On relief	−0.35	(0.35)	−0.20	(0.38)
Census region				
Midwest	−0.28	(0.21)	−0.28	(0.22)
South	0.55	(0.32)	−0.10	(0.36)
West	−0.12	(0.28)	0.15	(0.29)
Occupation				
Professional	0.13	(0.44)	−0.12	(0.47)
Farm	−0.60	(0.47)	−0.33	(0.51)
Labor	−0.10	(0.44)	0.01	(0.48)
Other	−0.36	(0.37)	−0.51	(0.40)

Source: Author analysis of AIPO 176 (November 1939).

Note: N = 1,548; LL = −1,292.82.

* $p < .10$; ** $p < .05$.

TABLE C.2 Support for U.S. Navy convoys, July–August 1941

Do you think the U.S. Navy should be used to guard [convoy] ships carrying war materials to Britain?

Variable	Yes vs. no opinion		No vs. no opinion	
	Coefficient	(SE)	Coefficient	(SE)
Constant	1.18	(0.21)**	1.25	(0.21)**
Support FDR	0.36	(0.18)*	−0.13	(0.19)
Oppose FDR	0.35	(0.30)	0.95	(0.30)**
Information	1.22	(0.33)**	0.66	(0.34)*
Info × support FDR	−0.65	(0.45)	−0.94	(0.48)**
Info × oppose FDR	−0.94	(0.65)	−0.35	(0.64)
Census region				
Midwest	0.08	(0.17)	0.16	(0.17)
South	0.87	(0.27)**	0.02	(0.28)
West	0.14	(0.22)	−0.05	(0.23)
Economic class				
Upper class	1.70	(1.02)*	0.56	(1.03)
Poor	−0.30	(0.17)*	−0.23	(0.18)
On relief	−0.47	(0.32)	−0.27	(0.33)
Occupation				
Professional	−0.14	(0.28)	−0.41	(0.29)
Farm	0.24	(0.38)	0.20	(0.39)
Labor	0.37	(0.21)*	0.35	(0.21)*
Unemployed	0.45	(0.35)	0.26	(0.35)
Male	0.55	(0.19)**	0.39	(0.20)**

Source: Author analysis of AIPO 243 (July–August 1941).

Note: N = 2,930; LL = −2,456.30.

* $p < .10$; ** $p < .05$.

TABLE C.3 Statistical test of differences: Support for the Neutrality Act, November 1939

Do you approve of the change which Congress made in the Neutrality Act which permits nations at war to buy arms and airplanes in this country?

Confidence intervals of endpoints on probability of "approve of changes" (standard error in parenthesis)

	FDR supporters	FDR opponents
Lowest information	0.65 (0.07)	0.68 (0.08)
Highest information	0.71 (0.05)	0.34 (0.06)

Source: Author analysis of AIPO 176 (November 1939).

Note: Likelihood-ratio test of equality of information terms is $\chi^2(2) = 11.51$; $Pr > \chi^2 = 0.03$. High-information FDR supporters are not statistically different from low-information FDR supporters. High-information FDR opponents are statistically different from low-information FDR opponents. High-information FDR supporters are statistically different from high-information FDR opponents. Low-information FDR opponents are not statistically different from low-information FDR supporters.

TABLE C.4 Statistical test of differences: Support for U.S. Navy convoys, July–August 1941

Do you think the U.S. Navy should be used to guard [convoy] ships carrying war materials to Britain?

Confidence intervals of endpoints on probability of "support convoy" (standard error in parenthesis)

	FDR supporters	FDR opponents
Lowest information	0.57 (0.03)	0.33 (0.03)
Highest information	0.75 (0.03)	0.33 (0.03)

Source: Author analysis of AIPO 243 (July–August 1941).

Note: Likelihood-ratio test of equality of information terms is $\chi^2(2) = 8.44$; $Pr > \chi^2 = 0.01$. High-information FDR supporters are statistically different from low-information FDR supporters. High-information FDR opponents are not statistically different from low-information FDR opponents. High-information FDR supporters are statistically different from high-information FDR opponents. Low-information FDR opponents are statistically different from low-information FDR supporters.

TABLE C.5 Probit results of the Iraq War Casualty Survey

U.S. made the right decision in using military force against Iraq

Variable	Coefficient	(SE)
Constant	0.62	(0.26)
Education	−0.06	(0.04)
Female	−0.00	(0.08)
Black	−0.71	(0.14)**
Hispanic	−0.09	(0.14)
Party identification	−0.29	(0.34)
Information	0.91	(0.27)**
Party identification information	−2.00	(0.42)**

Note: N = 1,205; LL = −666.35.

Current war with Iraq has been worth fighting

Variable	Coefficient	(SE)
Constant	0.27	(0.25)
Education	−0.02	(0.04)
Female	0.01	(0.08)
Black	−0.57	(0.14)**
Hispanic	−0.16	(0.14)
Party identification	−0.36	(0.33)
Information	0.73	(0.25)**
Party identification information	−1.66	(0.41)**

Note: N = 1,216; LL = −707.47.

(*continued*)

TABLE C.5 Probit results of the Iraq War Casualty Survey (*continued*)

War will be successful?

Variable	Coefficient	(SE)
Constant	0.88	(0.26)**
Education	−0.06	(0.04)
Female	−0.04	(0.08)
Black	−0.33	(0.13)**
Hispanic	0.15	(0.14)
Party identification	−0.06	(0.33)
Information	0.51	(0.26)*
Party identification information	−1.64	(0.41)**

Note: N = 1,221; LL = −708.88.

Source: Author analysis of the Iraq War Casualty Survey.

Note: The description of the coding of these variables is presented in Appendix B (with the exception of the "black" and "Hispanic" variables, which are simply dummy indicators).

* $p < .10$; ** $p < .05$.

STATISTICAL SIGNIFICANCE OF ETHNIC VARIABLES

In chapter 6, I present the substantive effect of the group attachment enmity variables on opinion about World War II. The full-model results used to estimate these effects are presented in the online appendix to this book (http://www.press.uchicago.edu/books/berinsky/). Although it is not technically possible to compute the standard errors needed to construct statistical tests, the consistency of the sign and magnitude of the ethnic effects speaks to their robustness across a number of data sets. In this appendix, I present examples of tests of the statistical significance of the ethnic variables (the full set of tests is available in the online appendix). In each of these tables, the entries represent the results of a likelihood-ratio test against the null hypothesis that each of the ethnic variables has "no effect."

TABLE D.1 The power of ethnic attachments, before the United States' entry into World War II, August 1939 (likelihood-ratio tests)

	Tend to own business	No question so important that U.S. should risk war	Don't allow England/France to buy food	Don't allow England/France to buy war supplies	Don't send U.S. Army and Navy abroad to help
English best	$\chi^2(3) = 27.20$; $\Pr > \chi^2 = 0.00$	$\chi^2(3) = 8.14$; $\Pr > \chi^2 = 0.04$	$\chi^2(3) = 14.72$; $\Pr > \chi^2 = 0.00$	$\chi^2(3) = 16.23$; $\Pr > \chi^2 = 0.00$	$\chi^2(3) = 30.91$; $\Pr > \chi^2 = 0.00$
Germans best	$\chi^2(3) = 0.19$; $\Pr > \chi^2 = 0.98$	$\chi^2(3) = 9.16$; $\Pr > \chi^2 = 0.03$	$\chi^2(3) = 1.93$; $\Pr > \chi^2 = 0.59$	$\chi^2(3) = 5.42$; $\Pr > \chi^2 = 0.14$	$\chi^2(3) = 12.92$; $\Pr > \chi^2 = 0.00$
Italians best	$\chi^2(3) = 2.63$; $\Pr > \chi^2 = 0.45$	$\chi^2(3) = 0.72$; $\Pr > \chi^2 = 0.87$	$\chi^2(3) = 0.62$; $\Pr > \chi^2 = 0.89$	$\chi^2(3) = 4.15$; $\Pr > \chi^2 = 0.24$	$\chi^2(3) = 3.70$; $\Pr > \chi^2 = 0.30$
Germans worst	$\chi^2(3) = 3.36$; $\Pr > \chi^2 = 0.34$	$\chi^2(3) = 4.26$; $\Pr > \chi^2 = 0.23$	$\chi^2(3) = 6.69$; $\Pr > \chi^2 = 0.08$	$\chi^2(3) = 9.08$; $\Pr > \chi^2 = 0.03$	$\chi^2(3) = 15.87$; $\Pr > \chi^2 = 0.00$
Italians worst	$\chi^2(3) = 11.96$; $\Pr > \chi^2 = 0.01$	$\chi^2(3) = 14.05$; $\Pr > \chi^2 = 0.00$	$\chi^2(3) = 9.13$; $\Pr > \chi^2 = 0.03$	$\chi^2(3) = 34.58$; $\Pr > \chi^2 = 0.00$	$\chi^2(3) = 26.00$; $\Pr > \chi^2 = 0.00$
Restrict rights of Jews in America[a]	$\chi^2(3) = 4.11$; $\Pr > \chi^2 = 0.25$	$\chi^2(3) = 17.06$; $\Pr > \chi^2 = 0.00$	$\chi^2(3) = 17.16$; $\Pr > \chi^2 = 0.00$	$\chi^2(3) = 10.30$; $\Pr > \chi^2 = 0.02$	$\chi^2(3) = 6.47$; $\Pr > \chi^2 = 0.09$

Source: Author analysis of Roper Survey 7 (August 1939).

[a] Those who would restrict the right of Jews in America have rejected the statement, "In the United States the Jews have the same standing as any other people, and they should be treated in all ways exactly as any other Americans."

TABLE D.2 The power of ethnic attachments, before the United States' entry into World War II, 1941 (likelihood-ratio tests)

European theater

Date	Axis variable test	Allies variable test
	Help England rather than stay out	
January 28, 1941	$\chi^2(1) = 27.65$; Pr>χ^2 = 0.00	$\chi^2(1) = 12.03$; Pr>χ^2 = 0.00
March 12, 1941	$\chi^2(1) = 74.26$; Pr>χ^2 = 0.00	$\chi^2(1) = 3.78$; Pr>χ^2 = 0.05
March 28, 1941	$\chi^2(1) = 76.21$; Pr>χ^2 = 0.00	$\chi^2(1) = 2.41$; Pr>χ^2 = 0.125
	Defeat Germany rather than stay out	
January 28, 1941	$\chi^2(1) = 12.22$; Pr>χ^2 = 0.00	$\chi2(1) = 2.29$; Pr>χ^2 = 0.13
	Willing to fight in Europe if U.S. gets involved?	
March 12, 1941	$\chi^2(2) = 17.99$; Pr>χ^2 = 0.00	$\chi^2(2) = 6.19$; Pr>χ^2 = 0.05
	Vote to go to war?	
January 28, 1941	$\chi^2(2) = 10.93$; Pr>χ^2 = 0.00	$\chi^2(2) = 6.66$; Pr>χ^2 = 0.04
	Favor war if convoy is sunk?	
January 28, 1941	$\chi^2(3) = 14.09$; Pr>χ^2 = 0.00	$\chi^2(2) = 3.82$; Pr>χ^2 = 0.28

Proximate questions

Date	Axis variable test	Allies variable test
	U.S. should fight preemptive wars?	
March 12, 1941	$\chi^2(2) = 23.51$; Pr>χ^2 = 0.00	$\chi^2(2) = 5.17$; Pr>χ^2 = 0.08
	U.S. should risk war to keep Japan down	
March 28, 1941	$\chi^2(2) = 12.08$; Pr>χ^2 = 0.00	$\chi^2(2) = 5.07$; Pr>χ^2 = 0.08
	U.S. should defend Latin America if attacked by European power?	
March 28, 1941	$\chi^2(2) = 4.67$; Pr>χ^2 = 0.10	$\chi^2(2) = 0.81$; Pr>χ^2 = 0.67

Sources: Author analysis of OPOR 806 (January 28, 1941), OPOR 807 (March 12, 1941), and OPOR 808W (March 28, 1941).

TABLE D.3 The power of ethnic attachments, after the United States' entry into World War II (likelihood-ratio tests)

If the German army overthrew Hitler and then offered to stop the war and discuss peace terms with the Allies, would you favor or oppose accepting the offer of the German army?

OPOR survey number	Date	Axis test	Allies test
811T	January 1942	$\chi^2(3) = 15.08$; $\mathrm{Pr} > \chi^2 = 0.00$	$\chi^2(3) = 5.06$; $\mathrm{Pr} > \chi^2 = 0.08$
817	June 1942	$\chi^2(2) = 32.94$; $\mathrm{Pr} > \chi^2 = 0.00$	$\chi^2(2) = 0.25$; $\mathrm{Pr} > \chi^2 = 0.88$
6	April 1943	$\chi^2(2) = 2.91$; $\mathrm{Pr} > \chi^2 = 0.23$	$\chi^2(2) = 0.97$; $\mathrm{Pr} > \chi^2 = 0.62$
15	August 1943	$\chi^2(2) = 5.12$; $\mathrm{Pr} > \chi^2 = 0.08$	$\chi^2(2) = 4.97$; $\mathrm{Pr} > \chi^2 = 0.08$
21	January 1944	$\chi^2(2) = 14.12$; $\mathrm{Pr} > \chi^2 = 0.00$	$\chi^2(2) = 2.62$; $\mathrm{Pr} > \chi^2 = 0.27$
26	April 1944	$\chi^2(2) = 20.55$; $\mathrm{Pr} > \chi^2 = 0.00$	$\chi^2(2) = 0.16$; $\mathrm{Pr} > \chi^2 = 0.92$
27	June 1944	$\chi^2(1) = 2.38$; $\mathrm{Pr} > \chi^2 = 0.30$	$\chi^2(1) = 6.55$; $\mathrm{Pr} > \chi^2 = 0.04$
30	August 1944	$\chi^2(2) = 6.49$; $\mathrm{Pr} > \chi^2 = 0.04$	$\chi^2(2) = 1.47$; $\mathrm{Pr} > \chi^2 = 0.48$
33K	October 1944	$\chi^2(2) = 7.87$; $\mathrm{Pr} > \chi^2 = 0.02$	$\chi^2(2) = 0.43$; $\mathrm{Pr} > \chi^2 = 0.80$
38	February 1945	$\chi^2(2) = 1.17$; $\mathrm{Pr} > \chi^2 = 0.56$	$\chi^2(2) = 0.77$; $\mathrm{Pr} > \chi^2 = 0.68$
43	April 1945	$\chi2(2) = 6.46$; $\mathrm{Pr} > \chi^2 = 0.04$	$\chi^2(2) = 1.84$; $\mathrm{Pr} > \chi^2 = 0.40$

Sources: Author analysis of OPOR surveys.

ECONOMIC POLICY ANALYSIS

The coding of the variables for the analysis of the 1986 South Africa sanctions can be found in the online appendix. The coefficients I used to generate the predicted probabilities in chapter 6 are presented in the following table.

TABLE D.4 Bivariate probit selection model analysis of sanctions against South Africa

Variable	Coefficient	(SE)
Outcome equation		
Constant	0.12	(0.31)
Black feeling thermometer (rescaled)	0.71	(0.27)**
Black	0.64	(0.17)**
Party identification	0.64	(0.16)**
Liberal	0.34	(0.14)**
Conservative	0.10	(0.12)
No ideology	0.22	(0.17)
Male	−0.22	(0.10)
Education	0.45	(0.24)*
Age	−1.32	(0.32)**
Selection equation		
Constant	−1.59	(0.20)**
Black feeling thermometer (rescaled)	0.53	(0.20)**
Black	0.62	(0.13)**
Party identification	−0.20	(0.13)
Liberal	0.19	(0.12)
Conservative	−0.17	(0.10)
No ideology	−0.29	(0.12)**
Male	0.28	(0.08)**
Education	0.62	(0.19)**
Age	0.19	(0.26)
Political information	2.75	(0.24)**
Discuss politics	0.69	(0.18)**
Interviewer experience	0.17	(0.09)*
Refusal conversion	−0.23	(0.26)
Correlation parameters		
ρ	−0.24	(0.17)
N/LL	1,346/−1,164.12	

Source: Author analysis of the 1986 National Elections Study.

* $p < .10$; ** $p < .05$.

RELATIONSHIP BETWEEN SUPPORT FOR WAR AND SUPPORT FOR RESTRICTING CIVIL LIBERTIES

In chapter 7, I present the substantive relationship between support for war and support for restricting civil liberties. The full-model results used to estimate these effects are presented in the online appendix to this book (http://www.press.uchicago.edu/books/berinsky/). In this appendix, I present examples of these analyses for the interested reader.

In the analyses, all variables except political interest (in the January 2006 analysis) and support for the Vietnam War (for the Harris analysis) were entered as a series of dummy variables. A few other notes about the analysis are in order. First, as mentioned in the text, the analyses in figure 7.4 do not control for partisanship because Pew did not ask a party identification question in its September 2001 survey. Second, the measure of war support employed in the analysis in figure 7.5 shifted across the period covered here. Before the United States invaded Iraq, I used a prospective measure of support for the (possible) war: "Would you favor or oppose taking military action in Iraq to end Saddam Hussein's rule?" or "Would you favor or oppose taking military action in Iraq to end Saddam Hussein's rule, even if it meant that U.S. forces might suffer thousands of casualties?"[1] After the United States' invasion, I used a retrospective measure, "Do you think the U.S. made the right decision or the wrong decision in using military force against Iraq?" Finally, as was the case with the analysis in chapters 5 and 6, I present tests of the statistical significance, although it is not technically possible to compute the standard errors needed to construct statistical tests for the World War II–era data.

I present below a subset of the analyses used to generate figures 7.3–7.6.

TABLE E.1 Partisan polarization on civil liberties restrictions, 2006

What concerns you more about the government's anti-terrorism policies, that they have not gone far enough to adequately protect the country or that they have gone too far in restricting the average person's civil liberties?

	Go too far vs. don't go far enough		Other response vs. don't go far enough	
	Coefficient	(SE)	Coefficient	(SE)
Constant	−0.13	(0.52)	0.92	(0.51)*
Region				
Midwest	0.00	(0.29)	−0.48	(0.31)
South	−0.32	(0.28)	−0.35	(0.29)
West	0.26	(0.30)	−0.14	(0.32)
Education				
Some high school	−0.38	(0.34)	−0.68	(0.34)**
Some college	−0.13	(0.35)	−0.68	(0.36)*
College graduate +	−0.22	(0.34)	−0.26	(0.34)
Size				
Suburban	−0.30	(0.25)	−0.24	(0.25)
Urban	0.43	(0.27)	−0.10	(0.29)
Black	0.15	(0.31)	−0.35	(0.41)
Female	−0.12	(0.19)	0.30	(0.20)
Democrat	−0.19	(0.51)	−0.45	(0.53)
Republican	−0.51	(0.61)	−0.84	(0.54)
Political interest	0.48	(0.58)	−1.29	(0.62)**
Democrat × interest	0.65	(0.81)	0.22	(0.93)
Republican × interest	−1.83	(1.04)*	0.37	(0.93)

Source: Author analysis of Pew Research Center for the People and the Press (January 2006).
Note: N = 746; LL = −714.49.
* $p < .10$; ** $p < .05$.

TABLE E.2 Support for war and support for civil liberties, 2002

What concerns you more right now? That the government will fail to enact strong, new anti-terrorism laws, or that the government will enact new anti-terrorism laws which excessively restrict the average person's civil liberties?

Variable	Fail to enact vs. enact		Other response vs. enact	
	Coefficient	(SE)	Coefficient	(SE)
Constant	−0.83	(0.35)*	−1.66	(0.50)**
Attack Iraq	**0.68**	**(0.16)****	**0.62**	**(0.25)****
Black	−1.06	(0.29)**	−1.63	(0.62)**
Female	0.22	(0.14)	0.60	(0.22)**
Democrat	−0.11	(0.17)	−0.07	(0.26)
Republican	0.26	(0.16)	0.02	(0.26)
Census region				
Midwest	0.24	(0.20)	0.72	(0.32)**
South	0.10	(0.19)	0.18	(0.32)
West	−0.04	(0.21)	0.19	(0.34)
Education				
High school graduate	−0.25	(0.29)	−0.79	(0.36)**
Some college	0.00	(0.29)	−0.92	(0.38)**
College graduate +	0.02	(0.28)	−1.02	(0.36)**
Size				
Suburban	0.21	(0.21)	−0.26	(0.36)
Urban	0.30	(0.18)*	0.31	(0.27)

Source: Author analysis of Pew Research Center for the People and the Press and Council on Foreign Relations (January 2002).

Note: N = 1,055; LL = −972.21.

* $p < .10$; ** $p < .05$.

TABLE E.3 Effect of support for the Vietnam War on civil liberties judgments

Do you think people have the right to conduct peaceful demonstrations against the war in Vietnam, or do you feel people don't have that right?

November 1965

	Don't have right vs. have right		Not sure vs. have right	
	Coefficient	(SE)	Coefficient	(SE)
Constant	−0.31	(0.24)	−0.10	(0.36)
Vietnam support	**0.73**	**(0.27)****	**−1.89**	**(0.54)****
Black	−0.75	(0.23)**	0.07	(0.29)
Female	−0.02	(0.14)	−0.74	(0.24)**
Republican	0.26	(0.22)	0.35	(0.36)
Democrat	0.34	(0.20)*	−0.10	(0.34)
Education				
Some high school	−0.39	(0.21)	−0.87	(0.31)**
High school graduate	−0.72	(0.18)**	−1.78	(0.30)**
Some college +	−1.72	(0.21)**	−2.23	(0.36)**

Note: N = 1,123; LL = −921.84.

* $p < .10$; ** $p < .05$.

May 1967

	Don't have right vs. have right		Not sure vs. have right	
	Coefficient	(SE)	Coefficient	(SE)
Constant	−0.90	(0.21)**	−0.52	(0.27)*
Vietnam support	**1.15**	**(0.25)****	**−0.60**	**(0.39)**
Black	−0.68	(0.22)**	0.84	(0.23)**
Female	−0.13	(0.13)	−0.20	(0.20)
Republican	0.09	(0.18)	−0.69	(0.29)**
Democrat	0.31	(0.16)**	−0.32	(0.23)
Education				
Some high school	−0.00	(0.19)	−0.79	(0.25)**
High school graduate	−0.43	(0.17)**	−1.17	(0.24)**
Some college +	−0.93	(0.19)**	−1.90	(0.32)**

Note: N = 1,418; LL = −1,172.74.

* $p < .10$; ** $p < .05$.

Sources: Author analysis of Harris Poll 1561 (November 1965) and Harris Poll 1735 (May 1967).

TABLE E.4 Effect of support for World War II on negative civil liberties judgments, November 1940

Do you believe in freedom of speech? [If yes,] Do you believe in it to the extent of allowing Fascists and Communists to hold meetings and express their views in this community?

Variable	Oppose vs. support	
	Coefficient	(SE)
Constant	−0.66	(0.16)**
War support	**0.38**	**(0.11)****
Male	−0.12	(0.15)
Occupation		
Professional	−0.04	(0.19)
Farm	0.24	(0.23)
Labor	0.13	(0.20)
Unemployed	0.06	(0.28)
Region		
Midwest	−0.19	(0.13)
South	0.64	(0.19)**
West	0.12	(0.17)
Class		
Upper class	0.20	(0.34)
Middle class	−0.08	(0.12)
On relief	0.14	(0.27)

Source: Author analysis of AIPO 224 (November 1940).

Note: The "war support" independent variable is a combination of two split-sample variables. One of the sample was asked, "Which of these two things do you think is the more important for the United States to try to do: to keep out of war ourselves, or to help England win, even at the risk of getting into the war?" The other half of the sample was asked, "Which of these two things do you think is the more important: that this country keep out of war, or that Germany be defeated." The variable is scored 0 if the respondent thinks it is more important to keep out of war and 1 if the respondent thinks it is more important to help England or defeat Germany. I performed the analysis separately for each form and, because the results were essentially the same, combined the two forms for the purposes of analysis. N = 1,439; LL = −943.39.

* $p < .10$; ** $p < .05$.

NES ANALYSIS OF RETROSPECTIVE WAR SUPPORT

In chapter 8, I present an analysis of the relationship between support for war and individuals' presidential vote choice. In the online appendix, I present the full analyses used to construct those effects (http://www.press .uchicago.edu/books/berinsky/). Here, I present a subset—those analyses that use data from the National Elections Study (NES).

In these analyses , all variables except party identification are entered as a series of dummy variables. The income quintile classifications were generated from the percentile groupings in the NES cumulative file. The omitted categories for the dummy variable groupings are region (Northeast), education (grade school only, except in 2004, when "high school graduate" is the omitted category), and income (bottom quintile). Party identification is measured using a branching seven-point scale, rescaled to the 0–1 interval, with Strong Democrats as 1 and Strong Republicans as 0. All analyses are probit results.

War-support variable: Do you think we did the right thing in getting into the fighting in Korea two years ago or should we have stayed out?

	Vote Eisenhower vs. Stevenson	
	Coefficient	(SE)
Constant	−1.88	(0.20)**
Korea a mistake	**0.22**	**(0.11)****
Party identification	3.17	(0.19)**
Female	0.07	(0.11)
Black	0.99	(0.29)**
Region		
Midwest	−0.10	(0.13)
South	−0.38	(0.16)**
West	−0.09	(0.19)
Education		
Some high school	0.12	(0.15)
High school graduate	−0.29	(0.14)**
Some college	−0.68	(0.21)**
College graduate	−0.00	(0.21)
Income		
Second quintile	0.09	(0.20)
Third quintile	0.03	(0.13)
Fourth quintile	−0.18	(0.18)
Fifth quintile	0.09	(0.27)
Income not reported	−0.41	(0.43)

Note: N = 975; LL = −393.88.
* $p < .10$; ** $p < .05$.

TABLE F.2 1952 NES election analysis of the prospective war-support measure

War-support variable: Which of the following things do you think it would be best for us to do now in Korea? Pull out of Korea entirely, keep on trying to get a peaceful settlement, or take a stronger stand and bomb Manchuria and China.

	Vote Eisenhower vs. Stevenson	
	Coefficient	(SE)
Constant	−1.90	(0.19)**
Pullout of Korea	**−0.12**	**(0.19)**
Escalate in Asia	**−0.29**	**(0.10)**
Party identification	3.19	(0.18)**
Female	−0.01	(0.10)
Black	1.09	(0.27)
Region		
Midwest	−0.06	(0.12)
South	−0.33	(0.15)**
West	−0.08	(0.17)
Education		
Some high school	0.21	(0.14)
High school graduate	−0.23	(0.13)*
Some college	−0.49	(0.19)**
College graduate	−0.05	(0.20)
Income		
Second quintile	0.05	(0.19)
Third quintile	0.01	(0.12)
Fourth quintile	−0.25	(0.17)
Fifth quintile	0.08	(0.27)
Income not reported	−0.35	(0.40)

Note: N = 1,095; LL = −440.29.

* $p < .10$; ** $p < .05$.

War-support variable: Do you think we did the right thing in getting into the fighting in Vietnam or should we have stayed out?

	Vote Nixon vs. Humphrey	
	Coefficient	(SE)
Constant	−0.33	(0.26)
Vietnam a mistake	−0.20	(0.12)
Party identification	1.65	(0.11)**
Male	0.02	(0.12)
Black	1.55	(0.37)**
Region		
North central	−0.37	(0.16)**
South	−0.68	(0.18)**
West	−0.41	(0.18)**
Education		
Some high school	−0.53	(0.23)**
High school graduate	−0.36	(0.21)*
Some college	−0.31	(0.23)
College graduate	−0.21	(0.23)
Income		
Second quintile	0.57	(0.25)**
Third quintile	0.50	(0.24)**
Fourth quintile	0.65	(0.25)**
Fifth quintile	0.82	(0.35)**
Income not reported	0.25	(0.54)

Note: N = 759; LL = −284.51.

* $p < .10$; ** $p < .05$.

1968 NES election analysis of the prospective war-support measure

War-support variable: Which of the following do you think we should do now in Vietnam? Pull out of Vietnam entirely, keep our soldiers in Vietnam but try to end the fighting, or take a stronger stand even if it means invading?

	Vote Nixon vs. Humphrey	
	Coefficient	(SE)
Constant	−0.09	(0.23)
Escalate	−0.54	(0.13)**
Withdraw	−0.31	(0.15)**
Party identification	1.76	(0.10)**
Male	−0.04	(0.12)
Region		
North central	−0.31	(0.15)**
South	−0.56	(0.16)**
West	−0.56	(0.18)**
Education		
Some high school	−0.41	(0.20)**
High school graduate	−0.34	(0.19)*
Some college	−0.40	(0.21)*
College graduate	−0.34	(0.22)
Income		
Second quintile	0.34	(0.22)
Third quintile	0.30	(0.21)
Fourth quintile	0.49	(0.22)**
Fifth quintile	0.46	(0.32)
Income not reported	0.25	(0.44)

Note: N = 862; LL = −329.71.

* $p < .10$; ** $p < .05$.

War-support variable: There is much talk about "hawks" and "doves" in connection with Vietnam, and considerable disagreement as to what action the United States should take in Vietnam. Some people think we should do everything necessary to win a complete military victory, no matter what results. Some people think we should withdraw completely from Vietnam right now, no matter what results. And, of course, other people have opinions somewhere between these two extreme positions. Suppose the people who support an immediate withdrawal are at one end of this scale at point number 1. And suppose the people who support a complete military victory are at the other end of the scale at point number 7. At what point on the scale would you place yourself?

	Vote Nixon vs. Humphrey	
	Coefficient	(SE)
Constant	−0.59	(0.25)**
Dovishness	**0.45**	**(0.19)****
Party Identification	1.67	(0.10)**
Male	0.07	(0.12)
Region		
North central	−0.35	(0.15)**
South	−0.64	(0.17)**
West	−0.44	(0.18)**
Education		
Some high school	−0.44	(0.21)**
High school graduate	−0.32	(0.19)*
Some college	−0.44	(0.22)**
College graduate	−0.33	(0.22)
Income		
Second quintile	0.48	(0.23)**
Third quintile	0.39	(0.22)*
Fourth quintile	0.62	(0.23)**
Fifth quintile	0.67	(0.32)**
Income not reported	0.30	(0.55)

Note: N = 840; LL = −308.76.

* $p < .10$; ** $p < .05$.

TABLE F.6 1972 NES election analysis of the retrospective war-support measure

War-support variable: Do you think we did the right thing in getting into the fighting in Vietnam or should we have stayed out?

	Vote McGovern vs. Nixon	
	Coefficient	(SE)
Constant	−0.69	(0.17)**
Vietnam a mistake	**0.58**	**(0.09)****
Party identification	1.22	(0.07)**
Male	−0.18	(0.08)**
Region		
North central	−0.13	(0.11)
South	−0.48	(0.11)**
West	−0.27	(0.13)**
Education		
Some high school	−0.11	(0.14)
High school graduate	0.17	(0.13)
Some college	0.27	(0.14)*
College graduate	0.67	(0.15)**
Income		
Second quintile	−0.16	(0.16)
Third quintile	−0.16	(0.13)
Fourth quintile	−0.26	(0.13)**
Fifth quintile	−0.94	(0.23)**
Income not reported	−0.54	(0.29)*

Note: N = 1,359; LL = −647.00.
* $p < .10$; ** $p < .05$.

TABLE F.7 1972 NES election analysis of the hawk–dove war-support measure

War-support variable: There is much talk about "hawks" and "doves" in connection with Vietnam, and considerable disagreement as to what action the United States should take in Vietnam. Some people think we should do everything necessary to win a complete military victory, no matter what results. Some people think we should withdraw completely from Vietnam right now, no matter what results. And, of course, other people have opinions somewhere between these two extreme positions. Suppose the people who support an immediate withdrawal are at one end of this scale at point number 1. And suppose the people who support a complete military victory are at the other end of the scale at point number 7. At what point on the scale would you place yourself?

| | Vote McGovern vs. Nixon | |
	Coefficient	(SE)
Constant	−1.23	(0.18)**
Dovishness	**1.71**	**(0.14)****
Party identification	1.17	(0.07)**
Male	−0.11	(0.08)
Region		
North central	−0.10	(0.11)
South	−0.43	(0.11)**
West	−0.27	(0.13)**
Education		
Some high school	−0.13	(0.15)
High school graduate	0.10	(0.13)
Some college	0.20	(0.14)
College graduate	0.51	(0.16)**
Income		
Second quintile	−0.12	(0.16)
Third quintile	−0.25	(0.13)*
Fourth quintile	−0.36	(0.14)**
Fifth quintile	−0.86	(0.23)**
Income not reported	−0.77	(0.30)**

Note: N = 1,465; LL = −628.53.
* $p < .10$; ** $p < .05$.

TABLE F.8 2004 NES election analysis of the retrospective war-support measure

War-support variable: Taking everything into account, do you think the war in Iraq has been worth the cost or not?

	Vote Kerry vs. Bush	
	Coefficient	(SE)
Constant	−2.71	(0.30)**
Iraq not worth cost	**1.64**	**(0.17)****
Party identification	3.31	(0.26)**
Black	0.79	(0.24)**
Female	−0.13	(0.15)
Education		
Some high school	0.93	(0.38)**
Some college	0.12	(0.19)
College graduate	0.36	(0.20)*
Region		
Midwest	0.03	(0.23)
South	−0.36	(0.22)*
West	−0.09	(0.24)
Income		
Second quintile	−0.16	(0.26)
Third quintile	−0.22	(0.22)
Fourth quintile	−0.35	(0.21)
Fifth quintile	−0.56	(0.29)*
Income not reported	−0.02	(0.28)

Note: N = 790; LL = −181.29.

* $p < .10$; ** $p < .05$.

NOTES

CHAPTER ONE

1. CBS/New York Times polling, available at http://www.pollingreport.com/iraq .htm (accessed May 12, 2006).

2. *Washington Post,* March 30, 2006.

3. Feaver joined the NSC staff as a special advisor in June 2005, and the "National Strategy for Victory in Iraq" report posted on the White House website in November 2005 showed that the document's author was "feaver-p." White House officials confirmed that Feaver played a significant role in drafting the plan (Shane 2005).

4. See Herbst (1993) for a description of strategies employed by congressmen to measure public opinion in the 1930s and 1940s. For instance, FDR employed a clipping service that monitored 350 newspapers and 43 magazines to track trends in editorial opinion (Steele 1974).

5. See, for instance, Baum 2003; Belknap and Campbell 1951; Burk 1999; Eichenberg 2005; Foyle 1999; Gartner and Segura 1997, 2000; Gartner, Segura, and Wilkening 1997; Gelpi, Feaver, and Reifler 2005–6; Holsti 1992, 2004; Kull, Ramsay, and Lewis 2003–4; Larson 1996; Mueller 1973, 1994; Nincic 1988, 1992; Page and Shapiro 1992; Popkin 1991; Schwarz 1994; Sobel 2001; Zaller 1992, 1994.

6. Certainly, partisan and group-based attachments are not the only factors that shape opinion on international policy. For instance, Hurwitz and Peffley (1987) convincingly demonstrate that foreign policy attitudes are structured by core values and abstract beliefs regarding appropriate general governmental strategies.

CHAPTER TWO

1. I briefly mention the U.S. involvement in Kosovo in chapter 5 but do not discuss the larger conflict. I refer interested readers to more detailed treatment, such as Larson and Savych (2007).

2. For more detailed historical treatments of the Korean War, see Casey (2008) and Halliday and Cumings (1988).

3. Mueller (1973, 25–27) presents a complete chronology of the major events of the Korean War.

4. The Soviets were absent since January 1950 because they had boycotted the United Nations over the issue of seating communist China's representative in the UN.

5. On average, 15 percent of Gallup respondents and 9 percent of NORC respondents declined to give a substantive response (Mueller 1973).

6. This narrative of the Vietnam War draws heavily on my description of that war (Berinsky 2004). For further detail, see Hallin (1986). For more on public opinion concerning Vietnam, see Mueller (1973) and Rosenberg, Verba, and Converse (1970).

7. Mueller (1973, 29–31) provides a list of the major events of the Vietnam War.

8. President Johnson's Message to Congress, August 5, 1964, published in *Department of State Bulletin*, August 24, 1964.

9. Thomas L. Friedman, "Standoff in the Gulf; U.S. Says General's Remark Is Hurting Its Gulf Strategy," *New York Times*, December 20, 1990.

10. Gallup survey, November 15–16, 1990. Of the remaining respondents, 23 percent thought that Bush should commence military action, and 6 percent did not offer a response.

11. Specifically, in a Gallup poll taken December 6–7, 1990, 41 percent of respondents wanted to begin military action after January 15, compared to 53 percent who wanted to wait longer to see if the economic and diplomatic sanctions were effective.

12. Adam Clymer, "Confrontation in the Gulf; Bush Asks Congress to Back Use of Force if Iraq Defies Deadline on Kuwait Pullout," *New York Times*, January 8, 1991.

13. "Confrontation in the Gulf: Excerpts from Gulf Resolutions before Congress," *New York Times*, January 12, 1991.

14. ABC News/ *Washington Post* poll, January 13, 1991.

15. Gallup poll, January 3–6, 1991.

16. "The Unfinished War: A Decade since Desert Storm" (2001), CNN.com (accessed May 30, 2008). At the same time, the human and monetary costs of the war were unclear. During the run up to the war, casualty estimates had been in the tens of thousands. In December 1990, General Norman Schwarzkopf was directed by the White House to aim for casualty levels of no more than 10 percent of the fighting force (which would translate into about 10,000 troops). John H. Cushman, "Pentagon Report on Persian Gulf War: A Few Surprised and Some Silences," *New York Times*, April 11, 1992.

17. See, for example, Burk 1999; Eichenberg 2005; Foyle 1999; Holsti 2004.

18. Thom Shanker, "U.S. Senses a Rise in Activity by Al Qaeda in Afghanistan," *New York Times*, December 4, 2007; www.nytimes.com/2007/12/04/world/asia/04gates.html (accessed December 21, 2007).

19. Presidential debate transcripts, MSNBC, http://www.msnbc.msn.com/id/18296908 (accessed December 21, 2007). During speeches, Barack Obama has called for increased troop levels, funding, and economic development in Afghanistan, although these topics were not discussed in the presidential debates.

20. "President Says Saddam Hussein Must Leave Iraq within 48 Hours," White

House statement transcript, March 17, 2003, http://www.whitehouse.gov/news/releases/2003/03/20030317–7.html (accessed December 21, 2007).

21. "President Delivers State of the Union," January 28, 2003, http://www.white house.gov/news/releases/2003/01/20030128–19.html (accessed December 21, 2007).

22. "U.S. Secretary of State Colin Powell Addresses the U.N. Security Council," February 5, 2003, http://www.whitehouse.gov/news/releases/2003/02/20030205–1. html (accessed December 21, 2007).

23. "U.S.-Europe Rifts Widen over Iraq," *Washington Post*, February 11, 2003.

24. Http://www.cnn.com/2003/US/05/01/bush.transcript/ and http://www.cnn .com/2003/ALLPOLITICS/10/28/mission.accomplished (accessed October 29, 2007).

25. I had a research assistant collect all articles in *Newsweek* magazine from February 2004 to November 2004 that mentioned the Democratic candidate(s) and their discussion of the war (pending or actual).

26. Trends are created using the lowess smoothing algorithm. Jacobson uses a bandwidth of .05, meaning that he uses 5 percent of the data range to create the trend estimate. Given the richness of the data in this graph, this choice is appropriate.

CHAPTER THREE

1. Http://transcripts.cnn.com/TRANSCRIPTS/0606/18/le.01.html (accessed August 20, 2007).

2. Here—and elsewhere in this book—I report survey marginals that have been re-weighted to correct for the problems associated with the quota-sampling methods used during this time (see Berinsky 2006 for details). As a result, the figures presented here may not match the marginals presented in other academic work—by and large other authors have drawn on the unweighted data presented in Cantril and Strunk (1951).

3. These surveys were designed and implemented in conjunction with the fledgling National Opinion Research Center (NORC).

4. These polls are also extremely difficult to work with. Most of these surveys have not been touched for almost sixty years, and as a result, the data sets are not easily usable. The data contain numerous miscodings and other errors. For example, in one data set from 1940, I ferreted out twenty different keypunch errors. Only with a tremendous amount of preparatory work—in conjunction with Eric Schickler and a team of research assistants—have I been able to make the data suitable for analysis. In addition, some codebooks do not include the codes necessary to decipher important questions, such as the respondent's occupation and education. However, by comparing and compiling variable codes across data sets I have been able to reconstruct the proper coding for almost all variables. I undertook this data reclamation project for the purposes of writing this book, but my efforts serve a larger purpose as well. This NSF-funded project will make these valuable surveys available to the community of scholars.

5. For a detailed description of quota-sampling methods, see Berinsky (2006). Although some pollsters used quotas in seeking a descriptively representative group of citizens (Roper 1940), others designed quotas to produce sample proportions that differed systematically from the population. George Gallup was most interested in predicting elections, so he drew samples to represent each population segment in proportion to the votes it usually cast in elections. Because southerners, African Americans,

and women turned out at low rates during this period, these groups were deliberately underrepresented in opinion polls. For example, the 1940 census found that 50 percent of the U.S. population (aged twenty-one and over) were women, 9 percent were African American, and 25 percent lived in the South. By contrast, a December 1940 Gallup poll included only 33 percent women, 3 percent African Americans, and 12 percent southerners. These figures are typical of the polls through the early 1940s. By the mid-1940s, however, Gallup had adjusted his gender quotas to interview equal numbers of men and women. This change in the composition of the sample makes it difficult to track real changes in opinion over time. The important point is that the Gallup data from the 1930s and 1940s that scholars use to represent the voice of the public came, in fact, from a skewed sample of that public.

6. For example, the 1940 census indicated that about 11 percent of the population aged twenty-one and over had at least some college education, whereas almost 30 percent of a typical 1940 Gallup sample had attended college.

7. The methods used in this book to correct for the deficiencies of quota-controlled surveys are discussed in Appendix A. For a detailed description of the methodology, see Berinsky (2006).

8. Revisionist views of World War II are often summarily dismissed. In 2008, novelist Nicholson Baker's book *Human Smoke* implicitly made the case that FDR provoked Japan into war and that Churchill played an active role in escalating the brutality of the war. Reaction to the book was controversial to say the least. For instance, William Grimes ended his *New York Times* review by concluding, "World War II was a deeply unfortunate conflict in which many lives were lost. Mr. Baker is right about that, but not about much else in this self-important, hand-wringing, moral mess of a book" (March 12, 2008). Questions of historical accuracy aside, the harsh criticism generated by Baker's book speaks to the strength of the view of World War II as a "good war."

9. Author analysis of AIPO 335 (November 1944).

10. These data are taken from OPOR 819 (July 17–23, 1942).

11. These data are taken from OPOR 817 (June 17, 1942).

12. For a discussion of newsmagazine coverage of the Vietnam War, see Landers (2004).

13. Although satellite technology had been available since the early 1960s—the 1964 Tokyo Olympic Games, for instance, were transmitted via satellite—the cost of such transmission was prohibitive for use on a regular basis until the mid-1970s (DeLuca 1980).

14. Victor Davis Hansen, "2,000 Dead, in Context," *New York Times*, October 27, 2005.

15. Specifically, f IAW Change 3, DoD Directive 5122.5, states, "Names, video, identifiable written/oral descriptions or identifiable photographs of wounded service members will not be released without the service member's prior written consent." David Carr, "Not to See the Fallen Is No Favor," *New York Times*, May 28, 2007, C1.

16. Not all such images were deemed fit for public consumption. Roeder (1993) notes that the military censors withheld all pictures that showed dead American soldiers being handled like inanimate objects, such as images of GIs piling corpses into trucks for removal from the front.

17. The *New York Times*, for one, regularly catalogued casualties from the tristate area.

18. "Navy Reports 1218 in Casualty List," *New York Times*, January 20, 1943, 11

19. Pew found that 22 percent of independents watched Fox News.

20. Pew Center for the People and the Press, "Online News Audience Larger, More Diverse: News Audiences Increasingly Politicized," June 8, 2004, http://people-press .org/reports/pdf/215.pdf (accessed November 13, 2007).

21. "Red Media, Blue Media: Evidence for a Political Litmus Test in Online News Readership," http://www.washingtonpost.com/wp-dyn/content/article/2006/05/03/ AR2006050300865.html (accessed November 8, 2007).

22. Ansolabehere, Lessem, and Snyder (2006) found that the pro-Republican balance of endorsements extended beyond presidential contests to other elections throughout the 1940, and, indeed, through the late 1960s.

23. Some papers, in fact, were established to further particular political viewpoints. In response to the *Chicago Tribune*'s isolationist perspective in the 1930s, the Field family founded the *Chicago Sun* to further an internationalist voice. Illinois Newspaper Project, "History of Newspaper Publishing in Illinois," http://www.library.uiuc.edu/ inp/ilhistory.html (accessed November 10, 2007).

24. A few notes are in order here. First, a similar split is found when "likely vote" in 1936 is used in place of "previous vote." Second, although the pattern of candidate support by newspapers differs somewhat by region of the country in predictable ways— Landon's support was highest in the Midwest and FDR's support was highest in the South—the results concerning the self-selection of media outlets by the survey respondents hold in every region of the country. Finally, I use unweighted cross-tabulations in these analyses.

25. Moreover, a survey taken in September of that same year found a difference of a similar size; the gap between media favorable and unfavorable to FDR was 3 percent among FDR voters and 39 percent among Landon voters.

26. Of course it is difficult to assess the direction of causality given this cross-sectional data. Even reports of a previous vote could be contaminated by contemporaneous persuasion—people might have misremembered their previous vote, bringing their recall of previous behavior in line with their current behavior. However, some evidence suggests that a self-selection mechanism was at work. Comparing the 1932 and 1936 votes, I find that 18 percent of citizens who voted for Hoover in 1932 voted for Roosevelt in 1936, and 17 percent of citizens who voted for Roosevelt in 1932 switched their vote to Landon—a nearly identical rate of defection. More important for present purposes, these defection rates were not significantly different—in either a statistical or a substantive sense—when the sample was broken down by the types of newspapers the respondent read. In any case, the data clearly show that Republican voters and Democratic voters gravitated to different news sources.

27. Roper also asked respondents to identify their favorite radio commentators in the same November 1939 survey. I performed a similar analysis on this question but did not find any partisan differences. One possible reason for the lack of variation is the fact that unlike newspaper columnists—for whom there was a near even balance of mentions of Democratic and Republican commentators—Democratic mentions outnumbered Republican mentions by a factor of four to one.

28. I had a research assistant prepare short biographies of all the names recorded by Roper and asked him to code the partisanship of the commentators, if possible. A second research assistant coded these biographies as well. If both coders thought a particular commenter was a partisan, I labeled that commentator a Democrat or a Republican. In no case did one coder label a commentator a Democrat and another coder label the same commentator a Republican. In 6 of the 44 cases, however, one coder labeled a political commentator a partisan, while the other coder did not ascribe partisan leanings to that commentator. As a robustness check, I added the split decisions to the pool of partisan columnists, but the results reported here did not change with the alternative coding scheme.

29. The media environment during the Vietnam War was considerably more homogenous than that found during either World War II or the Iraq War. The newspaper industry had consolidated during the 1950s and 1960s, constraining the media choices of the public. Moreover, the three major networks dominated the broadcast media before the rise of cable. That said, I still find considerable consistency in the structure of opinion across all the conflicts from the 1930s to the present, indicating that changes in the media do not fundamentally alter the way that the public responds to foreign conflicts.

30. The exact wording of the question was, "If you had to vote on the question of the U.S. entering the war now against Germany and Italy, how would you vote—to go into war now, or stay out of the war?"

31. I use the final date the survey was in the field rather than the date the survey was reported as the value for the survey date. The data presented here are the weighted estimates with the exception of one data point. The July 1944 OPOR survey does not contain any of the measures needed to properly weight the data. I therefore performed a back-of-the envelop correction for this data point. First, I computed the average difference between the weighted and unweighted levels of opposition in the "discuss peace" form of the German army question (which was 3 percent). I then subtracted this figure from the unweighted estimate of support for the policy of unconditional surrender.

32. In January 1942, OPOR asked one-half of its sample, "If the German army overthrew Hitler and then offered to stop the war and discuss peace terms with the Allies, would you favor or oppose accepting the offer of the German army?" Fifty-nine percent of respondents opposed making peace. The other half of the sample was first asked, "If Hitler offered to stop the war now and discuss peace terms with the Allies, would you favor or oppose accepting Hitler's offer?" and then asked the question about making peace with the German army. Under this scenario, opposition to making peace stood at 47 percent. This question-wording experiment is complicated by the fact that only those respondents who supported peace with Hitler were supposed to be asked about making peace with the German army. However, the survey marginals indicate that over half the sample were asked the follow-up question, thereby rendering a greater degree of comparability between the two forms. In any case, an analysis of the data suggests that asking the "German army" question after the "Hitler" question reduced support for taking a hard line, thereby indicating that the dip in support for unconditional surrender in 1944, even if genuine, is not as significant as it appears from the graph.

33. The question of whether it was more important to stay out of the war or "help England" (or "help England and France") was actually first asked in March 1940. The raw data for this survey are unavailable, however.

34. In the November 20, 1941, survey, Gallup asked a slightly different form of the question: "Which of these two things do you think is the more important? To do everything we can to defeat Germany, even if that means getting into war ourselves, or to stay out of war, even at the risk of letting Germany win?"

35. A few notes about the data contained in the graph are in order. First, at two points in time—October 29, 1940, and December 11, 1940—two surveys were reported on a single day. In both of these cases, support for war differed by less than 3 percent across the two polls. For presentational purposes, I average the polls reported on a given date. Second, one of the October 29, 1940, polls did not contain information about the respondent's region of residence. It was therefore not possible to perform the weighting for this survey. Instead, I adjusted the reported percentage of support for helping England by the average difference between the weighted and unweighted estimates during the 1940 campaign season.

36. FDR's appointment of Republicans Henry Stimson to the post of secretary of war and William Franklin Knox to that of secretary of the navy may have also played a role in turning support among his opponents in the public.

37. Although the particular interviewing methods used by Gallup during the campaign season complicate comparisons of opinion within the campaign to opinion outside the campaign, the opinion trends are suggestive. The Gallup polls conducted during the campaign used the same methodology and sampling frame as other Gallup polls from this time. Unlike other polls presented here, however, Gallup only inter-viewed those respondents who said they would "be able to vote in the presidential election this year." As discussed further in chapter 5, there is strong reason to believe that these limited samples are actually comparable to the regular Gallup samples from this time.

38. This figure is not weighted because of the complications involved with match-ing the Roper data to census data. An even more strongly worded question asked by Gallup in September 1941 also yielded similar sentiments, however. Specifically, 56 percent of respondents agreed that "the United States is already in the war," compared with 38 percent who disagreed with that statement.

39. Citizens who approved of FDR's performance as president remained more sup-portive of the stated war aims of the U.S. government than did opponents of FDR even after Pearl Harbor. The size of the differences between these two groups diminished greatly after 1941, however.

40. I define a supporter of FDR as an individual who voted for FDR in 1940 and, at the time of the survey, expressed approval of the president. An opponent of FDR is an individual who voted against FDR and expressed disapproval of the president at the time of the poll. I use the composite measure to avoid potential endogeneity concerns but get similar—although smaller—differences if I use FDR approval or 1940 vote choice in place of this composite measure (see chap. 5 for further discussion).

41. Indeed, many Americans thought that Japan acted as Germany's lackey. Specifi-cally, 69 percent of respondents to a December 1941 Roper poll thought that "the

Japanese government is doing her part as Hitler's ally, and her move was part of German strategy." This figure is not weighted because of the difficulties involved with matching the Roper data to census data.

42. As with the NORC poll, the margin of those who identified Germany as the number-one enemy, compared to those who identified Japan as the number-one enemy in the March 1942 poll, was smaller among residents of the West Coast. Even there, however, Germany led Japan by 42 percent to 38 percent. Casey (2001) reports that in April 1942, the percentage of respondents who said that the United States ought to focus on Japan was almost three times the percentage of respondents who said that the United States should focus on Germany. Even if this reading of public opinion accurately reflected a brief "Japan first" sentiment among the American public, by July of that year, twice as many respondents said that the United States should focus on Germany as said the United States should focus on Japan.

43. Contemporary observers of public opinion—most notably Cantril—recognized the true meaning of the change arising from the attack at Pearl Harbor. Over time, however, the importance of such insights has been overwhelmed by the myths discussed here.

44. The response categories for these questions were "yes," "no," and "it depends."

45. Because men and women vary greatly in their propensity to choose the "don't know" response (Berinsky 2004; Krosnick 2002)—especially in this time period—I computed the difference among only those respondents who provided an answer to the question.

46. A similar gap exists on the "defeat Germany" form of the question

47. To preserve continuity with the data presented in figure 3.1, I include "don't know" responses in the response base. Because women were more likely than men to abstain from survey questions, this decision has the effect of somewhat magnifying the differences between the sexes. The strong and consistent gender differences persist, however, even if "don't know" responses are excluded from the analysis.

48. Specifically, the question asked, "Which of these two things do you think the United States should try to do after the war is over: (1) stay out of world affairs as much as we can, or (2) take an active part in world affairs?"

49. The raw survey responses from the open-ended probes are not available. Here I analyze the categories generated by the coders for OPOR.

50. The "isolationist" responses are "Mind our own business, keep out of European affairs," "Let Europe settle its own arguments," and "We have enough problems of our own to solve." The "war aversion" responses are "Dislike war (general)," "Futility of war—what did the last war accomplish, etc.," "We are not prepared to risk a war," "We have nothing to gain by going in," "Don't want to send our boys over to be killed," "Object to fighting abroad," and "Can't afford a war." The "anti-England" responses are "No obligations to help England" and "England doesn't need our help."

CHAPTER FOUR

1. In other words, I use a "method of agreement" case selection design (Przeworski and Teune 1970; Van Evera 1997). World War II and Iraq are very different conflicts in terms of their instigating causes and the scope of the U.S. military effort. Yet I find

a similar poverty of knowledge of basic facts concerning the war and—as I discuss further in chapter 5—a similar structuring influence of partisan political attachments.

2. As Burk notes, precise statements of the casualties hypothesis are hard to find. Burk defines the casualties hypothesis as having three claims; "first, that the public will not support military deployments which result in casualties; second, that public support for a deployment would be abruptly withdrawn if casualties unexpectedly occurred; and, finally, that public opinion on this issue is so powerful that it constrains the use of force by—indeed, effectively debilitates—great powers" (1999, 77). Clearly, this is an extreme statement of the hypothesis. But references to the general mechanism at the heart of this hypothesis—that war deaths directly drive down public support for war—permeate popular discourse concerning war and even the writings of military strategists (the memoirs of Casper Weinberger, for instance). For a review of occurrences of this sentiment among elites, see Burk (1999).

3. In the academic community, the best recent statement of the relationship between casualties and support for war argues, "Wars tend to start popularly, with a rally-around-the-flag effect, but then become increasingly unpopular as they become more costly. The human costs of a conflict provide a powerful explanation of wartime opinion" (Gartner and Segura 1998, 295). Policymakers share the belief that casualties shape public opinion concerning the wisdom of war. In a series of interviews with political elites, Kull and Destler (1999) found that three-fifths of congressional staff members in 1995 believed that the loss of U.S. lives during a UN peacekeeping operation would lead to the immediate withdraw of U.S. troops. Even leaders of other countries subscribe to Mueller's logic. In the lead-up to the first Gulf War, for instance, Saddam Hussein claimed, "In the event of war, there will be great losses . . . when 5,000 Americans have fallen, Bush will have to end such a war" (*St. Louis Dispatch*, December 22, 1990).

4. Jentleson (1992) and Jentleson and Britton (1998) argue that the policy objective of a mission plays a large role in determining whether the costs of intervention weigh greatly in the public mind. He argues that a military intervention that is designed to stop foreign aggression against America and its allies will engender greater support than missions designed to affect internal political change, such as supporting an existing government allied with the United States (see also Oneal, Lian, and Joyner 1996). Jentleson's theory is different than other theories relating to the ongoing costs and benefits of war because it considers the overall justification that leads to war, not the continuing development of the war. Put another way, Jentleson's theory speaks to the baseline levels of support for interventions sparked by different initiating events, but it cannot explain the dynamics of support for a given intervention, short of a change in the policy objective of that intervention. Thus, although the objective of a mission may play a role in determining absolute levels of public support, that consideration is distinct from other theories of war discussed here.

5. In a related vein, Hurwitz and Peffley (1987) look more generally at foreign policy attitudes and advance an individual-level hierarchical model of attitude structure. This model is incompatible with the event-driven theories of war support but is complementary to the elite-driven view advanced in this book. Hurwitz and Peffley argue, in fact, that "among the various policy domains that comprise the political

environment of the average citizen, the international sphere is exceptionally complex and ambiguous. . . . Consequently, citizens are forced to rely on the assessments of U.S. political elites and media commentators, who interpret world events but who also, quite often, disagree with one another" (1987, 1103). Furthermore, I agree with Hurwitz and Peffley's contention that factors other than elite discourse play a role in structuring opinion on war. In chapter 6, I examine the role played by group attitudes in determining the public's stance on military intervention. Other scholars have also assessed the relationship between war support and domestic concerns. Liberman (2006), for example, finds that retributiveness—as indexed by support for the death penalty—was positively correlated with support for the Gulf War.

6. As Converse (1990), among others, has shown, aggregate opinion can look rational if citizens merely follow the cues of political elites who share their political predispositions, a line of reasoning I discuss further in the next section.

7. Wood (2007) discusses how presidential rhetoric can indirectly influence economic perceptions. Using time-series analysis, Wood finds that when presidents talk more optimistically about the economy, the public reports hearing less negative economic news and, as a result, evaluates the economy more positively. Wood does not break down his findings by partisan groupings, but his work does show how elite rhetoric can externally influence even economic evaluations.

8. Zaller does not explicitly contrast his theory with that of Mueller. Burk (1999), on the other hand, inspired in part by Zaller's work, draws clear distinction between the "casualties" hypothesis and an "elite consensus" hypothesis. Burk states that the "elite consensus" model holds that the public will "withhold or withdraw its support from peacekeeping deployments when there is division among elites about the necessity for deployment or the availability of alternatives to military action; and this will occur even if there are no casualties. At the same time, we expect the public to continue support for a deployment, despite casualties, if elite opinion is solidly behind it" (1999, 72). Burk carries out case studies of the U.S. interventions in Lebanon and Somalia and finds little support for either the casualties hypothesis or the elite consensus hypothesis. These cases are, however, both short-term interventions with relatively few casualties. In addition, Burk carries out his analysis at a highly aggregated level, making it difficult to properly distinguish between these two hypotheses.

9. Zaller (1992) measures a respondent's placement on the hawk–dove continuum based on the predicted answers to the question "Which do you think is the better way for us to keep the peace—by having a very strong military so that other countries won't attack us, or by working out our disagreements at the bargaining table?" Specifically, Zaller employs an instrumental variable technique developed by Franklin (1990) to generate a measure of hawk–dove based on the demographic characteristics of the respondents and the relationship of those characteristics to military hawkishness in the present day.

10. Some evidence suggests that Zaller's story is a better predictor of the dynamics of public support for the Vietnam War than event-driven theories of public opinion and war. Gartner, Segura, and Wilkening (1997) find that casualties did not play a role in determining opinion concerning the war after 1970. The differential performance

of this variable pre- and post-1970 could reflect the solidification of the two-message flows in elite discourse after 1968 (see Zaller 1992).

11. The Vietnam case illustrates nicely the impact of changes in elite cues. I discuss this matter further in chapter 5.

12. Zaller (1994) used education levels to proxy political engagement.

13. Bennett's (1990) "indexing" theory provides a mechanism for the transmission of elite discourse. Bennett argues that the output of the mass media is indexed to the balance of debate within government. Thus the media provides an accounting of elite discourse to the public. For a somewhat different view, see Entman (2004).

14. This position was actually advanced in a somewhat different form by Mueller (1973). Mueller discusses the importance of partisan cues in structuring wartime opinion and notes that as the Korean War proceeded, partisan differences increased in magnitude. He attributes this difference to the use of partisan cues and argues that well-informed partisans are most likely to adopt the positions of the political leaders of their respective parties (see 1973, 120–21).

15. To be clear, Zaller (1992) recognized the importance of cuing messages in his work. He argues, however, that citizens use cuing messages primarily to decide whether to accept or reject the persuasive messages that become the "considerations" that individuals use to form opinions. I argue instead that citizens can use the cuing messages themselves to form opinion.

16. Clearly, further explanation of the relative power of the RAS theory and the elite cue theory is in order. I hope this book will spur further work on this topic.

17. Zaller is ambiguous on a central question; it is not clear who constitutes an "elite." For Zaller, both the media and political actors can be classified as elites. But, especially in discussions of war, it may be important to distinguish between the discourse of actors in the political system (political leaders) and the mediators of that discourse (the press). Perhaps these two groups sometimes speak the same message, but the media is not necessarily a mere transmitter. When discussing "elite discourse" it is important to specify just who is an elite—different definitions may lead to different empirical indicators and different conclusions. Here I define "elite" as partisan political actors—leading Democrat and Republican politicians.

18. Month-by-month measures of war deaths are not available. The Department of the Army, however, recorded monthly casualties (which included war dead and injured soldiers) from December 7, 1941, to December 31, 1946. From December 1941 until December 1943, casualties did not exceed 10,000 in one month (except for May 1942, when approximately 30,000 casualties were recorded). Over the course of 1944, however, monthly casualty rates increased greatly, reaching 55,000 in June. Monthly casualty figures ranged from 50,000 to 80,000 until April 1945 (Department of the Army 1953).

19. OWI officials took this stance because they believed that a focus on Nazi atrocities committed against Jews might be counterproductive to generating public support for the war. Officials thought that focusing attention on the plight of European Jews might contribute to Americans' fears that the war was being fought to save Jews, a problematic cause in their minds given the levels of anti-Semitism in the United States

as measured in opinion polls in the 1940s. (See Leff 2005, chap. 8, for further discussion.)

20. The question read, "It is said that two million Jews have been killed in Europe since the war began. Do you think this is true, or just a rumor?"

21. Cobb (2007) comes to somewhat different conclusions regarding the media's coverage of casualties. He analyzes stories about Iraq appearing on NBC News and finds that NBC only infrequently provided cumulative casualty totals.

22. This question is part of a 2×2 experimental design in which one-half of respondents were asked the casualty knowledge question (see Appendix B for details of this treatment). I thank Time-Sharing Experiments for the Social Sciences (TESS) for funding the fieldwork for this experiment.

23. The mean and median estimates were generated using the poststratification weights provided by Knowledge Networks. Fewer than 2 percent declined to answer the initial questions and, following a probe asking respondents to provide their best guess even if they were not sure of the correct answer, every respondent answered the question.

24. With the extreme responses included, the standard deviation was 3,012.

25. I tried other methods of scoring a "correct" response—increasing and decreasing the band of acceptable answers incrementally from +/– 50 deaths to +/– 200 deaths—and found essentially the same results. The robustness of these findings extends beyond this particular data set. Cobb (2007) examines a number of surveys that measure knowledge of cumulative casualty rates from the year 2003 to 2006, using errors greater than 20 percent as his cutoff for a "correct" answer, and finds similar patterns of misperception.

26. In other words, even if such experiments are internally valid, they may have limited external validity.

27. Ideally, I would have measured the respondent's approval of George Bush to more directly account for the process of cue taking. Because I did not include an approval measure on the survey for cost considerations, however, I use partisanship as a proxy. As I demonstrate later in my discussions of casualty perception and opinion concerning the war, the use of Bush approval would likely only strengthen my results.

28. Specifically, I used multinomial logit (MNL) to analyze the data. I use MNL rather than an ordered estimation routine because, although the casualty estimate levels can be ordered, I expect that the independent variables will have nonlinear effects. For instance, political information should increase the probability of giving a correct answer, while decreasing the probability of being both an underestimator and an overestimator.

29. The full results of this analysis (and relevant question wordings) are presented in Appendix B. Political knowledge was measured by the number of correct answers to three factual questions. I estimated my models using alterative measures of partisanship, including a five-point scale, in which leaners were collapsed in with weak partisans, a three-point scale that did not distinguish strength of partisanship, and dummy variables for Democrats and Republicans. In all cases, the results were essentially the same as those reported here.

30. The "typical" respondent is one whose characteristics are set at the mean (for continuous variables) and the mode (for discrete variables).

31. I found no interactive effect between partisanship and information, indicating that partisans at all levels of political sophistication are equally likely to misperceive the reality of the level of war deaths in Iraq. (For similar accounts of partisan bias, see Bartels 2002.)

32. Gaines et al. (2007) also study levels of casualty knowledge but find no significant differences between Democrats and Republicans in estimates of casualties, although they do find that strong Democrats consistently gave higher casualty estimates than did strong Republicans. They also found that both Democrats and Republicans adjusted their casualty estimates over time to track changes in the actual casualty numbers from the war. There are, however, a number of important differences between my study and theirs that might explain some of these divergences. First, Gaines and his colleagues use a convenience sample of college students rather than the nationally representative sample employed in my study. Perhaps the college sample is simply better tied into current events, mitigating partisan differences in the cross-sectional data. Second, Gaines and his colleagues used a shifting categorical response variable rather than the continuous open-ended probe I employed in my study. This categorical probe may have had the effect of inducing an upward shift in casualty estimates over time, regardless of the respondent's perception of the true casualty number. As they concede, "our data may exaggerate the accuracy of beliefs, since the intervals from which respondents selected changes over time, as casualties grew. The survey questions thus induced updating" (2007, 962).

33. From August 8 to September 13, 2004, 90 American soldiers were killed in Iraq, as compared to 58 in the period from July 8 to August 7 and 45 in the period from June 8 to July 7; http://www.antiwar.com/casualties/list.php, which compiles American military death from May 1, 2003, to the present from the U.S. Department of Defense Web site.

34. Consistent with the elite cue theory, I found that the effect of judgments of George Bush on casualty misperceptions is even stronger than that of partisanship. Among respondents who said they had a "very favorable" opinion of George Bush, 34 percent gave the correct answer against 65 percent of respondents who said they had a "very unfavorable" opinion of Bush (this gap is larger than the gap between strong Republicans and strong Democrats). Furthermore, the casualty misperception results along partisan lines reported here were replicated with independent data collected by the Program on International Policy Attitudes (PIPA) for Kull, Ramsay, and Lewis in August 2004. Furthermore, as expected, these results grow stronger when a measure of strong support or opposition to Bush is used as an independent variable in place of partisanship (and replicated also in a separate PIPA study conducted in March 2004). Cobb (2007) replicates my findings concerning the effect of partisanship on the perceptions of marginal casualties, but he comes to different conclusions regarding the effect of partisanship on cumulative casualties.

35. On the same March 2006 survey, Kull and also found that "the number of Americans giving accurate estimates [of casualties] has dropped somewhat since

October 2004." The authors do not, however, provide the partisan breakdown of casualty estimates.

36. These two items are highly correlated ($r = 0.75$), indicating that they tap a latent dimension of support for the war. Each of these questions also included a follow-up probe that ascertained the strength with which the respondents held their views about the war. Using a four-point scale that differentiates between strong and weak attitudes on these two questions does not change the results reported here.

37. Specifically, I used the log (base 10) transformation of the respondents' casualty estimates in my runs to conform to Mueller's (1973) formulation of the casualty hypothesis. The results do not change if I use the raw casualty estimates in place of the transformed casualty estimates.

38. The full-model estimates are presented in Appendix B. I estimated more fully specified models that included other control variables, but the coefficient on the casualty variable was virtually identical.

39. Unlike the present study, Mueller's found no significant demographic correlates of casualty estimates.

40. There are other problems with the experiment as well, including the lack of reference to casualties in what Gartner terms the "negative casualties trend treatment" and the absence of a control condition.

41. This number was updated once on July 30, moving the casualty figure to 908. In the analyses presented in the paper, I set the range of the one "correct answer" (independent of the range of acceptable answers that were scored as "correct" estimates) from the low point (901) to the high point (915) of war deaths from this period.

42. I employed a between-subjects design rather than a within-subjects design (in which support for the war would be measured both before and after the treatment) because I was worried that respondents would try to maintain consistency in their answers to the war question, given the short time-span of the interview. In other words, a within-subjects design might artificially reduce the impact of the treatments because respondents would be giving two answers to same question in the span of a couple minutes. The between-subjects design employed here is therefore more likely to produce results supporting the casualties hypothesis than is a within-subjects design. The lack of significant findings in my analysis is therefore especially telling.

43. To check for balancing across conditions, I estimated a probit on the assignment to the "corrected" condition on a series of variables I knew to affect support for the war, including partisanship and gender. There were no reliable differences in the composition of the respondents in the two conditions on these variables. Due to random assignment, these two groups should not differ systematically in their background characteristics, including their perceptions of benefits arising from the war. The experimental design therefore holds constant the benefit side of the cost-benefit equation.

44. In addition, there are no statistically significant differences between the "estimated" condition and the "corrected" condition for those respondents who gave a correct casualty estimate. In addition, I estimated these models using the four-point scale that distinguishes strong and weak supporters of the war and found no significant differences between the conditions.

45. Admittedly, the difference in casualty figures here is on the smaller side. It could be that correcting the casualty figures has no effect on respondents' positions toward the war because that correction is not sufficiently large to change their views regarding the war. I am constrained in my ability to manipulate casualty figures because I am dealing here with an ongoing conflict. That said, the tethering of my study to reality is a strength; respondents have incomplete knowledge of ongoing events, and correcting those misperceptions has no effect on support for this ongoing conflict. Perhaps the treatment has no effect because casualty levels simply do not affect support for the war, no matter how small or large the differences. From this standpoint, the small differences are not a fatal flaw. Indeed, other scholars have found that even small variations in casualty figures can influence individuals' assessments of the wisdom of war (McGraw and Mears 2004).

46. I also ran this analysis broken down by the partisanship of the respondent. I found that, among overestimators, the treatment had no effect for any group. Among underestimators, the treatment had no effect for either independents or Republicans. The treatment, however, *increased* the level of support for Democratic underestimators (thereby driving the full sample result). I do not believe that this result represents a systematic effect for several reasons. First, there is no theoretic reason to expect such a pattern of results. Second, given the small sample size of the subgroup analysis, it is difficult to have much faith in the reliability of these results given the nonfindings in the other partisan subsamples. Finally, it appears that any treatment effect is a result of the peculiar nature of the Democrats in the "estimate war death condition." The level of support for the Iraq War among Democrats in this condition is much lower than among Democrats in the control condition. In fact the level of support for the war among Democrats in the "corrected" condition is equivalent to that of Democrats in the control condition. I also estimated the direct effect of casualty estimates on support for the war and found no relationship for either form of the dependent variable. This analysis is presented in Appendix B.

47. It has been suggested that these effects are small and in the incorrect direction because they aggregate individuals who greatly underestimate the casualty levels with those who give casualty figures closer to the true levels. Although the small sample size makes such subgroup analysis difficult (especially among overestimators), I performed the cross-tabulation presented in table 4.2 for only those respondents who underestimated casualty rates by 500 or more soldiers. I found that the effect of the information treatment among these respondents was almost identical to the effects in the full sample. Following Gilens (2001), I also sought to see if the effect of introducing policy-specific information (here the number of casualties) was conditional on the general information level of the respondent. Gilens found that knowledge of policy-specific facts had a significant influence on the political judgments of members of the public, especially among citizens with the highest levels of general political knowledge. Although I found conditional effects in the expected direction, these differences were not reliably significant. These results may indicate that in the realm of war, unlike other areas of politics, policy-specific information has little effect on the policy judgments of individual citizens. It could also be, however, that the sample sizes of these experiments were too small to reliably assess the types of effects Gilens identified.

48. This survey of 1,173 individuals was conducted from October 31, 2005, to November 10, 2005, by Polimetrix as part of the 2005 Public Opinion Research Training Lab survey. The Polimetrix sample is not, strictly speaking, a random sample. The sample is adequate for my purposes, however, because it represents a diverse sample and the experimental treatment was randomly assigned. It is possible that the treatment would have different effects in a different sample, thereby threatening the external validity of the experiment (through the interaction of selection and the treatment, to use the language of Campbell and Stanley 1966). Even in that case, however, the experiment would be internally valid. In any case, the same pattern of results was found in the 2004 experiment, which has fewer concerns with external validity, thereby strengthening my confidence in the conclusions of the 2005 study. Also, the basic pattern of results is the same with and without the use of the Polimetrix weighting scheme.

49. I thank Paul Brewer for suggesting that I include the baseline form of the question in the experiment.

50. The differences among conditions are statistically insignificant as well [$\chi^2(10)$ = 9.48; Pr = 0.49]. Moreover any differences that appear to exist—in particular, the level of support for war in the "200 billion dollars" condition relative to the other five conditions—are largely driven by the unequal distribution of "don't know" responses across the conditions, ranging from 1 percent in the "standard survey condition" to 5 percent in the "200 billion dollars" condition. If the "don't know" responses are excluded from the analysis, the difference between the conditions is completely insignificant [χ^2 (5) = 1.26; Pr = 0.94].

CHAPTER FIVE

1. All quotations are drawn from the *Congressional Record*.

2. This trend line was generated using a lowess smoothing algorithm with a bandwidth of .20.

3. Of course, members of Congress are not the only—or even the primary—partisan cue-givers in this period. In my account of the 1940 election, I discuss the effect of the pro-interventionist shift in war rhetoric by the Republican nominee for president, Wendell Willkie, on mass attitudes toward the war. Congressional rhetoric, however, functions well as a general index of sentiment among partisan political elites.

4. These patterns are consistent with Zaller's theory as well as my elite cue theory.

5. It would be ideal to examine more directly the relationship among elite cues, wartime events, and public support for war. Unfortunately, the data from the era are thin, and the polls with the necessary measures are limited to those presented here.

6. I use a measure of support for FDR, the primary partisan cue-giver during this time. Partisanship was not asked consistently during this period.

7. In cases where I lack one of the two measures, I use the single measure—past vote choice or presidential approval—in my analyses. The specific measures used in the different analyses are presented in Appendix C. In all cases, however, the basic results presented are robust to the specific predisposition measure used (approval, past vote choice, or the composite measure).

8. The online appendix to this volume (http://www.press.uchicago.edu/books/

berinsky/) details the items used to construct the information measures. These measures vary in quality across different surveys, but for both time periods analyzed here—pre–Pearl Harbor and post–Pearl Harbor—some surveys with deep information scales exist. The consistency of the results across different surveys—those with slim measures and those with deep measures—in a given time period bolsters my case that there was a fundamental change in the dynamics of opinion after December 1941.

9. I also performed an initial set of analyses in which I included information level squared (and interactions between the quadratic term and the FDR predisposition measures) to capture potential nonlinearities in patterns of support. If the quadratic terms were jointly significant—as they were in two cases—I used the results of the runs with the quadratic terms to generate figures similar to those presented later in the chapter. In both of these cases (and unlike the Vietnam graphs presented in figs. 5.12A–D and 5.13A–E), the figures were nearly identical in form to those presented in figures 5.2A–E and 5.3A–E. To preserve continuity across analyses, I used only the linear information specification in these figures.

10. I estimated my models using multinomial logit analysis because I do not delete those persons who fail to give a response to the war-support questions. Instead, I capture the full response set and explicitly model the decision to give a "don't know" response (see Berinsky 2004 for a discussion of the importance of "don't know" responses). Thus respondents were asked to choose an answer from a set of categorical nonordered options (for instance, support, oppose, and don't know).

11. I also conducted this analysis using the raw data. Following Zaller (1992), I plotted the percentage of respondents who supported the war, by partisanship, at different information levels. The results are noisier than the predicted probability graphs presented here but yield the same general pattern of results.

12. These patterns of results would also be predicted by Zaller (1992).

13. By "significant" I mean that the effect of information among supporters of FDR is significantly different from the effect of information among opponents of FDR in a statistical sense at the .10 level (and at the .05 level in most cases). I conducted these statistical tests in two ways. First, I conducted an F-test to see if the interaction term between FDR supporter and information was statically distinguishable from the interaction term between FDR opponent and information. I also used CLARIFY (King, Tomz, and Wittenberg 2000) to compute predicted levels of war support for FDR supporters and opponents at different levels of information, and confidence intervals around those predicted levels. This analysis is presented with the coefficients used to generate the figures in the online appendix. These statistical tests, however, are only suggestive because the data were collected using quota-sampling methods, not probability sampling as significance tests require (see Appendix C for more detail).

14. Gallup conducted a separate poll using the identical dependent variable during late January 1941 (AIPO study 229, January 24–29, 1941). Although Gallup conducted the fieldwork for OPOR at this time, the Gallup survey contained different information items—"Have you followed discussions of lend-lease?" "Do you read a daily newspaper regularly?" and "Can you recall which presidential candidate the paper supported in its editorials?"—allowing for a robustness check of the results. I find that the analysis of the Gallup data yields a nearly identical polarization pattern to that found in figures

5.2A–E. The result is especially important because the Gallup information scale is thin, whereas the OPOR scale is thick with factual knowledge questions. The convergence of the results across the two surveys provides evidence for the general robustness of my findings across surveys containing information scales of varying quality.

15. It should be noted that Willkie's message changed in the closing days of the campaign. At the end of October, Willkie sought to gain traction in the campaign by appealing to the Republican base through claims that FDR's aid to Britain policy would mire the United States in the European conflict. On October 23, for instance, Willkie said about FDR, "On the basis of his past performance with pledges to the people, if you reelect him, you may expect war in April 1941." Barnes claims that this shift in strategy was the work of party professionals who "sold him [Willkie] on the reverse technique of calling Roosevelt a war monger. . . . The continued gloomy reports from opinion polls and Willkie's gambling instinct led him to try it" (1952, 225). The Gallup poll I examine here was conducted on October 11–16 and captures the single-message dynamics that prevailed during most of the 1940 presidential campaign.

16. The message emanating from Willkie's campaign, it should be acknowledged, differed significantly from the one coming from congressional Republicans (see fig. 5.1). Given the relative salience of the two messages—the presidential campaign versus speeches on the floor of the House and Senate—it should not be surprising that Willkie's message had a greater effect.

17. The remaining 46 percent of respondents did not know where Willkie stood, which indicates that a significant portion of the public was unengaged with the change in the elite signal, a necessary condition for the existence of significant differences between high- and low-information voters. The mainstream and polarization patterns, after all, are caused by differential behavior of informed segments of the public relative to the uniformed segments of that public. Unfortunately, the individual-level data from this survey are unavailable, so it is impossible to perform the weighting adjustments described in Appendix C. Weighting of similar questions in other surveys suggests that the raw data presented here probably overstate the proportion of the population that was politically informed. There is no reason to believe, however, that the ratio of correct to incorrect answers would be dramatically altered by weighting; in all likelihood the proportion of respondents who did not know where Willkie stood would increase relative to the other two categories.

18. As noted in chapter 3, this Gallup poll was conducted using the same methodology and sampling frame used by other Gallup polls from this time. Unlike other polls presented here, however, Gallup only interviewed those respondents who said they would "be able to vote in the presidential election this year." That said, any differences between this poll and the other polls I examine here should not change the over-time inferences I draw in this book for two reasons. First, as discussed elsewhere (Berinsky 2006), Gallup's sampling procedure highly overrepresented the voting population. The 1940 postelection poll, for instance, reported a turnout rate of 89 percent among the entire sample. Less than 2 percent of the sample reported that they did not vote because they were ineligible to do so. The number of respondents excluded by Gallup's screen was therefore almost certainly quite small relative to other surveys from this time. Second, even in the unlikely event that the October 1940 survey greatly over-

represents voters relative to other surveys examined in this book, it is unlikely that the over-time patterns of opinion polarization would change. The difference between the mainstream and the polarization pattern, after all, manifests itself among subgroups of the most informed segments of the population. Considering the strong link between political participation and information, it is highly unlikely that excluding those ineligible to vote would change the composition of the highly informed segment of the sample enough to reverse the mainstream pattern found in figures 5.5A–B.

19. The graphs present the predicted positions for a white male with some college education. The full analyses are presented in Appendix C. I also ran the analysis using ordered probit and regression, with the full four-point scales as dependent variables. The results were substantively identical to those presented here. Finally, I estimated the models separately for each of the four experimental conditions and found that the results were nearly identical across each of the conditions.

20. The trend lines were generated using a lowess smoothing algorithm with a bandwidth of 0.25.

21. In fact the coefficients for the probit analysis predicting estimates of war success are nearly indistinguishable from the analogous coefficients for the probits predicting support for war.

22. It could be that pollsters stopped asking about support for the Afghanistan War because of the high levels of support reported in polls taken through early 2002.

23. This difference is also found in the raw data.

24. There are similar differences in information effects between support for the wars in Iraq and Afghanistan in data collected in 2005 by the Public Opinion Research Training Lab (PORTL) and in January 2006 by the Pew Center for the People and the Press. In both surveys, the interaction between information levels and partisanship is significant in the Iraq support model and insignificant in the Afghanistan support model. Moreover, a large baseline partisan gap exists in these surveys, confirming the existence of the gap uncovered in the 2004 NES.

25. Zaller, in fact, classifies Vietnam as a "partisan issue" in 1972 (1992, 108).

26. Specifically, Zaller used an NES question that asked, "Which of the following do you think we should do now in Vietnam? (1) pull out entirely, (2) keep our soldiers in Vietnam, but try to end the fighting, or (3) take a stronger stand even if it means invading North Vietnam." Zaller coded the first response—"pull out"—as opposition to the war and the other two options as support for the war.

27. Strictly speaking, I do not replicate Zaller's model. Instead, following the strategy advanced by Zaller (1994) and used elsewhere in this chapter, I model opinion as a function of information, predisposition (here party identification), and the interaction between predispositions and information. Because likelihood-ratio tests indicated that the addition of quadratic information terms significantly improved the model fit for 1966, 1968, and 1970, I included information level squared and relevant interactions to capture nonlinearities.

28. The graphs present the predicted positions for a white male at a given information level.

29. Zaller also argues that the change of administration in 1968 changed the dynamics of opinion. As he argues, "with the war effort being led by a Republican

rather than a Democrat, many doves found it easier to oppose the war" (1992, 204). He further argues that the biggest change in liberal opinion occurs between 1968 and 1970. Looking at Zaller's ideology-based analysis (as opposed to my partisanship-based analysis), however, it appears that the basic dynamics of public opinion changed from 1964 to 1968, when Johnson was president, indicating that the split within the Democratic Party, rather than the change in the occupant of the White House, was a more important determinant of changes in patterns of opinion expression among liberals.

30. I thank Time-Sharing Experiments for the Social Sciences (TESS) for funding the fieldwork for this experiment.

31. I employ hypothetical scenarios to maximize my control over the experimental treatments (see Herrmann, Tetlock, and Visser 1999).

32. The design therefore consisted of sixteen cells and two control groups. The design and full scenario wordings are presented in the online appendix.

33. To arrive at these numbers, I looked to media reports of estimated deaths in the months leading up to recent U.S. military action. For the high number, I searched Lexis-Nexis in the month before the start of the 1991 Gulf War for estimates of the number of war dead. Within this time period, I identified six reports with eight different casualty estimates. The projected number of dead ranged from 500 (by the chairman of the House Committee on Armed Services, Les Aspin) to 10,000 (by the Center for Defense Information, a private nonpartisan research organization). I took the median of these estimates—3,000 +/- a 500-casualty range. Arriving at the low number was more difficult because the media by and large did not report casualty estimates for the second Gulf War (in all likelihood following the lead of government officials, who—unlike their counterparts during the first Gulf War—essentially refused to talk about estimates of war dead). Still, I managed to find two estimates of the number of dead. The first, 400–800 dead, was by Daryl Press, a professor of government at Dartmouth College. The second was by Michael O'Hanlon, a senior fellow at the Brookings Institution, and ranged from 100 to 5,000 dead. I took the median of the range—400 casualties +/- a 100-casualty range (to be precise, I took the low end of the median, which is 400–800). As noted in the previous chapter, it is possible that the rate of casualty loss is more important than the aggregate number of deaths. I use the aggregate numbers here because most work on this topic has—consistent with Mueller's original hypothesis—looked at aggregate deaths (although see Gartner and Segura 1998). Future work should certainly consider this dimension, but given resource constraints, a focus on aggregate numbers is a good first step.

34. These scenarios are drawn from Feaver and Gelpi (2004) but were modified to keep the target country constant. Jentleson has also identified a third foreign policy goal of interest, humanitarian intervention (Jentleson and Britton 1998), which, like foreign policy restraint missions, is more popular than actions with an internal policy change goal. Because the crucial distinction is between the internal policy change goal and the other goals, I use the original typology here.

35. The order of the presentation of the parties was randomized within the conditions.

36. Some have argued that this design pushes respondents to rely on partisan cues because the scenario presented here is sparse. Admittedly, respondents are not pro-

vided with the details of the strategic situation surrounding the situation. For instance, possible actions by China and the potential for nuclear warfare are all left aside. The scenario design, however, is similar to other studies of the determinants of war (Feaver and Gelpi 2004; Herrmann, Tetlock, and Visser 1999). More important for present purposes, I provide subjects with salient information concerning two sets of factors that scholars have argued determine support for intervention: (1) the costs (in terms of human lives) and the benefits (the principle policy objective of the mission) on the one hand, and (2) partisan cues (the position of various actors in Congress) on the other. The low-information nature of the treatment makes all relevant cues stark and clear. Thus, the elite-driven theory can only be advantaged if the cost-benefit calculation naturally plays a small role in determining support for war.

37. In a more expansive design, for instance, it would undoubtedly be interesting to consider different rationales for party positions. But given the resource constraints I was operating under, I chose to keep the design as stark as possible.

38. This design admittedly ignores some prominent event-centered theories discussed in the previous chapter, such as Feaver and Gelpi's "perceived success" theory (2004). A more comprehensive design would require tens of thousands of cases, however. The design here is sufficient to provide a critical test of the relative merit of situational explanations of war support against elite-driven explanations. I checked the randomization by running a series of chi-square tests to see whether the characteristics of the respondents varied by condition. All of these tests indicated that I could not reject the null hypothesis of "no difference" across all of the following respondent characteristics: gender, census region, age, education, partisanship, and race.

39. These results were generated from a probit model predicting support for war. The results do not differ if I use the four-point support–opposition measure as the dependent variable in an ordered probit analysis. To determine if there were any consistent interactive effects, I also included interactions between conditions and examined mean support level (by partisanship) for each of the experimental conditions. I did not find any such effects. For instance, the highest level of support for intervention among Democrats is found in the case in which Democrats support intervention, Republicans oppose intervention, the mission's principle objective is foreign policy restraint, and casualties are low. The second highest level of support, however, is the case in which both Democrats and Republicans support intervention, the mission's principle objective is foreign policy restraint, and the casualty estimates are high.

40. Although the effect size varies by scenario, in every experimental condition Republicans are more likely to support intervention than are Democrats.

41. "Zogby Poll: 52% Support U.S. Military Strike against Iran," October 29, 2007, http://www.zogby.com/news/ReadNews.dbm?ID=1379 (accessed November 2, 2007).

42. Perhaps, then, the current political climate influences not only the baseline levels of support among partisans but the effect of the treatments as well.

43. This effect holds, even controlling for the respondent's beliefs concerning the desirability of international involvement abroad more generally.

44. Specifically, neither interaction term was even three-quarters as large as its standard error, and a joint test of significance of the terms can be rejected at the .40 level.

45. In the foreign policy restraint scenario, support for the intervention was 6 percent less in the high-casualty scenario as compared to the low-casualty scenario. In the internal policy change scenario, support for intervention was 3 percent less in the high-casualty scenario as compared to the low-casualty scenario

46. These results makes sense if, as argued here, Democrats would be more likely to oppose any intervention given their recent opposition to Bush over the Iraq War.

47. In fact, given the relative malleability of elite positions on war, the study of public opinion and war more clearly illustrates the general relationship between mass and elite positions.

CHAPTER SIX

1. Many of the ideas presented in this chapter were inspired by my graduate advisor, Don Kinder.

2. The next largest group, "nature of the times" composed 24 percent of the sample. These respondents made simple associations between the condition of the economy or the state of international affairs on the one hand and the incumbent administration on the other. These statements largely consisted of uninformed references to controversies over public policy. For instance, of the Republican Party, one respondent said, "Seems a lot like they helped to stop the [Korean] war" (Campbell et al. 1960, 243).

3. Converse (1964) himself did not mention the large proportions of respondents who fell in the "group interest" level of conceptualization when he discussed the role of groups and opinion. Kinder (2003) speculates that Converse may have overlooked this evidence because, by relying on reference group theory, Converse focused primarily on groups in society apart from the respondents' own. Much of the rhetoric concerning likes and dislikes of candidates and the parties, however, concerned the group to which a respondent belonged. I argue that references to a respondent's own group as well as references to other groups are consistent with Converse's general approach; in both cases, relying on groups allows one to arrive at decisions on complex political issues.

4. Individuals do not have to be aware of their affect toward various groups in order for those groups to play a role in political decision-making. Recent work has found that groups can play a role outside of consciousness (Berinsky and Mendelberg 2005; Mendelberg 2001).

5. Hurwitz and Peffley (1987) find that the core value of "ethnocentrism" structures foreign policy beliefs. Their definition of ethnocentrism, however, is different from the one I employ here. Hurwitz and Peffley measure ethnocentrism at the national level, defining the concept as "the belief that one's country is superior to all others" (1987, 1108).Thus, their use of the term bears little relation to the concept of domestic ethnocentrism used by Kinder and myself.

6. The material for this section is drawn from the Digital National Security Archive, http://nsarchive.chadwyck.com/saessayx.htm (accessed March 6, 2006).

7. The South Africa case is especially advantageous for present purposes, because it avoids completely the questions of endogeneity that might be raised by the World War II–era analyses presented later in the chapter. It is simply not plausible to argue that feelings toward blacks in the United States arose from attitudes toward the government

in South Africa; the flow of the causal arrow from domestic groups to foreign policies is indisputable.

8. Kinder and Sanders (1996) also find that racial resentment is a significant predictor of opinions on sanctions in 1986.

9. Hill uses the 1988 NES for his analysis. I use the 1986 data for two reasons. First, I wish to confirm that Hill's findings replicate in an independent data set. Second, I wish to create a more difficult test by situating the controversy in a deeper, explicitly partisan context. In 1986, the battle lines over the sanctions issue were clear; the Democratic Congress and the Republican president were at odds. To the extent that group membership and attitudes structure opinion in this heavily partisan context, we can have greater confidence of their independent predictive power.

10. The precise wording of the question was, "Lately, South Africa has been in the news a lot. Have you read or heard enough about what's going on there to have an opinion about what U.S. policy toward South Africa should be? [If yes,] Some people think that the U.S. should apply economic pressure to get the South African government to change its racial laws. Others think that the U.S. should not do this. What do you think—should the U.S. apply economic pressure or not?" Given the structure of the question-answering decision and the large portion of respondents who did not answer the question, I estimated jointly the decision to offer a response and the direction of response using a bivariate probit selection model (Dubin and Rivers 1989–90; Greene 1997; for a similar application, see Berinsky 1999, 2002a, 2004).

11. I adjusted the black feeling-thermometer score to control for interpersonal differences in the use of the feeling thermometer scale by including the mean of the feeling thermometer rating given to four balanced groups, namely, liberals, conservatives, Democrats, and Republicans (Winter and Berinsky 1999). I also ran my analysis using the racial resentment scale, which is designed to measure racial animosity through the use of subtle questions (Kinder and Sanders 1996). Although this measure is widely used to tap attitudes toward blacks, it remains controversial. Some researchers claim that racial resentment is essentially just a measure of opposition to government assistance (Schuman 2000; Sniderman and Tetlock 1986). Others find that the racial resentment scale measures different concepts for liberals and conservatives (Feldman and Huddy 2005). For my purposes, this controversy is not directly relevant because I am interested in measuring affect toward blacks in the domestic setting. In any event, this analysis replicates the findings obtained using the feeling thermometer measure.

12. I also included a series of demographic and attitudinal control variables in my analysis, although the tenor of the results does not change if the controls are removed. See Appendix D for the full model results. The bivariate probit selection model requires an exclusion restriction to identify the model. Specifically, at least one variable must be included in the selection equation but excluded from the outcome equation. Here I follow the strategy employed in my previous work on racial questions and social welfare policy (Berinsky 1999, 2002a, 2002b, 2004) and use measures of political information and political discussion to identify the model. As with my earlier work, I also included measures indicating how difficult it was to contact the respondents, on the assumption that those who are difficult to reach would also be less likely to answer specific survey questions (Brehm 1993). It should be noted that a likelihood-ratio test

on ρ indicates that selection bias exists in the question-answering process. The estimates presented here correct for that bias. I measure statistical significance here with a likelihood ratio test across the two-equation system. Thus, although the race variable fails to reach conventional levels of significance in the outcome equation, the effect of race is significant across the selection and outcome equations. Overall, then, the effect of race on the question-answering process is significant.

13. In this chapter, unlike earlier chapters, I do not consider opinion concerning other wars of the twentieth century because the cases that provide the most appropriate modern analogues lack appropriate data. Measures of feelings toward Vietnamese Americans during Vietnam and exogenous measures of feelings toward Arab Americans in the post 9/11 period simply do not exist. Surveys did not begin asking about feelings toward Arab Americans until after September 2001. Given the salience of the events of 9/11, it is not plausible to assume that attitudes about domestic groups structure opinion about foreign policy rather than the reverse. As I discuss in the conclusion, however, these data might illuminate the process by which international events influence affect toward domestic groups.

14. Rieselbach (1960) examined the effect of congressional district composition on the voting records of members of Congress from 1938 to 1941. He theorized that congressional districts with high concentrations of Irish and German immigrants would be represented by congressmen with antiwar voting records (because of anti-British sentiment in the Irish case). The data did not support this hypothesis. Given the multiple sources of isolationist voting behavior and the problems of ecological inference, however, it is difficult to draw definitive conclusions from this study.

15. Much work on race and gender adopts a similar "mere membership" approach to analysis.

16. To be specific, I created a fourfold typology: (1) respondents whose parents were both born in the United States (on average about 65–70 percent of respondents); (2) respondents whose parent or parents had been born in an Axis country (approximately 4–8 percent of the sample, depending on the stage of the war, with the majority of German descent); (3) respondents whose parent or parents had been born in an Allied country (approximately 8–10 percent of the sample, with the majority of English descent); and (4) respondents who did not fit into any of the first three categories—including those with foreign-born parents who did not come from an Axis or an Allied country or who came from countries occupied by the Allies or Axis (Italy after September 1943, for instance). This last, residual category also included respondents who might be subject to crosscutting cleavages, namely, those respondents who had one parent born in an Axis country and one parent born in an Allied country. In practice, however, almost no respondents met such a standard. For instance, in a January 1941 survey, only 8 of 3,168 respondents traced their lineage to both Axis and Allied countries. In general, the 1930s and 1940s were simply a different time, when ethnic groups tended not to intermarry. A majority of individuals with parents from one foreign country tended to marry others from that country, with the rest mostly marrying U.S.-born partners. To test the robustness of my results, I estimated a set of models in which I separated people with one foreign-born parent from those with two foreign-born parents and the results remained the same. The results also are similar if I remove Ger-

man Jews from the sample. Given the relatively small number of individuals in these groups, it is not surprising that these estimates are noisy, but I generally find that these analyses replicated the results reported here. I updated the Allied/Axis classification on a survey-by-survey basis to reflect the contemporaneous balance of the warring powers. For instance, after September 1943, respondents whose parents were born in Italy moved from the "Axis" group to the "other" group.

17. Sometimes, however, surveys asked respondents where they themselves were born. Using these measures in place of the parental variables yields results that are similar in magnitude to the second-generation results presented later. It appears, then, that first- and second-generation ethnics exhibited similar patterns of political behavior.

18. After the United States entered the war, the Office of War Information (OWI) established a Surveys Division, whose assigned task was to monitor civilian morale and collect data on public attitudes and behavior concerning the war. Although OWI, like other wartime government agencies, employed social scientists, the office did not have a national field staff or persons experienced in survey operations. The NORC organization was therefore awarded a contract to run surveys for OWI. Several OWI reports presented the relationship between a respondent's parental heritage and opinion concerning the war. One report, "How the People of the United States Would Fight This War" (January 12, 1942), presented breakdowns of prospective war opinion by the same Allied/Axis distinction used here. Another report, "How the Populace Regards the Government's Handling of War News" (January 22, 1942), examined breakdowns on opinion by ethnicity concerning the way the news of the attack on Pearl Harbor was handled. Other contemporary observers were interested in the role of ethnicity as well. Cantril, for instance, traced group influence by examining the Catholic–Protestant split on the question of whether we should help England and concluded, "When Catholics looked toward Europe, they tended to look on the European scene as both Americans and Catholics, whereas when they looked toward the East, their religious frames of reference did not apply and they held essentially the same nationalistic opinion as did Europeans" (1944, 183).

19. These analyses control for the region of residence, size of town, occupation, gender, race, and education of the respondent, following the strategy outlined by Berinsky (2006). Because measures of partisanship were not included on these surveys, it is not possible to control for the respondents' political predispositions. I find, however, that the ethnic identity variables do not reliably predict the respondents' vote choice or approval of FDR (controlling for the other demographic characteristics of the respondents). Thus, I can be confident that the ethnic variables are not simply picking up the effect of support or opposition to FDR. These findings are not fully consistent with those of Bean, Mosteller, and Williams (1944). These authors argue that beliefs about the war among Italians and Germans led these groups to shift away from the Democratic Party in the 1940 election. These authors, however, used aggregate data in only eight states, and their inferences may suffer from an aggregation bias.

20. A word here about the role of religion is in order. In the 1930s and 1940s, different ethnic groups had distinct religious identities. For instance, English immigrants tended to be Protestant, and Italian immigrants tended to be Catholic. It could therefore be the case that the effects I attribute to ethnic lineage in fact measure

religious differences. Furthermore, a "religious" interpretation is not consistent with my theoretical expectations; I argue here that it is visible social groupings and the mapping of those groupings to the foreign stage that structure opinion. A closer examination of the data, however, indicates that the ethnic effects are largely independent of religious effects. The Allied and Axis groupings used in the analysis cut across religious lines. For instance, although respondents of Italian descent were overwhelmingly Roman Catholic, the respondents from other countries had more heterogeneous religious leanings. For instance, 30 percent of those of English descent were Catholic. (It should be noted that if one were interested in the behavior of groups from countries with large and clear religious cleavages—such as Ireland—it would be important to jointly account for the religious and ethnic background of the respondent; see Cantril 1944 for discussion.) As a result, although there were somewhat distinct religious identities to the ethnic groups used in the analysis—the pool of "Axis" respondents had more Catholics than the pool of "Allied" respondents, and there were more Jews among the Allied than the Axis—the overall religious profile of the two groups was not that different. Including measures of denominational attachment diminished somewhat the Allied and Axis effects, but these effects were still consistent and strong.

21. The precise wordings of these questions are as follows (in the order in which they appear in table 6.2): (1) "Which side do you think is winning the war now—Germany and Italy or England?" (2) "Which side do you think will win the war if no other countries go into it—Germany and Italy or England?" (3) "If Germany and Italy defeat England in the present war, do you think that Germany and Italy will start a war with the United States within the next 10 years?" (4) "If Germany defeats England in the present war, do you think you will be as free to do what you want to as you are now?" (5) "Do you think that, if England falls, Germany will soon be in control of all of our trade and foreign markets?" (6) "Which side do you think will win the war—Germany and Italy, or England?" (7) "If Germany and Italy should defeat England in the present war, do you think Germany and Italy would start a war against the United States within the next 10 years?" (8) "Which of these two things do you think is the more important for the United States to try to do? To keep out of war ourselves or to help England win, even at the risk of getting into the war?" (9) "Which of these two things do you think is the more important? That this country keeps out of war, or that Germany be defeated, even at the risk of our getting into the war?" (10) "Would you be willing to fight or have any man of military age in your family fight overseas if the United States gets involved in the war in Europe?" (11) "If you were asked to vote today on the question of the United States entering the war against Germany and Italy, how would you vote—to go into the war, or to stay out of the war?" (12) "If American merchant ships with American crews are used to carry war materials to Britain, and some of them are sunk by the Germans on the way over, would you be in favor of going to war against Germany?" (13) "Do you think the United States should go to war only after it has actually been invaded, or do you think that there are times when we should fight before we are invaded?" (14) "Should the United States take steps now to keep Japan from becoming more powerful, even if this means risking a war with Japan?" (15) "If Brazil, Argentina, Chile or any other Central or South American country is actually

attacked by any European power, do you think the United States should fight to keep that European power out?"

22. When Germany is specifically mentioned (in the split-sample experiment in the January 28, 1941, OPOR survey), the effect of Axis-country parentage is smaller than in the "help England" form of the question. It appears, therefore, that the mention of England is a trigger for both positive affect among those from Allied countries and negative affect for those respondents from Axis countries.

23. Specifically, in a series of multivariate analyses (available from the author upon request), the interactions between information and the ethnic heritage variables were not significant.

24. This finding is consistent with the bottom-up perspective advanced by Lee (2002) in the realm of civil rights in the United States.

25. This is not to say that those of Japanese, German, or Italian background were somehow disloyal. Rather I merely argue that ambivalence regarding the war was largest among these groups.

26. I use a lowess smoothing algorithm to trace opinion trends over time. The temporal thickness of the data is not as great as for the other analysis in this book for which I use the smoothing algorithm. This technique, however, is appropriate given the relative noisiness of the data. The data points in the figures are based on a relatively small number of cases for two reasons. First, I removed Italian Americans from the "Axis" category for the period beginning September 1943, which sharply reduced the number of respondents in that category. Second, after the United States entered the war, fewer respondents were interviewed in the surveys (approximately 1,000 per survey, as opposed to the 3,500-case surveys analyzed earlier). As a result, the estimates of the effects of ethnic background are based on fewer cases than are those for the prewar data.

27. These differences remain, even if we strip out those ethnic groups referred to in the question. For instance, I get the same results on the "trust Russia" question after removing those respondents of Russian heritage from the analysis.

28. Specifically, the question asks, "If the German Army overthrew Hitler and then offered to stop the war and discuss peace terms with the allies, would you favor or oppose the offer of the German army?"

29. OPOR also asked respondents, "If Hitler offered peace now to all countries on the basis of not going farther, but of leaving matters as they are now, would you favor or oppose such a peace?" The differences between the ethnic groups are largely the same as those presented in figure 6.4. At a couple of points in figure 6.4, opposition to making peace with the German army is relatively low. In these two cases, as discussed in chapter 3, respondents were first asked if they would be willing to make peace with Hitler. A question-wording experiment performed early in the war demonstrates that the net effect of asking the "Hitler" variant of the question before the "German army" variant is to see the opposition to making peace drop by about 10 percent from the first question to the second.

30. An examination of data from the Korean War effort indicates that the conditions surrounding the activation of ethnic identity during World War II were indeed unique. The 1952 NES contains a measure of the ethnicity of the respondents' parents.

Analysis parallel to that presented here indicates that—as in the 1940s—descendants of parents from Axis countries were less supportive of military action than were those respondents whose parents were born in the United States. This effect was small and statistically insignificant, however. When the focus of inquiry shifts to future U.S. action, the differences among the groups are even smaller. Moreover, the rates of intermarriage between respondents of Allied and Axis lineage were significantly larger in the early 1950s than they were in the 1940s, diminishing the aggregate impact of the differences between the various ethnic groups. In short, although it may be that the groups described here naturally tend toward the hawkish or dovish side of the spectrum, the effect of group membership on opinion during World War II was largely unique. That is, while German Americans were somewhat dovish with regards to the Korean War, they were especially dovish in the context of the war against Germany.

31. I do not mean to draw a stark distinction between these two sets of analyses. It is not possible to identify the ethnic identity of the respondents to the Roper survey discussed later in the chapter. Thus, it could be that the respondents who say that a particular group makes the "best" citizens are members of that group. What distinguishes the analysis in this section from the results presented earlier is that here I am able to identify precise ethnic attachments. Put another way, the Roper survey allows us to tap likes and dislikes of particular groups, although we do not know the particular ethnic identity of the respondents. Of the surveys examined earlier, we might not be able to measure closeness to particular groups, but we can measure the ethnic identity of the respondents.

32. Unfortunately, the survey did not ask respondents to identify their own nationality.

33. For the purpose of the analysis that follows, I keep the Sicilian group separate from the Italian group. Combining the two groups—as Roper did when reporting the results in *Fortune* magazine—yields nearly identical results.

34. For instance, although anti-Italian sentiment ran highest in New England, as we might expect from patterns of immigrant migration (26 percent of respondents named them the worst group), a plurality of respondents named Italians the "worst" group in each census region. The same patterns of dislike can be found in divisions along gender, age, urbanicity, and racial lines.

35. The states in this region are Iowa, Kansas, Minnesota, Missouri, Nebraska, North Dakota, and South Dakota. The census information was generated using the Integrated Public-Use Microdata Series: Version 3.0 (http://www.ipums.org).

36. Although Roper did not measure the education levels of the respondents, polls from this era consistently drew samples that had higher mean levels of educational attainment than did the U.S. Census estimates (see Berinsky 2006 for details).

37. It may also be that highly educated respondents disliked distinct groups of immigrants. If this were the case, then perhaps in the full sample there would appear a different distribution of ethnic dislikes altogether. Without a measure of education in this survey, it is impossible to tell which scenario properly captures the sentiments of the public.

38. Furthermore, the large gap in the dislike of immigrants from the two European Axis countries—Italians were mentioned as the most disliked group by 18 percent more respondents than were Germans—indicates that it is not attitudes toward the

impending war alone that determined the patterns of likes and dislikes of the different ethnic groups.

39. *Life*, May 1, 1939, 69.

40. Further evidence of the exogenous nature of the structure of ethnic likes and dislikes comes from the Roper survey. If, in fact, the pattern of likes and dislikes were structured by the war, we would expect a strong relationship between expressions of fondness for the English and dislike of the Germans. In fact, these measures are only weakly related—the correlation between the two measures is 0.08.

41. The other sixteen references were to unnamed aggressors or dictatorships.

42. The variables measuring the "best" and "worst" ethnic groups were all entered into a single equation. Replicating the analysis with these variables entered one at a time yields nearly identical results.

43. It appears that anti-Axis citizen sentiment is not a reflection of general hostility toward ethnic minorities in the United States. Given that only 2 percent of the sample expressed dislike of more than one group—almost certainly as a result of the design of the question—it is impractical to correlate the different dislike measures. It is, however, possible to correlate the dislike measures with a measure of anti-Semitism (described in further detail later in the chapter). Support for the proposition that there should be a policy to deport Jews from this country to some new homeland "as fast as it can be done without inhumanity" is not correlated with dislike of Italians and Germans. The correlation between the anti-Semitism item and the dislike of Italians is 0.04, whereas the correlation with dislike of Germans is 0.004. These results indicate that anti-Axis immigrant sentiment is distinct from dislike of other ethnic groups.

44. I used the question that specifically asked about Jews in America so that I could directly tap anti-Semitism, rather than using the indirect ethnic dislike question. In addition, because only 2 percent of the sample expressed dislike for more than one ethnic group, use of this measure also allows me to tap overall dislike of Jews with a less discriminating probe. I reran my analysis using the ethnic dislike question in place of the anti-Semitism measure and obtained similar, although somewhat weaker, results. I do, however, find stronger results in the expected direction if I use a measure that combines the two items concerning Jews.

45. The precise wording of the question is as follows:

> Which of the following statements most nearly represents your general opinion on the Jewish question:
>
> 1. In the United States the Jews have the same standing as any other people, and they should be treated in all ways exactly as any other Americans.
> 2. Jews are in some ways distinct from other Americans but they make respected and useful citizens so long as they don't try to mingle socially where they are not wanted.
> 3. Jews have somewhat different business methods and therefore some measures should be taken to prevent Jews from getting too much power in the business world.
> 4. We should make it a policy to deport Jews from this country to some new homeland as fast as it can be done without inhumanity.

Respondents who chose any answer except the first were given a "nontolerant" score; those choosing the first answer were assigned a tolerant score. Additional analysis, in which the different response categories were entered as a series of dummy variables yields similar results; the higher-numbered (less tolerant) answers exhibited stronger effects, but all the effects were in the same direction.

46. Because respondents were allowed to give answers that followed no particular ordering, I used an unordered multinomial logit (MNL) model to derive coefficient estimates of the effect of the group like and dislike variables. I then generated estimates of the effects of these variables on the probability of choosing various response categories. Following the analytic strategy outlined in Berinsky (2006), I included controls for the quota categories of gender, region, urbanicity, and class. The MNL analysis uncovered some interesting results—for example, the ethnic like and dislike variables had the effect in some cases of mobilizing respondents from the "don't know" category to a pro-intervention or anti-intervention position. However, the tenor of the results does not change if I collapse the response categories and use probit analysis instead.

47. I present the probability of giving an anti-interventionist response rather than a pro-interventionist one because it is easiest to distinguish the isolationist responses from the set of possible responses. For instance, it is difficult to determine if selling arms for "credit" is a strictly pro-interventionist response, but the "not at all" response is a clear anti-interventionist response. In addition, I do not report significance tests here or for other analyses in this chapter for reasons discussed in earlier chapters. I do, however, report in Appendix D the results of significance tests on the relevant coefficients.

48. It could be that the results concerning ethnic dislikes are even stronger than the analysis in table 6.4 indicates, because there may be omitted variable bias in these analyses. The respondents' education was not measured on this survey. We know, however, that the well educated tend to be more tolerant of racial and ethnic groups, and therefore should report fewer ethnic dislikes, than the less-educated respondents. These highly educated respondents also tend to be interventionist in outlook. Thus, in this case, the omitted variable of education is negatively correlated with the dependent variable and negatively correlated with the ethnic hatred variable. In such a case, the coefficient on the ethnic dislike variable would be attenuated toward zero.

CHAPTER SEVEN

1. Robin Toner and Neil A. Lewis, "A Nation Challenged: Security and Liberty; A Familiar Battle Fought and Won," *New York Times,* October 26, 2001.

2. Pew Center for the People and the Press, Survey Report, September 19, 2001, http://people-press.org/reports (accessed May 18, 2007).

3. These findings are largely consistent with other polls taken at that time (see Huddy, Khatib, and Capelos 2002), although some polling organizations found a shallower commitment to civil liberties (see the later discussion).

4. As I note later in the chapter, there are no data from the Korean War that speak to this question. Unfortunately, the polls conducted during that conflict did not include measures of support for civil liberties. Stouffer's (1955) classic study of tolerance, for instance, was not conducted until more than a year after the war had ended.

5. Sullivan, Pierson, and Marcus (1982) also find that belief in democratic norms was one of the strongest predictors of political tolerance.

6. Similarly, Schildkraut (2002) finds that support for granting the police the power to stop and search (1) anyone, (2) people who fit a terrorist profile, or (3) any Arab or Muslim is predicted by many of the same independent variables, most notably worry about being a victim of an attack. As I demonstrate later, I find similar empirical overlap in the context of World War II and the post-9/11 cases.

7. Mueller (1988) notes, however, that because Communists were not the most disliked group for *all* citizens in the 1950s, general tolerance almost certainly had risen since that time.

8. Stouffer (1955) did not measure respondents' dislike of Communists.

9. Sullivan, Pierson, and Marcus (1982), by use of a series of paired polar adjectives—for instance, "violent/nonviolent" and "unpredictable/predictable"—measured threat by asking respondents to describe the group they liked the least. Mueller (1988) argues that this measure, in fact, is better conceived as a measure of group dislike than as a measure of group threat.

10. Feldman and Stenner (1997) also find that the effect of threat is highest among those respondents prone to authoritarian predispositions.

11. Both sets of authors found that personal threat—the level of concern for one's own safety—had only a small effect on civil liberties judgments, but that sociotropic threat—fear that the United States might suffer another terrorist attack—had a large effect on opinion.

12. Consistent with this position, Hutchison and Gilber (2007) find that cross-national variation in the objective level of threat from territorial disputes explains levels of political tolerance. Specifically, individuals in societies that face severe territorial threats are less willing to allow disliked groups to demonstrate publicly or hold political office.

13. Specifically the GSS asks if the target group should be permitted to engage in three public activities: (1) deliver public speeches, (2) have books that they write be available in public libraries, and (3) teach in colleges and universities. This measurement strategy is consistent with Sullivan, Pierson, and Marcus's (1982) admonition not to focus questions on political targets of one ideological stripe. In effect, the GSS casts a wide net, hoping to find some disliked target group for every respondent. As Gibson notes, "the use of a broad range of fringe groups, as in the GSS, provides everyone an opportunity to express his or her intolerance" (1992, 574). Gibson demonstrated that although the GSS battery and the content-controlled "least-liked" tolerance questions advanced by Sullivan Pierson, and Marcus were not highly correlated, the use of either variable led to similar conclusions regarding the determinants of tolerance. Gibson concludes that either measurement approach is adequate for measuring tolerance. I therefore use the GSS data to measure variation in levels of intolerance, both across individuals and over time.

14. Recently, Mondak and Sanders (2003, 2005) and Gibson (2005) carried out a debate about the best way to analyze trends in tolerance over time. Mondak and Sanders note that assessing trends in tolerance through the GSS battery is difficult because changes in tolerance might arise though true increases or decreases in tolerance or

it might arise through changes in affect toward the specific target groups used by the GSS. In essence Mondak and Sanders argue that the problems identified by Sullivan, Pierson, and Marcus (1982) might contaminate the GSS data. Proceeding from Sullivan and colleagues' definition of tolerance—"Political tolerance exists when respondents allow the full legal rights of citizenship to groups they themselves dislike"—Mondak and Sanders argue that tolerance is inherently dichotomous; advocating the restriction of the rights of any group constitutes intolerance. Adopting a dichotomous measurement strategy, the authors argue, sidesteps the problem caused by changing attitudes toward groups regardless of their true underlying attitudes. As long as there is one group that a respondent dislikes, one can measure tolerance and changes in tolerance. Gibson writes that this position is incorrect, arguing that a continuous measure is preferable on theoretical grounds. Here I adopt Gibson's strategy but check my results using Mondak and Sanders's dichotomous measure. This strategy, of course, does not account for changes over time in people's willingness to admit they dislike particular groups. The expression of a desire to severely curtail the liberties of Arabs in the months after 9/11 (see below) indicates, however, that citizens are willing to express hostility, given the right circumstances.

15. GSS included the item on the 1973, 1974, 1976, 1977, 1980, 1982, 1984, 1985, 1987, 1988, 1989, 1990, 1994, 1996, 1998, 2000, 2002, and 2004 surveys.

16. This item may be limited in another way. It could be that the threat component of the GSS "fear of crime" item is, in part, a measure of racial threat. In this case, any predictive power of the item may reflect omitted race-based hostility among white respondents, rather than the pure threat I wish to measure. To assess this possibility, I estimated a model to see if the threat item had different effects for whites and blacks. I found that the differences between the two groups were insignificant in both a statistical and a substantive sense.

17. The control variables were ideology, age, gender, race, education, region, and city size. At the suggestion of other scholars, I also included controls for income, religion (including self-identification as a fundamentalist), and the strength of religion. None of these variables affected the results. The full model results are presented in the online appendix. I pooled the data across all years, including fixed effects for the study year, using 1973 and 1974 as the baseline (the model would not converge if I included a separate dummy variable for 1974). I also ran these analyses separately in each year. The effect of the fear variable varied somewhat from year to year and was not always statistically significant. The effect was always positive, however, ranging from 0.02 to 0.08.

18. I also ran my analysis with a measure of authoritarianism that was available in some of the surveys, under the assumption that individuals who scored high on the authoritarianism scale would be both more threatened by their neighborhood and less tolerant of political dissent. Although authoritarianism had a large effect on intolerance, the inclusion of that measure did not change the effect of the threat variable.

19. I also conducted analysis on trends in mean intolerance levels and mean threat over the last thirty years. These two trends follow somewhat different trajectories but are clearly related. The correlation between the two series is .60, and a bivariate regression of intolerance levels on the threat measure indicates that a 10 percent increase in the proportion of people expressing fear in a given year is associated with a .08

movement on aggregate intolerance score (where 0 represents the most tolerant position and 1 is the least tolerant position). Moreover, these results hold, even accounting for the mid-1990s increase in the fear of crime. Using 1990 as the breaking point for the analysis, I find that the correlation between tolerance and threat actually increases after 1989. Before 1990, the two series are correlated at 0.57, but after 1990, the correlation rises to 0.69. The effect of a 10 percent increase in fear level drops from 0.06 in the first time period to 0.03 in the second period but remains statistically significant. Using the Mondak and Sanders approach, I find the same basic results, although the relationships are somewhat weaker. The threat and intolerance measures are correlated at 0.45, and regression analysis indicates that a 10 percent increase in the proportion of people expressing fear is associated with a .03 increase on aggregate intolerance score—an increase of more than one standard deviation. The convergence of the two sets of results should not be surprising because the continuous tolerance measure and the binary tolerance measure are correlated at 0.86. In any case, the data suggest that increases in aggregate levels of threat are related to increased support for restrictions on civil liberties.

20. Specifically, the GSS asked, "Are the following threats [nuclear war] to the United States greater, about the same, or less today than they were 10 years ago?" The fear of neighborhood and fear of nuclear war variables are correlated at .10 (a correlation that is statistically significant at the .05 level). If both threat variables are included in the regression, both variables have significant effects, although—as expected—the effect of each diminishes in the presence of the other.

21. This measure also extends the scope of examination into the international realm, assessing the effects of threats from abroad.

22. This effect is statistically significant as well. I also ran the analysis using the three responses to the nuclear war variable as dummy variables and confirmed that the effect of the nuclear war threat variable is linear.

23. Jenkins-Smith and Herron (2006) also find that trust in government is positively related to preferences for security over liberty. Unlike Davis and Silver (2004), however, the authors do not explore the relationship between trust in government and threat.

24. The GSS trust item reads, "How much of the time do you think you can trust the government in Washington to do what is right—just about always, most of the time, only some of the time, or almost never?" This item is identical to one of the two items used by Davis and Silver (2004) in their analysis discussed earlier. (The other item read, "Is the government run by a few big interests, or is it run for the benefit of all people?")

25. These analyses control for the political and demographic characteristics of the respondents. Given the potential importance of partisan judgments in determining political trust, I was sure to include party identification as a control variable in this analysis. Until recently, however, there was no statistical relationship between trust in government and partisanship (Hetherington 2008). The same is true of political ideology as well.

26. Davis (2007) explores change in civil liberties judgments from 2001 to 2004, using panel data. Some of this work is discussed later in the chapter.

27. See also Goux, Egan, and Citrin (2008) for a discussion of the Pew data.

28. The Pew general civil liberties item indicates a lower level of support for the civil liberties position than does the Davis and Silver survey (2004). Recall that Davis and Silver found majority support for the civil liberties position in the trade-off between security and civil liberties. The different outcomes of the two surveys might be a result of slight differences in question wording. The outcomes might also result from a fluke of the data, however. Davis and Silver replicated the general civil liberties/ security trade-off question in a 2003 survey. Although aggregate support for most of the civil liberties items remained stable across the two surveys (Davis 2007), there was a ten-point drop in the civil liberty position in the general question. This pattern runs counter to both the expected results and the Pew data. Perhaps, then, the initial Davis and Silver results represent something of an outlier.

29. A factor analysis of these items indicates that they all tap a single dimension. Specifically, the factor analysis yielded a single-factor solution. The eigenvalue for the first dimension is 1.22, and no other factor has an eigenvalue greater than 0.25. Providing further support for the link between the general trade-off question and the target items is the fact that the factor scores for the "worry" question (0.30) and the question concerning immigrant camps (0.25) are roughly equivalent. Similar factor analyses of British data from February 2003 and August 2005 yield nearly identical results; questions about general civil liberties trade-offs and specific questions about what to do with immigrants scaled on the same factor.

30. As noted earlier, the question "Do you think it will be necessary for the average person to give up some civil liberties?" was not asked after 2004. The parallel item, however, measuring whether "the government has gone too far in restricting civil liberties," followed the same upward trend in support as the general civil liberties question in the period after 9/11. There is reason to think, therefore, that the third Pew question—which is worded in a manner similar to the government anti-terrorism question asked in 2001 and 2002—captures general trends in civil liberties. Because support for the civil liberties position has been increasing since 2004, it stands to reason that general support for civil liberties has been rising as well.

31. Interestingly, at the same time that there was a large increase in support for the protection of civil liberties, from January 2002 to August 2003, sociotropic threat dropped only marginally. In January 2002, 62 percent of respondents were "very worried" or "somewhat worried" that there would soon be a terrorist attack in the United States. In August 2003, 58 percent of respondents took such a position.

32. Sullivan, Pierson, and Marcus (1982) used partisan attachment to estimate the "least-liked" groups of respondents but did not explore the direct effects of partisan identification.

33. This question was asked in two ways as part of a question-wording experiment. Half the sample was asked the retaliation question. The other half were asked the same question but with the qualification "even if it means that U.S. armed forces might suffer thousands of casualties?" Including the casualty caveat reduced support for retaliation somewhat, but the effect of the retaliation variable on support for civil liberties was the same for both forms. I estimated an alternative model, including a dummy for question

form and an interaction between form and the question. The coefficients were nonsignificant, and I therefore combined the two for purposes of analysis.

34. Huddy et al. (2005) found that sociotropic threat increased both support for military intervention and restrictions on civil liberties. To account for the possibility that the relationships I find here are spurious, I included measures of threat—both individual-level and sociotropic threat—in my analyses, when available. Including the threat measure diminished somewhat the effect of war support on support for civil liberties, but the relationship between the two variables remained statically and substantively significant. To preserve continuity, I present the estimates (figs. 7.4 and 7.5) without the controls for threat. As noted earlier, Pew did not ask about partisanship on the September 2001 survey. The analysis of data from this survey does not therefore include party identification. This fact does not invalidate the results presented here. Indicators are that in the wake of 9/11, partisanship had little effect on civil liberty judgments. Davis and Silver (2004) find no partisan differences on civil liberties questions in their late 2001 survey. Furthermore, the Pew data suggest that these differences took several months to develop into a significant cleavage; as figure 7.2 shows, the partisanship gap on civil liberties questions was only about five points in January 2002.

35. These first differences are generated from logit analysis, which controls for the demographic characteristics of the respondents, including the their gender, race, education level, and the census region and size of the metropolitan area of residence.

36. For instance, Stouffer's (1955) study of political tolerance, conducted in the aftermath of the Korean War, does not contain a single question about attitudes toward military action.

37. Respondents could also say they were "not sure" where they stood. These data are therefore analyzed using multinomial logit (see Appendix E for details).

38. Harris conducted a poll in 1970 that, in addition to the Vietnam protester question described earlier, asked a long battery of questions about civil liberties. Unfortunately, this survey did not ask about support for the Vietnam War, so it is not possible to perform comparable analyses in this survey. I did, however, correlate the Vietnam question used in my analyses with the more general questions and found a significant correlation. Thus, even granting problems with the dependent variables used here, I find that the Vietnam protest item does relate to the more general concept of interest.

39. Scale details are available from the author upon request.

40. Specifically, Republicans were about 4 percent more supportive than Democrats of the pro–civil liberty position.

41. These questions were the second stage in a branching question. Gallup first asked, "Do you believe in freedom of speech?" Upward of 94 percent of respondents said they did believe in free speech. As in the present day, the introduction of specific target groups dropped support greatly.

42. It could also be that individuals who did not trust Russia felt more threatened by radicals, which would lead to the same effects in the trend data.

43. Figure 7.7 therefore contains both trade-off items and tolerance items.

44. In later surveys, Gallup asked about Fascists and Communists together, but in 1938 Gallup used a split sample format in which one-half of respondents were asked

about Communists and the other half were asked about Fascists. The level of support for civil liberties was within 1 percent between the two groups, so in figure 7.7 I present a tolerance score that averages across the two items.

45. These trends could be an artifact of changes in the international sphere. Although Communists and Fascists were disliked in the late 1930s, in 1940 and early 1941 they were increasingly seen as the enemy. However, the readings in January 1941 and July 1941 on support for unconditional free speech show a downward trend as well, indicating that the decline in support for the questions relating to Communists and Fascists reflects a general trend.

46. This individual-level analysis employs procedures described in Berinsky (2006). The multivariate results are included in Appendix E.

CHAPTER EIGHT

1. Edward Epstein, "War's Outcome Often Dictates President's Fate," *San Francisco Chronicle*, October 22, 2004; http://www.sfgate.com/cgi-bin/article.cgi?file=/chronicle/archive/2004/10/22 (accessed August 7, 2007).

2. For the 1968 election, I present the results of a model involving the choice between Humphrey and Nixon. I use the two-party vote share to ensure comparability across the different elections. Including Wallace as a third choice in a multinomial logit model does not change the results reported in table 8.1.

3. See Appendix F for the full results.

4. For the seven-point escalation/de-escalation scales used in the 1968 and 1972 NES, I compute the effect of moving from a position of support for doing "everything necessary to win a complete military victory, no matter what results" to saying that the United States "should withdraw completely from Vietnam right now, no matter what results."

5. The full results of this analysis are presented in Appendix F. A few notes are in order here. Because retrospective and prospective opinions are often highly correlated, I ran my analysis as a series of regressions, using each measure of war support in turn as a single independent variable (along with the relevant control variables). Including multiple measures of war support, where available, changed the magnitude of the coefficients (as expected, given the correlations between the different measures of war support). The pattern of these coefficients did not change appreciably, however. I do not present in this table the full future action scale results (although the probit and logit analyses used to generate these predicted effects contain dummy variables marking both the escalation and de-escalation positions). Following the strategy of Zaller (1992), I considered the "pull out" option as the option most distinct from the other two. Because the "status quo" answer represented the official policy of both the Johnson and Nixon administrations, like Zaller I take that position to be akin to war support. Considering the range of response options leads to some interesting results, however. Both Stevenson in 1952 and Humphrey in 1968 found their greatest levels of support among respondents who favored the status quo. That is, both respondents who wanted to escalate the war *and* respondents who wanted to de-escalate the war were less likely to vote for the candidates of the incumbent's party. These effects are not strong and do not extend to an analysis that uses the seven-point scale recoded into

similar hawk/dove/status quo positions. Thus, the findings are more suggestive than anything else. These results, however, seem to demonstrate that respondents who were dissatisfied with the war, whatever their reasons, were less likely to vote for the party of the incumbent president.

6. Although some of the questions concerning Iraq were not precisely comparable to earlier questions, the questions asked by the CBS News/*New York Times* poll were almost exactly the same as the questions asked during Korea and Vietnam. The "effect of war support" on the 2004 election results is very similar to the other questions. We may, therefore, have confidence in the continuity of the results presented in table 8.1.

7. Because I employ probit models in the analysis reported in table 8.1, I use a modified version of the level importance statistic in figure 8.1, multiplying the potential maximum importance of the contribution of a variable by its mean. The intuition behind the measure is identical to Achen's (1982) proposed quantity, however.

8. The loss for the 2004 election was computed by averaging the effect from all the polls.

9. The correlation of the Johnson and Humphrey feeling thermometer measures was .71. By comparison, the correlation between the Humphrey feeling thermometer and that of Muskie—his vice presidential candidate—was .59. By way of comparison, the correlation between Nixon and his vice presidential candidate, Spiro Agnew, was also .59.

10. The average respondent believed all three candidates stood just to the "escalate" side of the midpoint of the scale. The mean placement for Johnson was 4.46, for Nixon 4.43, and for Humphrey 4.14.

11. A similar relationship can be found on the "urban unrest" scale—the question of whether the government should use force to solve problems of urban unrest versus solving the root problems of that unrest, such as poverty. This result indicates that respondents assumed that the political positions of Johnson and Humphrey were consistent across domestic as well as international issues.

12. Equivalent measures do not exist in the 1952 study. Responses to the open-ended "candidate likes/dislikes" question are suggestive, however. Among respondents who gave a reason for their decision to vote against Stevenson, 26 percent said they cast their vote because of his connection with Truman. That category was by far the highest single response, even greater than those who voted against Stevenson because he was a Democrat—16 percent.

13. See, for instance, Abramowitz 1988, 1996; Campbell 2000; Fair 1978, 1988, 2002; Hibbs 2000; Holbrook 1996; Lewis-Beck and Tien 2000; Rosenstone 1983; Wlezien 2001; and Wlezien and Erikson 2000, 2004.

14. I focus here on economic variables because I wish to model election outcomes as a function of external events so as to identify the occurrence of deviant elections. Thus, I want to avoid including factors that might be endogenous to the process, such as presidential approval. Put another way, to identify elections that are deviant results, I take Hibbs to be correct when he argues that "approval ratings and other poll readings of voter sentiments about the incumbent president, his party, candidates at elections, and so forth are logically inadmissible in behavioral models of voting" (2000, 171).

15. The estimate of the discount rate used to compute the weighted RDI in figure

8.1 comes from a model that also includes casualty measures for the war years (Hibbs 2000, 2007). However, omitting the casualty variable (Hibbs 2000; Bartels and Zaller 2001) or removing the war elections of 1952 and 1968 from the sample (Hibbs 2000) results in a very similar estimate of the temporal discount term. For instance, the 95 percent confidence interval of the weighted RDI discount term overlaps with the point estimate of the same model with the war dummy variable omitted (and vice versa) (Bartels and Zaller 2001).

16. The measure of change in RDI over the last two quarters advanced by Achen and Bartels (2002) also puts the 2004 election almost precisely on the regression line.

17. In Hibbs' (2000) original analysis, which covered the elections from 1952 to 1996, the elections of 1968 and 1972 were the biggest outliers. If we exclude the two elections most directly touched by war—1952 and 1968—the weighted change in RDI predicts the election outcomes with near perfect precision.

18. Although they use different measures to account for the effects of wars, Rosenstone and Hibbs come to a common conclusion regarding the effects of those wars on presidential elections. Rosenstone (1983) finds that an increase of 10 percent in disapproval of the handling of war leads to a 1.6 percent decrease in the vote share of the incumbent's party. Rosenstone estimates that Korea cost the Democrats 6 percent of the vote in 1952, whereas Vietnam cost the Democrats 8 percent in 1968. Hibbs (2000) uses cumulative casualties in 1952, 1964, 1968, and 1976 and estimates that the Democrats were disadvantaged by 11 percent in both 1952 and 1968 because of the ongoing wars.

19. Specifically, Bartels and Zaller (2001) find that including a dummy variable marking the war years of 1952 and 1968 reduces the standard error of the regression relative to the model in which just the economic indicator is used to predict the vote, for each of the following six economic indicators: (1) percentage change in RDI per capita during the election year; (2) percentage change in RDI per capita in the twelve months before the election; (3) average percentage change in RDI per capita for the term of the incumbent's party, with temporal discounting; (4) percentage change in GDP per capita during the election year; (5) percentage change in GDP per capita in the twelve months before the election; and (6) average percentage change in GDP per capita for the term of the incumbent's party, with temporal discounting. Bartels and Zaller (2001) find a somewhat smaller effect for war than do Hibbs (2000) and Rosenstone (1983). Specifically, they report a model-averaged parameter estimate (where the parameters are combined across all forty-eight models, they estimate using Bayesian model averaging) of –3.94 percent—roughly one-half of the Hibbs estimate and one-third of the Rosenstone estimate. I believe their estimate is in part a function of the use of a variable measuring the number of terms the incumbent's party has been in power, which should correct for some of the underperformance of the incumbent in 1952, given that that election was held after twenty years of uninterrupted Democratic rule.

20. The lack of systematic attention to the wartime elections, in fact, has obscured the incongruence of the results of individual-level election results. Compare, for example, Miller et al.'s (1976) discussion of the 1972 election with Converse et al.'s (1969) analysis of the 1968 election.

21. Similarly, Converse et al. note that although 40 percent of the electorate cited

the war in Vietnam as the most important problem facing the government in Washington, the contest between Nixon and Humphrey was decided above all on the grounds of party loyalty, where "the central 1968 issues tend to give rather diminutive relationships" (1969, 1097).

22. Furthermore, the minority of voters who did see large differences between the candidates could not agree on which candidate was a hawk and which a dove.

23. This is not to say that opinions on the war are exactly like economic evaluations—unlike aggregate evaluations in the economic realm, there is no "true answer" about whether a particular war is right or wrong. But because partisan predispositions can so heavily influence beliefs about war—as discussed in chapter 4—it is difficult to separate out the independent effect of war on candidate choice.

24. Put another way, the analysis here underscores the lessons of chapter 5. In that chapter, I demonstrated that attitudes about war are endogenous to evaluations of political leaders. Therefore any analysis that treats such attitudes as causally prior to vote choice is inherently flawed.

25. The tension between these two statements is evident in some academic work published on this topic. For instance, Klinkner spends the first half of his article arguing that attitudes about the Iraq War were central to explaining Bush's victory in the 2004 election and the second half of the same article arguing that those opinions were "shaped largely by opinions of its chief architect—George W. Bush" (2006, 295). In cases where opinion is elite-led—especially on this, the most polarizing war in the history of polling—it is extremely difficult to peel apart the causal pathways with cross-sectional data.

26. Many scholars in the realist tradition, on the other hand, argue that domestic politics do not influence foreign policy.

27. For a thorough review of existing studies, see Levy (1989).

28. For instance, Merolla, Ramos, and Zechmeister (2007) point to examples, such as Peron in Argentina, where charismatic leaders were able to trade on domestic crises.

29. Merolla and Zechmeister (2009) argue that the lack of a rally in the Spanish case is the result of a perception that the administration mishandled the crisis, in particular, by immediately and mistakenly attempting to place the blame on the domestic terrorist group ETA.

30. In this figure I follow the analytic strategy advanced by Jacobson (2008) and combine many polls from several organizations, each using slightly different question wordings. The different individual subseries trend together, as expected. To generate the trend lines, I employed a lowess smoothing algorithm with a bandwidth of 0.2.

31. It is not possible to compute a correlation for the two series because no organization simultaneously asked about the likelihood of an attack and the extent to which people were worried about an attack. If we interpolate the missing data with a linear trend, the correlation is 0.63.

32. Although the trend on the "very likely" question is upward at the end of the series, it seems to be a modest upward tick. Indeed, with the exception of a single high reading in July 2007, most of the "very likely" percentages in 2007 tend toward the low point of the distribution.

33. These trends remain stable even if I adjust for interpersonal differences in the

use of thermometer scores. I computed these trends by subtracting the mean thermometer score across six balanced groups from the Bush feeling thermometer, following procedures outlined in Winter and Berinsky (1999).

34. This upward trend held for both Republicans and Democrats.

35. I also control for the mean feeling thermometer. Specifically, I regress Bush's feeling thermometer score on party identification (measured in 2000), gender, and race. The full results are presented in Appendix F.

36. The same pattern holds if I compare the relationship between Bush leadership scores and vote choice; from 2000 to 2004 there was a large increase in the impact of leadership on support for Bush. The panel structure of the data allows for the examination of more complicated causal paths. In additional analysis, I used lagged values of the independent variables in place of the contemporaneous measures. Given that the argument here is that the meaning of leadership changed from 2000 to 2004, such analysis is not especially telling. In any case, when I ran this analysis, the coefficient for the leadership scores increased in both 2002 and 2004, but the difference between the effect in those years remained stable.

37. I also assessed the effects of panel attrition on my results. Bush opponents dropped out at higher rates than did Bush supporters from 2000 to 2004, perhaps in part because panel attrition is most likely to affect respondents of low socioeconomic status (Bartels 1999). Although conducting the analysis only for those respondents who were in all three waves might ensure a disproportionately pro-Bush sample, this possibility should not effect the trends presented here. In any case, the same basic pattern of results holds if I use the full samples—both panel respondents and new cross-sectional respondents—in all years rather than restricting myself to the panel participants.

38. Even FDR's supporters were hesitant to grant him a third term. As early as July 1937, 27 percent of respondents said they opposed granting Roosevelt a third term, even though they supported him, because they thought that no president should have a third term. This figure is not weighted because of the difficulties involved with matching the Roper data to census data.

39. The four response options were as follows: (1) "Roosevelt has done an excellent job and it's very important that he should be president during the next four years"; (2) "While he has made mistakes and he's been in office a long time, it is still better to elect Roosevelt president again for the next four years"; (3) "Although Roosevelt has done some good things, he has been president long enough and the country would be better off to elect Dewey for the next four years"; and (4) "It would be a very bad thing for this country to reelect Roosevelt for another four years."

40. Churchill again became prime minister when the Conservatives returned to power in 1951.

41. Specifically, respondents were asked, "If there was a general election tomorrow, which party would you vote for?" The opinion polls presented in figure 8.7 are drawn from King (2001). These polls were conducted using face-to-face interviews, and samples were drawn using quota-sampling methods. Many of these individual-level polls have been lost to time. Moreover, unlike the U.S. public opinion data presented in this book, even for those polls for which we have individual-level data we do not have detailed records of the sampling procedure or the census data, which permit correc-

tions for sample biases. The data presented here should therefore be taken with a grain of salt. Still, for the purposes of this book, these data are useful for tracking trends over time and examining cross-tabulations of relationships between variables.

42. The reasons for these changes are twofold according to Franklin and Ladner (1995). First, a large new group of voters entered the electorate, and second, these voters were the first to have had any significant chance of growing up in a Labour household. Whereas in previous elections the Labour Party had to rely on the conversion of existing voters, in 1945 it was finally able to enjoy the same benefits of other established parties and gain voters who supported Labour by inheritance. A significant number of older voters passed away in the years between the last election in 1935 and the one in 1945. Twenty percent of the electorate in 1945 were too young to have voted in a previous election, yet the electorate had increased in size by only 5 percent since 1935. Together, these figures imply that about 15 percent of those who had voted in 1935 were not members of the electorate in 1945.

43. In fact, in many ways, the British general election is the best illustration in this chapter of the continued primacy of domestic politics during times of war.

CHAPTER NINE

1. CBS News Poll, "Five Years in Iraq," March 19, 2008. The survey was conducted during March 15–18, 2008.

2. ABC News Transcripts, *Good Morning America*, 7:14 a.m. (EST), March 19, 2008.

3. For instance, in every one of eight surveys of Cuban Americans in the Miami area conducted from 1991 to 2007 by the Cuban Research Institute of Florida International University, a majority of respondents strongly or mostly favored "direct U.S. military action to overthrow the Cuban government"; http://www.fiu.edu/orgs/ipor/cuba8/CubaComp.htm (accessed July 8, 2008).

4. An intellectual model here could be the development of "two-level games" (Putnam 1988), which emphasizes the importance of treating domestic and international relations as interrelated rather than as mutually exclusive realms of politics.

5. Feinstein and Schickler (2008) demonstrate that in the north, this process of sorting began earlier. Northern Democrats began to embrace racial liberalism in the 1940s and were more liberal than northern Republicans from the late 1940s onward. Therefore, the process of change on the issue of race may have been even more gradual than Carmines and Stimson (1989) suggest, underscoring the gradual nature of political change in domestic politics.

6. The lowest level of support among Republicans during the Johnson administration was 31 percent, in August 1968.

7. In 2002, the NES asked respondents: "Some people feel the government in Washington should see to it that every person has a job and a good standard of living. Others think the government should just let each person get ahead on their own. Which is closer to the way you feel or haven't you thought much about this?" A large portion—30 percent of the sample—said they hadn't thought about it. In 2004, NES asked the more traditional seven-point-scale version of the question: "Some people feel the government in Washington should see to it that every person has a job and a good standard of living (suppose these people are at one end of a scale, at point 1).

Others think the government should just let each person get ahead on their own (suppose these people are at the other end, at point 7). And, of course, some other people have opinions somewhere in between, at points 2, 3, 4, 5, or 6. Where would you place yourself on this scale, or haven't you thought much about it?" Only 9 percent did not answer this form of the question. Removing the "don't know" responses does not change the size of the partisan gap on this question.

8. For a competing view, however, see Fiorina, Abrams, and Pope (2005).

9. To be precise, the graph is a function of the DW-NOMINATE scores, as advanced by Poole and Rosenthal (see McCarthy, Poole, and Rosenthal 2006). NOMINATE scores are derived directly from all available roll call votes. The points in the figure represent the differences between the mean positions of all Republican members of Congress and the mean positions of all Democratic members of Congress.

APPENDIX A

1. These figures are based on an analysis of AIPO 225 (December 1940). They are typical of the polls I examined through the early 1940s. By the mid-1940s, however, Gallup had adjusted his gender quotas to interview equal numbers of men and women. This change in the composition of the sample makes it difficult to track real changes in opinion over time.

2. The use of weighting adjustments can lower the precision of survey estimates because we trade off a reduction in bias for an increase in variance (Kalton and Flores-Cervantes 2003). Given the compositional imbalance in the quota samples, I believe this is a worthwhile trade-off.

3. The poststratification weights I employ are different from probability weights, which are known at the time the survey is designed and are used to adjust for nonconstant probability of sample inclusion. It is not possible to employ probability weights for the quota samples I examine here.

4. More formally, let w_{ij} represent the weight for each cell in the three-by-two cross-classification table of interest. The goal is to estimate $\hat{w}_{ij}$ from the marginal proportions in the population, w_i ($i = 1, 2, 3$) and w_j ($j = 1, 2$), respectively. This can be achieved with the following algorithm (Little and Wu 1991):

1. Initialize the weights by setting each $\hat{w}_{ij}^{(0)}$ equal to n_{ij}/n, which is the sample cell count over the sample size.

2. Calculate $\hat{w}_{ij}^{(1)} = w_i * \dfrac{\hat{w}_{ij}^{(0)}}{\sum_j \hat{w}_i^{(0)}}$ for each i. Here we are "raking" over the rows.

3. Calculate $\hat{w}_{ij}^{(2)} = w_j * \dfrac{\hat{w}_{ij}^{(1)}}{\sum_i \hat{w}_j^{(1)}}$ for each j. Here we are "raking" over the columns.

4. Repeat steps 2 and 3 until $\sum_j \hat{w}_i = w_i$ and $\sum_i \hat{w}_j = w_j$ for each i and j, which is when "convergence" is achieved. Although the process can be slow, generally the raking algorithm converges reliably.

5. The estimate of the weighted mean is then $\hat{\theta} = \sum_i \sum_j w_{ij} \hat{\theta}_{ij}$.

5. In some surveys, it appears that African Americans may have been excluded from the sampling scheme. It is not possible, however, to make a definitive statement on this point given the sampling procedure descriptions.

6. I included race as a separate weighting category for those surveys that had at least 20 African Americans in the sample. When race was used as a weighting variable for the purpose of creating cell weights, whites were weighted using the full stratification table (gender by region by occupation/education), whereas blacks were only weighted on the basis of gender due to small sample sizes. In some cases—most notably the OPOR surveys conducted after 1942—there were no blacks in the sample. In those cases, race was ignored and the surveys were weighted to the full population.

APPENDIX C

1. The entry for "World War Two" varies from year to year; in one year it may read "World War Two," whereas in others it reads as "World War 2" or "World War no. 2."

2. The index sometimes refers to a page number that includes only part of a speech, debate, or other exchange on the war; in those cases it was necessary to backtrack to the beginning of the debate and then follow through to the end.

3. For example, an isolationist tone may be inferred from a statement that compares German imperialism in eastern Europe to British imperialism in India, questions the moral difference between Hitler and Stalin, or suggests that America should not concern itself over who wins the war.

4. The concern here with the use of weights in regression analysis is distinct from the regression estimation methods discussed earlier.

5. As Gelman counsels, "In a regression context, the analysis should include as 'X variables' everything that affects sample selection or nonresponse. Or, to be realistic, all variables should be included that have an important effect on sampling or nonresponse, if they also are potentially predictive of the outcome of interest" (2005, 3).

6. In the 1940 analysis, I found that information has a greater effect among opponents of FDR. This result makes sense given the context of the 1940 election. With the stability of the pro-FDR war message and the sudden change in the anti-FDR war message, we would expect that opponents of FDR would be more responsive to changes in the balance of political cues.

APPENDIX E

1. Pew asked these different questions in a split-sample format. Although support for action was slightly lower when the possibility of casualties were mentioned, the effect of support for action on support for restricting civil liberties was nearly identical across the forms.

REFERENCES

Abramowitz, Alan I. 1988. "An Improved Model for Predicting Presidential Election Outcomes." *PS: Political Science and Politics*. 21: 843–47.

———. 1996. "Bill and Al's Excellent Adventure: Forecasting the 1996 Presidential Election." *American Politics Quarterly*. 24: 434–42.

Abramson, Paul R., John H. Aldrich, Jill Rickershauser, and David W. Rohde. 2007. "Fear in the Voting Booth: The 2004 Presidential Election." *Political Behavior* 29: 197–220.

Achen, Christopher H. 1982. *Interpreting and Using Regression*. Beverley Hills: Sage Publications.

———. 1986. *The Statistical Analysis of Quasi-Experiments*. Berkeley: University of California Press.

Achen, Christopher H., and Larry M. Bartels. 2002. "Blind Retrospection: Electoral Responses to Drought, Flu, and Shark Attacks." Prepared presented at the Annual Meeting of the American Political Science Association, Boston.

Adams, Michael C. C. 1994. *The Best War Ever: America and World War II*. Baltimore: Johns Hopkins University Press.

Alba, R. D. 1985. *Italian Americans: Into the Twilight of Ethnicity*. Englewood Cliffs, NJ: Prentice-Hall.

Aldrich, John H., John L. Sullivan, and Eugene Borgida. 1989. "Foreign Affairs and Issue Voting: Do Presidential Candidates 'Waltz before a Blind Audience?'" *American Political Science Review* 83: 123–41.

Aldrich, John H., Christopher Gelpi, Peter Feaver, Jason Reifler, and Kristin Thompson Sharp. 2006. "Foreign Policy and the Electoral Connection." *Annual Review of Political Science* 9: 477–502.

Almond, Gabriel A. 1960. *The American People and Foreign Policy*. New York: Praeger.

Anderson, Christopher J., Silvia Mendes, and Yuliya V. Tverdova. 2004. "Endogenous

Economic Voting: Evidence from the 1997 British Election." *Electoral Studies* 23: 683–708.

Ansolabehere, Stephen, Rebecca Lessem, and James M. Snyder Jr. 2006. "The Orientation of Newspaper Endorsements in U.S. Elections, 1940–2002." *Quarterly Journal of Political Science* 1: 393–404.

Ansolabehere, Stephen, Erik C. Snowberg, and James M. Snyder Jr. 2005. "Unrepresentative Information: The Case of Newspaper Reporting on Campaign Finance." *Public Opinion Quarterly* 69: 213–31.

Arena, Philip. 2008. "Success Breeds Success? War Outcomes, Domestic Opposition, and Elections." *Conflict Management and Peace Science* 25: 136–51.

Arlen, Michael J. 1982. *Living Room War.* Syracuse, NY: Syracuse University Press.

Baker, Nicholson. 2008. *Human Smoke: The Beginnings of World War II, the End of Civilization.* Rockefeller Center, NY: Simon and Schuster.

Ball, Stuart. 2003. *Winston Churchill.* New York: New York University Press.

Barnes, Joseph F. 1952. *Willkie: The Events He Was Part Of, the Ideals He Fought For.* New York: Simon and Schuster.

Bartels, Larry M. 1999. "Panel Effects in the American National Election Studies." *Political Analysis.* 8: 1–20.

———. 2002. "Beyond the Running Tally: Partisan Bias in Political Perceptions." *Political Behavior* 24: 117–50.

———. 2003. "Democracy with Attitudes." In *Electoral Democracy*, ed. Michael B. MacKuen and George Rabinowitz, 48–82. Ann Arbor: University of Michigan Press.

Bartels, Larry M., and John Zaller. 2001. "Presidential Vote Models: A Recount." *PS: Political Science and Politics.* 34: 9–20.

Baum, Matthew A. 2002. "The Constituent Foundations of the Rally-`round-the-Flag Phenomenon." *International Studies Quarterly* 46: 263–98.

———. 2003. *Soft News Goes to War: Public Opinion and American Policy in the New Media Age.* Princeton: Princeton University Press.

———. 2004. "Going Private: Public Opinion, Presidential Rhetoric, and the Domestic Politics of Audience Costs in U.S. Foreign Policy Crises." *Journal of Conflict Resolution* 48: 603–31.

Baum, Matthew A., and Tim Groeling. 2004. "What Gets Covered? How Media Coverage of Elite Debate Drives the Rally-`round-the-Flag Phenomenon, 1979–1998." Paper presented at the Annual Meeting of the American Political Science Association.

Baum, Matthew A., and Phil Gussin. 2008. "In the Eye of the Beholder: How Information Shortcuts Shape Individual Perceptions of Bias in the Media." *Quarterly Journal of Political Science* 3: 1–31.

Baum, Matthew A., and Samuel Kernell. 2001. "Economic Class and Popular Support for Franklin Roosevelt in War and Peace." *Public Opinion Quarterly* 65: 198–229.

Bean, Louis H., Frederick Mosteller, and Frederick Williams. 1944. "Nationalities and 1944." *Public Opinion Quarterly* 8: 368–75.

Belknap, George, and Angus Campbell. 1951. "Political Party Identification and Attitudes toward Foreign Policy." *Public Opinion Quarterly* 15(4): 601–23.

Bennett, W. Lance. 1990. "Toward a Theory of Press–State Relations in the United States." *Journal of Communication* 40: 103–27.

Berinsky, Adam J. 1999. "The Two Faces of Public Opinion." *American Journal of Political Science* 43: 1209–30.

———. 2002a. "Political Context and the Survey Response: The Dynamics of Racial Policy Opinion." *Journal of Politics* 64: 567–84.

———. 2002b. "Silent Voices: Social Welfare Policy Opinions and Equality in America." *American Journal of Political Science* 46: 276–87.

———. 2004. *Silent Voices: Opinion Polls and Political Representation in America*. Princeton: Princeton University Press.

———. 2006. "American Public Opinion in the 1930s and 1940s: The Analysis of Quota-Controlled Sample Survey Data." *Public Opinion Quarterly* 70: 499–529.

Berinsky, Adam J., and James N. Druckman. 2007. "Public Opinion Research, Presidential Rhetoric, and Support for the Iraq War." *Public Opinion Quarterly* 71: 126–41.

Berinsky, Adam J., and Tali Mendelberg. 2005. "The Indirect Effects of Discredited Stereotypes in Judgments of Jewish Leaders." *American Journal of Political Science* 49: 845–64.

Bethlehem, J. G. 2002. "Weighting Nonresponse Adjustments Based on Auxiliary Information." In *Survey Nonresponse*, ed. R. M. Groves, D. A. Dillman, J. L. Eltinge, and R. J. A. Little. New York: Wiley.

Bobo, Lawrence. 1983. "Whites' Opposition to Busing: Symbolic Racism or Realistic Group Conflict?" *Journal of Personality and Social Psychology* 45: 1196–1210.

Boyd, Richard W. 1972. "Popular Control of Public Policy: A Normal Vote Analysis of the 1968 Election." *American Political Science Review.* 66: 429–49.

Brady, Henry E., and Paul M. Sniderman. 1985. "Attitude Attribution: A Group Basis for Political Reasoning." *American Political Science Review* 79: 1061–68.

Braumoeller, Bear F. 2008. "The Myth of American Isolationism" Manuscript. Ohio State University.

Breen, Richard. 1996. *Regression Models: Censored, Sample Selected, or Truncated Data.* Sage University Paper Series on Quantitative Applications in the Social Sciences, 07-111. Thousand Oaks, CA: Sage Publications.

Brehm, John. 1993. *The Phantom Respondents: Opinion Surveys and Political Representation.* Ann Arbor: University of Michigan Press.

Brody, Richard A. 1991. *Assessing the President: The Media, Elite Opinion and Public Support.* Stanford: Stanford University Press.

Burk, James. 1999. "Public Support for Peacekeeping in Lebanon and Somalia: Assessing the Casualties Hypothesis." *Political Science Quarterly* 114: 53–78.

Caldeira, Gregory A. 1987. "Public Opinion and the U.S. Supreme Court: FDR's Court-Packing Plan." *American Political Science Review* 81: 1139–53.

Campbell, Angus, Philip E. Converse, Warren E. Miller, and Donald E. Stokes. 1960. *The American Voter.* New York: Wiley.

Campbell, Donald T., and Robert A. LeVine. 1961. "A Proposal for Cooperative Cross-Cultural Research on Ethnocentrism." *Journal of Conflict Resolution* 5: 82–108.

Campbell, Donald T., and Julian C. Stanley. 1966. *Experimental and Quasi-Experimental Designs for Research*. Chicago: Rand McNally.

Campbell, James E. 2000. "The Science of Forecasting Presidential Elections." In *Before the Vote: Forecasting American National Elections*, ed. James E. Campbell and James C. Garand, 169–88. Thousand Oaks, CA: Sage Publications.

Campbell, Joel T., Leila S. Cain, Anatol Rapoport, and Philip E. Converse. 1965. "Public Opinion and the Outbreak of War." *Journal of Conflict Resolution* 9: 318–33.

Cantril, Hadley. 1944. *Gauging Public Opinion*. Princeton: Princeton University Press.

———. 1948. "Opinion Trends in World War II: Some Guides to Interpretation." *Public Opinion Quarterly* 12: 30–44.

———. 1967. *The Human Dimension: Experiences in Policy Research*. New Brunswick, NJ: Rutgers University Press.

Cantril, Hadley, and Mildred Strunk. 1951. *Public Opinion; 1935–1946*. Princeton: Princeton University Press.

Carmines, Edward G., and James A. Stimson. 1989. *Issue Evolution*. Princeton: Princeton University Press.

Casey, Steven. 2001. *Cautious Crusade: Franklin D. Roosevelt, American Public Opinion, and the War against Nazi Germany*. New York: Oxford University Press.

———. 2008. *Selling the Korean War: Propaganda, Politics, and Public Opinion 1950–1953*. New York: Oxford University Press.

Chiozza, Giacomo, and H. E. Goemans. 2004. "International Conflict and the Tenure of Leaders: Is War Still Ex Post Inefficient?" *American Journal of Political Science* 48: 604–19.

Chong, Dennis. 1993. How People Think, Reason, and Feel about Rights and Liberties. *American Journal of Political Science* 37: 867–99.

———. 1996. "Creating Common Frames of Reference on Political Issues." In *Political Persuasion and Attitude Change*, ed. Diana C. Mutz, Paul M. Sniderman, and Richard A. Brody. Ann Arbor: University of Michigan Press.

Cleveland, William S. 1979. "Robust Locally-Weighted Regression and Scatterplot Smoothing." *Journal of the American Statistical Association*. 74: 829–36.

Cole, G. D. 1948. *A History of the Labour Party since 1914*. London: Routledge and Kegan Paul.

Conover, Pamela Johnston. 1988. "The Role of Social Groups in Political Thinking." *British Journal of Political Science* 18: 51–76.

Conover, Pamela Johnston, and Virginia Sapiro. 1993. "Gender, Feminist Consciousness, and War." *American Journal of Political Science* 37: 1079–99.

Converse, Jean M. 1987. *Survey Research in the United States: Roots and Emergence 1890–1960*. Berkeley: University of California Press.

Converse, Philip E. 1964. "The Nature of Belief Systems in the Mass Publics." In *Ideology and Discontent*, ed. David Apter. New York: Free Press.

———. 1965. "Comment on: Public Opinion and the Outbreak of War." *Journal of Conflict Resolution* 9: 330–33.

———. 1975. "Public Opinion and Voting Behavior." In *Handbook of Political Science*, ed. Fred W. Greenstein and Nelson W. Polsby, 4:75–169. Reading, MA: Addison-Wesley.

———. 1990. "Popular Representation and the Distribution of Information." In *Information and Democratic Processes*, ed. John A. Ferejohn and James H. Kuklinski, 369–88. Urbana: University of Illinois Press.

Converse, Philip E., Warren E. Miller, Jerrold G. Rusk, and Arthur C. Wolfe. 1969. "Continuity and Change in American Politics: Parties and Issues in the 1968 Election." *American Political Science Review* 63: 1083–1105.

Cobb, Michael D. 2007. "Dispelling Casualty Myths: Citizens' Knowledge and News Media's Coverage about Casualties." Paper presented at the Annual Meeting of the Midwest Political Science Association, Chicago.

Dallek, Robert. 1995. *Franklin D. Roosevelt and American Foreign Policy, 1932–1945.* New York: Oxford University Press.

Dawson, Michael C. 1994. *Behind the Mule: Race and Class in African-American Politics.* Princeton: Princeton University Press.

Davis, Darren W. 2007. *Negative Liberty: Public Opinion And the Terrorist Attacks on America.* New York: Russell Sage Foundation.

Davis, Darren W., and Brian D. Silver. 2004. "Civil Liberties vs. Security in the Context of the Terrorist Attacks on America." *American Journal of Political Science* 48: 28–46.

Davis, James. A. 1975. "Communism, Conformity, Cohorts, and Categories: American Tolerance in 1954 and 1972–73." *American Journal of Sociology* 81: 491–513.

Delli Carpini, Michael X., and Scott Keeter. 1996. *What Americans Know about Politics and Why It Matters.* New Haven: Yale University Press.

DeLuca, Stuart M. 1980. *Television's Transformation.* New York: Barnes.

Department of the Army. 1953. Army Battle Casualties and Nonbattle Deaths in World War II: Final Report, 7 December 1941–31 December 1946. Report prepared by the Statistical and Accounting Branch, Office of the Adjutant General, under direction of the Program Review and Analysis Division, Office of the Comptroller of the Army, OCS (June 1, 1953), Report Control Symbol CSCAP (OT) 87.

Deville, J., and C. Sarndal. 1992. "Calibration Estimators in Survey Sampling." *Journal of the American Statistical Association* 87: 376–82.

Deville, J., C. Sarndal, and O. Sautory. 1993. "Generalizing Raking Procedures in Survey Sampling." *Journal of the American Statistical Association* 88: 1013–20.

Divine, Robert A. 1979. *The Reluctant Belligerent: American Entry into World War II.* New York: Wiley.

Dower, John. 1986. War without Mercy. New York: Pantheon Books.

Doyle, Michael W. 1983. "Kant, Liberal Legacies, and Foreign Affairs." *Philosophy and Public Affairs* 12: 205–35.

———. 1986. "Liberalism and World Politics." *American Political Science Review* 80: 1151–69.

Druckman, James N. 2001. "The Implications of Framing Effects for Citizen Competence." *Political Behavior.* 23: 225–56.

Dubin, Jeffrey A., and Douglas Rivers. 1989–90. "Selection Bias in Linear Regression, Logit and Probit Models." *Sociological Methods and Research* 18 (2–3): 360–90.

Edwards, George C., and Tami Swenson. 1997. "Who Rallies? The Anatomy of a Rally Event." *Journal of Politics* 59: 200–212.

Eichenberg, Richard. 2003. "Gender Differences in Attitudes toward the Use of Force by the United States, 1990–2003" *International Security* 28: 110–41.

——. 2005. "Victory Has Many Friends: American Public Support for the Use of Military Force, 1980–2005" *International Security* 30: 140–77.

Entman, Robert M. 2004. *Projections of Power: Framing News, Public Opinion, and U.S. Foreign Policy.* Chicago: University of Chicago Press.

Erikson, Robert S. 2004. "Macro- vs. Micro-Level Perspectives on Economic Voting: Is the Micro-Level Evidence Endogenously Induced?" Paper presented at the 2004 Political Methodology Meetings, Stanford University.

Erikson, Robert S., Michael B. MacKuen, and James A. Stimson. 2002. *The Macro Polity.* New York: Cambridge University Press.

Erskine, Hazel. 1970. "The Polls: Freedom of Speech." *Public Opinion Quarterly* 34 (3): 483–96.

Fair, Ray C. 1978. "The Effect of Economic Events on Votes for President." *Review of Economics and Statistics* 60: 159–73.

——. 1988. "The Effect of Economic Events on Votes for President: 1984 Update." *Political Behavior* 10: 168–79.

——. 2002. *Predicting Presidential Elections and Other Things.* Stanford: Stanford University Press.

Fearon, James. 1994. "Domestic Political Audiences and the Escalation of International Conflict." *American Political Science Review* 88: 577–92.

Feaver, Peter D., and Christopher Gelpi. 2004. *Choosing Your Battles: American Civil-Military Relations and the Use of Force.* Princeton: Princeton University Press.

Feinstein, Brian, and Eric Schickler. 2008. "Platforms and Partners: The Civil Rights Realignment Reconsidered." *Studies in American Political Development* 22: 1–31.

Feldman, Stanley. 1989. "Measuring Issue Preferences: The Problem of Response Stability." *Political Analysis* 1:25–60.

Feldman, Stanley, and Leonie Huddy. 2005. "Racial Resentment and White Opposition to Race-Conscious Programs: Principles or Prejudice?" *American Journal of Political Science* 49 (1): 168–83.

Feldman, Stanley, and Karen Stenner. 1997. "Perceived Threat and Authoritarianism." *Political Psychology* 18: 741–70.

Field, Harry H., and Louise M. Van Patten. 1945. "If the American People Made the Peace." *Public Opinion Quarterly* 8: 500–512.

Fiorina, Morris P. 1981. *Retrospective Voting in American National Elections.* New Haven: Yale University Press.

Fiorina, Morris P., with Samuel J. Abrams and Jeremy C. Pope. 2005. *Culture War? The Myth of a Polarized America.* New York: Pearson Longman Publishing Group.

Fischoff, Baruch. 1991. "Value Elicitation: Is There Anything in There?" *American Psychologist* 46: 835–47.

Folly, Martin. 2002. *The United States and World War II: The Awakening Giant.* Edinburgh: Edinburgh University Press.

Foyle, Douglas C. 1999. *Counting the Public In: Presidents, Public Opinion, and Foreign Policy.* New York: Columbia University Press.

Franklin, Charles H. 1990. "Estimation across Data Sets: Two-Stage Auxiliary Instrumental Variables Estimation (2SAIV)." *Political Analysis* 1: 1–24.

Franklin, Charles H., and John E. Jackson. 1983. "The Dynamics of Party Identification." *American Political Science Review* 77: 957–73.

Franklin, Mark, and Matthew Ladner. 1995. "The Undoing of Winston Churchill: Mobilization and Conversion in the 1945 Realignment of British Voters." *British Journal of Political Science* 25: 429–52.

Gaines, Brian J., James H. Kuklinski, Paul J. Quirk, Buddy Peyton, and Jay Verkuilen. 2007. "Same Facts, Different Interpretations: Partisan Motivation and Opinion on Iraq." *Journal of Politics* 69 (4): 957–74.

Gartner, Scott Sigmund. 2008. "The Multiple Effects of Casualties on Public Support for War: An Experimental Approach." *American Political Science Review* 102 (1): 95–106.

Gartner, Scott Sigmund, and Gary M. Segura. 1997. "Appearances Can Be Deceiving: Self-Selection, Social Group Identification, and Political Mobilization." *Rationality and Society* 9: 133–61.

———. 1998. "War, Casualties and Public Opinion." *Journal of Conflict Resolution* 42 (3): 278–300.

———. 2000. "Race, Casualties, and Opinion in the Vietnam War." *Journal of Politics* 62: 115–46.

Gartner, Scott Sigmund, Gary M. Segura, and Bethany Barratt. 2004. "War Casualties, Policy Positions, and the Fate of Legislators." *Political Research Quarterly* 53 (3): 467–77.

Gartner, Scott Sigmund, Gary M. Segura, and Michael Wilkening. 1997. "All Politics Are Local: Local Losses and Individual Attitudes toward the Vietnam War." *Journal of Conflict Resolution* 41 (5): 669–94.

Gaubatz, Kurt Taylor. 1999. *Elections and War: The Electoral Incentive in the Democratic Politics of War and Peace.* Stanford: Stanford University Press.

Gelman, Andrew. 2005. "Struggles with Survey-Weighting and Regression Modeling." Department of Statistics and Department of Political Science, Columbia University, New York.

Gelman, Andrew, and John B. Carlin. 2002. "Poststratification and Weighting Adjustments." In *Survey Nonresponse*, ed. R. M. Groves, D. A. Dillman, J. L. Eltinge, and R. J. A. Little. New York: Wiley.

Gelman, Andrew, and Gary King. 1993. "Why Are American Presidential Election Campaign Polls so Variable When Votes Are so Predictable?" *British Journal of Political Science* 23: 409–51.

Gelpi, Christopher, Peter D. Feaver, and Jason Reifler. 2005–6. "Casualty Sensitivity and the War in Iraq." *International Security* 30: 7–46.

Gelpi, Christopher, Jason Reifler, and Peter D. Feaver. 2007. "Iraq the Vote: Retrospective and Prospective Foreign Policy Judgments on Candidate Choice and Casualty Tolerance." *Political Behavior* 29: 151–74.

Gibson, James L. 1992. "Alternative Measures of Political Tolerance: Must Tolerance Be "Least-Liked"?" *American Journal of Political Science* 36: 560–77.

———. 2005. "On the Nature of Tolerance: Dichotomous or Continuous?" *Political Behavior* 27: 313–23.

———. 2006. "Enigmas of Intolerance: Fifty Years after Stouffer's Communism, Conformity, and Civil Liberties." *Perspectives on Politics* 4: 21–34.

Gibson, James L., and Richard D. Bingham. 1985. *Civil Liberties and Nazis: The Skokie Free Speech Controversy.* New York: Praeger.

Gilens, Martin. 1999. *Why Americans Hate Welfare.* Chicago: University of Chicago Press.

———. 2001. "Political Ignorance and Collective Policy Preferences." *American Political Science Review* 95: 379–96.

Gleason, Philip. 1981. "Americans All: World War II and the Shaping of American Identity." *Review of Politics* 43: 483–518.

Gowa, Joanne S. 1999. *Ballots and Bullets: The Elusive Democratic Peace.* Princeton: Princeton University Press.

Goux, Darshan, Patrick J. Egan, and Jack Citrin. 2008. "The War on Terror and Civil Liberties." In *Public Opinion and Constitutional* Controversy, ed. Nathaniel Persily, Jack Citrin, and Patrick J. Egan. New York: Oxford University Press.

Green, Donald, Bradley Palmquist, and Eric Schickler. 2002. *Partisan Hearts and Minds: Political Parties and the Social Identities of Voters.* New Haven: Yale University Press

Greene, William H. 1997. *Econometric Analysis.* 3rd ed. New York: Macmillan.

Gschwend, Thomas. 2005. "Analyzing Quota Sample Data and the Peer-Review Process." *French Politics* 3: 88–91.

Hale, Henry E. 2004. "Explaining Ethnicity." *Comparative Political Studies* 37: 458–85.

Halliday, Jon, and Bruce Cumings. 1988. *Korea: The Unknown War.* New York: Pantheon Books.

Hallin, Daniel C. 1986. *The Uncensored War: The Media and the Vietnam.* New York: Oxford University Press.

Heckman, James J. 1979. "Sample Selection Bias as a Specification Error." *Econometrica* 47: 153–61.

Heinrichs, Waldo H. 1988. *Threshold of War: Franklin D. Roosevelt and American Entry into World War II.* New York: Oxford University Press.

Herbst, Susan. 1993. *Numbered Voices: How Opinion Polling Has Shaped American Politics.* Chicago: University of Chicago Press.

Herrmann, Richard K., Philip E. Tetlock, and Penny S. Visser. 1999. "Mass Public Decisions on Going to War: A Cognitive-Interactionist Framework." *American Political Science Review* 93: 553–74.

Hetherington, Marc J. 2001. "Resurgent Mass Partisanship: The Role of Elite Polarization" American Political Science Review 95: 619–31.

———. 2008. "Turned Off or Turned On? How Polarization Affects Political Engagement." In *Red and Blue Nation?* vol.: *Consequences and Correction of America's Polarized Politics,* 1–33 . Washington, DC: Brookings/Hoover.

Hibbs, Douglas A., Jr. 2000. "Bread and Peace Voting in U.S. Presidential Elections." *Public Choice* 104: 149–80.

———. 2007. "Bread and Peace Voting in U.S. Presidential Elections: The Economy, the

War in Iraq and the Vote for Bush in 2004." http://www.douglas-hibbs.com/ Election2004/election2004_update.htm (accessed January 21, 2008).

Higham, John. 2002. *Strangers in the Land*. Piscataway, NJ: Rutgers University Press.

Hill, Kevin A. 1993. "The Domestic Sources of Foreign Policymaking: Congressional Voting and American Mass Attitudes toward South Africa." *International Studies Quarterly* 37: 195–214.

Hillygus, D. Sunshine, and Todd G. Shields. 2005. "Moral Issues and Voter Decision Making in the 2004 Presidential Election." *PS: Political Science and Politics* 38: 201–9.

Holbrook, Thomas. 1996. "Reading the Political Tea Leaves: A Forecasting Model of Contemporary Presidential Elections. *American Politics Quarterly* 24: 506–19.

Holsti, Ole R. 1992. "Public Opinion and Foreign Policy: Challenger to the Almond-Lippmann Consensus—Mershon Series: Research Programs and Debates." *International Studies Quarterly* 36: 439–66.

———. 2004. *Public Opinion and American Foreign Policy*. Ann Arbor: University of Michigan Press.

Holt, D., and D. Elliot. 1991. "Methods of Weighting for Unit Non-Response." *Statistician* 40: 333–42.

Howell, William, and Douglas Kriner. 2008. "Political Elites and Public Support for War." Typescript. University of Chicago.

Howerth, Ira W. 1894. "Present Condition of Sociology in the United States." *Annals of the American Academy of Political and Social Science* 5.

Huddy, Leonie, and Stanley Feldman. 2006. "Personal Threat, Domestic Security, and the Erosion of Civil Liberties." Paper presented at the 2006 Annual Meeting of the International Society of Political Psychology, Barcelona.

Huddy, Leonie, Stanley Feldman, Charles Taber, and Gallya Lahav. 2005. "Threat, Anxiety, and Support of Antiterrorism Policies." *American Journal of Political Science* 49: 593–608.

Huddy, Leonie, Nadia Khatib, and Theresa Capelos. 2002. "The Polls—Trends: Reactions to the Terrorist Attacks of September 11, 2001." *Public Opinion Quarterly* 66: 418–51.

Hurwitz, Jon, and Mark Peffley. 1987. "How Are Foreign Policy Attitudes Structured? A Hierarchical Model." *American Political Science Review* 81: 1099–1120.

———. 1998. "Whites' Stereotypes of Blacks: Sources and Political Consequences. In *Perception and Prejudice: Race and Politics in the United States*, ed. Jon Hurwitz and Mark Peffley. New Haven: Yale University Press.

Hutchings, Vincent L. 2003. *Public Opinion and Democratic Accountability: How Citizens Learn about Politics*. Princeton: Princeton University Press.

Hutchison, Marc L., and Douglas M. Gilber. 2007. "Political Tolerance and Territorial Threat: A Cross-National Study." *Journal of Politics* 69: 128–42.

Huth, Paul K., and Todd L. Allee. 2003. *The Democratic Peace and Territorial Conflict in the Twentieth Century*. Cambridge: Cambridge University Press.

Hyman, Herbert H., and Eleanor Singer, eds. 1968. *Readings in Reference Group Theory and Research*. New York: Free Press.

Iyengar, Shanto, and Donald Kinder. 1987. *News That Matters: Television and American Opinion*. Chicago: University of Chicago Press.

Iyengar, Shanto, and Richard Morin. 2007. "Red Media, Blue Media: Evidence of Ideological Polarization in Media Use." http://pcl.stanford.edu/common/docs/research/iyengar/2007/ica-redmedia-bluemedia.pdf (accessed May 12, 2008).

Jackson, John E. 1975. "Issues, Party Choices, and Presidential Votes." *American Journal of Political Science* 19: 161–85.

Jacobs, Lawrence R., and Robert Y. Shapiro. 1999. "Lyndon Johnson, Vietnam, and Public Opinion: Rethinking Realists' Theory of Leadership." *Presidential Studies Quarterly* 29: 592–616.

Jacobson, Gary, C. 2008. *A Divider, Not a Uniter: George W. Bush and the American People.* New York: Pearson/Longman.

Jenkins, Roy. 2001. *Churchill.* New York: Farrar, Straus and Giroux.

Jenkins-Smith, Hank C., and Kerry Herron. 2006. "Rock and a Hard Place: Public Willingness to Trade Civil Rights and Liberties for Greater Security." Paper presented at the 2006 Annual Meeting of the American Political Science Association, Philadelphia.

Jentleson, Bruce W. 1992. "The Pretty Prudent Public: Post Post-Vietnam American Opinion on the Use of Military Force." *International Studies Quarterly* 36: 49–73.

Jentleson, Bruce W., and Rebecca L. Britton. 1998. "Still Pretty Prudent: Post–Cold War American Public Opinion on the Use of Military Force." *Journal of Conflict Resolution* 42: 395–417.

Kalton, Graham, and Ismael Flores-Cervantes. 2003. "Weighting Methods." *Journal of Official Statistics* 19: 81–97.

Karol, David, and Edward Miguel. 2007. "The Electoral Cost of War: Iraq Casualties and the 2004 U.S. Presidential Election." *Journal of Politics* 69: 631–46.

Kam, Cindy, and Donald R. Kinder. 2007. "Terror and Ethnocentrism: Foundations of American Support for the War on Terrorism." *Journal of Politics* 69: 318–36.

Keith, Bruce E., David B. Magleby, Candice J. Nelson, Elizabeth Orr, Mark C. Westlye, and Raymond E. Wolfinger. 1992. *The Myth of the Independent Voter.* Berkeley: University of California Press.

Kennedy, David M. 1999. *Freedom from Fear: The American People in Depression and War, 1929–1945.* New York: Oxford University Press.

Kinder, Donald R. 2003. "Belief Systems after Converse." In *Electoral Democracy,* ed. Michael MacKuen and George Rabinowitz. Ann Arbor: University of Michigan Press.

Kinder, Donald R., Gordon S. Adams, and Paul W. Gronke. 1989. "Economics and Politics in the 1984 American Presidential Election." *American Journal of Political Science* 33: 491–515.

Kinder, Donald R., and Lynn M. Sanders. 1996. *Divided by Color: Racial Politics and Democratic Ideals.* Chicago: Chicago University Press.

King, Anthony, ed. 2001. *British Political Opinion, 1937–2000: The Gallup Polls.* London: Politico's.

King, Gary, Michael Tomz, and Jason Wittenberg. 2000. "Making the Most of Statistical Analyses: Improving Interpretation and Presentation." *American Journal of Political Science* 44: 347–61.

Klapper, Joseph. 1960. *The Effects of Mass Communication.* Glencoe, IL: Free Press.

Klarevas, L. 2002. "The 'Essential Domino' of Military Operations: American Public Opinion and the Use of Force." *International Studies Perspectives* 3: 417–37.

Klingberg, Frank. 1952. "The Historical Alternation of Moods in American Foreign Policy." *World Politics* 4 (2): 239–73.

———. 1983. *Cyclical Trends in American Foreign Policy Moods: The Unfolding of America's World Role.* New York: University Press of America.

Klinkner, Philip A. 2006. "Mr. Bush's War: Foreign Policy in the 2004 Election." *Presidential Studies Quarterly* 36: 281–96.

Kramer, Gerald H. 1983. "The Ecological Fallacy Revisited: Aggregate- versus Individual-Level Findings on Economics and Elections, and Sociotropic Voting." *American Political Science Review* 77: 92–111.

Krosnick, Jon A. 2002. "The Causes of No-Opinion Responses to Attitude Measures in Surveys: They Are Rarely What They Appear to Be." In *Survey Nonresponse,* ed. R. M. Groves, D. A. Dillman, J. L. Eltinge, and R. J. A. Little. New York: Wiley.

Kull, Steven. 2006. "Iraq: The Separate Realities of Republicans and Democrats." World Public Opinion Organization; http://www.worldpublicopinion.org/pipa/articles/brunitedstatescanadara/186.php?nid=&id=&pnt=186 (accessed June 15, 2008).

Kull, Steven, and I. M. Destler. 1999. *Misreading the Public: The Myth of a New Isolationism.* Washington, DC: Brookings.

Kull, Steven, and Clay Ramsay. 2001. 'The Myth of the Reactive Public: American Public Attitudes on Military Fatalities in the Post–Cold War Period." In *Public Opinion and the International Use of Force,* ed. Phillip Everts and Pierangelo Isneria. London: Routledge.

Kull, Steven, Clay Ramsay, and Evan Lewis. 2003–4. "Misperceptions, the Media, and the Iraq War." *Political Science Quarterly* 118: 569–98.

Landers, James. 2004. *The Weekly War: Newsmagazines and Vietnam.* Columbia: University of Missouri Press.

Larson, Eric V. 1996. *Casualties and Consensus: The Historical Role of Casualties in Domestic Support for U.S. Wars and Military Operations.* Santa Monica: Rand Corporation.

Larson, Eric V., and Bogdan Savych. 2007. *Misfortunes of War: Press and Public Reactions to Civilian Deaths in Wartime.* Santa Monica: Rand Corporation.

Lebow, Richard N. 1981. *Between Peace and War: The Nature of International Crisis.* Baltimore: Johns Hopkins University Press.

Lewis-Beck, Michael S., and Charles Tien. 2000. "The Future in Forecasting: Prospective Presidential Models." In *Before the Vote: Forecasting American National Elections,* ed. James E. Campbell and James C. Garand, 83–102. Thousand Oaks, CA: Sage Publications.

Lee, Taeku. 2002. *Mobilizing Public Opinion: Black Insurgency and Racial Attitudes in the Civil Rights Era.* Chicago: University of Chicago Press.

Leff, Laurel. 2005. *Buried by The Times: The Holocaust and America's Most Important Newspaper.* New York: Cambridge University Press.

Legro, Jeffrey W. 2000. "Whence American Internationalism?" *International Organization* 54: 253–89.

Leigh, Michael. 1976. *Mobilizing Consent: Public Opinion and American Foreign Policy, 1937–1947*. Westport, CT: Greenwood Press.

Levy, Jack S. 1989. "The Diversionary Theory of War: A Critique." In *Handbook of War Studies*, ed. Manus I. Midlarsky. Boston: Unwin Hyman.

Liberman, Peter. 2006. "An Eye for an Eye: Public Support for War against Evildoers." *International Organization* 60: 687–722.

Lippmann, Walter. 1922. *Public Opinion*. New York: Harcourt, Brace.

Little, R. J. A. 1993. "Post-Stratification: A Modeler's Perspective." *Journal of the American Statistical Association* 88: 1001–12.

Little, R. J. A., and D. B. Rubin. 2002. *Statistical Analysis with Missing Data*. 2nd ed. New York: Wiley.

Little, R. J. A., and Mei-Miau Wu. 1991. "Models for Contingency Tables with Known Margins When Target and Sampled Populations Differ." Journal of the American Statistical Association 86: 87–95.

Lohr, Sharon 1999. *Sampling: Design and Analysis*. Pacific Grove, CA: Duxbury Press.

Lord, Charles G., Lee Ross, and Mark R. Lepper. 1979. "Biased Assimilation and Attitude Polarization: The Effects of Prior Theories on Subsequently Considered Evidence." *Journal of Personality and Social Psychology* 37: 2098–2109.

Lupia, Arthur. 1994. "Shortcuts versus Encyclopedias: Information and Voting Behavior in California Insurance Reform Elections." *American Political Science Review* 88: 63–76.

Maoz, Ze'ev. 1998. "Realist and Cultural Critiques of the Democratic Peace." *International Interactions* 24: 3–89.

Marcus, George E., John L. Sullivan, Elizabeth Theiss-Morse, and Sandra L. Wood. 1995. *With Malice towards Some: How People Make Civil Liberties Judgments*. New York: Cambridge University Press.

McCarthy, Nolan M., Keith T. Poole, and Howard Rosenthal. 2006. Polarized America: The Dance of Ideology and Unequal Riches. Cambridge: MIT Press.

McClosky, Herbert. 1964. "Consensus and Ideology in American Politics." *American Political Science Review* 58: 361–82.

McClosky, Herbert, and Alida Brill. 1983. *Dimensions of Tolerance: What Americans Believe about Civil Liberties*. New York: Russell Sage Foundation.

McGraw, Kathleen M., and Zachary M. Mears. 2004. "Casualties and Public Support for U.S. Military Operations: An Interactionalist Perspective." Working paper. Ohio State University.

Meernik, James, and Michael Ault. 2001. "Public Opinion and Support for U.S. Presidents' Foreign Policies." *American Politics Research* 29: 352–73.

Mendelberg, Tali. 2001. *The Race Card: Campaign Strategy, Implicit Messages, and the Norm of Equality*. Princeton: Princeton University Press.

Merolla, Jennifer L., Jennifer M. Ramos, and Elizabeth J. Zechmeister. 2007. "Crisis, Charisma, and Consequences: Evidence from the 2004 U.S. Presidential Election." *Journal of Politics* 69: 30–42.

Merolla, Jennifer L., and Elizabeth J. Zechmeister. 2009. *Democracy under Stress: Crises, Evaluations, and Behavior*. Chicago: University of Chicago Press.

Miller, Arthur H., Warren E. Miller, Alden S. Raine, and Thad A. Brown. 1976. "A

Majority Party in Disarray: Policy Polarization in the 1972 Election." *American Political Science Review* 70: 753–78.

Miller, Warren E., and J. Merrill Shanks. 1996. *The New American Voter*. Cambridge: Harvard University Press.

Modigliani, Andre. 1972. "Hawks and Doves, Isolationism and Political Distrust: An Analysis of Public Opinion on Military Policy." *American Political Science Review* 66: 960–78.

Mondak, Jeffery J. 2001. "Developing Valid Knowledge Scales." *American Journal of Political Science* 45:224–38.

Mondak, Jeffrey J., and Mitchell S. Sanders. 2003. "Tolerance and Intolerance, 1976–1998." *American Journal of Political Science* 47: 492–502.

———. 2005. "The Complexity of Tolerance and Intolerance Judgments: A Response to Gibson." *Political Behavior* 27: 325–37.

Morrow, James D. 2002. "The Laws of War, Common Conjectures, and Legal Systems in International Politics." *Journal of Legal Studies* 31: S41–S60.

Mueller, John E. 1973. *War, Presidents, and Public Opinion*. New York: Wiley.

———. 1988. "Trends in Political Tolerance." *Public Opinion Quarterly* 52: 1–25.

———. 1994. *Policy and Opinion in the Gulf War*. Chicago: University of Chicago Press.

Mutz, Diana C. 1998. *Impersonal Influence: How Perceptions of Mass Collectives Affect Political Attitudes*. New York: Cambridge University Press.

Mutz, Diana C., and Jeffery J. Mondak. 1997. "Dimensions of Sociotropic Behavior: Group-Based Judgments of Fairness and Well-Being." *American Journal of Political Science* 41: 284–308.

Nincic, Miroslav. 1988. "The United States, the Soviet Union, and the Politics of Opposites." *World Politics* 40: 452–75.

———. 1992. *Democracy and Foreign Policy: The Fallacy of Political Realism*. New York: Columbia University Press.

Norrander, Barbara, and Clyde Wilcox. 1993. "Rallying around the Flag and Partisan Change: The Case of the Persian Gulf War." *Political Research Quarterly* 46: 759–70.

Nunn, Clyde Z., Harry J. Crockett, and J. Allen Williams. 1978. *Tolerance for Nonconformity*. San Francisco: Jossey-Bass.

Oneal, John R., Bradley Lian, and James Joyner Jr. 1996. "Are the American People 'Pretty Prudent'? Public Responses to U.S. Uses of Force, 1950–1988." *International Studies Quarterly* 40: 261–79.

Page, Benjamin I., and Richard A. Brody. 1972. "Policy Voting and the Electoral Process: The Vietnam War Issue." *American Political Science Review* 66: 979–95.

Page, Benjamin I., and Marshall M. Bouton. 2006. *The Foreign Policy Disconnect: What Americans Want from Our Leaders but Don't Get*. Chicago: University of Chicago Press.

Page, Benjamin I., and Robert Y. Shapiro. 1992. *The Rational Public: Fifty Years of Trends in Americans' Policy Preferences*. Chicago: University of Chicago Press.

Parker, Suzanne L. 1995. "Toward an Understanding of 'Rally' Effects: Public Opinion and the Persian Gulf War." *Public Opinion Quarterly* 59: 526–46.

Pelling, Henry. 1967. *A Social Geography of British Elections, 1885–1910*. London: Macmillan.

Perlmutter, Philip. 1996. *The Dynamics of American Ethnic, Religious, and Racial Group Life: An Interdisciplinary Overview.* Westport, CT: Praeger.

Popkin, Samuel L. 1991. *The Reasoning Voter.* Chicago: University of Chicago Press.

Price, Vincent. 1989. "Social Identification and Public Opinion: Effects of Communicating Group Conflict." *Public Opinion Quarterly* 53: 197–224.

Prior, Markus. 2007. *Post-Broadcast Democracy: How Media Choice Increases Inequality in Political Involvement and Polarizes Elections.* Cambridge: Cambridge University Press.

Prothro, James W., and Charles M. Grigg. 1960. "Fundamental Principles of Democracy: Bases of Agreement and Disagreement." *Journal of Politics* 22: 276–94.

Przeworski, Adam, and Henry Teune. 1970. *The Logic of Comparative Social Inquiry.* New York: Wiley.

Putnam, Robert D. 1988. "Diplomacy and Domestic Politics: The Logic of Two-Level Games. *International Organization* 42: 427–60.

Reiter, Dan, and Allan C. Stam. 2002. *Democracies at War.* Princeton: Princeton University Press.

Rieselbach, Leroy N. 1960. "The Basis of Isolationist Behavior." *Public Opinion Quarterly* 24: 645–57.

Robinson, Daniel J. 1999. *The Measure of Democracy: Polling, Market Research, and Public Life, 1930–1945.* Toronto: University of Toronto Press.

Roeder, George H., Jr. 1993. *The Censored War: American Visual Experience during World War Two.* New Haven: Yale University Press.

Roper, Elmo. 1940. "Sampling Public Opinion." *Journal of the American Statistical Association* 35 (210, pt. 1): 325–34.

Rosenberg, Milton J., Sidney Verba, and Philip E. Converse. 1970. *Vietnam and the Silent Majority: The Dove's Guide.* New York: Harper and Row.

Rosecrance, Richard N. 1963. *Action and Reaction in World Politics; International Systems in Perspective.* New York: Little, Brown.

Rosenstone, Steven J. 1983. *Forecasting Presidential Elections.* New Haven: Yale University Press.

Ruggles, Steven, Matthew Sobek, Trent Alexander, Catherine A. Fitch, Ronald Goeken, Patricia Kelley Hall, Miriam King, and Chad Ronnander. 2004. "Integrated Public Use Microdata Series: Version 3.0." Minneapolis, MN: Minnesota Population Center.

Russett, Bruce M. 1960. "Demography, Salience, and Isolationist Behavior." *Public Opinion Quarterly* 24: 658–64.

———. 1993. *Grasping the Democratic Peace: Principles for a Post–Cold War World.* Princeton: Princeton University Press.

Schafer, Sarah. 1999. "To Politically Connect, and Profitably Collect; Ron Howard's Web Site Wants to Get People Involved—and to Sell the Results of Its Internet Polls. The Question: Will It Work?" *Washington Post*, December 13, F10.

Schildkraut, Deborah J. 2002. "The More Things Change . . . American Identity and Mass Elite Responses to 9/11." *Political Psychology* 23: 511–35.

Schlozman, Kay Lehman, and Sidney Verba. 1979. *Injury to Insult: Unemployment, Class, and Political Response.* Cambridge: Harvard University Press.

Schultz, Kenneth. 1998. "Domestic Opposition and Signaling in International Crises." *American Political Science Review* 92: 829–44.

———. 2001. *Democracy and Coercive Diplomacy.* Cambridge: Cambridge University Press.

Schuman, Howard. 1972. "Two Sources of Antiwar Sentiment in America." *American Journal of Sociology* 78: 513–36.

———. 2000. "The Perils of Correlation, the Lure of Labels, and the Beauty of Negative Results. " In *Racialized Politics: The Debate about Racism in America*, ed. David O. Sears, Jim Sidanius, and Lawrence Bobo. Chicago: University of Chicago Press.

Schwarz, Benjamin. 1994. *Casualties, Public Opinion, and U.S. Military Intervention: Implications for U.S. Regional Deterrence Strategies.* Santa Monica: Rand Corporation.

Sears, David O., Jim Sidanius, and Lawrence Bobo. 2000. *Racialized Politics: The Debate about Racism in America.* Chicago: University of Chicago Press.

Shane, Scott. 2005. Bush's Speech on Iraq Echoes Analysts Voice. *New York Times*, December 4, 1, 35.

Sharot, T. 1986. "Weighting Survey Results." Journal of the Market Research Society 28: 269–84.

Sherif, M. 1966. *Common Predicament: Social Psychology of Intergroup Conflict and Cooperation.* Boston: Houghton-Mifflin.

Skitka, Linda J., Christopher W. Bauman, and Elizabeth Mullen. 2004. "Political Tolerance and Coming to Psychological Closure Following the September 11, 2001, Terrorist Attacks: An Integrative Approach." *Personality and Social Psychology Bulletin* 30: 743–56.

Slovic, Paul. 1995. "The Construction of Preference." *American Psychologist* 50: 364–71.

Small, Melvin, and J. David Singer. 1982. *Resort to Arms: International and Civil Wars, 1816–1980.* Beverly Hills: Sage Publications.

Smith, M. Brewster. 1947–48. "The Personal Setting of Public Opinions: A Study of Attitudes toward Russia." *Public Opinion Quarterly* 11: 507–23.

Smith, Tom W. 1987. "The Art of Asking Questions, 1936–1985." *Public Opinion Quarterly* 51: S95–S108.

Sniderman, Paul M., Richard A. Brody, and Philip E. Tetlock. 1991. *Reasoning and Choice.* Cambridge: Cambridge University Press.

Sniderman, Paul M., Joseph F. Fletcher, Peter H. Russell, and Philip E. Tetlock. 1996. *The Clash of Rights: Liberty, Equality, and Legitimacy in Pluralist Democracy.* New Haven: Yale University Press.

Sniderman, Paul M., and Thomas Piazza. 1993. *The Scar of Race.* Cambridge: Harvard University Press.

Sniderman, Paul M., and Philip E. Tetlock. 1986. "Symbolic Racism: Problems of Motive Attribution in Political Analysis." *Journal of Social Issues* 42: 129–50.

Sobel, Richard. 2001. *The Impact of Public Opinion on U.S. Foreign Policy since Vietnam: Constraining the Colossus.* New York: Oxford University Press.

Steele, Richard W. 1974. "The Pulse of the People: Franklin D. Roosevelt and the Gauging of American Public Opinion." *Journal of Contemporary History* 9: 195–216.

Stenner, Karen. 2005. *The Authoritarian Dynamic, Cambridge Studies in Public Opinion and Political Psychology.* New York: Cambridge University Press.

Stimson, James A. 2004. *Tides of Consent: How Public Opinion Shapes American Politics.* New York: Cambridge University Press.

Stouffer, Samuel Andrew. 1955. *Communism, Conformity, and Civil Liberties: A Cross-Section of the Nation Speaks Its Mind.* Garden City, NY: Doubleday.

Sullivan, John Lawrence, James Pierson, and George E. Marcus. 1982. *Political Tolerance and American Democracy.* Chicago: University of Chicago Press.

Sunstein, Cass R. 2007. *Republic.com 2.0.* Princeton: Princeton University Press.

Tajfel, Henri. 1981. *Human Groups and Social Categories.* Cambridge: Cambridge University Press.

Tajfel, Henri, and John C. Turner. 1979. "An Integrative Theory of Intergroup Conflict." In *The Social Psychology of Intergroup Relations*, ed. W. G. Austin and S. Worchel. Monterey: Brooks-Cole.

Terkel, Studs. 1984. *The Good War: An Oral History of World War II.* New York: New Press.

Thompson, Steven K. 2002. *Sampling.* New York: Wiley.

Toner, Robin A., and Neil A. Lewis. 2001. "A Nation Challenged: Security and Liberty; A Familiar Battle Fought and Won." *New York Times*, October 26, 5.

Tourangeau, Roger, Lance Rips, and Kenneth Rasinski. 2000. *The Psychology of Survey Response.* Cambridge: Cambridge University Press.

Van Evera, Stephen. 1997. *Guide to Methods for Students of Political Science.* Ithaca, NY: Cornell University Press.

Valentino, Nicholas, Vincent Hutchings, and Ismail White. 2002. "Cues That Matter: How Political Ads Prime Racial Attitudes during Campaigns." *American Political Science Review* 96: 75–90.

Verba, Sidney, Richard A. Brody, Edwin B. Parker, Norman H. Nie, Nelson W. Polsby, Paul Ekman, and Gordon S. Black. 1967. "Public Opinion and the War in Vietnam." *American Political Science Review* 61: 317–33.

Verba, Sidney, and Kay Lehman Schlozman. 1977. "Unemployment, Class Consciousness, and Radical Politics: What Didn't Happen in the Thirties." *Journal of Politics* 39: 291–323.

Voeten, Erik, and Paul R. Brewer. 2006. "Public Opinion, the War in Iraq, and Presidential Accountability." *Journal of Conflict Resolution.* 50: 809–30.

Walsh, Katherine Cramer. 2004. *Talking about Politics: Informal Groups and Social Identity in American Life.* Chicago: University of Chicago Press.

Weatherford, M. Stephen, and Boris Sergeyev. 2000. "Thinking about Economic Interests: Class and Recession in the New Deal." *Political Behavior*, 22: 311–39.

Weisberg, Herbert F., and Dino P. Christenson. 2007. "Changing Horses in Wartime? The 2004 Presidential Election." *Political Behavior* 29: 279–304.

West, Darrel M. 2003. "Comparing Wars." http://www.insidepolitics.org/heard/westreport303.html (accessed April 12, 2008).

Winfield, Betty Houchin. 1994. *FDR and the News Media.* New York: Columbia University Press.

Winship, Christopher, and Larry Radbill. 1994. "Sampling Weights and Regression Analysis." *Sociological Methods and Research* 23 (2): 230–57.

Winter, Nicholas, and Adam J. Berinsky. 1999. "What's Your Temperature? Thermometer Ratings and Political Analysis." Paper presented at the 1999 Meeting of the American Political Science Association, Atlanta.

Wlezien, Christopher. 2001. "On Forecasting the Presidential Vote." *PS: Political Science and Politics* 34: 29–35.

Wlezien, Christopher, and Robert S. Erikson. 2000. "Temporal Horizons and Presidential Election Forecasts." In *Before the Vote: Forecasting American National Elections*, ed. James E. Campbell and James C. Garand, 103–18. Thousand Oaks, CA: Sage Publications.

———. 2004. "The Fundamentals, the Polls, and the Presidential Vote." *PS: Political Science and Politics* 37: 747–51.

Wlezien, Christopher, Mark Franklin, and Daniel Twiggs. 1997. "Economic Perceptions and Vote Choice: Disentangling the Endogeneity." *Political Behavior* 19: 7–17.

Wong, Cara. 2007. "'Little' and 'Big' Pictures in Our Heads: Race, Local Context and Innumeracy about Racial Groups in the U.S." *Public Opinion Quarterly* 71: 392–412.

Wood, B. Dan. 2007. *The Politics of Economic Leadership: The Causes and Consequences of Presidential Rhetoric*. Princeton: Princeton University Press.

Zaller, J. R. 1992. *The Nature and Origins of Mass Opinion*. New York: Cambridge University Press.

———. 1994 "Elite Leadership of Mass Opinion: New Evidence from the Gulf War." In *Taken By Storm: The Media, Public Opinion, and U.S. Foreign Policy in the Gulf War*, ed. Lance Bennett and David Paletz. Chicago: University of Chicago Press.

———. 2003. "Coming to Grips with V. O. Key's Concept of Latent Opinion." In *Electoral Democracy*, ed. Michael MacKuen and George Rabinowitz. Ann Arbor: University of Michigan Press.

Zaller, J. R., and Stanley Feldman. 1992. "A Simple Theory of the Survey Response." *American Journal of Political Science* 36: 579–616.

INDEX

ABC News, 42, 178, 181, 184, 207, 266n14, 305n2
Achen, Christopher H., 182, 189, 191–93, 201, 204, 223, 301n7, 302n16
Adams, Gordon S., 129, 130
Adams, Michael C. C., 36
Afghanistan War: elite positions, 27, 105, 109, 266n19 (*see also* elite discourse on war); end of initial conflict, 26; origin of U.S. involvement, 25–26; public opinion, 27–29, 105, 109–11, 283n22
African Americans, 132–34, 244–45, 250, 252, 253, 254, 257, 258, 259, 264, 286–87n7, 287n11, 296n16, 306n5, 306n6
al Qaeda, 26, 29, 78
Alba, R. D., 146
Almond, Gabriel A., 3, 66
American Institute of Public Opinion (AIPO), 33, 34, 90, 198, 199, 201, 237, 238, 239, 240, 241, 242, 243, 255, 281–82n14, 306n1; Gallup, George, 15, 17, 23, 34, 35, 37, 43, 44, 46, 48, 50, 52, 63, 74, 75, 79, 83, 90, 93, 94, 95, 97, 100, 101, 119, 125, 150, 171, 172, 173, 197, 198, 199, 200, 222, 223, 266n5,

266nn10–11, 266n15, 267n5, 268n6, 271n34, 272nn37–38, 281–82nn14–15, 282n18, 299n41, 299n44, 306n1
apartheid, 132
Arena, Philip, 192, 201, 204
Arlen, Michael J., 39,
Associated Press, 41, 75
Atlee, Clement, 202
audience costs, 2
Authorization for Use of Military Force against Iraq Resolution of 1991, 24
Authorization for Use of Military Force against Terrorists Act, 26
auxiliary information, 223–28
Axis of Evil, 29

Baath Party, 30
Baghdad, 24, 30
Ball, Stuart, 201
Barratt, Bethany, 125
Bartels, Larry M., 66, 186, 187, 191–93, 201, 204, 302n16, 302n19, 304n37
Battle of the Bulge, 33
Baum, Matthew A., 40
Bauman, Christopher W., 159
BBC (British Broadcasting Company), 42
Belknap, George, 68, 111

Bennett, Robert, 86, 216
Bennett, W. Lance, 275n13
Berinsky, Adam J., 19, 91, 222, 266n6, 281n10, 287n12
between-subjects design, 118, 199, 278n42
bin Laden, Osama, 26
Bingham, Richard D., 158
Botha, P. W., 132
Boyd, Richard W., 184
Brady, Henry E., 129
Brill, Alida, 158
British Institute of Public Opinion (BIPO), 202–4
Brody, Richard A., 88, 112, 158, 184, 188, 189
Burk, James, 7, 63, 273n2, 274n8
Bush, George H. W., 22, 23, 27, 266n42
Bush, George W., 1–2, 9, 29–31, 70, 77, 78, 102, 109, 121, 123, 166, 178–79, 180, 184, 185, 186, 190, 193–96, 207, 208, 209, 219, 264, 277n34, 303n25, 303–4n33, 304nn35–37

Cambodia, 20
Campbell, Angus, 67, 68, 73, 111, 129, 286n2
Campbell, Donald T., 148, 286n2
Cantril, Hadley. See Office of Public Opinion Research (OPOR)
Carmines, Edward G., 133, 215, 305n5
Casey, Steven, 34, 99, 147, 198, 272n42
casualties, 19, 25, 27, 40–42, 62, 65, 72, 73, 74, 75, 76–84, 85, 118–23, 125–26, 181, 218, 230, 233, 251, 266n16, 269n17, 274n10, 275n18, 276nn21–22, 276n25, 276n27, 277nn32–34, 278nn37–41, 278n44, 279nn45–47, 284n33, 285n39, 286n45, 298n33, 301n15, 302n18, 307n1
casualties hypothesis, 7, 63–65, 72, 73–74, 76–84, 118–23, 124, 125–26, 273nn2–3, 274n8, 278n37, 278n42
CBS News, 42, 181, 207, 265n1, 301n6, 305n1
cell-weighting, 224, 225, 236
censorship, 40–41

Cheney, Dick, 29, 207–8
Chicago, 38
Chicago Daily, 43
Chicago Tribune, 43, 87–88, 269n23
China, 16–17, 29, 181, 258, 266n4
Chiozza, Giacomo, 192
Chirac, Jacques, 29
Chong, Dennis, 158
Churchill, Winston, 200–205, 268n8, 304n40
civil liberties judgments, 5, 8, 155–77, 209, 212, 216, 294nn3–4, 295n11, 296n19, 297n26, 298nn28–31, 298n33, 299n34, 299n38, 299n40, 299n44, 300n1, 307n1 (appendix E)
civil liberties judgments, feelings toward: atheists, 159, 161; Communists, 159, 160, 161, 173; Fascists, 172, 173; homosexuals, 161; militarists, 161; racists, 161; radicals, 172, 173, 175, 176; socialists, 159
civil liberties judgments, war: Iraq War, 163–71, 252, 253; Vietnam War, 168, 170–71, 254; World War II, 171–76, 255
Clark, Wesley, 30
class politics, 203–4
Clinton, William J., 29, 105, 220
CNN, 33, 42
Coalition Provisional Authority in Iraq, 30
Cobb, Michael D., 79, 276n21, 276n25, 277n34
Cole, G. D., 201
columnists, 44, 269n27
Comprehensive Anti-Apartheid Act of 1986, 132
Congressional Black Caucus, 132
Congressional Record, 88, 234
Conover, Pamela Johnston, 53, 55, 130, 131, 139, 146
Conservative Party, 200–205
considerations, 82, 275n15
Converse, Philip E., 35, 71, 128, 129, 130, 132, 139, 214, 274n6, 286n3, 302n20

crime, 161, 296n16, 296n19
Cuban-Americans, 212, 305n3
cue givers, 70, 72, 75, 124, 280n3; presidents, 70, 75
cue taking, 69, 70, 77, 214, 276n27
culture war issues, 178–79, 219

Dallek, Robert, 51
D'Ambrosio, Lisa, 131
Davis, Darren W., 155, 160, 162, 163, 164, 165, 297nn23–24, 297n26, 298n28, 299n34
Dean, Howard, 30
Democratic Party, 19, 20, 22, 23, 24, 27, 29, 30, 68, 70, 72, 79, 86, 88, 89, 102, 111–12, 115, 119, 123, 129, 132, 170–71, 178, 179, 183, 184, 189, 190, 198, 215, 267n25, 275n17, 287n9, 289n19, 302n18, 305n5
democratic peace theory, 3
DiMaggio, Joe, 146
discrimination, 146–47
diversionary war theory, 192
domestic policy attitudes, influence on foreign policy attitudes, 2, 4–5, 7–8, 64–66, 69–71, 72, 126, 179, 207–9, 220–21. *See also* civil liberties judgments; civil liberties judgments, feelings toward; civil liberties judgments, war; elections, influence of war on; group attachments; group attachments, group prejudice; party identification, partisan leanings; threat perception
Druckman, James N., 66

economy, perceptions of, 65, 129, 189, 274n7
education, 77, 138, 145, 158, 175, 182, 223, 227–28, 232, 233, 244, 245, 250, 252, 253, 254, 256, 257, 258, 259, 260, 261, 262, 263, 264, 267n4, 268n6, 275n12, 283n19, 285n38, 289n19, 292nn36–37, 294n48, 296n17, 299n35, 306n6

Eisenhower, Dwight D., 17, 18, 20, 111, 185, 257, 258
elderly, war support among, 55
elections, influence of war on, 5, 9, 178–206, 209
elite cue theory, 69–71, 72, 79, 88, 89, 90, 92, 100, 102, 111, 115, 124, 189, 210, 275n16, 277n34, 280n4; definition, 70
elite discourse on war, 5, 7, 66–71, 72, 73, 85–86, 119, 121, 124, 126, 190–91, 220–21; Afghanistan, 27, 105, 109, 266n19; Gulf War, 24, 68; Iraq War, 30, 102, 111; Vietnam War, 19–20, 68, 111–12, 188–89, 190; World War II, 87–89, 92, 95, 99–100
elite divisions on foreign policy, 7, 20, 24, 30, 62, 69, 70, 73, 85–86, 87–89, 92, 111, 112, 115, 125, 190
embassy bombings in Kenya and Tanzania, 26
endogeneity of vote choice and war support, 90–91, 189–90, 212–13
England, 48–55, 89, 92, 94, 95, 100, 101, 111, 136, 137, 147, 148, 149, 200, 209, 211, 238, 247, 248, 255, 271n33, 271n35, 272n50, 289n18, 290n21, 291n22
Epstein, Edward, 178
Erikson, Robert S., 35, 65
Eritrea, 123
ethnic groups, 71, 127–51, 217, 247
ethnic groups, attitudes toward American ethnic groups: African Americans, 133–34, 250; descendants of immigrants from Allied/Axis countries, 8, 135–43, 248, 249, 288n16, 290n18; English, 144, 145, 147, 148, 149, 247; Germans, 8, 144, 145, 147, 148, 149, 247, 289n19, 292n38, 293n40; Irish, 145; Italians, 8, 134, 144, 145, 146, 147, 148, 149, 247, 292n34, 292n38, 293n43; Japanese, 145, 150–51; Jews, 8, 134, 145, 146, 147, 148, 247; Scandinavians, 145; Sicilians, 144, 145; Swedes, 145
ethnocentrism, 130, 131, 148, 286n5

event-response theory, 6–7, 61–66, 69, 71–72, 73, 79, 102, 122, 124, 208, 210

Executive Order 9066, 149

experimental treatment, 79–80, 81, 82–83, 118–20, 121, 230–31

Fascist government in Italy, 134, 147

fear, 5, 9, 193, 194; civil liberties, 161–63; election outcomes, 9

Feaver, Peter D., 1–2, 3, 64, 65, 103, 180, 191, 265n3, 284n34, 285n38

Feldman, Stanley, 82, 295n10

Field, Harry H. *See* National Opinion Research Center (NORC)

Fortune, 34, 50, 143, 198, 292n33

Fox News, 42, 77, 230, 233, 269n19

France, 18, 29, 52, 53, 147, 149, 247, 271n33

Franklin, Charles H., 202, 204, 305n42

freedom of speech, 157–59, 170, 171, 173–76, 255, 299n41, 300n45

Fulbright, William, 19, 112

Gaines, Brian J., 65–66, 124, 277n32

Gallup, George. *See* American Institute of Public Opinion (AIPO)

Gaubatz, Kurt Taylor, 192

Gelpi, Christopher, 3, 64, 65, 103, 180, 191, 284n32

gender gap in public opinion, 52–56

General Social Survey (GSS), 161–62, 295nn13–14, 296nn15–16, 297n20, 297n24

Geneva Peace Accords, 18

Gephardt, Richard, 24

German-American Bund, 134

Germany, 29, 33, 37, 38, 46, 48, 49, 50, 51, 52, 74, 91, 92, 94, 95, 97, 98, 136, 137, 138, 147, 148, 172, 199, 201, 235, 248, 255, 270n30, 271n34, 271n41, 272n42, 272n46, 290n21, 291n22

Gibson, James L., 158, 295nn13–14

Gilens, Martin, 63, 76, 279n47

Gleason, Philip, 134–35

Goemans, H. E., 192

Grenada, 21

Gronke, Paul W., 129, 130

group attachments, 5, 8, 62, 66, 71, 72, 73, 127–51; attitudes toward other groups, 8, 71, 133–34, 143–51, 158, 211; group cues, 71, 129, 131; group identity and foreign policy attitudes, 8, 71, 131, 135–43, 211; group interest, 129, 286n3

group attachments, group prejudice: anti-Italian sentiment, 146, 292n34; anti-Japanese sentiment, 145–46, 150–51; anti-Semitism, 146, 147, 149, 275n19, 293nn43–44

Gulf of Tonkin resolution, 18, 183

Gulf War, 21–25, 39, 40, 55, 220; casualties, 25; origins, 21–23; public opinion on, 23–24, 25, 52, 68, 124; U.S. invasion, 24

Hamilton, Lee, 24

Hansen, Victor Davis, 40

hawk-dove measure, 112, 116, 117, 118, 261, 263, 274n9

hawks and doves, 68, 115, 181, 291n30, 300n5

Hetherington, Marc J., 220, 297n25

Hill, Kevin A., 133, 287n9

Hitler, Adolf, 33, 46, 47, 95, 96, 97, 98, 147, 175, 209, 235, 249, 270n32, 271n41, 291nn28–29, 307n3 (appendix C)

Holocaust, 74–75, 147

Holsti, Ole R. , 3, 4

Hoover, Herbert, 44, 269n26

House of Commons, 200

Howell, William, 123

Howerth, Ira W., 146

Humphrey, Hubert, 112, 184, 185, 188, 189, 206, 259, 260, 261, 300n2, 300n5, 301nn9–11, 302n21

Hurwitz, Jon, 5, 61, 273n5, 286n5

Hussein, Saddam, 22, 23, 29, 30, 183, 251, 273n3

ideology, 71, 128, 129, 283n29, 296n17, 297n25

Il-Sung, Kim, 14

immigration, 131, 134, 135, 146
information, 5, 6, 37–38, 61–62, 63–64,
    73–84, 118–21, 279n47, 284n36
in-groups, 130, 131, 133
interest in politics. *See* political awareness
International Convention on the Suppres-
    sion and Punishment of the Crime of
    Apartheid, 132
interstitial information, 128, 130, 139
Iran, 21, 29, 122
Iraq War, 1, 27–32, 33, 40, 41, 62, 65, 70,
    73, 75–84, 86, 100–111, 163–71, 178,
    179, 180, 181, 182, 183–84, 185, 190,
    210, 212, 216, 217, 218–20, 252, 253,
    264, 277n31, 277n33, 279n46, 286n46,
    303n25; censorship, 41; declaration of
    victory in, 30; elite positions, 30, 102,
    111; Iraqi resistance, 30, 31; lead-up,
    29; opposition outside of United
    States, 29; public opinion, 1, 31–32,
    100, 104, 106–10; U.S. invasion, 30
Iraq War Casualty Survey, 76–84, 103,
    105, 109, 124, 229–33
issue publics, 128
Italy, 46, 136, 137, 147, 270n30, 288n16,
    290n21
Iyengar, Shanto, 42

Jacobson, Gary C. , 31, 65, 100, 109, 111,
    124, 166, 180, 190, 218, 220, 267n26,
    303n30
Japan, 14, 37, 38, 46, 50, 51, 138–39, 268n8,
    290n21
Japanese internment during World War
    II, 149–51
Jenkins, Roy, 202
Jentleson, Bruce W., 119, 122, 273n4,
    284n34
Johnson, Lyndon B., 2, 6, 18, 19, 111, 115,
    124, 184, 185, 206, 220, 266n8, 283n29,
    300n5, 301nn9–11, 305n6

Kabul, 26
Kandahar, 26
Karzai, Hamid, 26

Keith, Bruce E., 67, 191
Kennedy, David M., 99
Kennedy, John F., 18, 124
Kerry, John, 30, 178, 180, 264
Kinder, Donald R., 39, 129, 130, 131, 133,
    286n3, 286n5, 287n8, 297n11
Kissinger, Henry, 20
Klingberg, Frank, 45
Klinkner, Philip A., 179, 180, 182, 188,
    303n25
Knowledge Networks, 76, 276n23
knowledge of politics. *See* political aware-
    ness
knowledge of wartime events. *See* infor-
    mation
Korean War: armistice, 17; Chinese
    involvement, 16; degree of partisan-
    ship, 220; elections, 179, 181–82, 185,
    302n18; ethnic attachments, 291–29;
    history of the conflict, 266nn2–3; ori-
    gins, 14; public opinion, 15, 16–17, 20,
    52, 56, 68, 72–73, 111, 257, 258, 275n14;
    US/UN invasion during, 15
Kosovo, U.S. military involvement in,
    85–86, 105, 126, 215–16, 220, 265n1
Kramer, Gerald H., 189
Kriner, Douglas, 123
Kull, Steven, 64, 70, 77, 78, 273n3,
    277nn34–35
Kuwait, 21–22, 24

Labour Party, 200–204, 305n42
Ladner, Matthew, 202, 204, 305n42
Landon, Alf, 43–44, 269n26
Laos, 20
Larson, Eric V., 3, 37, 63, 64, 74, 125
Latin America, 138–39, 248
leadership, 9, 180, 190, 191–96, 197, 213,
    304n36
Lebanon, 21, 274n8
Legro, Jeffrey W., 55, 87–88, 91
level of importance statistic, 182
Levin, Carl, 86
LeVine, Robert A., 148
Lewis, Evan, 77

Liberal Party, 203, 204
Liberia, 123
Life, 146
Lippmann, Walter, 3
London bombing, 194
Louis Harris and Associates, 170

MacArthur, General Douglas, 15–16
MacKuen, Michael B., 35
mainstream pattern in public opinion, 68,
    88, 89, 90, 93, 95, 96, 100, 101, 109, 113,
    114, 115, 116, 282nn17–18
Marcus, George E., 159, 160, 295n5, 295n9,
    295nn13–14, 298n32
Massimino, Elisa, 155
McCarthy, Eugene, 19
McClosky, Herbert, 158
McGovern, George, 112, 185, 186, 262,
    263
media: Internet, 39, 40, 42, 43; media
    diversity, 42–44; media partisan-
    ship, 42–43; newspapers, 38–39,
    269n24, 269nn26–27, 270n29, 281n14;
    newsreels, 39; radio, 39, 202, 269n27;
    selective media exposure, 43–44;
    television, 39
Merolla, Jennifer L., 193, 194, 195, 197,
    303n28
Michel, Rob, 24
Mitchell, George, 24
Mondak, Jeffrey J., 130, 231, 295n14,
    296n19
Morin, Richard, 42
Moscow Conference of Foreign Minis-
    ters, 14
MSNBC, 42
Mueller, John E., 4, 7, 13, 15, 17, 18, 22,
    38, 53, 63, 79, 115, 118, 266n7, 275n14,
    278n37, 278n39, 295n7, 295n9
mujahideen, 25
Mullen, Elizabeth, 159
Muskie, Edmund, 184, 301n9
Mussolini, Benito, 134, 147
Mutz, Diana C., 130

National Assembly in Iraq, 31
National Elections Study, 109, 110, 115, 133,
    194, 232, 250, 256, 257, 258, 259, 260,
    261, 262, 263, 264, 283n24, 283n26,
    287n9, 291n30, 300n4, 305n7
National Liberation Front, 18
National Opinion Research Center
    (NORC), 15, 50, 135, 150, 151, 266n5,
    267n3, 272n42, 289n18; Field, Harry
    H., 34
National Public Radio (NPR), 42
National Strategy for Victory in Iraq, 1,
    208, 265n3
NATO (North Atlantic Treaty Organiza-
    tion), 26, 27, 215
Nazi atrocities, 37, 74–75, 87, 124, 275n19
Nazi regime, 37, 99, 147, 209
New Deal, 99
New Hampshire primary, 19, 186
New York Times, 1, 40, 41, 269n18,
    301n294
Newsweek, 30, 267n25
Nickles, Don, 86
Nielsen, 42
Nixon, Richard M., 6, 20, 21, 30, 112, 115,
    184–86, 188–90, 215, 259, 260, 261,
    262, 263, 300n2, 300n5, 301nn9–10,
    302n21
North Korea, 14–16, 29, 119
North Vietnam (Democratic Republic of
    Vietnam), 18–20, 283
Northern Alliance, 25, 26
Nunn, Sam, 22, 24

Office of Public Opinion Research
    (OPOR), 34, 38, 46, 48, 51, 52, 55, 56,
    75, 90, 93, 96, 98, 135, 136, 171, 173,
    197, 199, 238, 248, 249, 270nn31–32,
    272n49, 281n14, 291n22, 291n29,
    306n6; Cantril, Hadley, 34, 48, 75, 198,
    272n43, 289n18
Office of War Information, 34, 74, 136,
    289n18
Operation Desert Shield, 22

Operation Desert Storm, 24
opinion polls from 1930s and 1940s, 2,
3, 4, 34–35, 43, 135, 222–28, 236–39,
267n5, 306n1
out-groups, 130, 131, 133, 143

Page, Benjamin I., 35, 112, 140, 184,
188–89, 209, 214
Panama, 21
parallel publics, 140
party identification, 50, 66, 67–68, 79,
99, 250, 276n27, 276n29, 277nn31–35,
283nn24–25, 283n27, 285nn38–39
party identification, effects on: civil liberties judgments, 156, 165–66, 167, 175;
perceptions of war success, 103, 105;
recall and interpretation of facts, 65,
72, 73, 77–78, 124, 218; selection of
media outlets, 43–44; war support, 5,
6, 7, 9, 50, 62, 69–71, 72, 73, 79, 84, 86,
91–124, 210–11, 217, 244, 245, 257–64,
279n46, 281n11
party identification, partisan leanings:
Democrats, 22, 42, 65, 68, 73, 77, 78,
100, 102–11, 113–24, 129, 165–66, 170,
207, 211, 215, 218, 219, 252–54, 276n29,
277n32, 277n34, 279n46, 285nn39–40,
286n46, 287n11, 299n40, 304n34,
305n5; independents, 67, 77, 121, 122,
123, 165, 191, 269n19, 279n46; Republicans, 1, 22, 24, 42, 65, 68, 77, 78, 100,
102–11, 113–19, 121–24, 165–66, 170,
207, 211, 218, 219, 252–54, 277n32,
277n34, 279n46, 285n39, 287n11,
299n40, 304n34, 305n5
party identification, projection effects,
65, 72
Patriot Act, 155, 177
Pearl Harbor, 7, 34, 36, 37, 45–52, 53, 72,
74, 87, 88, 90, 91, 98–99, 100, 126,
127, 134, 140, 149, 173, 209, 218, 237,
271n39, 280n8, 289n18
Peffley, Mark, 5, 61, 273n5, 286n5
Pentagon, 26, 41, 157

performance issues, 186, 189; war, 9,
179–80, 192
Perlmutter, Philip, 135
Pew Research Center for the People and
the Press, 42, 76, 77, 105, 159, 163, 164,
165, 166, 168, 251, 252, 253, 269nn19–
20, 283n24, 294n2, 298nn27–28,
298n30, 299n34, 307n1 (appendix E)
Pierson, James, 159, 160, 172, 295n5,
295n14, 298n32
polarization pattern in public opinion,
68, 69, 70–71, 88, 89, 90, 92, 93, 94,
95, 102, 104, 105, 106, 107, 108, 109,
110, 111, 112, 114, 115, 116, 117, 118, 170,
281n14, 282nn17–18
political awareness, 45, 62, 63,
66–67, 68, 70, 77, 89, 90–118, 139,
167, 211, 218, 240–45, 250, 252,
277n31, 281n9 281n11, 281nn13–14,
282nn17–18, 283n24, 283nn27–28,
287n12, 307n6
Potsdam Conference, 14
Powell, Colin, 29
pragmatic isolationism, 55
presidential forecasting models, 186–88
principle policy objectives of war, 119, 121,
122, 284n36, 285n39
Prior, Markus, 39, 42, 43
probability sampling, 35, 222, 237, 281n13

question ordering, 55
question wording, 15, 47, 80, 82, 83,
270n32, 276n29, 291n29, 298n28,
303n30
quota-controlled sampling, 35, 222–28,
268n7

race, 128, 129, 133–34, 228, 285n38, 287n12,
288n14, 289n19, 296nn16–17, 299n35,
304n35, 305n5, 306n6
Raddatz, Martha, 207
rally effects, 64, 88, 193–96
Ramos, Jennifer M., 193, 194, 195, 303n28
Ramsay, Clay, 64, 70, 77

rationality of the public, 62, 63, 64, 69, 125, 191, 208, 213; cost-benefit analysis, 61, 62, 63, 72, 125, 210, 213

Reagan, Ronald W., 132

realistic group conflict theory, 129

Reception-Acceptance-Sampling (RAS) theory, 70, 275n16

reference group cues, 71, 128–30, 135–36

Reifler, Jason, 3, 65, 103, 180, 191

Reiter, Dan, 3, 125

Republican Party, 17, 20, 24, 27, 30, 49, 68, 70, 72, 86, 87, 88, 89, 99, 102, 109, 111, 112, 119, 120, 123, 175, 183, 184, 197, 211, 213, 215, 216, 218, 271n36, 275n17, 280n3, 282nn15–16, 286n2, 287n9, 305n5, 306n9

Rhee, Syngman, 14

Rivers, Douglas, 35

Roeder, George H., 40, 41, 268n16

Roosevelt, Franklin D., 9, 43–44, 49, 50–52, 70, 87, 88, 99, 138, 147, 149, 197–200, 201, 205, 209, 211, 216, 217, 268n8, 269nn24–25, 271n36, 282n15, 304n38; definition of opponent and supporter, 90–91, 238–39, 271n40; effect of FDR support, 90–92, 95, 98, 175, 237, 238, 240, 241, 242, 243, 271n39, 280n6, 281n9, 281n13, 289n19, 307n6 (appendix C); public opinion polling, 2, 34, 48, 265n4

Roper (organization), 35, 44, 52, 43, 90, 95, 97, 99, 143, 145, 147, 197, 199, 200, 201, 222, 223, 237, 247, 267n5, 269n27, 270n28, 271n38, 292n31, 292n33, 292n36, 293n40, 304n38

Roper, Elmo, 34

Rosenstone, Steven J., 187, 302n19

Russia. See Soviet Union

Sanders, Lynn M., 133, 287n8, 287n11

Sapiro, Virginia, 53, 55

Saudi Arabia, 22, 24

Schultz, Kenneth, 3, 126, 192

Schuman, Howard, 55–56, 287n11

security, tradeoff between civil liberties and, 155–56, 163–64, 165, 166, 168, 169, 252, 253, 298n28

Segura, Gary M., 63, 125, 273n3, 274n10, 284n33

Seoul, 14–16

September 11, 2001, 25, 26, 72, 78, 163–66, 168

17th parallel, 18

Shapiro, Robert Y., 35, 140, 208, 214

Silver, Brian D., 155, 160, 162, 163, 164, 297n23, 298n28

Skitka, Linda J., 159

Sniderman, Paul M., 129, 158

Snow, Tony, 33

Sobel, Richard, 45, 72

social identity theory, 129

soft news, 40

Somalia, 25, 274n8

South Africa, 128, 131–34, 249, 250, 286n7, 287n10

South Korea, 14–15, 118–20

South Vietnam (Republic of Vietnam), 18, 20

southerners, 222, 226, 227, 267n5

Soviet Union, 14, 25, 29, 140, 141, 172, 173, 291n27, 299n42

Spain 2004 general election, 193

Stam, Allan C., 3, 125

stereotypes, 71, 131, 146, 148

Stevens, Ted, 86

Stevenson, Adlai, 185, 257, 258, 300n5, 301n12

Stimson, James A., 35, 215, 305n5

Stouffer, Samuel Andrew, 159–60, 294n4, 295n8, 299n36

Sudan, 26

Sullivan, John Lawrence, 159, 295n9, 295nn13–14, 298n32

Sunstein, Cass R., 42, 43

survey experiments, 47, 76–84, 118–23, 198, 229–33, 270n32, 276n22, 276n26, 278n43, 279n47, 280n48, 283n19, 285nn39–40, 291n22, 291n29, 298n33

Taft, Robert, 98
Taliban, 25–27
Terkel, Studs, 36
Tet offensive, 19
Tetlock, Philip E., 158
38th parallel, 14–16
Tho, Le Duc, 20
threat perception: civil liberties, 5, 8, 151,
    156, 157, 161, 162, 164, 173, 216; crime,
    161; evaluations of leaders, 9, 193–95;
    measure, 296n19, 299n34; sociotro-
    pic threat, 161–62, 164, 174, 298n31,
    299n34; threat predisposition, 160;
    trust in government, 162
Thuy, Xuan, 20
tolerance, 157, 158, 159, 162, 212, 216
Treaty of Versailles, 142
trust in foreign governments, 140–42,
    173, 291n27, 299n41
trust in government, 156, 157, 162–63, 166,
    297nn23–25

U.K. 1945 general election, 200–205, 305n42
United Nations, 15–16, 27, 70, 266n4;
    General Assembly, 132; Security
    Council, 29, 30; Security Council
    Resolutions, 15, 22
United Press Association, 41
U.S. presidential elections: 1940 election,
    43, 44, 49, 90, 95–100, 197, 198, 217,
    271n40, 280n3, 282n15, 289n19, 307n6;
    1944 election, 197–201; 1952 election,
    20, 111, 179, 181, 182, 183, 186, 187, 188,
    190, 300n5, 301n15, 302nn17–18; 1968
    election, 19, 112, 115, 181, 182, 183, 184,
    185, 186, 187, 188–90, 206, 215, 300n2,
    300n5, 301n15, 302nn17–20; 1972
    election, 112, 181, 182, 183, 184, 185, 186,
    187, 189, 190, 283n25, 302n17; 2000
    election, 193–94, 195, 196, 219; 2004
    election, 9, 30, 178, 180, 181, 182, 183,
    184, 186, 190, 193–95, 196, 212, 218,
    301n6, 301n8, 302n16, 303n35; 2008
    election, 27
USS Abraham Lincoln, 30

Vandenberg, Arthur, 45, 99
Vietnam War, 2, 18–21, 39, 40, 111–18,
    124, 125, 166, 168–71, 172, 181, 182,
    183, 184–85, 188–89, 190, 214, 215,
    218, 220, 254, 259, 260, 261, 262,
    263, 270n29, 283nn25–26, 288n13,
    299n38, 300n4, 302n18; elite posi-
    tions, 19–20, 68, 111–12, 188–89,
    190, 274n10 (see also elite discourse
    on war); end of hostilities, 20;
    opposition to, 19; origins of, 18;
    public opinion, 20–21, 52, 55, 68,
    72–73, 115, 119, 274n10; U.S. military
    involvement, 18–19; Vietnamization
    strategy, 20, 24

war aversion, 56, 272n50
war support: clarity of objectives, 63, 64;
    correctness of war, 1–2, 9, 20, 209;
    effect of on civil liberties judgments,
    156, 166, 168, 169, 172, 174, 175, 176;
    events of war, 62–66, 71–73, 79–80,
    118–19, 121; gender gap, 52–57; group
    attachments, 5, 8, 62, 66, 71, 72, 73,
    127–51, 136–43; likelihood of success,
    1–2, 63, 64–65, 66, 103; partisanship,
    5, 6, 7, 9, 50, 62, 69–71, 72, 73, 79,
    84, 86, 91–124, 210–11, 217, 244, 245,
    257–64, 279n46, 281n11; principle
    policy objectives, 119, 121, 122, 284n36,
    285n39
Warner, John, 24
Washington Post, 83, 86, 103, 105
weapons of mass destruction (WMD), 27,
    29, 78, 183, 218
Wellstone, Paul, 86
West, Darrell M., 37
whites, 132, 133, 296n16, 306n6
Willkie, Wendall, 43, 49, 99–100, 216,
    280n3, 282n15
Winfield, Betty Houchin, 43
within-subject design, 199–201, 278n42
women, 52–56, 215, 222, 225, 226, 227,
    267n5, 272n45, 306n1
World Trade Center, 26, 157

World War II, 3, 4, 6, 7, 13, 33–57, 62, 87–100, 126, 209, 211, 217, 268n8, 271nn34–35, 271nn38–39, 272n42, 275n18; conditions of termination, 91, 92, 94, 95, 96, 97, 98; content analysis, 234–35; data analysis, 236–39, 267n4; Destroyers for Bases program, 48; elections, 197–205, 213, 304n38, 305nn42–43; European theater, 137, 138; gender gap in public opinion, 52–56; internationalism, 55, 87–88, 91, 95, 96, 97, 99, 147–49; isolationism, 45, 46, 49, 50, 51, 55, 87, 89, 99, 131, 138, 147–49, 272n50, 288n14; Lend-Lease proposal, 48; media, 38–45, 270n29; myths, 13, 36–57; Neutrality Act and, 92, 93, 240; public opinion, 6, 33, 37–38, 46–51, 74, 87, 91, 92, 124, 135–38, 140–45, 148–49, 289n18, 290n21; reaction to war, 52–57; understanding of conflict, 140–42; U.S. aid to England, 48–49, 50, 53, 54, 55, 92, 93, 94, 95, 99, 100, 101, 137, 138–39, 149, 211, 247, 271n35, 272n50, 282n15, 290n21, 291n22; U.S. Navy convoy ships, 50, 92, 94, 95, 149, 241, 242, 243, 247; U.S. policy of unconditional surrender, 46–47, 74, 142, 175–76, 249; war aims, 53, 54, 75, 91, 142, 249, 270n32, 290n21, 291n29

Yugoslavia, former, 25

Zaller, John R., 5, 19, 22, 66–67, 68, 69, 70, 72, 82, 102, 103, 112, 119, 124, 186, 187, 274nn8–10, 275n12, 275n15, 275n17, 281nn11–12, 283nn25–27, 283n29, 300n5, 302n19
Zechmeister, Elizabeth J., 193, 194, 195, 197, 303n28
Zedong, Mao, 16
Zogby, 122